Automaticity and Control in
Language Processing

Advances in Behavioural Brain Science
Series Editor: Glyn W. Humphreys
Professor of Cognitive Psychology, University of Birmingham

This book series aims to present state-of-the-art research in behavioural brain science—specifically documenting progress in current cognitive, neuroscientific, and computational approaches to substantive topics. The series is based on a biennial series of international meetings in the Behavioural Brain Sciences Centre at the University of Birmingham, where international researchers are brought together for 2–3 days to review their research. The topics to be covered will vary from attention and action, to language processing, computational modelling of vision and action, learning, and neural plasticity, to aspects of the development and neural implementation of theory of mind and aspects of social cognition. In each case, an interdisciplinary perspective is emphasized, covering work at several levels of analysis.

Also available in this series:

Attention in Action: Advances from Cognitive Neuroscience
edited by Glyn W. Humphreys and M. Jane Riddoch

Automaticity and Control in Language Processing

Edited by
Antje S. Meyer, Linda R. Wheeldon
and Andrea Krott

Psychology Press
Taylor & Francis Group
HOVE AND NEW YORK

First published 2007 by Psychology Press
27 Church Road, Hove, East Sussex, BN3 2FA

Simultaneously published in the USA and Canada
by Psychology Press
270 Madison Avenue, New York, NY 10016

*Psychology Press is an imprint of the Taylor & Francis Group,
an Informa Business*

© 2007 Psychology Press

Typeset in Goudy by RefineCatch Limited, Bungay, Suffolk
Printed and bound in Great Britain by
MPG Books Ltd, Bodmin, Cornwall
Cover design by Anú Design

British Library Cataloguing in Publication Data
A catalogue record for this book is available from the British Library

Library of Congress Cataloging in Publication Data
Automaticity and control in language processing / edited by Antje S.
Meyer, Linda R. Wheeldon, and Andrea Krott.
    p. cm.
Includes bibliographical references and index.
ISBN 1-84169-650-1
1. Psycholinguistics. I. Meyer, Antje. II. Wheeldon, Linda. III. Krott,
Andrea, 1969–
P37.A88 2006
401'.9–dc22
                              2006013262

ISBN: 978-1-84169-650-8

Contents

Contributors

Kathryn Bock, University of Illinois at Urbana-Champaign, Beckman Institute for Advanced Science and Technology, 405 N Mathews, Urbana, IL 61801, USA

Catherine Connelly, Behavioural Brain Sciences, School of Psychology, University of Birmingham, Birmingham B15 2TT, UK

Gary S. Dell, University of Illinois at Urbana-Champaign, Beckman Institute for Advanced Science and Technology, 405 N Mathews, Urbana, IL 61801, USA

Andrew W. Ellis, University of York, Department of Psychology, York YO10 5DD, UK

Victor S. Ferreira, Department of Psychology, University of California, San Diego, La Jolla, CA 92093-0109, USA

Joanne K. Fillingham, Department of Psychology, The University of Manchester, Oxford Road, Manchester M13 9PL, UK

Emer M. E. Forde, Neurosciences Research Institute, School of Life and Health Sciences, Aston University, Birmingham B4 7ET, UK

Susan M. Garnsey, University of Illinois at Urbana-Champaign, Beckman Institute for Advanced Science and Technology, 405 N Mathews, Urbana, IL 61801, USA

Simon Garrod, University of Glasgow, Department of Psychology, Glasgow G12 8QT, UK

Peter Hagoort, F. C. Donders Centre for Cognitive Neuroimaging, Radboud University Nijmegen, Adelbertusplein 1, 6525 EK Nijmegen, The Netherlands

Robert J. Hartsuiker, Department of Experimental Psychology, Ghent University, Henri Dunantlaan 2, 9000 Ghent, Belgium

Glyn W. Humphreys, Behavioural Brain Sciences, School of Psychology, University of Birmingham, Birmingham B15 2TT, UK

Arthur F. Kramer, University of Illinois at Urbana-Champaign, Beckman Institute for Advanced Science and Technology, 405 N Mathews, Urbana, IL 61801, USA

Tate T. Kubose, University of Illinois at Urbana-Champaign, Beckman Institute for Advanced Science and Technology, 405 N Mathews, Urbana, IL 61801, USA

Matthew A. Lambon Ralph, School of Psychological Sciences, University of Manchester, Oxford Road, Manchester M13 9PL, UK

Martijn Lamers, University of Nijmegen, Nijmegen Institute for Cognition and Information, Montessorilaan 3, 6525 HR Nijmegen, The Netherlands

Randi C. Martin, Department of Psychology, Rice University, PO Box 1892, Houston, TX 77251-1892, USA

Martin J. Pickering, The University of Edinburgh, School of Philosophy, Psychology and Language Sciences, 7 George Square, Edinburgh EH8 9JZ, UK

Friedemann Pulvermüller, MRC Cognition and Brain Sciences Unit, 15 Chaucer Road, Cambridge CB2 2EF, UK

Julia Rayner, 250 Devon Street East, PO Box 492, New Plymouth, New Zealand

Ardi Roelofs, Nijmegen Institute for Cognition and Information, Radboud University Nijmegen, Spinoza Building B.02.32, Montessorilaan 3, 6525 HR Nijmegen, The Netherlands

Dana Samson, Behavioural Brain Sciences, School of Psychology, University of Birmingham, Birmingham B15 2TT, UK

Yury Shtyrov, MRC Cognition and Brain Sciences Unit, 15 Chaucer Road, Cambridge CB2 2EF, UK

Eleanor Steer, Behavioural Brain Sciences, School of Psychology, University of Birmingham, Birmingham B15 2TT, UK

Preface

Most people would probably agree that it can be useful and pleasurable to talk to others. Some might say that they also enjoy listening to others. We often talk or listen while doing other things, and the accompanying speech is rarely perceived to be a burden. In fact, many people are distressed if, for some length of time, they have nobody to talk to (although, interestingly, less distress seems to result from having nobody to listen to). Speaking and listening usually feel effortless and easy, supporting, rather than hindering us in our daily activities.

The lay view that using language is easy has a counterpart in the scientific discipline of psycholinguistics. This is the assumption that the core linguistic processes involved in speaking and listening are carried out by cognitive modules (defined roughly along the lines proposed by Fodor, 1983; see also Coltheart, 1999), which function largely automatically and independently of other cognitive processes. This assumed modularity sets linguistic processes apart from the "higher-level", more controlled conceptual processes that occur when speakers decide whether to talk at all and what to say, and when listeners work hard to make sense of a muddled argument or a poorly told joke. Modularity can therefore explain why we tend to think that speaking and listening are easy: It is because these processes are largely taken care of by autonomous and automatically functioning modules.

The notion of modularity has had a pervasive influence on psycholinguistic theories and experimental research (e.g., Bock, 1982; Frazier, 1987; Levelt, 1989; Levelt, Roelofs, & Meyer, 1999). However, it is obviously not the case that all contemporary models of speech production and comprehension are modular. In fact, many are distinctly nonmodular, including the families of interactive models of lexical access proposed by Dell and collaborators (e.g., Dell, 1986; Dell, Burger, & Svec, 1997) and by Caramazza and colleagues (e.g., Caramazza, 1997; Caramazza & Miozzo, 1997), as well as interactive approaches to sentence comprehension (e.g., Altmann & Steedman, 1988; Tanenhaus & Trueswell, 1995). So far, much of the modularity debate has concerned one specific aspect of modularity, namely the relationships of the components *within* the linguistic processing system; for instance, the relationship between semantic and phonological processing in word production, or the relationship between syntactic and semantic analysis in sentence comprehension. Important questions are whether these processes are strictly ordered in time, and whether they are autonomous or interact with each other (see Hagoort, Chapter 11, for a detailed discussion leading to the rejection of the "internal modularity" assumption for speech comprehension). By contrast, the "external" relations between linguistic processes and other cognitive processes have received less attention. A tacit assumption underlying much of the empirical research on language processing is that the linguistic components are largely independent of other cognitive processes. One implication of this view is that language processing can justifiably and conveniently be studied in isolation, using tasks such as rapid naming of large sets of line drawings or listening to statements such as "She spread her sandwich with socks", followed by "On the way to work she saw the neighbours' shark", which are somewhat different from the way language is used in everyday life. Of course, the fact that sophisticated models of speaking and listening have been based on the results of such studies demonstrates that this approach is not entirely unreasonable.

However, does the modular view really capture the way people use language? Do core linguistic processes run automatically, in isolation from other cognitive processes and outside the influence of executive control? These were the issues that formed the focus of a workshop held at the School of Psychology of the University of Birmingham in September 2004. We invited leading researchers working on questions of language processing to discuss the relationships between the core processes of language production and comprehension and other cognitive processes. The present volume is based on the presentations and discussions that took place during the workshop.

The chapters address diverse psycholinguistic issues. These include differences in speech planning for monologues and dialogues (Garrod and Pickering, Chapter 1), differences and similarities between speech production and comprehension (Bock, Dell, Garnsey, Kramer, and Kubose, Chapter 2), the detection and repair of speech errors (Hartsuiker, Chapter 5), the ways speakers and listeners deal with conceptual and linguistic ambiguities (Ferreira, Chapter 4), the mechanisms underlying language choice and code switching in bilinguals (Rayner and Ellis, Chapter 3), the processes underlying naming and categorization in healthy and brain-damaged persons (Roelofs and Lamers, Chapter 6; Humphreys, Forde, Steer, Samson, and Connelly, Chapter 7; Lambon Ralph and Fillingham, Chapter 9), the role of short-term memory in language comprehension and production (Martin, Chapter 8), and the time course and neural correlates of lexical, semantic, and syntactic processing in comprehension (Hagoort, Chapter 11; Pulvermüller and Shtyrov, Chapter 10). The empirical research described in the chapters used a wide range of methods, including analyses of speech errors and repairs; recording of response latencies, eye movements, and evoked potentials; and case studies of brain-damaged patients.

With respect to our theme, a number of key issues can be identified. One of them is how automaticity should be defined and measured. This is taken up by Garrod and Pickering (Chapter 1), who argue for a graded notion of automaticity; by Bock and colleagues (Chapter 2), who report on a study using a dual task paradigm to assess the capacity demands arising during the production and comprehension of complex spatial utterances; and by Pulvermüller and Shtyrov (Chapter 10), who explain how evoked brain potentials can be used in studies of spoken language comprehension in order to distinguish early automatic processes and later capacity-demanding processes (see also Hagoort, Chapter 11). Roelofs and Lamers (Chapter 6) explain how eye tracking can be used to tap the allocation of visual attention during an object-naming task.

A second issue is which, if any, of the processes involved in language processing are capacity demanding. There appears to be consensus that the core linguistic processes involved in speaking and listening do not pose strong capacity demands, in line with the lay view that speaking and listening are easy. By contrast, the processes involved in the mapping between linguistic and conceptual structures require capacity. In language production, these processes tend to precede the linguistic formulation of an utterance, whereas in comprehension they follow the linguistic processing of the utterance (Bock and colleagues, Chapter 2). Hartsuiker (Chapter 5) and Ferreira (Chapter 4) discuss an additional capacity-demanding component involved in speaking: the speakers' self-monitoring processes.

A third issue is whether the speech-processing components are autonomous; that is, whether, once triggered by appropriate input, they are immune to outside influences, or whether they can be affected by such influences. Speaking often serves a goal; speakers may, for instance, want to instruct listeners in exactly what to do or where to go, or they may want to tell an entertaining story. Therefore, the speakers' goals and motives must in some way affect what they say and how they say it. Similarly, though perhaps less obviously, a listener's goals (e.g., to be able to carry out the instructions given by the speaker or to judge whether or not the speaker has a pleasant character) must in some way affect the way speech is processed. Several authors consider this issue, from quite different perspectives. Ferreira (Chapter 4) discusses how speakers and listeners deal with conceptual and linguistic ambiguity and concludes, in line with a strict autonomy assumption, that choices leading to the avoidance of ambiguity are implemented only at the conceptual level and during monitoring. Rayner and Ellis (Chapter 3) discuss how bilingual speakers switch between languages. Confirming earlier evidence, the results of their experiments show that the costs involved in switching from one language to the other depend on the relative activation levels of the languages involved, with switches into the stronger language being more costly than switches into the weaker language. Interestingly, the results also suggest that high activation of a few items of the weaker language can trigger the inhibition of the entire weaker lexicon. Roelofs and Lamers (Chapter 6) discuss the relationship between visual orienting, selective stimulus processing, and response preparation in Stroop-like tasks and explain how the effects of selective attention are represented in Roelofs' computational model, WEAVER++. Martin (Chapter 8) presents the case of patient MC, who shows difficulties in inhibiting irrelevant verbal information but not nonverbal information, suggesting that executive functions might be specific to particular processing domains. Finally, Humphreys and colleagues (Chapter 7), and Lambon Ralph and Fillingham (Chapter 9) show how executive function deficits can affect language processing: Humphreys and colleagues report that their patient FK was unable to name objects at a superordinate level (an ability which is usually spared in patients with a semantic deficit), and that their patients DS and PW were unable to override automatic but task-irrelevant lexicosemantic processing. With those three cases, the authors discuss how executive processes operate on language processes. Lambon Ralph and Fillingham show how attentional/executive deficits in aphasic patients affect their relearning of picture names.

Producing and understanding utterances necessarily involves holding various types of information in working memory. For instance, speakers must remember whom they are talking to; keep track of what they have said already; and, according to many theories, temporarily buffer utterance fragments before producing them. Similarly, listeners must remember what they have been told already, and keep utterance fragments in a buffer, minimally until semantic and syntactic processing is possible. Therefore, an important issue is how the role of working memory should be conceptualized in models of speech processing. Based on a large number of patient studies, Martin (Chapter 8) argues for the existence of different working memory buffers: a semantic buffer that is involved in both language comprehension and language production, and two phonological buffers, one for language comprehension and one for language production. She also presents evidence for the hypothesis that deficits in semantic short-term memory might be associated with problems of inhibiting irrelevant information.

A final issue, taken up in several papers, concerns the cortical representations and mechanisms underlying the specific linguistic processes involved in speaking and listening and the general cognitive control processes. Pulvermüller and Shtyrov (Chapter 10) review the results of event-related brain potentials (ERP) studies demonstrating that spoken words immediately, and without requiring attention, activate phonological, syntactic, and semantic processes in the listener's mental lexicon. These processes may be followed by later analyses that depend on attention and task-related strategies. Hagoort (Chapter 11) presents the MUC (memory, unification, and control) model of spoken sentence processing, which is also largely based on ERP evidence, and which offers a novel psychologically and neurobiologically plausible account of syntactic and semantic integration processes occurring during spoken sentence processing. Roelofs and Lamers (Chapter 6) and Humphreys and colleagues (Chapter 7) discuss the cortical basis of attentional control processes, Roelofs focusing on the role of the anterior cingulate cortex (ACC) for selective stimulus processing and Humphreys and colleagues discussing the specific roles of the left and right frontal lobes in controlled language processing.

As must now be clear, the workshop presentations represented a wide range of data and theoretical positions relevant to the issue of automaticity and control in language processing. The interactions between such a distinguished set of researchers led to a stimulating meeting, which it was our pleasure to host. We are very grateful to all participants, the authors of the present chapters as well as the other presenters and discussants, for their contributions. We hope that both the workshop and the book help advance our understanding of the relationship between speaking and listening and other cognitive processes and stimulate further research. We also thank the Experimental Psychology Society for their support.

Antje S. Meyer, Linda R. Wheeldon, and Andrea Krott
Birmingham, March 2006

References

Altmann, G. T. M., & Steedman, M. (1988). Interaction with context during human sentence processing. *Cognition, 30*, 191–238.

Bock, J. K. (1982). Towards a cognitive psychology of syntax: Information processing contributions to sentence formulation. *Psychological Review, 89*, 1–47.

Caramazza, A. (1997). How many levels of processing are there in lexical access? *Cognitive Neuropsychology, 14*, 177–208.

Caramazza, A., & Miozzo, M. (1997). The relationship between syntactic and phonological knowledge in lexical access: Evidence from the "tip-of-the-tongue" phenomenon. *Cognition, 64*, 309–343.

Coltheart, M. (1999). Modularity and cognition. *Trends in Cognitive Sciences, 3*, 115–120.

Dell, G. S. (1986). A spreading-activation theory of retrieval in sentence production. *Psychological Review, 93*, 283–321.

Dell, G. S., Burger, L. K., & Svec, W. R. (1997). Language production and serial order: A functional analysis and a model. *Psychological Review, 104*, 123–147.

Fodor, J. D. (1983). *The modularity of mind*. Cambridge, MA: MIT Press.

Frazier, L. (1987). Sentence processing: A tutorial review. In M. Coltheart (Ed.), *Attention and performance XII* (pp. 559–585). Hove, UK: Lawrence Erlbaum Associates Ltd.

Levelt, W. J. M. (1989). *Speaking: From intention to articulation*. Cambridge, MA: MIT Press.

Levelt, W. J. M., Roelofs, A., & Meyer. A. S. (1999). A theory of lexical access in speech production. *Behavioral and Brain Sciences, 22*, 59–60.

Tanenhaus, M. K., & Trueswell, C. (1995). Sentence comprehension. In J. L. Miller & P. D. Eimas (Eds.), *Speech, language, and communication* (pp. 217–262). San Diego, CA: Academic Press.

1 Automaticity of language production in monologue and dialogue

Simon Garrod
University of Glasgow, UK

Martin J. Pickering
University of Edinburgh, UK

Over the last decade, there has been much discussion among social psychologists about automaticity in relation to the control of social behaviour. In this chapter, we discuss automaticity in the context of language production, a key aspect of social behaviour. We consider automaticity and control in the context of both monologue and dialogue. The discussion is motivated by a recent claim by Pickering and Garrod (2004) that the fundamental mechanism underlying dialogue is an automatic process known as interactive alignment. We review this claim, and then analyse in more detail automaticity and language production.

Pickering and Garrod (2004) argued that successful dialogue involves the alignment of situation models, and that this occurs via three processes: (1) an automatic mechanism of alignment involving priming at all levels of linguistic representation and percolation between these levels; (2) a mechanism that repairs alignment failure; (3) alignment via explicit "other modelling", which is used as a last resort. One criticism of the model is that language comprehension and production are clearly not automatic, and that they involve different kinds of strategic processing, conscious guidance and monitoring, and so on. For example, Shintel and Nusbaum (2004) stated in their commentary that dialogue cannot be as automatic as we claim, because "automaticity implies a passive process in which the input is processed in an invariable, inflexible manner" (p. 210). In response, our claim is not that language processing is largely automatic (which would be ludicrous) but rather that alignment is largely automatic.

In this chapter, we focus on language production. We propose that when one interlocutor produces an utterance, the other interlocutor is likely to produce an utterance that reflects some of the linguistic properties of the first utterance. For example, if A produces *chef*, B is more likely to produce *chef* when he comes to speak; but if A produces *cook*, B is then more likely to produce *cook* (Brennan & Clark, 1996; Garrod & Anderson, 1987). Our claim is that a major reason for this alignment is that the comprehension of *chef* (or alternatively *cook*) activates representations corresponding to this stimulus in B's mind (roughly corresponding to a lexical entry). These representations remain active, so that when B comes to speak, it is more likely that these representations will be employed, and hence it is more likely that he will utter *chef* (or *cook*). Whereas other factors of course affect whether B will actually utter a particular word, the tendency is enhanced by prior comprehension of that particular word. Our proposal is similar at other levels of linguistic representation, such as syntax (Branigan, Pickering, & Cleland, 2000) or phonology (Pardo, 2006). We assume that this tendency to alignment is automatic.

This account contrasts with an account in which alignment is a strategic process. If B wants to talk about cooking, he may have to select between *cook* and *chef*. If A has just uttered *chef*, then B is more likely to decide to use *chef* as well. There may be many reasons for this. For example, Giles and Powesland (1975) proposed that people speak in the same way as their interlocutors when they wish to affiliate to them. On their account, alignment is the result of a decision to behave like one's interlocutor for social reasons. Somewhat similarly, Brennan and Clark (1996) proposed that interlocutors set up tacit "conceptual pacts" to use the same term to refer to the same thing. For instance, if A refers to a shoe as a *pennyloafer* and B does not query this use but rather responds to A's instruction, then both A and B assume (1) that B has accepted this referential term, and (2) that both know (1). (In contrast, if B queried A's expression, then the pact would not be formed.) On their account, alignment is therefore the result of a process of negotiation that is specialized to dialogue and involves inference.

Strategic accounts assume that alignment is entirely the result of additional social or inferential processes. In contrast, interactive alignment proposes that there is an automatic tendency to align underlying all dialogue. Strategic decisions to align particularly strongly or not to align at all occur "on top of" this basic tendency, which we argue is automatic. The goal of this chapter is to explicate this notion of automaticity in relation to more general claims about automaticity in language production.

The chapter falls into three sections. First, we explicate the notion of automaticity as a graded property of cognitive processes (Bargh, 1994; Cohen, Dunbar, & McClelland, 1990). We then apply this graded notion of automaticity to language production in relation to standard models whose motivation is primarily research in monologue (e.g., Levelt, 1989), and then show how they need to be modified in the context of dialogue. Finally, we address the question of the automaticity of alignment.

The decomposition of automaticity

In cognitive psychology, automaticity and control were traditionally treated as all-or-none phenomena (Posner & Snyder, 1975; Shiffrin & Schneider, 1977). Automatic processes were considered to be involuntary, not drawing on general resources, and resistant to interference from attended activities or other automated activities (Johnson & Hasher, 1987). Controlled processes were just the opposite: voluntary, interfering, and subject to interference. More recently, this view has been challenged. For instance, Cohen et al. (1990) proposed that processes exhibit different degrees of automaticity as a function of what they call their *strength of processing*. They defined strength of processing in relation to processing pathways within a connectionist network. Strong processing pathways have strong connections between units and modules, leading to fast and accurate transmission of information along the pathway. One aspect of such pathways, which we consider below, is that they offer less optional choices than weaker processing pathways. Cohen et al. (1990) argued that strength of processing determines the extent to which processes are open to interference from other processes that may share portions of the same pathway. So a strong process is likely to be considered automatic because it tends to be efficient and resistant to interference. A weaker process is likely to be considered more controlled because it is less efficient and more likely to suffer from interference from the stronger process.

Another challenge to the all-or-none view of automaticity comes from researchers in social cognition, notably Bargh (1994). He argued that any processes as complex as those studied by social psychologists are bound to be made up of different components, some automatic and some controlled. He identifies four criteria, what he calls the "four horseman of automaticity". The first horseman is *awareness*. Automatic processes are likely to be those of which the subject is not aware. Examples of automaticity at this level include the effects of subliminally presented stimuli, as in subliminal priming of attitudes or activation of stereotypes (Bargh & Pietromonaco, 1982). The second horseman is *intentionality*: whether the subject needs voluntarily to instigate the process. For example, Stroop interference effects are considered automatic because they occur whether the person wants them to or not (Pratto & John, 1991). The third horseman is *efficiency*. Automatic processes are more efficient than controlled processes: they are faster, require less focal attention, and so on. Bargh's final horseman is *controllability*. Automatic processes are those which a subject cannot easily control in the sense of stopping or modifying the process once it is under way. However, to avoid confusion with the more normal contrast between automatic and controlled processes, we will refer to this as *interruptibility* instead (notice that efficiency and interruptibility are also key properties of strong and weak processing pathways in Cohen et al.'s (1990) terms).

Bargh's horsemen sometimes ride together, but sometimes do not. For example, evidence suggests that stereotypes are accessed unintentionally but that use of the stereotype to support a judgement is subject to some degree of control (Fiske & Neuberg, 1990). Hence, automaticity is a graded notion. Because language production is a complex activity with many distinct components, it is also appropriate to consider whether it, too, might exhibit graded automaticity.

The components of language production and their automaticity

This section is in two parts. We first discuss standard models of language production, principally that of Levelt (1989), in relation to the automaticity of their components. However, such models were developed largely to provide an account of production in monologue. Hence, we then discuss how such models need to be developed in order to account for language production in dialogue and how such models now relate to automaticity.

Automaticity in models of language production

It should be clear that language production involves both automatic and controlled processes. On the one hand, some decisions about what to talk about are clearly controlled, but some aspects of constructing the particular form of what one says are automatic. In order to determine the extent to which production is automatic, we need to decompose accounts of language production with respect to the four "horsemen". To do this, we focus on Levelt's account of production, making reference both to the general account (Levelt, 1989) and to the account of lexical encoding (Levelt, Roelofs, & Meyer, 1999).

Such accounts assume that language production involves converting a nonlinguistic representation of what a person wants to talk about into a sequence of speech sounds (or writing or signs). Levelt (1989) divides production into three broad stages: conceptualization (deciding what to talk about), formulation (constructing linguistic representations), and articulation. In his framework, speakers construct a series of intermediate representations as they move from message to sound, and also monitor this process. Each step in this process could be automatic to a greater or lesser degree with respect to Bargh's four criteria, as we shall see. One important point is that most aspects of language production involve some degree of choice between alternatives. It may be that degree of automaticity is related to the extent to which the speaker has to make such choices because choice relates both to intentionality and strength of processing.

In Levelt's first stage, the speaker conceptualizes the message that she wishes to convey. This seems to be controlled with respect to all four criteria. It is clearly amenable to introspection. It is generally assumed that people intend to convey the message they produce (Levelt's book is subtitled *Speaking: From Intention to Articulation*). (Any exceptions, such as echoing a previous speaker without understanding her message, are presumably highly atypical.) It is not efficient, in the sense that people can put considerable effort into deciding what to talk about next (or, indeed, whether to talk at all). Finally, it is interruptible, because people can decide to abandon or change what they are planning to talk about. Note, however, that thought is of course not an entirely controlled process, with associations between ideas occurring spontaneously, it being impossible to suppress unintended thoughts (Wenzlaff & Wegner, 2000) and so on. Hence, even deciding what to talk about has some automatic components.

Of course, there is a considerable difference between situations where a speaker's decision about what to say is not obviously driven by any external stimulus and situations where the speaker responds to a particular stimulus, as in picture-naming experiments. In cases of the former, such as preparing and giving a speech, the four criteria are obviously met. In the latter case, it is still true that people are aware of responding, have to decide to respond to the stimulus (e.g., to follow instructions in an experiment), and can stop themselves midstream or change their description (e.g., if the picture changes: Van Wijk & Kempen, 1987). Picture naming presumably involves less effort than coming up with an idea from scratch, but almost certainly it is impossible to remove any effort from the process. There is also evidence from picture–word interference experiments that pictures do not automatically activate their names except when the task is to name the picture. In a word-to-word translation task, Bloem and La Heij (2003) found that semantically related word contexts interfered with translation, but semantically related picture contexts facilitated translation. They suggested that this is because the picture contexts automatically activate only semantic features (hence priming selection of semantically related words), whereas the word contexts automatically activate the word forms themselves (hence interfering with selection of semantically related words). In other words, there is no automatic lexical activation from pictures unless you intend to name them (see Roelofs, 2003, for a related argument about Stroop effects). In fact, Levelt (1989, p. 20) argued that conceptualization is the only truly controlled process in speech production; all subsequent stages he considered automatic.

One possibility is that the results of this conceptualization are fed into the formulator. For example, when deciding on the concept TIGER the speaker might simply activate the features that uniquely specify tigers, such as CAT-FAMILY, HAS-STRIPES, and so on. These features can be seen as corresponding to the (nonlinguistic) idea and are therefore part of the "vocabulary" of thinking. These would then be used in performing lexical access on the word *tiger*. However, Levelt (1989) assumed that the prelinguistic idea is converted into a linguistic concept (principally to avoid the hyperonym problem), and that this representation is the input to the formulation process (see also Levelt et al., 1999). So we can ask whether the process of accessing the concept TIGER from features like CAT-FAMILY and HAS-STRIPES is automatic or not. Although there is no research that directly addresses this question, there is indirect evidence from models of Stroop interference results that establishing the linguistic concept is a controlled process (Roelofs, 2003). This is used to explain why conflicting ink colour (e.g., green) does not interfere with naming the word written in that colour (e.g., RED), whereas the conflicting word does interfere with naming the ink colour. In other words, whereas reading words is automatic and not subject to interference, naming colours is not automatic and so is subject to interference.

In Levelt's model, speakers then formulate their utterance, turning the message into a series of linguistic representations. Although specific models differ on exactly the levels proposed, they tend to agree that there is a stage of grammatical encoding, a stage of phonological encoding, and an interface with lexical items encoded as lemmas, which inform both grammatical and phonological encoding. Crudely, the speaker has to decide the grammatical form of what she is saying, decide what words (and morphemes) to use, and decide what phonological form to employ. Here, the question of automaticity becomes more complex.

Choice of lexical items appears to be the most controlled. For example, in describing a particular dog crossing a road the speaker needs to choose an appropriate level of description for the dog. Should she say *Rover, a spaniel, a dog* or even *a four-legged mammal*? Similarly, she has to decide between synonyms and near synonyms (*chair* vs. *seat*, *cook* vs. *chef*, etc.). To the extent that speakers are always presented with the problem of choosing an appropriate level of lexical specification, the process cannot be completely automatic. In terms of the four horsemen, speakers can become aware of lexical choice, before, during, and after uttering a word. It is less clear whether they have to be aware of all word choices. For example, they might never be aware of some short function words that they produce. But there is no doubt that people can be aware of lexical selection and, presumably, normally are. They can also be aware of making a choice between alternatives, without necessarily being aware of all the factors that bias them toward one choice or the other. Lexical access must surely be intentional: it is hard to see how it could take place without voluntary instigation of the process. Again, however, one possible exception involves function words without any inherent meaning (e.g., the complementizer *that*), for which Levelt (1989) and others propose "indirect election": such words are selected on the basis of the compatibility with other words, and do not require prior activation of a concept.

Lexical access is clearly not entirely efficient, in that there are some conditions under which access is impaired by processing load, where people get into tip-of-the-tongue states, and so on. There is also evidence that lexical access (i.e., lemma selection) takes up central attentional resources. V. Ferreira and Pashler (2002) investigated dual-task interference between word naming and tone discrimination. They showed that when the verbal context interfered with naming (attributed to influence at the level of lemma selection) it also slowed down tone discrimination in the secondary task even with long stimulus-onset asynchronies. By the logic of the psychological refractory period (PRP), this means that lemma selection calls on central resources and so interferes with performance on the nonlinguistic tone-discrimination task. Activities that call on central attentional resources are usually considered to be controlled rather than automatic. Finally, lexical selection is normally interruptible, in that speakers can correct or modify their choice of lexical item during the course of speaking (e.g., "It's the re——— uh green one"). This involves mechanisms of monitoring, which we turn to below. In summary, lexical selection appears to be largely controlled, although the selection of function words without inherent meaning may sometimes be an exception to this.

It is much less clear whether grammatical encoding is automatic or not. Consider awareness first. Speakers can be aware of the grammatical form they are using, but need not be. On the one hand, fairly literate speakers may sometimes realize when they are using a passive. But they are almost certainly not aware of their choice in all cases. Less educated speakers may use a passive without consciously realizing that it is a passive; nonlinguists are rarely aware of the dative alternation, and so on. They can of course be aware of some differences between possible forms, without necessarily appreciating the full linguistic subtleties of their choices. This seems to point to an awareness of the output of the production process, but, crucially, not to awareness of the process itself. Likewise, they are certainly not aware of all the factors that lead them to produce one form rather than another (e.g., syntactic or lexical priming; Bock, 1986a, 1986b). Intentionality is tricky to assess, because speakers clearly decide to produce utterances, but whether they then make a separate decision about which construction to use given the particular pattern of activation at the conceptual stratum is unclear. For example, a conceptual representation of John hitting Mary, with Mary focused, makes a passive likely (*Mary was hit by John*) (Tomlin, 1995). But is there an intention to produce the passive beyond that used to activate the conceptual representation? There certainly can be for literate speakers deciding to employ a passive for particular effect, but it is unclear whether this is generally the case. Next, we suspect that grammatical encoding involves processing effort, with more complex constructions being subject to more disruption than less complex ones, but there is little definitive evidence for this (though of course there is evidence that more complex constructions are harder to produce than simpler ones; F. Ferreira, 1991). However, there is evidence from V. Ferreira and Pashler's (2002) interference task that accessing morphophonemic word forms (an aspect of grammatical encoding) uses central resources in the same way as lemma access. They tested interference from word-form access by manipulating the frequency of the words in the naming task and found that frequency affected performance on the secondary tone-discrimination task to the same degree as the naming task. This indicates that grammatical encoding is not entirely efficient. Finally, grammatical encoding seems normally interruptible, in that speakers can correct or modify their choice of construction during production (a case in point being where they realize that they are getting into a grammatical dead end; F. Ferreira, 2004). However, it is hard to know whether the process of grammatical encoding is being monitored or just its results (see below).

In summary, grammatical encoding shows some features that point to its being a controlled process, such as being partly open to awareness and competing for central resources. But it also seems more automatic than some earlier processes such as identifying the concept and the lemma. The fact that grammatical encoding inevitably involves choices between alternative forms would suggest that the process is unlikely to involve a direct strong pathway in Cohen et al.'s (1990) terms. In other words, it is not likely to be of high automaticity in their terms.

It is also difficult to be certain what aspects of phonological encoding are automatic. Aspects of phonological encoding that are associated with meaning differences are less likely to be automatic. A good example is stress and intonation, as in cases like contrastive stress or the intonational effect on the meaning of words such as *only*. Speakers can also deliberately stress particular words, just as they appear to choose those words themselves, and presumably they can at least sometimes modify faulty stress. In fact, Levelt (1989, ch. 10) proposed a prosody generation module that was under executive control with respect to encoding intonational meaning. At the other extreme, however, it is much more likely that the process of selecting syllables and phonemes for words that have been selected is largely automatic. Thus, V. Ferreira and Pashler (2002, Experiment 2) showed that phoneme selection, unlike lemma access or word-form selection, did not compete for central resources. Although phonemic priming speeded the naming task, it did not have a comparable effect on their secondary tone-discrimination task. This may partly reflect the fact that there is normally no choice in phonological form, except with respect to stress.

Aspects of articulation seem automatic, such as the way in which phonological and phonetic representations are converted into tongue movements and the like. But on the other hand, people can clearly choose to speak at a fast rate, with a posh accent, or with a sarcastic tone of voice. We suspect that automaticity occurs in those aspects of articulation that involve mapping from earlier stages in the production process (e.g., a particular phone has to be articulated in a particular way), but not in those that come from separate intentions on the part of the speaker (e.g., a tone of voice). Finally, of course, speakers may also become aware of certain phonological properties of their own speech via the monitoring process (e.g., use of a posh accent). In general, aspects of articulation that relate to a whole expression or utterance (such as tone of voice) are less likely to be automatic than aspects that relate to a smaller fragment such as a phone.

We have repeatedly referred to monitoring as providing evidence for the interruptibility of a process. More strictly, monitoring itself may be automatic, but there may be a controlled process of interrupting production (to allow an aspect of speech to be corrected or abandoned). In Levelt's (1989) model, monitoring takes place via the comprehension system, and therefore is presumably automatic to the extent that comprehension itself is automatic. Whereas this chapter focuses on production, we note that the case for automaticity in comprehension seems pretty strong, as it is difficult to prevent language comprehension except at levels of interpretation and inference without blocking up one's ears ("What you have to remember about parsing is that basically it's a reflex"; ascribed to Garrett by Fodor, 1983). So comprehension-based monitoring may well be automatic, but, clearly, the speaker can decide what to do at that point, and there is good evidence that correcting speech is affected by processing load (Oomen & Postma, 2002). However, Levelt (1989, ch. 12; see also Roelofs, 2004) argued that self-monitoring is a controlled process in terms of both detecting when an error has occurred and correcting it. There is clear evidence for control of monitoring as a whole, in that speakers can tune their monitor according to the context (e.g., speakers monitor for lexicality only when producing real words; Baars, Motley, & MacKay, 1975; cf. Hartsuiker, Corley, & Martensen, 2005). The main argument for control at the level of detection is that many important errors are missed, suggesting that speakers do not automatically attend to everything they say. It is hard to imagine that a theory of production-based monitoring would differ in this respect.

However, theories differ with respect to which stages in the production process can be monitored. Levelt (1989) assumed monitoring within the conceptualizer, plus an "inner" and an "outer" loop, with the outer loop involving actual speech. The inner loop monitors a phonological (Wheeldon & Levelt, 1995) or phonetic (Levelt, 1989) representation, but, crucially, does not have access to grammatical encoding. If this is correct, it would suggest that some, but not all, aspects of production are interruptible. Presumably, the interruptible stages are conceptualization, phonological/phonetic encoding, and articulation, but not aspects of grammatical encoding, for example. However, Pickering and Garrod (2004) challenged this claim, and argued that it should be possible to monitor any level of representation constructed during speech.

Altogether, language production in monologue involves a mixture of both controlled and automatic processes. In general, processes at the instigation of speaking in Levelt's framework (e.g., message formulation and lexical access) are more controlled than those downstream (e.g., syntactic formulation and articulation). Yet, even for these lower-level processes, not everything is automatic, as Shintel and Nusbaum (2004) pointed out. One possible account is that many stages of production involve some input from the situation model, as well as input from earlier stages in the production process. For example, phonological encoding involves a mapping from the lemma (the lemma *tiger* has to be converted into /tIger/), but also involves the mapping of focus (in the situation model) into an intonation pattern. On this account, the mapping from the lemma is automatic, at least with respect to awareness, intentionality, and perhaps efficiency, but the mapping from the situation model is not automatic.

What changes in dialogue?

Above, we have considered which aspects of standard models of language production are automatic and in what sense. But this is quite a long way from our main question, which is to determine the sense in which processes of alignment in dialogue are automatic. One concern is that standard production models are principally designed to deal with monologue, and focus on the modelling of data acquired from monological paradigms such as picture description. Before considering automaticity in relation to alignment, we need to ask whether models of language production can be accommodated to dialogue data, and whether this accommodation makes any difference to the automaticity of different components of such a model.

In order to address this question, we start by considering how standard assumptions about dialogue might affect the characterization of automaticity discussed above for monologue. We use Clark's (1996) account of language use as a basis for examining production in dialogue. One of his central claims is that dialogue, unlike monologue, is a joint activity. In other words, it involves two interlocutors working together to establish the meaning of what is being communicated. This has two consequences in relation to automaticity of language production. First, it means that speakers have to take their particular interlocutor into account in planning and formulating their utterances. In principle, this could affect any stage of production from constructing the message (choosing to tell your interlocutor only about things you know that she does not already know) to choosing appropriate lexical items (referring to someone as *my next door neighbour Mary* rather than just *Mary* or *her* according to your assessment of how accessible the referent may be to your interlocutor). Because such "audience design" requires speakers to tailor their choices about what to produce to their addressee, dialogue entails less automaticity than a monologue-based account might suggest. Although even speaking in isolation requires decisions about what to say (e.g., how to describe a picture), the isolated speaker does not need to pay attention to potentially changing evidence about addressee understanding, as occurs throughout dialogue.

But in other respects, dialogue may be more automatic than monologue. In dialogue, what one interlocutor says imposes constraints on what her partner can say next. For example, a question usually requires an answer. This means that, to a certain extent, message planning is distributed between interlocutors. Such distributed planning may make production more automatic. For example, the appropriate response to a question is normally to produce an answer (Schegloff & Sacks, 1973), and so the choice about what to say next is reduced in comparison to monologue.

More generally, one would expect language processing in dialogue to be automatized to some degree, because, as Garrod and Pickering (2004) point out, conversation seems more straightforward than producing speeches, for instance. The apparent ease of conversation is surprising because there are so many features of dialogue which should present additional processing problems. First, there is the problem that conversational utterances tend to be elliptical and fragmentary. If we assume, as most accounts of language processing do, that complete utterances are "basic" (because all information is included in them), ellipsis should present difficulty. Second, conversation presents a whole range of interface problems. These include deciding when it is socially appropriate to speak, being ready to come in at just the right moment (in one study interlocutors started speaking about 0.5 s before their partner finished (Sellen, 1995)), planning what you are going to say while still listening to your partner, and, in multiparty conversations, deciding whom to address. To do this, you have to keep task switching (one moment speaking, the next moment listening). Yet, we know that multitasking and task switching are challenging and effortful (Allport, Antonis, & Reynolds, 1972). Interestingly, Roelofs and Hagoort (2002) use this multitasking feature of dialogue to motivate the need for control in language production (i.e., speakers need to be able to block out the interference from their interlocutor's speech while planning what they are going to say themselves). However, the apparent ease of conversation would suggest a greater automatization of production processes in dialogue than in monologue. In addition, the fact that most people have much more experience with conversation than producing speeches means that there is more opportunity to automatize processes in dialogue than in monologue (Shiffrin & Schneider, 1977). This is one of the motivations behind the interactive-alignment account.

Automaticity and alignment

We now turn to the question that we began with, namely, whether alignment itself constitutes an automatic mechanism. The first part of this section discusses the "short-term" process of alignment via channels of alignment. We then contrast this short-term process with longer-term mechanisms involved in the construction of routines.

Automaticity in the channels of alignment

Pickering and Garrod (2004) argued that interlocutors align situation models during dialogue. Such models are assumed to capture what people are "thinking about" while they understand a discourse, and therefore are in some sense within working memory (they can be contrasted with linguistic representations, on the one hand, and general knowledge, on the other hand). We proposed that the basic mechanism of alignment is automatic and primarily unconscious, with interlocutors tending to produce and interpret expressions in the same ways that their partners have just done. In other words, alignment is largely the result of priming. For example, interlocutors tend to produce words they have just heard, to assume that ambiguous words have meanings that they have recently given to those words, to use grammatical constructions they have recently used, and so on.

This account is supported by a great deal of evidence showing alignment at a range of different linguistic levels. For example, Garrod and Anderson (1987) found that participants in a cooperative maze game tended to describe their positions in the maze in similar words and interpretations for those words (e.g., *line* to mean horizontal row of nodes in the maze), and to employ similar description schemes (e.g., referring to position by coordinates with the same origin). Likewise, Branigan, Pickering, and Cleland (2000) found that participants in an interactive card-sorting task tended to describe a card in the same grammatical structure that their partner had just used when describing a card to them. This tendency was especially strong when both prime and target descriptions employed the same verb. Hence, Pickering and Garrod (2004) argued that alignment at one level (here, the same verb) leads to more alignment at other levels (here, the same syntax). On this basis, alignment at "lower" levels is likely to lead to alignment at the level of the situation model.

A key idea behind the interactive alignment account is that dialogue (unlike monologue) supports automatic alignment channels at different linguistic levels (e.g., phonological, syntactic, semantic).[1] Let us consider how these channels are automatic in relation to Bargh's (1994) "four horsemen". Take the *chef/cook* example from the beginning of the chapter. First, in order for the alignment channel to operate, B presumably has understood A's previous use of *chef* and to this extent may be aware of the fact that A used that term. However, it may not be strictly necessary for B to have understood A's mention of *chef* for the channel to operate, because under the right circumstances repetition priming can be demonstrated with subliminal primes (and, presumably, comparable priming should be possible in dialogue). The point here is that whether or not interlocutors are aware of the expressions operating on the alignment channels, the channels are automatic. In much the same way that people automatically project their own goals to others whether those goals are explicit or implicit (Kawada, Oettingen, Gollwitser, & Bargh, 2004), the fact that B may have been aware of A's prior mention of *chef* does not make the alignment channel less automatic.

How about the second horseman of intentionality? Again, as we argued in the introduction, there is no reason to think that B's increasing tendency to say *chef* following A's prior mention is primarily intentional. Even though the lexical choice as such may involve some control, the channel is responsible only for increasing the tendency to choose *chef* rather than, say, *cook* in this situation; it is not responsible for instigating that choice.

In relation to the third horseman of efficiency, to the extent that alignment channels involve priming, they presumably increase the efficiency of the production process. Furthermore, alignment involves a kind of imitation, and there is evidence that imitation is extremely efficient because it can occur very rapidly. For example, Goldinger (1998) had participants shadow words, and found that not only did the acoustic characteristics of the produced word reflect those of the stimulus, but also this imitation was greater when the words were produced immediately after the stimulus. Fowler, Brown, Sabadini, and Weihing (2003) found that imitating a string of phonemes is almost as fast as making a simple reaction time judgement to the same stimulus. Fadiga, Craighero, Buccino, and Rizzolatti (2002) found that listeners activated appropriate muscles in the tongue while listening to speech (but not during nonspeech). All of this points to the potential efficiency of interactive alignment channels.

The question of interruptibility may be slightly more complicated. However, we would suggest that, in general, interlocutors are not easily able to interfere with alignment channels. In other words, they cannot easily override the tendency to imitate their interlocutor. Our reason for hedging about interruptibility is that there is some evidence that the degree of alignment seen in dialogue may be affected by other social factors. We consider this issue in more detail below.

Short-term vs. long-term alignment

Thus far, we have treated alignment channels as contributing to a single process of alignment. However, we suspect that the alignment mechanism may be more complex than this and have both a short-term and a long-term aspect. Short-term alignment between comprehension and production explains the ease with which interlocutors can complete their partners' utterances and get the syntax and semantics right. Because production processes are primed by the alignment channels during comprehension, speakers do not have to go through all the stages of production outlined above in order to complete their partners' utterances. One can think of alignment as presetting parameters in the production mechanism and so reducing the decision space confronting a speaker in dialogue compared to that confronting a speaker of monologue. Hence, the short-term effect of alignment channels is to automatize production. Of course, short-term alignment facilitates production not only when completing an interlocutor's utterance but also when responding to that interlocutor. Morgan (1973) noted syntactic constraints between utterances and responses in dialogue. For example, *Being called "your highness"* is a well-formed reply to the question *What does Tricia enjoy most?*, whereas *That she be called "your highness"* is not. This is because you cannot say *Tricia enjoys that she be called "your highness"*. As interactive alignment predicts, speakers reuse the structures that they have just interpreted as listeners when formulating their response. Again, this is consistent with the idea that the alignment channels preset syntactic parameters used in production and so reduce the decision space confronting the speaker. Similarly, in lexical production, a speaker's first reference to *chef* or *cook* involves a choice between these alternatives. But following an interlocutor's use of one of these terms, the speaker can now simply repeat that term, without having to make a choice to the same extent. Alignment reduces the decision space, and this increases automaticity.

The long-term aspect of alignment relates to what we have called *routines*. A routine is an expression that is "fixed" to a relatively large extent. It occurs at a much higher frequency than the frequency of its components would lead us to expect (e.g., Aijmer, 1996). Stock phrases, idioms, and some clichés are routines. However, other expressions can be less extreme forms of routines, as for example, if they contain some fixed elements and some elements that vary (. . . *sing/dance/drink your way through the day/evening*). Such cases are semiproductive. Most discussion of routines relates to expressions that are in some sense "permanent" within a language user or group (e.g., Aijmer, 1996; Kuiper, 1996; Nunberg, Sag, & Wasow, 1994). But routines may also be established during a particular dialogue, and therefore can have a temporary status. If one interlocutor starts to use an expression (either simple or complex) and gives it a particular meaning, the other will most likely follow suit.

Various experimental studies show this process of routinization. For example, Garrod and Anderson (1987) had participants play a collaborative "maze game" in which they had to describe their positions to each other. In one example, one participant says *It's like a right indicator* to refer to a box protruding from the maze on the right. The other participant accepts this novel use of the expression, and the first participant then repeatedly utters *right indicator* to refer both to this position and to other boxes protruding to the right. This suggests that both interlocutors develop this routine. Similar processes occur when interlocutors agree on a "shorthand" description of unfamiliar objects, as when referring to a geometric shape as *an ice skater* (Clark & Wilkes-Gibbs, 1986).

Pickering and Garrod (2005) interpret routines in terms of Jackendoff's (2002) linguistic framework (see also Jackendoff, 1999). Jackendoff assumes a "rich" lexicon, which not only contains individual words or morphemes, but also includes any form of complex expression that can be accessed directly, including idioms, constructions, and even whole speeches if they have been memorized. Lexical entries contain separate representations for syntax, semantics, and phonology, which are associated via "linking rules". For example, the "normal" interpretation of *right* is represented in Figure 1.1a, and that of *indicator* is represented in Figure 1.1b. These can be combined (during comprehension or production) to produce the representation for the complex expression given in Figure 1.1c. However, this representation might well not be lexicalized. In contrast, Pickering and Garrod proposed that the routinized interpretation of *right indicator* developed by the maze-game participants is as represented in Figure 1.1d, where the composite meaning is idiosyncratic and is not compositional (as indicated by the link between the composite meaning and the N' node). Whereas Jackendoff (2002) focused on the description of a relatively fixed lexicon, our assumption is that the lexicon changes all the time during dialogue, new expressions becoming routinized (and, presumably, other previously routinized expressions being "lost").

We assume that routines arise from the increased levels of activation associated with the operation of the alignment channels. However, they can be maintained only through implicit memory. Whereas alignment channels can be considered as pre-setting production parameters locally, routinization imposes long-term restrictions on choice in production. To this extent,

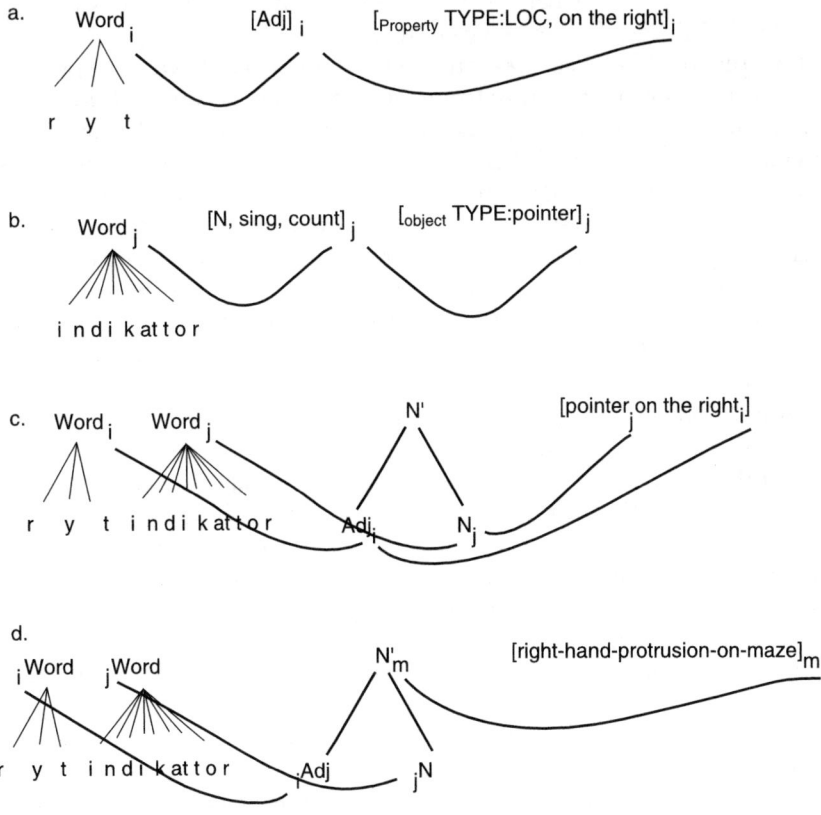

Figure 1.1 Phonological, syntactic, and semantic representations together with the links between them for (a) the word *right*, (b) the word *indicator*, (c) the phrase *right indicator*, and (d) the routine *right indicator*.

routinization increasingly automatizes the production process as the dialogue unfolds.

Conditional automaticity: Social influences on alignment

When discussing the automaticity of alignment channels, we hedged over the degree to which the alignment process may be subject to control in Bargh's (1994) sense. This was because there seem to be certain aspects of alignment that reflect social factors. For example, there is some evidence to suggest that alignment is stronger between interlocutors than between a speaker and side participant (Branigan, Pickering, McLean, & Cleland, in press). It has also been suggested that the degree of alignment between interlocutors may be affected by the degree to which the speakers want to affiliate (Giles & Powesland, 1975). Interestingly, similar effects have been reported in social cognition. For example, Lakin and Chartrand (2003) found that people are less likely to copy a partner's incidental movements (e.g., foot shaking, head nodding) when they find that partner unattractive.

It is still not clear what is responsible for these social effects. One possibility is that alignment and other forms of imitation depend to a degree upon the amount of attention that participants pay to the situation. The more they attend, the more effective the alignment channels are. This would suggest that the channels are conditionally automatic in that they operate "at full strength" only when interlocutors are really attending to each other. Another possibility is that interlocutors are able to inhibit alignment channels if they want to, but that this requires conscious effort. Hence, if they have no strong goal to affiliate or even have a goal not to affiliate with their partner, they consciously block the alignment process to the extent that they can. Danet (1980) discusses a case of the use of terms to refer to the result of pregnancy in an abortion trial. The prosecuting lawyer tended to employ terms like *baby* or *unborn child*, whereas the defendant tended to employ terms like *foetus*. It is clear that the different sides in the debate did not want to align on the same terms, because different terms would have had very different implications. For example, for the defendant to employ *baby* would have been taken to imply acceptance that the results of pregnancy were a person with the legal right not to be killed. We assume that the interlocutors modelled the implications of adopting a particular term for how they believed the relevant audience (whether judge, jury, or the wider public) was likely to perceive them.

Without going into the full implications of this interesting situation, we note that the participants had a strong interest in not aligning on each others' terms and that the effort needed to avoid alignment must have been considerable. In more mundane cases, interlocutors may on occasion try to impose their choice of expression on their interlocutor, when there is a conflict about who is right (e.g., the name of a car), whose dialectical expression is to be employed (e.g., *lunch* vs. *dinner* to refer to the midday meal), or the political implications of a choice of expression (e.g., *benefit claimants* vs. *scroungers*) (Jefferson, 1987). Attempting to impose one's term is effortful, and the "combatants" may hope that if they stick to their term, their interlocutor may give in and change hers.

We suggest that controlling alignment in this way is effortful and possibly interferes with effective communication, and that it is not automatic. However, as in the literature on social mimicry, we do not think that such examples of control undermine the basic claim that alignment is a largely automatic process.

Conclusion

The chapter began by noting the degree of interest among social psychologists in automaticity and how this contrasts with the situation in psycholinguistics. Social psychologists are interested in automaticity because it explains the apparent ease with which we make complex social judgements (Bargh & Chartrand, 1999). Conversation is a good example of a complex social activity which is apparently easy to perform (Garrod & Pickering, 2004). This was one of the reasons for Pickering and Garrod's (2004) proposal of automatic alignment channels as part of the interactive-alignment account. In this chapter, we have discussed in more detail what it means for language production to be automatized in both monologue and dialogue settings, using Bargh's (1994) graded notion of automaticity. We have argued that language production in monologue involves both controlled and automatic processes. In general, we have suggested that the degree of control of the process relates to the extent to which speakers need to make choices at any level. On this account, processes that occur at earlier stages in language production are more likely to be controlled than those that occur at later stages.

The situation appears to change in dialogue because of the interactive alignment process that occurs in dialogue. Although the basic processes of language production do not necessarily become completely automatic in dialogue, the interactive alignment channels serve to automatize processes at many levels, and they do so by effectively reducing the decision space at these levels.

References

Aijmer, K. (1996). *Conversational routines in English: Convention and creativity.* London: Longman.

Allport, D. A., Antonis, B., & Reynolds, P. (1972). On the division of attention: A disproof of the single channel hypothesis. *Quarterly Journal of Experimental Psychology, 24,* 225–235.

Baars, B. J., Motley, M. T., & MacKay, D. G. (1975). Output editing for lexical status from artificially elicited slips of the tongue. *Journal of Verbal Learning and Verbal Behavior, 14,* 382–391.

Bargh, J. A. (1994). The four horsemen of automaticity: Awareness, intention, efficiency, and control in social cognition. In R. S. Wyer & T. K. Srull (Eds.), *Handbook of social cognition* (Vol. 1, pp. 1–40). Hillsdale, NJ: Lawrence Erlbaum Associates, Inc.

Bargh, J. A., & Chartrand, T. L. (1999). The unbearable automaticity of being. *American Psychologist, 54,* 462–479.

Bargh, J. A., & Pietromonaco, P. (1982). Automatic information processing and social perception: The influence of trait information presented outside of conscious awareness on impression formation. *Journal of Personality and Social Psychology, 43,* 437–449.

Bloem, I., & La Heij, W. (2003). Semantic facilitation and semantic interference in word translation: Implications for models of lexical access in language production. *Journal of Memory and Language, 48,* 468–488.

Bock, J. K. (1986a). Meaning, sound, and syntax: Lexical priming in sentence production. *Journal of Experimental Psychology: Learning, Memory, and Cognition, 12,* 575–586.

Bock, J. K. (1986b). Syntactic persistence in language production. *Cognitive Psychology, 18*, 355–387.

Branigan, H. P., Pickering, M. J., & Cleland, S. (2000). Syntactic coordination in dialogue. *Cognition, 75*, B13–B25.

Branigan, H. P., Pickering, M. J., McLean, J. F., & Cleland, A. A. (in press). Participant role and syntactic alignment in dialogue. *Cognition.*

Brennan, S. E., & Clark, H. H. (1996). Conceptual pacts and lexical choice in conversation. *Journal of Experimental Psychology: Learning, Memory, and Cognition, 22*, 1482–1493.

Clark, H. H. (1996). *Using language.* Cambridge: Cambridge University Press.

Clark, H. H., & Wilkes-Gibbs, D. (1986). Referring as a collaborative process. *Cognition, 22*, 1–39.

Cohen, J. D., Dunbar, K., & McClelland, J. L. (1990). On the control of automatic processes: A parallel distributed processing account of the Stroop effect. *Psychological Review, 97*, 332–361.

Danet, B. (1980). "Baby" or "foetus"? Language and the construction of reality in a manslaughter trial. *Semiotica, 32*, 187–219.

Fadiga, L., Craighero, L., Buccino, G., & Rizzolati, G. (2002). Speech listening specifically modulates the excitability of tongue muscles: A TMS study. *European Journal of Neuroscience, 15*, 399–402.

Ferreira, F. (1991). Effects of length and syntactic complexity on initiation times for prepared utterances. *Journal of Memory and Language, 30*, 210–233.

Ferreira, F. (2004). Production-comprehension asymmetries. *Behavioral and Brain Sciences, 29*, 196.

Ferreira, V., & Pashler, H. (2002). Central bottleneck influences on the processing stages of word production. *Journal of Experimental Psychology: Learning, Memory and Cognition, 28*, 1187–1199.

Fiske, S. T., & Neuberg, S. E. (1990). A continuum of impression formation, from category-based to individuating processes: Influences of information and motivation on attention and interpretation. *Advances in Experimental Social Psychology, 23*, 1–74.

Fodor, J. A. (1983). *The modularity of mind.* Cambridge, MA: Bradford Books/MIT.

Fowler, C. A., Brown, J. M., Sabadini, L., & Weihing, J. (2003). Rapid access to speech gestures in perception: Evidence from choice and simple response time tasks. *Journal of Memory and Language, 49*, 396–413.

Garrod, S., & Anderson, A. (1987). Saying what you mean in dialogue: A study in conceptual and semantic co-ordination. *Cognition, 27*, 181–218.

Garrod, S., & Pickering, M. J. (2004). Why is conversation so easy? *Trends in Cognitive Sciences, 8*, 8–11.

Giles, H., & Powesland, P. F. (1975). *Speech styles and social evaluation.* New York: Academic Press.

Goldinger, S. D. (1998). Echoes of echoes? An episodic theory of lexical access. *Psychological Review, 105*, 251–279.

Hartsuiker, R. J., Corley, M., & Martensen, H. (2005). The lexical bias effect is modulated by context, but the monitoring account doesn't fly: Related Beply to Baars, Motley, and MacKay (1975). *Journal of Memory and Language, 52*, 58–70.

Jackendoff, R. (1999). Parallel constraint-based generative theories of language. *Trends in Cognitive Science, 3*, 393–400.

Jackendoff, R. (2002). *Foundations of language.* Oxford: Oxford University Press.

Jefferson, G. (1987). On exposed and embedded corrections in conversation. In G. Button & J. R. E. Lee (Eds.), *Talk and social organization* (pp. 86–100). Clevedon, UK: Multilingual Matters.

Johnson, M. K., & Hasher, L. (1987). Human learning and memory. *Annual Review of Psychology, 38,* 631–668.

Kawada, C. L. K., Oettingen, G., Gollwitser, P. M., & Bargh, J. A. (2004). The projection of implicit and explicit goals. *Journal of Personality and Social Psychology, 86,* 545–559.

Kuiper, K. (1996). *Smooth talkers: The linguistic performance of auctioneers and sportscasters.* Mahwah, NJ: Lawrence Erlbaum Associates, Inc.

Lakin, J. L., & Chartrand, T. L. (2003). Using non-conscious behavioral mimicry to create affiliation and rapport. *Psychological Science, 14,* 334–339.

Levelt, W. J. M. (1989). *Speaking: From intention to articulation.* Cambridge, MA: MIT Press.

Levelt, W. J. M., Roelofs, A., & Meyer, A. S. (1999). A theory of lexical access in speech production. *Behavioral and Brain Sciences, 22,* 1–75.

Morgan, J. L. (1973). Sentence fragments and the notion "sentence". In B. B. Kachru, R. B. Lees, Y. Malkiel, A. Pietrangeli, & S. Saporta (Eds.), *Issues in linguistics: Papers in honor of Henry and Renée Kahane* (pp. 719–752). Urbana, IL: University of Illinois Press.

Nunberg, G., Sag, I. A., & Wasow, T. (1994). Idioms. *Language, 70,* 491–538.

Oomen, C. C. E., & Postma, A. (2002). Limitations in processing resources and speech monitoring. *Language and Cognitive Processes, 17,* 163–184.

Pardo, J. S. (2006). On phonetic convergence during conversational interaction. *Journal of the Acoustical Society of America, 119,* 2382–2393.

Pickering, M. J., & Garrod, S. (2004). Toward a mechanistic psychology of dialogue. *Behavioral and Brain Sciences, 27,* 169–225.

Pickering, M. J., & Garrod, S. (2005). Establishing and using routines during dialogue: Implications for psychology and linguistics. In A. Cutler (Ed.), *Twenty-first century psycholinguistics: Four cornerstones* (pp. 85–102). Mahwah, NJ: Lawrence Erlbaum Associates, Inc.

Posner, M. I., & Snyder, C. R. R. (1975). Attention and cognitive control. In R. L. Solso (Ed.), *Information processing and cognition: The Loyola Symposium* (pp. 55–85). Hillsdale, NJ: Lawrence Erlbaum Associates, Inc.

Pratto, F., & John, O. P. (1991). Automatic vigilance: The attention-grabbing power of negative social information. *Journal of Personality and Social Psychology, 61,* 380–391.

Roelofs, A. (2003). Goal-referenced selection of verbal action: Modelling attentional control in the Stroop task. *Psychological Review, 110,* 88–125.

Roelofs, A., & Hagoort, P. (2002). Control of language use: Cognitive modeling of the hemodynamics of Stroop task performance. *Cognitive Brain Research, 15,* 85–97.

Schegloff, E. A., & Sacks, H. (1973). Opening up closings. *Semiotica, 8,* 289–327.

Sellen, A. J. (1995). Remote conversations: The effect of mediating talk with technology. *Human–Computer Interaction, 10,* 401–444.

Shiffrin, R., & Schneider, W. (1977). Controlled and automatic human information processing II: Perceptual learning, automatic attending, and a general theory. *Psychological Review, 84,* 127–190.

Shintel, H., & Nusbaum, H. C. (2004). Dialogue processing: Automatic alignment or controlled understanding? *Behavioral and Brain Sciences, 27,* 210–211.

Tomlin, R. S. (1995). Focal attention, voice, and word order. In P. Dowing & M. Noonan (Eds.), *Word order in discourse* (pp. 517–552). Amsterdam: John Benjamin.

Van Wijk, C., & Kempen, G. (1987). A dual system for producing self-repairs in spontaneous speech—evidence from experimentally elicited repairs. *Cognitive Psychology, 19*, 403–440.

Wenzlaff, E. M., & Wegner, D. M. (2000). Thought suppression. *Annual Review of Psychology, 51*, 59–91.

Wheeldon, L. R., & Levelt, W. J. M. (1995). Monitoring the time-course of phonological encoding. *Journal of Memory and Language, 34*, 311–334.

Note

1   Alignment channels operate only when people engage in dialogue. However, the mechanism underlying the channels is that of comprehension-to-production and production-to-comprehension priming. Hence, during monologue (isolated production or comprehension), the alignment channels are present but do not engage in the communication process as such. Furthermore, the channels cannot influence the automaticity or otherwise of language processing during monologue.

2 Car talk, car listen

Kathryn Bock, Gary S. Dell, Susan M. Garnsey, Arthur F. Kramer, and Tate T. Kubose
University of Illinois at Urbana-Champaign, USA

Among age-old speculations about the origins of human language is a sugges-tion that use of the oral channel evolved to leave the hands and the rest of the body free for other activities. True or not, there are few human activities that proceed unaccompanied by talking or listening. With the scope of everyday activities expanding to include some that are life-threatening unless performed with sufficient care, questions about the demands of language use on attention to other things have assumed new priority. This new priority runs up against an old, unresolved, but theoretically central psycholinguistic debate over how language production and language comprehension are related to each other. The terms of this relationship involve shared or div-ided components of linguistic knowledge and shared or divided resources of perceptual, motor, and cognitive skill. Our question in this chapter is how production and comprehension differ in their demands on attention or working memory (Baddeley, 2003), as reflected in how much production and comprehension interfere with other tasks. At bottom, we are interested in whether talking is harder than listening.

The automatic answer to this question seems to be "of course". Talking involves retrieving linguistic information from memory and assembling utterances in working memory, using only information from the intended meaning; listening benefits from specific form cues and accompanying rec-ognition processes. The retrieval challenges for speakers are imposing: The estimated vocabulary of an educated English speaker is over 45,000 words. Failures of retrieval are common enough to have inspired a famous observa-tion of William James (1890) about tip-of-the-tongue states and a large research literature on the phenomenon, beginning with Brown and McNeill (1966). Assembling utterances entails structuring and ordering the words into one of the infinite number of possible phrases or sentences of English, drawing on the 12,000-or-more syllables of which English words are com-posed, and articulating the syllables at a rate of three or four per second, using more muscle fibres than any other mechanical performance of the human body (Fink, 1986). It is ability to speak a foreign language, not ability to understand one, that constitutes the commonplace standard of bilingual competence: Every word uttered, indeed every sound, is on display for evaluation. Talking to an audience, public speaking, is many people's greatest fear. Public listening inspires no such terror.

This unreflective view of the challenges of language production overlooks the more subtle but no less vexing challenges of normal language understanding. Normal understanding involves the auditory modality, and audition has its own impressive accounting of peripheral mechanics, in the form of the 1,600,000 or so moving parts of the hair cells in the cochlea. Cognitively, listening to language means segmenting a continuous stream of sound into identifiable components and disambiguating the inevitably ambiguous products at whatever rates they are produced. As adventurous tourists testify, it means dealing with the uninterpretable cascades of sound that greet one's tentative efforts to converse in a foreign language. It is generally easier to produce "où est la toilette?" than it is to comprehend a fluently spoken response. One hopes instead for a pointed gesture.

Conceivably, intuitions about the greater difficulty of language production are due merely to differences in how readily we can evaluate our own performance. Talking provides multiple opportunities to compare our speech against standards ranging from how we sound and how fluent we are to how adequately we are conveying what we mean to say. After all, speakers know what meaning they intended. All of this is possible because we presumably listen to and comprehend what we say, fairly automatically and unstoppably. In comparison, diagnosing a problem in our comprehension of others' speech requires information to which we have no direct access. We become aware of ambiguity, incomplete understanding, and outright mistakes only when confronted with other evidence that conflicts with an initial interpretation, sometimes in the form of trying to say the same thing ourselves. This raises the suspicion that the major thing that makes production hard is the standard we hold ourselves to.

Still, the automatic reaction that speaking is harder has something going for it empirically. Beyond the patent information-processing challenges of language production, there is evidence that children's early comprehension vocabularies are 3 months ahead of their production vocabularies (Benedict, 1979). For adults, the active or productive vocabulary is vastly smaller than the passive or comprehension vocabulary, with estimates of 30,000 words for the former compared to 75,000 for the latter (Levelt, 1989). Language disorders of all kinds, from stuttering in children to aphasia in adults, are more strongly associated with problems of production than with deficits in comprehension. All of these things are consistent with the intuition that production is the harder and more fragile aspect of language performance.

Of course, these types of evidence are vulnerable to the differential-standards objection. Perhaps children are in principle capable of producing what they comprehend, but their articulatory apparatus stands in the way of making their speech comprehensible. What adults require as evidence of comprehension is simple and mastered much earlier: When infants reliably turn toward the referent of a word, they are likely to be credited with understanding it (Huttenlocher, 1974). Yet, there is next to nothing in the psychological literature, either about human perception and performance or about psycholinguistics, that allows the intuition of greater production difficulty to be quantified with respect to normal adult language use.

Reasons for the absence of rigorous comparisons are easy to come by. Auditory and articulatory events differ enormously at the periphery, with auditory comprehension involving auditory sensory systems and production involving oral motor systems. The events are subserved by different cortical regions in different parts of the human brain. There are differences in what the processing systems have to accomplish that require differences in how they work: Comprehension creates interpretations of utterances, construct-ing meaning from ambiguous input; production creates utterances, con-structing forms from *unambiguous* input (Bock, 1995). Comprehension requires perceptual analysis to segment and recognize words and parse struc-tures; production requires conceptual synthesis to recall and assemble words and structures. Finally, the demanding events seem to occur at different points in time, with the demands of comprehension peaking near the ends of utterances and the demands of production peaking near the beginnings, even prior to speech onset. These differences are a challenge to standards of experi-mental control on a par with the proverbial comparison of apples and oranges.

Dual-task comprehension and production

Because of the many intrinsic differences between comprehension and pro-duction, in the present work we applied dual-task logic to the question of their relative difficulty. Despite their pitfalls (Jonides & Mack, 1984), dual-task methodologies create a yardstick on which otherwise incommensurate types of cognitive performances can be roughly compared.

There have been a few controlled comparisons of the dual-task effects of speaking and hearing single words (Shallice, McLeod, & Lewis, 1985). The results of this work suggest that the systems for articulation and audition are separable and impose different demands (see also Martin, Lesch, & Bartha, 1999). Missing, however, are systematic comparisons of comprehension and production of connected speech, which is what normal adult language use consists of. Even when adults speak to babies, fewer than 10% of their utterances consist of isolated words (van de Weijer, 1999).

We know that hearing or reading a sentence interferes with performance on secondary tasks such as detecting a nonlinguistic auditory stimulus (Garrett, Bever, & Fodor, 1966; Holmes & Forster, 1970) or making a lexical decision to an unexpected letter string (Shapiro, Zurif, & Grimshaw, 1987). Importantly, this interference varies as a function of the sentence's complexity (Gordon, Hendrick, & Levine, 2002) and where in a sentence the secondary task is performed (Ford, 1983). Similar evidence of difficulty arises during speaking, but the timing differs. Ford and Holmes (1978) required speakers to respond with a button press to tones that occurred at unexpected times during extemporaneous monologues about general topics such as "family life". Response times were slower at ends of clauses only when the current clause was followed by at least one additional clause, suggesting that the planning or preparation of upcoming speech is more distracting than current execution. In spontaneous speech, pauses and hesitations tend to occur earlier rather than later in utterances (Clark & Wasow, 1998; Maclay & Osgood, 1959), suggesting that problems arise nearer the beginning than the end of speech, consistent with the preparation hypothesis.

A more rigorous illustration of the timing of production demands can be found in work by Bock, Irwin, Davidson, and Levelt (2003). They used a controlled task that elicited utterances of different complexity as descriptions of identical scenes, and speakers' eye movements were monitored as they described the scenes. The results showed increases in several measures of preparation at earlier utterance positions. More complex utterances were accompanied by longer speech onset latencies as well as increased eye–voice spans and longer gaze durations to parts of scenes mentioned earlier in the utterances.

The finding that production takes its toll early in utterances stands in contrast with long-standing evidence that the ends of sentences and clauses are sites of high comprehension demand (Mitchell & Green, 1978). Bock et al. (2003; see also Bock, Irwin, & Davidson, 2004) proposed a process of utterance *ground breaking* in production, analogous to the phenomenon of clause wrap-up in comprehension. Ground breaking requires that speakers (1) dis-integrate the elements of a scene or mental model from their perceptual or mental contexts, in order to refer to them in an upcoming utterance; and (2) map the elements to the words and structures of language. The harder the dis-integration and mapping, the more difficult the utterance preparation.

Clearly, there are demands of both comprehension and production, but existing research provides little basis for systematic comparison. As a result, it remains possible and perhaps even likely that, held to comparable, objective performance standards, comprehension and production differ relatively little in how much they disrupt concurrent nonlanguage activities. Successful listening and successful speaking may impose similar penalties on performance, with major implications for psycholinguistic theories of language processes. In addition, the issue of the normal demands of language use has increasingly important practical and societal implications for whether and how we prescribe (or proscribe) the ability to engage in conversation.

To address both the theoretical and the practical questions about the demands of different facets of language performance, we have begun to examine how hard speaking and listening are in terms of their comparative consequences for the performance of another common, fairly automatic, and culturally central adult activity, driving an automobile.

A growing body of research has considered the impact of talking on driving in a very specific context. With increasing use of cellular telephones by drivers, there is an urgent need to understand their effects on driving performance (see Alm & Nilsson, 2001, for a review). For the most part, these effects appear to be negative. For instance, epidemiological research has shown that the chances of being involved in an automobile collision are greater for drivers using wireless telephones (Redelmeier & Tibshirani, 1997; Violanti, 1998; Violanti & Marshall, 1996). The initial assumption was that physical manipulation of the telephone, and not actual conversation, presents the greatest danger to driving safety. Recent research has shown that this is not necessarily the case. McKnight and McKnight (1993) showed that both placing calls and holding a conversation resulted in poorer simulated driving performance than no distraction at all. Other studies have shown that hands-free telephones provide little added safety over handheld versions with respect to driving performance (Lamble, Kauranen, Laasko, & Summala, 1999; Strayer & Johnston, 2001). The conclusion from this work is that the major distraction in using cellular phones is not the manipulation of the telephone, but the perceptual or cognitive distractions of conversation.

Taking this research as a springboard, we set out to separate the relative demands of comprehending and producing connected speech on driving performance in a high-fidelity simulator. As in the existing psycholinguistic literature, applied research on driving has not separated comprehension and production difficulty under conditions that match them for the complexity of the linguistic materials. Recarte and Nunes (2003) conducted a remarkable study that ranged over many potential sources of driver distraction, including language comprehension and production, finding that comprehension was often no more disruptive than uninterrupted driving. However, Recarte and Nunes presented drivers with 2-minute passages of speech which the drivers had to recall aloud, with measures of driving performance taken during the comprehension and production (recall) episodes. There were no apparent requirements for recall accuracy, though, which would allow perfunctory comprehension to trade off with laboured, retrieval-intensive production. Without criteria for comprehension accuracy and matching of conceptual and linguistic complexity, it is impossible to tell whether the source of difficulty is the language task itself or the general memory and conceptual processes that accompany the encoding and retrieval of the material.

In our examination of the effects of speech production and speech comprehension on driving performance, we used a dual-task paradigm with simulated driving as the primary task and a language-production or language-comprehension task as the secondary task. That is, we compared driving performance under single-task (i.e., driving only) and dual-task (i.e., driving with a concurrent speech task) conditions, and we also compared driving performance when the secondary task, the concurrent speech task, involved chiefly language production or chiefly language comprehension. The advantage of driving as a primary task, apart from its social and applied significance, is that it offers multiple, continuous performance measures, extending over the same time course as speech itself. The measures include proximal aspects of driving skill, such as steering, braking, and moving the accelerator, as well as the distal consequences of these activities, including maintenance of lane position, following distance, and acceleration.

The secondary language tasks involved producing or understanding statements about the spatial relationships between pairs of buildings on the campus of the University of Illinois at Urbana-Champaign. Normative knowledge of campus buildings and locations was assessed in preliminary studies that determined which buildings could be queried in the task. The participants in the actual talk-and-drive tasks were also tested on their campus knowledge prior to performance of the experimental tasks, and their memory of building locations was refreshed with the map in Figure 2.1.

In the production task, participants were cued to formulate and produce two-clause statements about the buildings. They were given two building names (e.g., Foellinger Auditorium, English Building) and then a map direction (e.g., south). They then had 20 s to say what other campus buildings were closest to the named buildings in the given direction, using a structurally simple, two-clause sentence. For instance, a correct response to "Foellinger

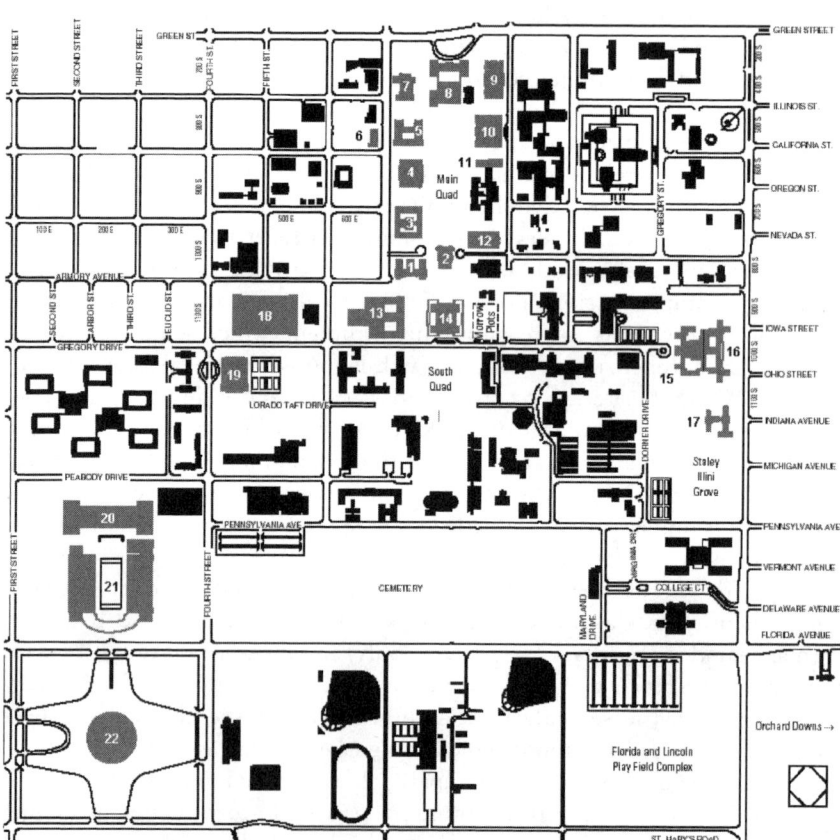

Figure 2.1 Map of area tested in the building location task.

Auditorium, English Building, South" would be "The Undergraduate Library is south of Foellinger Auditorium and Lincoln Hall is south of the English Building." Comprehension used recordings of the actual utterances generated during the production experiment, presented to different partici-pants. The participants listened to these utterances and had to verify whether each clause of the utterance was true. Figure 2.2 displays the sequence of events in the corresponding production and comprehension tasks.

Building Location Production Trial

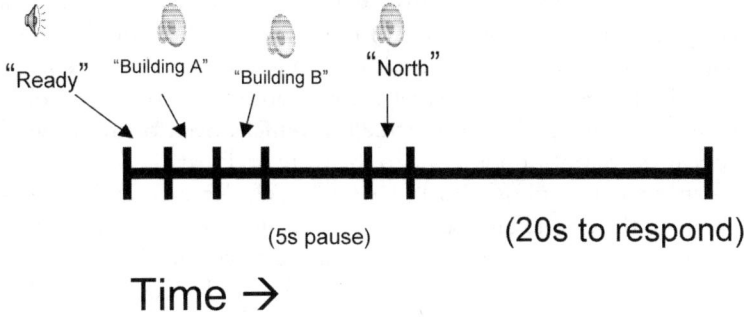

Building Location Comprehension Trial

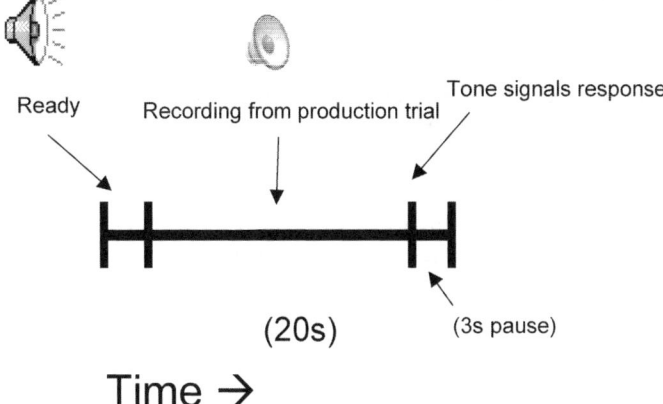

Figure 2.2 Events on production and comprehension trials.

In this way, production and comprehension were closely matched. The produced and comprehended sentences were the same. The same knowledge sources were called upon, and both tasks required participants to deal with exactly two building pairs. Both speech tasks required spatial reasoning of the kind that occurs when giving or receiving directions in the car, in person, or by telephone. This permitted a comparison of speaking and understanding under conditions that ensured similar cognitive processes, processes which are shared by production and comprehension.

The language and driving tasks were performed in the Beckman Institute Driving Simulator. The simulator is a real automobile, an automatic-transmission 1998 Saturn SL, positioned between eight projection screens displaying an integrated 260° view to the front and rear of the vehicle (Figure 2.3). The displays mimic movement through natural environments. The driving scenarios, the movements of the vehicle, and the behaviours of interacting vehicles were simulated with commercial simulation software adapted for the purposes of the experiment. Figure 2.4 shows a simulated environment photographed from outside the vehicle. Seen from inside, the display appears as a continuous scene to the front and rear.

In two experiments, Kubose, Bock, Dell, Garnsey, Kramer, and Mayhugh (2006) examined the effects of speech production and speech comprehension on continuous measures of velocity, lane maintenance, and headway maintenance (maintenance of a safe distance behind a lead vehicle). Simulated wind gusts, variable in strength and direction, made vehicle control more difficult, similar to a technique in a driving task designed by Graham and Carter (2001). In one experiment, driving was easy: Participants simply had to maintain their speed (55 miles per hour) and position in the right-hand lane of a straight, two-lane rural highway with intermittent oncoming traffic, compensating for wind gusts. In the second experiment, the driving task was similar but harder: On the same two-lane road, with the same intermittent oncoming traffic and wind gusts, drivers had to maintain a safe following distance (headway) from a lead vehicle. Headway maintenance was complicated by simulating the erratic slowing and acceleration of a box truck ahead of the driver's vehicle.

Kubose et al. (2006) found that driving was indeed worse under dual-task conditions than under single-task conditions, consistent with other dual-task driving studies (Rakauskas, Gugerty, & Ward, 2004). As Figure 2.5 (top panel) illustrates, in easy driving there was increased variability in velocity when driving was accompanied by a speech task than when driving was the only task, and in the harder driving task (bottom panel) there was increased variability in headway time when speech accompanied driving. However, counter to the expectation of greater difficulty due to production than to comprehension, the differences in the effects of the two secondary tasks were negligible. Figure 2.5 shows that the impact of production on driving was no worse than the impact of comprehension on driving. Paradoxically, on one measure, talking actually seemed to improve driving performance

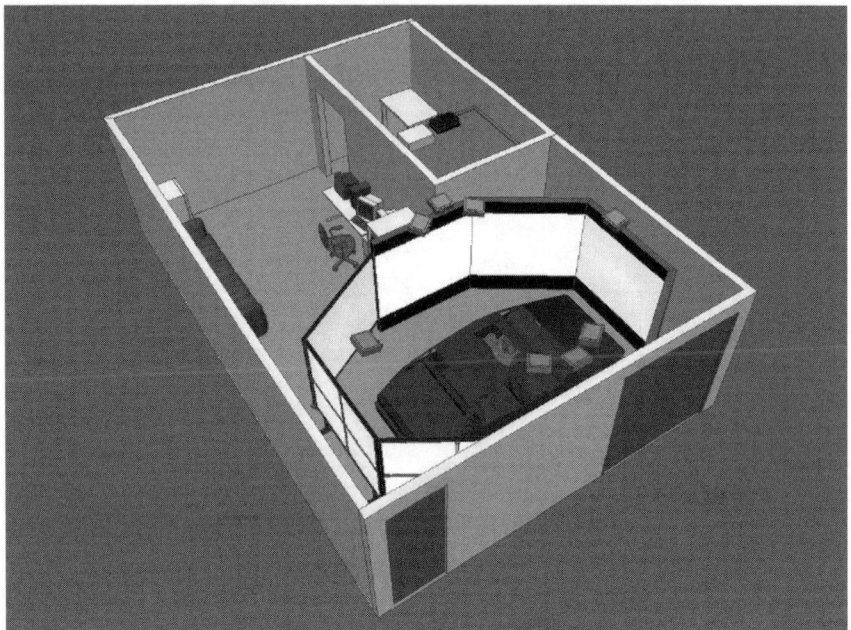

Figure 2.3 Beckman Institute Driving Simulator.

Figure 2.4 A simulated environment photographed from outside the vehicle.

Variability in Velocity, Easy Driving

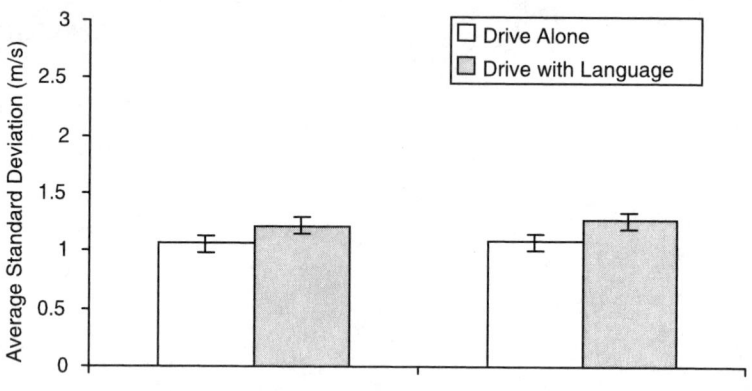

Variability in Headway Time, Harder Driving

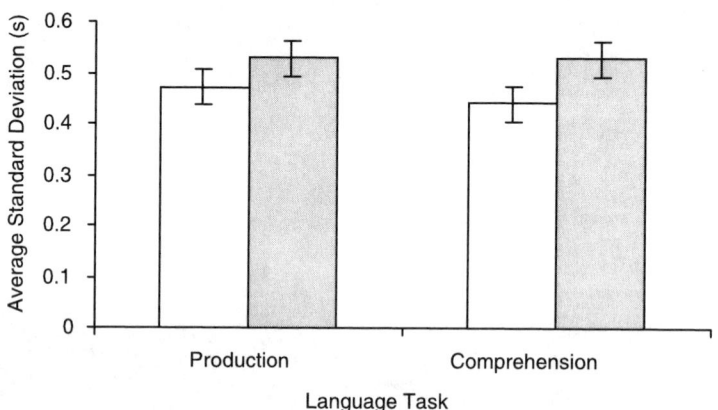

Figure 2.5 Change in variability of driving performance when driving alone or driving while talking (Production) or understanding (Comprehension) (from
Kubose et al., 2006).

relative to driving in silence. With an accompanying production task, there
was less variability in the maintenance of lane position for easier as well as
harder driving. Comprehension, in contrast, had no effect relative to silent
driving on either of these measures.

There are a number of ways to interpret these results. Routine driving is a
highly automated task for most young adults, and its performance may tend
to improve when attention is directed elsewhere. Experts can get worse when
they try to focus on the components of their skills (Beilock & Carr, 2001;
Beilock, Carr, MacMahon, & Starkes, 2002). This would account for the
unexpected reduction in the variability of lane position that accompanied

production, and would be consistent with the hypothesis that production demands more attention than comprehension. In light of the generally similar effects of production and comprehension on dual-task performance, however, another interpretation is that when the contents of the language (the messages, the syntax, the words, the phonology, and so on) for comprehension and production are well equated, the attentional demands are very much the same. Obviously, given the inherent disparities between understanding and generating language, this is a claim that deserves a sceptical reception and requires considerable buttressing. In the next section, we inspect it more closely, calling on finer-grained measures of driving performance time-locked to specific aspects of speech events.

Speaking and listening: Breaking ground and wrapping up

In terms of correct performance on the secondary language tasks, Kubose et al. (2006) found few differences between comprehension and production. Overall accuracy of producing and verifying building locations was better than 85%, with only a 1% decrease in accuracy under dual-task conditions. Comprehenders and producers showed similar levels of performance and similarly small reductions when the language tasks accompanied driving, consistent with their generally similar performance profiles.

These global similarities were found on measures recorded over fairly long intervals. The comprehension and production trials on which dual-task performance was assessed could take as long as 20 s; the utterances themselves consumed 8.6 s, less than a half of the whole period, on average. To determine how the peak local demands associated with comprehension and production compared under dual-task conditions, we determined the onsets and offsets of speech on every driving trial, time-locked the driving measures to the speech events, and examined the driving performance changes that accompanied the production and comprehension of the building location statements.

Figures 2.6 and 2.7 depict speech-localized variations in performance during production (top panel) and comprehension (bottom panel). Time 0 on each graph represents the onset of the 20-s data-recording periods. During the ensuing 20 s, the timing of the events during the production and comprehension tasks was as follows. On production trials, the offset of the recorded direction prompts (north, east, etc.) occurred at 7.25 s. The average onset of speaking came 2.74 s later, with the offset of the first clause occurring approximately 3.75 s after that. During these 3.75 s, speakers said things along the lines of "The Undergraduate Library is south of Foellinger Auditorium . . .". The utterance ended after another clause, on average, 8.5 s after speech began. Events on the comprehension trials occurred along the same timescale, with the important exception that the comprehenders did not hear the recorded direction prompts, but only what the speakers said. The onset of the audio for comprehenders occurred 6.25 s after trial onset.

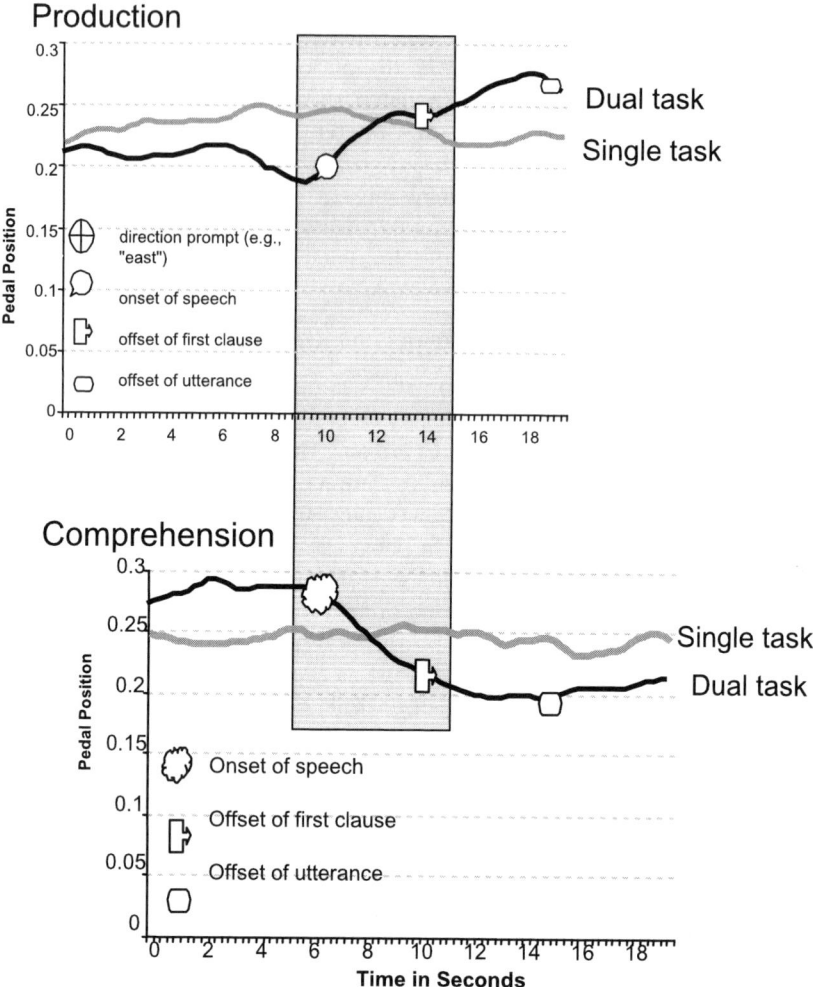

Figure 2.6 Localized changes in driving performance accompanying speech events.

The figures align speech onset across the two tasks, the onset of speaking in the production task and the onset of listening in the comprehension task. The graphed values are aggregates over performance during each quarter-second within the recording period. The heavy black line represents the dual-task condition, and the grey line represents the single-task condition. The boxed areas in each graph highlight the changes in the measures during production and comprehension of the first clauses of the building location descriptions.

The measures shown are direct reflections of the drivers' operation of the

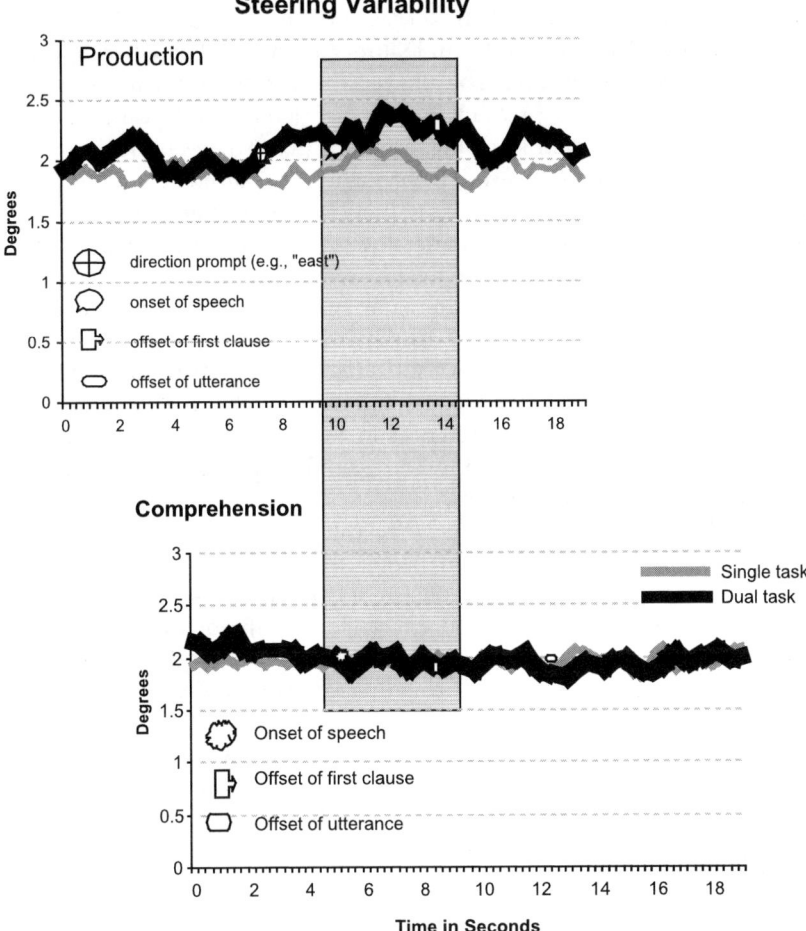

Figure 2.7 Localized changes in steering accompanying speech events.

vehicle's accelerator and steering wheel under the more challenging driving conditions that required headway maintenance. Steering variability is shown in degrees, and accelerator position in a range between 0 and 1, where 0 is no pressure and 1 is maximum pressure ("floored"). Because steering and acceleration both demanded continuous adaptations in order to deal with wind gusts and changes in the speed of the lead vehicle, they give a moment-by-moment picture of how drivers controlled the vehicle's perceived position and speed.

For accelerator position, shown in Figure 2.6, there were localized changes in driving performance accompanying speaking and listening at the expected points of greatest production and comprehension difficulty. Recall that, in production, we anticipated changes in driving occurring close to the onsets of clauses, whereas, in comprehension, we anticipated changes closer to the ends of clauses. The top panel of Figure 2.6 shows that when speakers received the direction prompt that allowed them to begin formulating their utterances, they reduced pressure on the accelerator and continued that reduction until they began speaking, at which point they began to increase pressure and continued increasing it throughout the utterance. For comprehenders, shown in the bottom panel, reduction in accelerator pressure began with the onset of the recorded utterance and continued through the end of the first clause. So, in production, the greatest reduction in accelerator pressure occurs during formulation, just prior to utterance onset; in comprehension, the greatest reduction begins close to the end of the clause and continues through the second clause. Both of these effects were statistically significant ($t(21) = -2.96$, $p < .01$ for production and $t(23) = 5.82$, $p < .001$ for comprehension) and, despite the differences in their timing, the magnitudes of the changes in accelerator position were similar relative to the negligible changes for the single-task controls.

The results for steering in Figure 2.7 revealed a different pattern. In comprehension, shown in the bottom panel, the absence of changes in the comprehenders' performance is consistent with the absence of dual-task effects in the maintenance of lane effects for comprehension. Producers, however, showed increased variability in steering ($t(21) = -2.728$, $p = .013$), beginning with the presentation of the direction prompt—again, the trigger for the onset of utterance formulation. However, in light of the better maintenance of lane position during dual-task than during single-task performance in production, the most viable interpretation of this increased variability is in terms of how successfully speakers dealt with wind gusts. To maintain lane position against unpredictable gusts of wind requires continuous adjustments to steering, and it appears that while they were speaking the drivers in the production condition did this better than when they were only driving.

The local variations in driving performance during speaking and listening disclose that the changes are concurrent with the accompanying speech events, and the nature of the changes is consistent with the broad differences measured over longer intervals. The process of production was accompanied by *improved* lane maintenance, and the changes in steering needed for better lane maintenance were temporally linked to the features of production that make the greatest demands. At analogous times, comprehension had no differential effect on steering. When talking and listening did interfere with driving, the interference came at different times, but the kinds and amount of disruption were similar. The times were linked to the beginnings and ends of clauses, the structures that correspond most closely to "idea units" in language. Apparently, in production, it was the mental ground breaking needed to assemble these units that was disruptive; in listening, it was the mental wrap-up that caused problems.

Implications

The time-course data showed the expected differences in the profiles of difficulty for comprehension and production. They also showed similarities in the amounts of disruption, when disruptions arose. An open, pressing question is how the contents of the language employed contributed to these similarities. The spatial thinking that was required in order to formulate and understand utterances in the building-location tasks may be more taxing, or simply different, than other messages conveyed in language, due to the special nature of the disruptions associated with spatial cognition (cf. Irwin & Brockmole, 2004). If so, messages with different contents could have different effects. Although Recarte and Nunes (2003) found very few content-associated variations in driving disruption in a comparison of concrete and abstract language, it is unclear whether their concrete passages called on spatial imagery. But even if other kinds of language impose fewer demands, the importance of spatial cognition to driving and to ordinary communication during driving makes any negative impact of spatial language on comprehension a finding to be reckoned with. It means that following verbal directions, whether from a passenger or from the audio of a telematic device, can be very hard.

As it stands, the tentative conclusion from the present findings is that when the linguistic and conceptual complexity of language is controlled, and accuracy of understanding is required, language comprehension can interfere just as much with driving as talking does. A second conclusion is that when production and comprehension differed in the magnitudes of their effects, production actually served to improve driving performance. There is nothing in these results to suggest substantial disparities in the degree to which speaking and listening interfere with other activities, except in their timing.

Whether we see speaking as being objectively more demanding than understanding depends on the interpretation of the paradox of improved lane position that accompanied speaking in two experiments (Kubose et al., 2006) and the corresponding changes in steering that were time-linked to the events of production. These changes could reflect an improved ability to perform expert, highly practised, routinized skills when attention is drawn away from them. This is compatible with Beilock's (Beilock & Carr, 2001; Beilock et al., 2002) interpretation of how and why conscious attention interferes with skilled performance. If it is right, we would expect to see production interfere more than comprehension with other, less routine, less automatic skills. Likewise, we might expect to see improvements in the performance of some other highly practised skills when they are accompanied by talking. These speculations remain to be tested.

An alternative interpretation of these effects is specific to driving and, perhaps, similarly dangerous activities. Alm and Nilsson (1994) proposed that drivers are sensitive to the problems that talking can cause, and therefore selectively increase attention to the elements of a task that are dangerous. Kubose et al. (2006) tried to test this by changing the most threatening elements of the driving task, but they found the same patterns of results over two experiments. When lane position was the most important factor in safety, drivers maintained lane position better when talking than when not. When headway maintenance was also essential to safety, drivers dropped further behind the lead vehicle while performing the language tasks, regardless of whether the task involved comprehension or production. Only the speakers showed improved lane maintenance at the same time.

So, drivers who were talking stayed more reliably in their lanes, coping better with wind gusts, than they did when they were not talking. Assuming that their increased variability in steering (Figure 2.7) reflected coping with the wind, the talkers did not exhibit improved lane maintenance throughout the driving trials. Instead, the improvements actually accompanied speaking. There was no similar reaction by the comprehenders, despite their similar tendency to drop behind the lead vehicle. Therefore, if compensation for increased danger is indeed a strategic reaction to the secondary language tasks, we could conclude that drivers regard speaking as more dangerous than listening and as requiring additional forms of compensation, a conclusion that would support an interpretation of speaking as the harder task. Alternatively, it could be that listening elicits fewer efforts to compensate for danger than speaking does. If so, one might reason that listeners must be *more* distracted than speakers, implying that understanding is harder than talking. Although this stretches credulity and strains the logic of dual-task performance, it is nonetheless fully consistent with a compensatory hypothesis.

A final interpretation is that something about the act of speaking supports more active steering, regardless of attentional demands. Without knowing precisely what that something could be or how it works, we point to a phenomenon called "motor overflow" in the human-performance literature. Motor overflow is a spread of motor system output to muscles that would otherwise be at rest (Bodwell, Mahurin, Waddle, Price, & Cramer, 2003). Failure to inhibit motor overflow could reflect demands on attention, too, but since comprehenders presumably have no motor overflow to inhibit, its workings are relevant only to the driving performance of the talkers. Motor overflow channelled through the natural skill of wayfinding and the acquired, well-practised skill of steering may transiently serve to enhance the ability to stay on course.

In short, there is no selective support in our findings for the hypothesis that producing language is harder than understanding it. We do have evidence from variations in velocity and headway maintenance that production and comprehension alike change driving safety for the worse, and that the changes are temporally linked to the acts of talking and understanding.

The mechanisms of production and comprehension

The simplest conclusion from our results is that talking and understanding are both hard, because on the simplest interpretation of our dual-task measures, they seem to be about equally disruptive. Because these findings come from a dual task that was designed to equate the linguistic complexity and cognitive contents of the language used, this conclusion implies that the peripheral channels, together with the underlying mechanisms, do not differ substantially in their demands on or interference with other processes.

The peripheral channels for speaking and hearing language are clearly different in many respects, and seem to take independent tolls on attention (Martin et al., 1999; Shallice et al., 1985). What is largely unknown and a subject of long-standing debate is whether and how the central mechanisms for comprehending and producing speech divide. Classical models of aphasia posit different neural underpinnings for comprehension and production (Martin, 2003), but modern research has blurred these boundaries with evidence that the differing problems of aphasics may be better explained in terms of the general severity of the impairment or specific linguistic deficits (i.e., deficits to components of language such as the lexicon or syntax) than in terms of modality.

If comprehension and production are subserved by identical cognitive mechanisms, it would make sense for them to be nearly equivalent in their ability to interfere with other activities. However, for many of the same reasons that we lack evidence about their relative difficulty, we do not know whether they work in the same ways. Theories about the relationship between production and comprehension run the gamut from near equation of the two systems (Kempen, 1999; MacKay, 1987) to endorsement of the substantial functional and neuroanatomical separation of modality-specific information (Caramazza, 1997). In between are claims that the systems are separate but intertwined in various ways. Bever (1970; Townsend & Bever, 2001) proposed that something similar to the production system serves as a backstop for language comprehension, checking its operation with analysis by synthesis. On this kind of view, the comprehension system normally relies on sophisticated lexical guesswork without much early reliance on syntax, bringing the production system's syntax into play during comprehension to verify candidate interpretations. Garrett (2000) argued not only that the production system may serve as an analysis-by-synthesis backstop for the comprehension system, but also that the comprehension system may serve as a synthesis-by-analysis backstop for production. In some theories of language production, comprehension operates to monitor the accuracy of the process (Levelt, 1989).

While falling short of establishing how production and comprehension differ or converge, there is growing evidence for similarities in their workings. Parallel findings for number agreement in English (Bock & Cutting, 1992; Pearlmutter, Garnsey, & Bock, 1999), for structural adaptations from language comprehension to language production that parallel adaptations within production (Bock, Chang, Dell, & Onishi, in press), and for similarities in lexical-structural preferences (Garnsey, Pearlmutter, Myers, & Lotocky, 1997), all indicate that whatever the differences between the systems, they must have a lot in common. To support the prosaic successes of human communication, they have to. Our preliminary results seem to extend the similarities of normal language comprehension and production to their capacity to interfere with other activities.

Some practical implications and some practical limitations

To return briefly to the practical goal of our work, we make one addition to the growing body of research showing that the use of automotive telematic devices can be hazardous to one's health. It is now fairly well established that the major disruptions to driving from the use of cellular telephones come not from the manipulation of the devices, but from the cognitive demands of ordinary conversation (Nunes & Recarte, 2002; Strayer & Johnston, 2001). This makes moot the current regulations in some states and cities that require the use of hands-free telephones in automobiles. Until the demands of conversation are better understood, we are in a poor position to legislate the details of when and how people should use the mobile communication apparatus that is available to them, down to and including the ubiquitous radio. We need safer, better-informed designs for the increasingly sophisticated and increasingly intrusive devices of the present and near future, including navigation aids and electronic mail. Current research hints that the use of cellular telephones is already more distracting than anything else we do while driving cars and can increase the probability of accidents by a factor of four (Redelmeier & Tibshirani, 1997). To this, our results provisionally add the bad news that the problems can be exacerbated as much by drivers' careful listening as by their talking.

The provision is that there is obviously much more to be done in order to establish how general (which is to say, how limited) this conclusion may be. The narrow range of driving situations we sampled, the artificiality of even a high-fidelity driving simulator, and the restricted nature of the messages that drivers produced and understood, all argue that strong conclusions would be premature. Our findings nonetheless offer good reasons to revisit the seductive idea that listening to language is little more distracting for drivers than doing nothing else at all (Recarte & Nunes, 2003).

Summary

A widely credited assumption about language is that producing it is much harder than comprehending it. The assumption is often treated as an explanation for why infants start to understand before they start to talk, for why second-language learners can understand languages that they cannot speak, and, more generally, for why the vocabulary and structural complexity accessible to comprehenders seem to exceed those accessible to speakers. But in spite of its intuitive appeal, the assumption of significant disparities in the difficulty of comprehension and production has scant empirical support. The record is thin for understandable reasons. There are problems in disentangling the component processes of comprehension and production, problems in equating the information called upon during task performance, and problems in pinpointing where variations in performance arise when someone hears or says a normal, structured sequence of words and phrases. We have begun to address these problems in experiments that equate the speech that is produced and understood within a task environment that provides continuous performance measures. Specifically, speakers and listeners respectively produce and understand the same utterances while driving in a simulator that provides continuous assessment of acceleration, velocity, lane position, steering, following distance, braking latency, and so on. Utterances are elicited with a task that controls utterance content while ensuring utterance novelty for the speakers who spontaneously produce them as well as the listeners who later understand them. Relative to single-task control conditions (driving only and speaking or listening only), we find differences between speakers and listeners in the management of component tasks, but no generalized, differential degradation in the driving performance of speakers compared to listeners. Performance degradation is time-locked to specific events of comprehension and production. The findings have implications for claims about the nature of the challenges that automotive telematic systems present to safe driving as well as for theories of executive processes in language use.

Acknowledgements

Authors are listed alphabetically. We are grateful to Pierre Wiltzius and the Beckman Institute, to Ko Kurokawa and General Motors, to the National Institutes of Health (grant numbers T32-MH18990 and R01-MH66089), and to the National Science Foundation (grant number BCS-0214270) for their support. We also thank Hank Kaczmarski, Braden Kowitz, Camille Goudeseune, Jim Farrar, and Debbie Carrier for helping to keep the simulator laboratory running smoothly; Jill Barr, Valerie Brisky, Natalie Hall, Christopher Johnson, Etienne Korvorst, Laura Matzen, Jeff Nelson, Ankur Patel, Erik Pedersen, Seth Redenbo, Brian Roland, and Aaron Yao for their help with data collection and analysis; Simon Garrod, Alan Baddeley, and other conference participants for helpful comments on the work; and Antje Meyer, Andrea Krott, and Linda Wheeldon for generously providing the venue, the funding, and the patience that made this chapter possible.

References

Alm, H., & Nilsson, L. (1994). Changes in driver behaviour as a function of hands-free mobile phones—a simulator study. *Accident Analysis and Prevention, 26,* 441–451.

Alm, H., & Nilsson, L. (2001). The use of car phones and changes in driver behaviour. *International Journal of Vehicle Design, 26,* 4–11.

Baddeley, A. (2003). Working memory: Looking back and looking forward. *Nature Reviews Neuroscience, 4,* 829–839.

Beilock, S. L., & Carr, T. H. (2001). On the fragility of skilled performance: What governs choking under pressure? *Journal of Experimental Psychology: General, 130,* 701–725.

Beilock, S. L., Carr, T. H., MacMahon, C., & Starkes, J. L. (2002). When attention becomes counterproductive: Divided versus skill-focused attention in performance of sensorimotor skills by novices and experts. *Journal of Experimental Psychology: Applied, 8,* 6–16.

Benedict, H. (1979). Early lexical development: Comprehension and production. *Journal of Child Language, 6,* 183–200.

Bever, T. G. (1970). The cognitive basis for linguistic structures. In J. R. Hayes (Ed.), *Cognition and the development of language* (pp. 279–362). New York: Wiley.

Bock, K. (1995). Sentence production: From mind to mouth. In J. L. Miller & P. D. Eimas (Eds.), *Handbook of perception and cognition. Vol. 11: Speech, language, and communication* (pp. 181–216). Orlando, FL: Academic Press.

Bock, J. K., Chang, F., Dell, G. S., & Onishi, K. H. (in press). Persistent structural priming from language comprehension to language production. *Cognition.*

Bock, J. K., & Cutting, J. C. (1992). Regulating mental energy: Performance units in language production. *Journal of Memory and Language, 31,* 99–127.

Bock, J. K., Irwin, D. E., & Davidson, D. J. (2004). Putting first things first. In J. M. Henderson & F. Ferreira (Eds.), *The integration of language, vision, and action: Eye movements and the visual world* (pp. 249–278). New York: Psychology Press.

Bock, J. K., Irwin, D. E., Davidson, D. J., & Levelt, W. J. M. (2003). Minding the clock. *Journal of Memory and Language, 48,* 653–685.

Bodwell, J. A., Mahurin, R. K., Waddle, S., Price, R., & Cramer, S. C. (2003). Age and features of movement influence motor overflow. *Journal of the American Geriatrics Society, 51,* 1735–1739.

Brown, R., & McNeill, D. (1966). The "tip of the tongue" phenomenon. *Journal of Verbal Learning and Verbal Behavior, 5,* 325–337.

Caramazza, A. (1997). How many levels of processing are there in lexical access? *Cognitive Neuropsychology, 14,* 177–208.

Clark, H. H., & Wasow, T. (1998). Repeating words in spontaneous speech. *Cognitive Psychology, 37,* 201–242.

Fink, B. R. (1986). Complexity. *Science, 231,* 319.

Ford, M. (1983). A method for obtaining measures of local parsing complexity throughout sentences. *Journal of Verbal Learning and Verbal Behavior, 22,* 203–218.

Ford, M., & Holmes, V. (1978). Planning units and syntax in sentence production. *Cognition, 6*, 35–53.

Garnsey, S. M., Pearlmutter, N. J., Myers, E., & Lotocky, M. A. (1997). The contributions of verb bias and plausibility to the comprehension of temporarily ambiguous sentences. *Journal of Memory and Language, 37*, 58–93.

Garrett, M. (2000). Remarks on the architecture of language processing systems. In Y. Grodzinsky, L. P. Shapiro, & D. Swinney (Eds.), *Language and the brain: Representation and processing* (pp. 31–69). San Diego, CA: Academic Press.

Garrett, M., Bever, T., & Fodor, J. (1966). The active use of grammar in speech perception. *Perception and Psychophysics, 1*, 30–32.

Gordon, P. C., Hendrick, R., & Levine, W. H. (2002). Memory-load interference in syntactic processing. *Psychological Science, 13*, 425–430.

Graham, R., & Carter, C. (2001). Voice dialling can reduce the interference between concurrent tasks of driving and phoning. *International Journal of Vehicle Design, 26*, 30–47.

Holmes, V. M., & Forster, K. I. (1970). Detection of extraneous signals during sentence recognition. *Perception and Psychophysics, 7*, 297–301.

Huttenlocher, J. (1974). The origins of language comprehension. In R. L. Solso (Ed.), *Theories in cognitive psychology: The Loyola Symposium* (pp. 331–368). Hillsdale, NJ: Lawrence Erlbaum Associates, Inc.

Irwin, D. E., & Brockmole, J. (2004). Suppressing *where* but not *what*: The effect of saccades on dorsal- and ventral-stream visual processing. *Psychological Science, 15*, 467–473.

James, W. (1890). *The principles of psychology* (Vol. 1). New York: Dover.

Jonides, J., & Mack, R. (1984). On the cost and benefit of cost and benefit. *Psychological Bulletin, 96*, 29–44.

Kempen, G. (1999). *Human grammatical coding.* Unpublished manuscript, Leiden University, Leiden, the Netherlands.

Kubose, T., Bock, J. K., Dell, G. S., Garnsey, S. M., Kramer, A. F., & Mayhugh, J. (2006). The effects of speech production and speech comprehension on simulated driving performance. *Journal of Applied Cognitive Psychology, 20*, 43–63.

Lamble, D., Kauranen, T., Laasko, M., & Summala, H. (1999). Cognitive load and detection thresholds in car following situations: Safety implications for using mobile (cellular) telephones while driving. *Accident Analysis and Prevention, 31*, 617–623.

Levelt, W. J. M. (1989). *Speaking: From intention to articulation.* Cambridge, MA: MIT Press.

MacKay, D. G. (1987). *The organization of perception and action: A theory for language and other cognitive skills.* Berlin: Springer-Verlag.

Maclay, H., & Osgood, C. E. (1959). Hesitation phenomena in spontaneous English speech. *Word, 15*, 19–44.

Martin, R. C. (2003). Language processing: Functional organization and neuro-anatomical basis. *Annual Review of Psychology, 54*, 55–89.

Martin, R., Lesch, M., & Bartha, M. (1999). Independence of input and output phonology in word processing and short-term memory. *Journal of Memory and Language, 41*, 3–29.

McKnight, A. J., & McKnight, A. S. (1993). The effect of cellular phone use upon driver attention. *Accident Analysis and Prevention, 25*, 259–265.

Mitchell, D. C., & Green, D. W. (1978). The effects of context and content on immediate processing in reading. *Quarterly Journal of Experimental Psychology, 30,* 609–636.

Nunes, L. M., & Recarte, M. A. (2002). Cognitive demands of hands-free-phone conversation while driving. *Transportation Research Part F, 5,* 133–144.

Pearlmutter, N. J., Garnsey, S. M., & Bock, J. K. (1999). Agreement processes in sentence comprehension. *Journal of Memory and Language, 41,* 427–456.

Rakauskas, M., Gugerty, L., & Ward, N. J. (2004). Effects of cell phone conversations on driving performance with naturalistic conversation. *Journal of Safety Research, 35,* 453–464.

Recarte, M. A., & Nunes, L. M. (2003). Mental workload while driving: Effects on visual search, discrimination, and decision making. *Journal of Experimental Psychology: Applied, 9,* 119–137.

Redelmeier, D. A., & Tibshirani, R. J. (1997). Associations between cellular-telephone calls and motor vehicle collisions. *New England Journal of Medicine, 336,* 453–458.

Shallice, T., McLeod, P., & Lewis, K. (1985). Isolating cognitive modules with the dual-task paradigm: Are speech perception and production separate processes? *Quarterly Journal of Experimental Psychology, 37A,* 507–532.

Shapiro, L. P., Zurif, E., & Grimshaw, J. (1987). Sentence processing and the mental representation of verbs. *Cognition, 27,* 219–246.

Strayer, D. L., & Johnston, W. A. (2001). Driven to distraction: Dual-task studies of simulated driving and conversing on a cellular telephone. *Psychological Science, 12,* 462–466.

Strayer, D. L., Drews, F. A., & Johnston, W. A. (2003). Cellphone-induced failures of visual attention during simulated driving. *Journal of Experimental Psychology: Applied, 9,* 23–32.

Townsend, D. J., & Bever, T. G. (2001). *Sentence comprehension: The integration of habits and rules.* Cambridge, MA: MIT Press.

van de Weijer, J. (1999). *Language input for word discovery.* Nijmegen, the Netherlands: MPI Series in Psycholinguistics.

Violanti, J. M. (1998). Cellular phones and fatal traffic collisions. *Accident Analysis and Prevention, 30,* 519–524.

Violanti, J. M., & Marshall, J. R. (1996). Cellular phones and traffic accidents: An epidemiological approach. *Accident Analysis and Prevention, 28,* 265–270.

3 The control of bilingual language switching

Julia Rayner and Andrew W. Ellis
University of York, UK

Introduction

Bilinguals regularly switch between languages when communicating with other bilinguals. This is referred to as "code switching" (Clyne, 1980; Poplack, 1980). A great deal of research has been carried out to explain how bilinguals are able to code switch and yet keep their two languages apart. Grosjean's (1997, 2001) conceptualization of a "language mode continuum" describes a range of forms of language mixing that can occur, depending on the "language mode" a bilingual speaker is in. That in turn depends on whether the bilingual is communicating with monolinguals or other bilingual speakers. In monolingual mode, the bilingual adopts the language of another monolingual speaker, with the nonshared language being deactivated or inhibited so that it does not intrude upon the language being spoken. According to Grosjean, bilinguals adopt a "bilingual mode" when communicating with other bilinguals who share the same languages. A base (or matrix) language is adopted and the other language (termed the "guest language") is brought in as and when needed. In this case, both languages will be activated but one more strongly than the other. The levels of activation of different languages will depend on factors such as the local language environment, the knowledge of other speakers, the demands of the processing task, and the proficiency of the speakers. Less proficient bilinguals will require greater control of the first language (L1) when operating in the second language (L2). Often there are insufficient resources to control the language not required, resulting in intrusions from the more dominant language.

A bilingual in bilingual mode will therefore be switching constantly between one language and the other. Penfield and Roberts (1959) were the first explicitly to propose the idea of a language switch in the brain. They described it as a device that is "curiously automatic", and has the effect of turning one language off when the other is on. Although bilinguals switch without apparent difficulty, cognitive-psycholinguistic research shows that there is generally a cost to switching between languages that takes the form of a slight pause when moving from one language into another. Using Penfield and Roberts' metaphor (which, as we shall see later, breaks down eventually), we could say that it takes time to throw the language switch. Kolers (1966) carried out some of the first experimental studies of language switching. Participants with a working knowledge of both French and English were asked to read aloud passages of text. The passages could be entirely in French or English, or could alternate between the two languages every few words. Kolers found that the reading speed for mixed text was slower than for pure texts and attributed the extra time to the cost of repeatedly switching between languages.

Dalrymple-Alford (1985) adapted this procedure and had French–English bilinguals read aloud lists of printed words that could be all-French or all-English ("pure lists"), or a mixture of French and English ("mixed lists"). The times taken to read the mixed lists were longer than the times taken to read the pure lists, providing further evidence of language-switching costs.

Kolers (1966) and Dalrymple-Alford (1985) avoided words that occur in both French and English, so that each written word dictated the language in which it was to be read (an exogenous cue). Macnamara, Krauthammer, and Bolgar (1968) used numbers (Arabic numerals) as their stimuli rather than words. The numbers had names in both the languages of their bilingual participants, so gave no intrinsic cue as to the language in which they should be named. In fact, each number was presented inside one of two geometric shapes that identified the language in which the number was to be named. This task places more emphasis on endogenously driven language switching than the tasks used by Kolers (1966) and Dalrymple-Alford (1985). The results showed an increase in response times and a greater number of errors for mixed naming than naming the digits in only one language. Macnamara et al. (1968) concluded that there were two distinct language systems and a device for switching between them which took time to operate.

An important study by Meuter and Allport (1999) sought to determine whether or not language switching should be regarded as simply one of many forms of task switching. Everyday life constantly requires us to switch between different tasks, and there is a substantial literature on the cognitive mechanisms that make such switching possible (see Allport & Wylie, 2000a, 2000b; Monsell, 2003). Many studies have looked at the speed of performing a given task to a given stimulus as a function of whether the same task was performed on the previous stimulus (a so-called nonswitch trial) or whether a different task was performed on the previous item (a switch trial). For example, participants may be required to alternate between deciding on some trials of an experiment whether a digit shown on a computer screen is odd or even, and deciding on other trials whether the digits are higher or lower than the number 7. There will be some cue on the screen for each trial to indicate which task is to be performed on that trial (e.g., the background colour of the screen or an accompanying auditory tone). A general finding is that reaction times tend to be faster when the task being performed on a given trial of the experiment is the same as the task performed on the previous trial (nonswitch trials) compared with when the task on the previous trial was different (switch trials). The difference between the speed of responding on switch and nonswitch trials provides a measure of the magnitude of the switching cost (e.g., Allport, Styles, & Hsieh, 1994; Rogers & Monsell, 1995). Studies show that if participants receive advance warning of the need to switch tasks on the next trial, switching costs are reduced. They are not, however, eliminated. It is as if participants can go some way toward instantiating the cognitive processes required for the new task by endogenous, preparatory task-switching processes, but external input is required to achieve a full switch-over from one set of processes to another. Rogers and Monsell (1995) argued that the preparatory component can be reduced if participants can anticipate the proceeding switch trial and therefore prepare for it. The residual component, however, is stimulus-related and independent of the amount of preparation that is possible for the upcoming trial. If the stimulus evokes cognitive processes that are no longer required, there will be competition between the old and the new processes, and the efficiency of switching will be impaired as a consequence. The residual persistence of one task set until an exogenous input requires a different form of response is sometimes known as "task set inertia" (see Allport & Wylie, 2000a, 2000b; Monsell, 2003, for reviews).

One of the findings to emerge from the task-switching literature concerns the relative costs of switching from an easier task to a harder task or from a harder task to an easier task. The well-known "Stroop effect" requires people to name the colour of the ink in which words are written (rather than reading the actual words). This becomes extraordinarily difficult when the words are themselves colour names. If you are faced with the word RED printed in green ink, it is easy to respond "red" by simply reading the word aloud, but very difficult to respond "green" by naming the colour of the ink. Allport et al. (1994) exploited this asymmetry in task difficulty. Depending on the cue they were given, participants had either to read colour names aloud (the easy task) or name the colours of the inks in which they were printed (the difficult task). The speed of responding on nonswitch trials (where the same task had been performed on the previous trial) was compared with the speed of responding on switch trials (where the other task had been performed on the previous trial). Ink colours were named at much the same speed irrespective of whether the previous trial had involved reading aloud (switch) or colour naming (nonswitch). In contrast, reading colour names was much faster when the previous trial had also involved (nonswitch) than when it had involved naming ink colours (switch). Thus, there was a substantial cost associated with switching from the easy to the difficult task and much less of a cost associated with switching from the difficult to the easy task. This pattern of results was replicated by Allport and Wylie (2000b) and fits with other reports of asymmetrical switch costs between pairs of tasks which differ on difficulty (e.g., De Jong, 1995; Harvey, 1984).

Allport et al. (1994) proposed that when participants are doing the easier of two tasks, little suppression of the more difficult task set is required because that task does not compete with the easier one. Thus, when participants are reading aloud written colour names, the names of the colours of the inks are not automatically activated, and so do not compete and do not need to be inhibited. When the task switches from word naming to colour naming, the level of activation of the colour-naming processes is the same as it would have been if the task on the previous trial had also been colour naming, so no switching cost is seen. If, on the other hand, participants are naming ink colours, then the written colour names will tend to be activated quickly and automatically, so that if a participant is trying to name the green ink in which the word *RED* is written, competition will be experienced between the target word "green" and the word "red". In order to perform the colour-naming task efficiently, the processes that would normally respond to the written words have to be actively suppressed. If there is a sudden switch from colour naming to word reading, it takes time to release ("deactivate") the inhibition that has been applied to the word-reading processes, and a switch cost will be seen in the form of slower word reading on switch trials than on nonswitch trials.

Most bilinguals find it easier to speak in one of their languages than the other. For example, their childhood may have been spent speaking one language and they may have begun to learn the other language only in late childhood, or even adulthood. Under such circumstances, the language of childhood would normally be the dominant language while the later-acquired language would be the subordinate language. Meuter and Allport (1999) argued that if language switching behaves in the same way as other types of task switching (and is controlled by the same mechanisms), then there should be more of a cost associated with switching from the second, subordinate language into the first, dominant language than from the first, dominant language into the second, subordinate language. Imagine, for example, an individual who spent their childhood in Spain speaking only Spanish. They began to learn English in school at the age of 10 or 12. Many of the textbooks they used in the course of their university studies in Spain were written in English, so they became reasonably proficient in the second language. They then travelled to Britain to study for a higher degree at university there. Their English improved still further, but they continued to mix socially with fellow Spanish speakers and, if asked, would say that they still found speaking in Spanish easier than speaking in English. When such a person was speaking in Spanish (L1), the words for the desired concepts and meanings in English (L2) would tend not to be activated automatically and would not compete for selection with Spanish words. English would not need to be inhibited in order to speak Spanish, so that if the person wanted to switch from Spanish into English, that second language should be immediately available. If, in contrast, the person was speaking in English (L2), the Spanish (L1) words for desired concepts and meanings *would* tend to be activated automatically and *would* tend to compete with English words for selection. Speaking fluent English would require the suppression or inhibition of Spanish. If the person wanted to switch from English into Spanish, that inhibition would need to be released, causing a momentary delay before normal Spanish fluency was resumed (i.e., a switching cost).

Meuter and Allport (1999) tested the somewhat counter-intuitive prediction that the cost of switching from L2 (difficult) to L1 (easy) should be greater than the cost of switching from L1 to L2. Their participants were people of the sort just described who had a definite first language to which had been added a later second language, and who remained more fluent in L1 than L2. Like Macnamara et al. (1968), Meuter and Allport (1999) used language-neutral digits (1 to 9) as stimuli. The digits were presented individually on a computer screen, and the participants were asked to name them as quickly as possible in one of their two languages depending on the colour of the background surrounding the digit. On approximately two-thirds of the experimental trials, the language required was the same as on the previous trial (nonswitch), while on the remaining one-third of trials a change of language was indicated (switch). The pattern of results predicted from previous studies of general task switching was confirmed. On nonswitch trials, digits were named faster in L1 than in L2. That was reversed, however, on switch trials where digits were named faster in L2 than in L1. What this means is that the participants were experiencing greater difficulty switching from L2 to L1 than from L1 to L2, just as participants in other studies had experienced greater difficulty switching from a difficult task to an easy task than from an easy task to a difficult task.

Comparable results were found by Kroll and Peck (1998). Their bilingual participants named pictures of objects as quickly as possible. Like digits, object pictures are language neutral. Each picture was accompanied by a tone that indicated the language in which it was to be named. In one block of trials, participants were required to name only in L1 or L2 (the pure condition). When there was a change of tone, they simply responded "No". In mixed blocks, participants had to pay attention to the tone and switch language when required. Kroll and Peck (1998) found that L1 naming speeds were slower in the mixed condition than in the pure condition, whereas L2 naming speeds were equally fast (or slow) in both conditions. This result is clearly in keeping with the findings of Meuter and Allport (1999).

The four experiments reported here used a similar experimental paradigm. The participants in each experiment were adults from Spain or South/Central America whose first language was Spanish and who had not begun to learn English until at least the age of 8 years. All had been living in Britain for at least 6 months, mostly as postgraduate students at the University of York. The experimental tasks all involved naming pictures that appeared on a computer screen. The pictures used in the experiments were black-and-white line drawings of familiar objects taken from a set published by Snodgrass and Vanderwart (1980). Critical items had high name agreement in both English and Spanish, meaning that different people tend to give the same names to those items. When the experiment called for different sets of items, they were matched on English and Spanish word frequencies, age of acquisition in Spanish as L1 and English as L2, and naming speeds for native speakers of the two languages.

The pictures were presented in sequences of three ("triplets"). The start of a new triplet was marked by the presentation of a red asterisk on the computer screen. Following Kroll and Peck (1998), each picture was accompanied by either a high tone or a low tone. Except for one condition of experiment 1 (the pure language blocks), the tone cued the participant as to whether the picture should be named in English or Spanish. The first two pictures of each triplet were always accompanied by the same tone, and so were both named in either Spanish or English. The third item could be accompanied by the same tone, indicating that the picture was to be named in the same language as the previous two (a nonswitch trial) or it could be accompanied by a different tone, indicating that the picture was to be named in the other language (a switch trial). Participants were made aware of the triplet structure of trials through instructions and a practice session. The presentation of each picture on the computer screen started a millisecond clock in the computer. The production of the spoken name was detected by a microphone attached to a voice key which stopped the clock. The naming latency on each trial was taken as the time between the appearance of the picture on the screen and the start of the spoken name. Only naming times on the third items in triplets are reported. They were the items that could be named in L1 or L2 under nonswitch or switch conditions. Error rates were generally low, and when differences were observed between conditions they were in the same direction as the differences in naming latencies.

Experiment 1 sought to demonstrate that this paradigm was effective in generating switch costs and to discover whether they were asymmetrical, as in the studies of Kroll and Peck (1998) and Meuter and Allport (1999). Experiments 2 to 4 built on the results of experiment 1, looking to see whether it was possible under certain circumstances to obtain costs of switching from L1 to L2 that were comparable with the costs of switching from L2 into L1. Full details of all four experiments can be found in Rayner (2004).

Experiment 1: Asymmetric switching costs between L1 and L2

Participants in experiment 1 attended two testing sessions separated by 2 weeks. As noted above, the experiment involved naming triplets of three pictures. The crucial items were the third pictures in each triplet. In blocks of mixed-language trials, the third items could be named in the same language as the first two (nonswitch trials) or in the other language (switch trials). In our first experiment, we were interested in comparing naming speeds in the nonswitch trials of mixed-language blocks with naming speeds in blocks of trials where there was no language switching at all (pure blocks). Accordingly, the participants began each session with a block of 20 triplets in which the tone that accompanied each picture was to be ignored and every picture named in the same language. (This was the only time this was done. In every other condition of the four experiments, the tone cued the required language.)

Half the participants named all the pictures in the pure blocks in Spanish in session 1. That was followed after a short break by a block of trials in which the first two pictures in each of 40 triplets were always named in Spanish, with the third picture being named in either Spanish (nonswitch) or English (switch), depending on whether the accompanying tone stayed the same or changed. When these participants returned for the second session, they began by naming all the pictures in a pure block in English. They then tackled a mixed block in which the first two items of each triplet were always named in English, with the third item being named in English (nonswitch) or Spanish (switch), depending on the accompanying tone. The remaining participants received the contents of the two sessions in the opposite order. This design allowed us to gauge the effect on picture naming speed in L1 and L2 of introducing language switching into mixed blocks compared with naming in pure blocks where no switching occurred and in which each of the critical experimental pictures occurred equally often in each of the experimental conditions.

Only responses to pictures occurring in the third position of triplets in the different experimental conditions were analysed. Table 3.1 shows the results. There was a tendency for naming speeds to be faster in the pure Spanish (L1) blocks than in the pure English (L2) blocks, although that difference did not reach significance. Turning to the comparison of nonswitch and switch trials in mixed language blocks, Table 3.1 shows that when the pictures on the third trial in a triplet were named in English (L2), naming latencies in the three conditions were similar whether the English naming trial occurred in the context of an English-only block (pure condition), followed two other English naming trials in a mixed-language block (nonswitch), or followed two Spanish naming trials (switch). That is, there was no discernible cost of switching from Spanish (L1) into English (L2) compared with remaining in English.

Table 3.1 Mean RT, standard deviation (S.D.), and percentage of errors (%) for picture-naming data in English (L2) and Spanish (L1) in the pure, nonswitch, and switch conditions of experiment 1

	English (L2)			Spanish (L1)		
	Pure	*Nonswitch*	*Switch*	*Pure*	*Nonswitch*	*Switch*
Mean	1055	1140	1090	1006	1095	1243
S.D.	137	180	132	173	168	210
% error	4.8	5.2	6.6	4.4	2.5	7.1

In contrast, when the pictures on the third trial of a triplet were named in Spanish (L1), naming latencies were significantly slower when a Spanish naming trial followed two English naming trials in a mixed-language block (switch) than when a Spanish naming trial followed two other Spanish naming trials in a mixed-language block (nonswitch) or occurred in an all-Spanish block (pure). That is, there was a significant cost of switching from English (L2) into Spanish (L1) compared with remaining in Spanish.

The results of experiment 1 match those of Meuter and Allport (1999). Naming was slowed when bilinguals switched from L2 into L1, but not when they switched from L1 into L2. This is compatible with the notion that in speakers with definite first (dominant) and second (subordinate) languages, L1 words compete for selection with L2 words when they are speaking in L2 and must therefore be inhibited in order to speak their second language fluently. Releasing that inhibition on a switch trial incurs a processing cost. In contrast, L2 words do not normally compete for selection with L1 words. There is no need to inhibit the second language, so there is no cost of switching from the first language into the second.

Experiment 2: An attempt to induce a cost of switching from L1 into L2 by priming L2 vocabulary

The results of experiment 1 fit with the theory that the natural level of activation of L2 words is such that they do not compete for selection with L1 words. In contrast, L1 words are naturally more highly activated and therefore prone to interfere with the selection of L2 words unless they are actively inhibited. The possibility explored in experiment 2 was that L2 words might come to compete with L1 words if activated sufficiently (e.g., through priming). If that could be done, we should see a cost of switching from L1 into L2 as well as from L2 into L1.

Experiment 2 retained the picture triplets with language cued by an accompanying tone, but dispensed with the pure language blocks of experiment 1. There were two sessions as before. In one session, the first two pictures of each triplet were named in English and the third picture in English (nonswitch) or Spanish (switch), depending on the tone. In the other session, the first two pictures of each triplet were named in Spanish and the third picture in Spanish (nonswitch) or English (switch). The order of the two sessions was counterbalanced across 24 bilingual participants.

The crucial difference from experiment 1 was that in half the triplets in each block the same picture appeared in positions 1 and 3 (the repeat conditions). When that happened, the tone accompanying the repeated picture in the third position could require it to be named either in the same language (nonswitch trials) or in the other language (switch trials). Naming the same picture in the same language in the first and third of a triplet should facilitate naming speed through the process of repetition priming (Wheeldon & Monsell, 1992). The more interesting question was what would happen when a picture that had just been named in one language on trial 1 had to be named in the other language on trial 3. In particular, would the act of naming a picture in L2 on trial 1 of a triplet interfere with naming the same picture when it appeared on trial 3 of the same triplet in the switch condition and now had to be named in L1? Would that then cause inhibition to be applied to L2, resulting in a cost of switching from L1 to L2?

The results are shown in Table 3.2. The nonrepeat conditions of experiment 2 are much like the mixed language conditions of experiment 1 and provided a replication of the findings of experiment 1. In the nonrepeat conditions, there was no significant difference between switch and nonswitch trials in English (L2), but switch trials were substantially slower than nonswitch trials in Spanish (L1), showing a switch cost of 156 ms (1252–1096 ms).

Inspection of Table 3.2 also shows that when pictures were repeated in positions 1 and 3 of triplets, the cost of switching from L2 into L1 was substantial. But there were also signs of a cost of switching from L1 to L2 (an 82-ms difference between naming a picture in English when the same picture had been named in English two trials previously (1096 ms) compared with naming a picture in English when the same picture had been named in Spanish two trials previously (1178 ms)). Unfortunately, the three-way interaction between language, repetition, and switch condition that would have been required to support a strong claim that repetition had differential effects on switch and nonswitch trials in L1 compared with L2 was not significant.

Certain theories of repetition priming suggest that when the same picture is named twice in the same language, there should be a dual benefit of both recognizing the same object twice and retrieving the same name twice (Ellis, Flude, Young, & Burton, 1996). When the same picture is seen twice but has to be named in different languages on each occasion, there may be some benefit of recognizing the same object twice, but no benefit for name

Table 3.2 Mean RT (M), standard deviation (S.D.), and percentage of errors (%) for picture-naming data in English (L2) and Spanish (L1) in experiment 2. The third trials of triplets could involve a switch from the previous two trials or no switch, and could involve the repetition of the picture that appeared on the first trial of the triplet (repeat) or a new picture (nonrepeat)

	English (L2)		Spanish (L1)	
	Nonswitch	Switch	Nonswitch	Switch
Nonrepeat				
Mean	1249	1266	1096	1252
S.D.	92	95	175	227
% error	17.7	13.2	6.6	13.5
Repeat				
Mean	1096	1178	980	1222
S.D.	91	84	186	217
% error	10.1	10.1	3.1	6.6

retrieval on the second occasion (because a different word is being retrieved). The benefit of naming the same picture twice in the same language can be seen by comparing the nonswitch naming latencies in the repeat and non-repeat conditions. In Spanish (L1), naming a picture on trial 3 of a triplet having named it in the same language on trial 1 reduced the mean naming latency by 116 ms (from 1096 to 980 ms). A comparable benefit was seen in English (L2), where naming a picture on trial 3 of a triplet having named it in the same language on trial 1 reduced the mean naming latency by 153 ms (from 1249 to 1096 ms). If, however, a picture was repeated but had to be named in the other language on the second occasion, the benefits of repetition were reduced (to 30 ms in Spanish (1252–1222 ms) and 88 ms in English (1266–1178 ms)). The results are compatible with the notion that repetition priming of object naming has two components—a perceptual component to do with object recognition and a lexical component to do with name retrieval (Ellis et al., 1996).

The results of experiment 2 were tantalizing, but fell short of a clear demonstration that it is possible to induce a cost of switching from L1 into L2 under conditions in which L2 vocabulary is activated to the point where it begins to compete during the selection of L1 vocabulary and so needs to be inhibited in order to respond fluently in L1. Experiments 3 and 4 explored the same possibility, but under conditions where there was considerably more repetition of items in experimental blocks.

Experiment 3: A further attempt to induce a cost of switching from L1 into L2 by priming L2 vocabulary

The goal of experiment 3 was the same as experiment 2—to induce a cost of switching into L2 by boosting the activation levels in L2 to the point where the bilingual participants were obliged to inhibit L2 when responding in L1.

As before, blocks of picture-naming trials were divided into triplets, with language being cued by a tone that accompanied each picture. There were four types of experimental blocks with 64 triplets (32 switch and 32 nonswitch). In two blocks, the first two pictures in each triplet were always named in English, with the third picture being named either in English (nonswitch) or in Spanish (switch). In another two blocks, the first two pictures in each triplet were always named in Spanish, with the third picture being named in Spanish (nonswitch) or English (switch).

Importantly, one version of each language condition used 16 pictures that were multiply repeated within a block in both languages. This was the *overlapping vocabularies* condition. The other version of each language condition split the 16 pictures into two, with eight pictures always being named in English and the other eight pictures always being named in Spanish. This was the *separate vocabularies* condition. The comparison of overlapping and separate vocabularies was done across subjects. The 36 bilinguals who participated in the experiment were divided into two groups. One group was given the overlapping vocabulary blocks where the same 16 pictures were presented across trials in both languages. The second group was given the separate vocabulary blocks with eight items that were only ever named in English and eight items were only ever in Spanish.

The results are shown in Table 3.3 and Figure 3.1. Participants were naming a small set of pictures repeatedly, so their mean naming latencies are generally quicker than in experiments 1 and 2. The separate vocabularies conditions replicated the pattern of results in experiment 1 and in the non-repeat conditions of experiment 2: switching from English (L2) into Spanish (L1) showed a significant 104-ms cost when the switch (876 ms) and non-switch (772 ms) conditions were compared. In contrast, there was no significant cost of switching from Spanish into English when switch (795 ms) and nonswitch (790 ms) conditions were compared. Participants in the group that received the separate vocabularies blocks therefore showed the standard asymmetry—a cost of switching from L2 into L1, but no cost of switching from L1 into L2. This was supported by a significant language by switch condition interaction in the analysis of the naming latencies of the separate vocabularies group.

The participants in the separate vocabularies group were never faced with the requirement to name in Spanish a picture which they had also named in English on previous trials. That, however, was precisely the experience of the participants in the overlapping vocabularies group. They would often find themselves trying to name a picture in one language which they had recently named in the other language, possibly several times. The overlapping vocabularies group showed a different pattern of results from that seen in the separate vocabularies group. This time, the 65-ms cost of switching from L2 into L1 (switch = 1008 ms; nonswitch = 943 ms) was matched by an 81-ms cost of switching from L1 into L2 (switch = 926 ms; nonswitch = 845 ms). While there were significant main effects of language (English faster overall than

Table 3.3 Mean RT, S.D., and percentage of errors for picture naming in English and Spanish in the nonswitch and switch trials of the separate and overlapping conditions in experiment 3 (between-groups comparison of separate and overlapping conditions)

	English (L2)		Spanish (L1)	
	Nonswitch	Switch	Nonswitch	Switch
Separate vocabularies				
Mean	790	795	772	876
S.D.	103	171	109	227
% error	2.3	2.6	1.9	4.5
Overlapping vocabularies				
Mean	845	926	943	1008
S.D.	125	150	199	217
% error	7.1	9.7	7.8	8.9

1A. Separate vocabularies

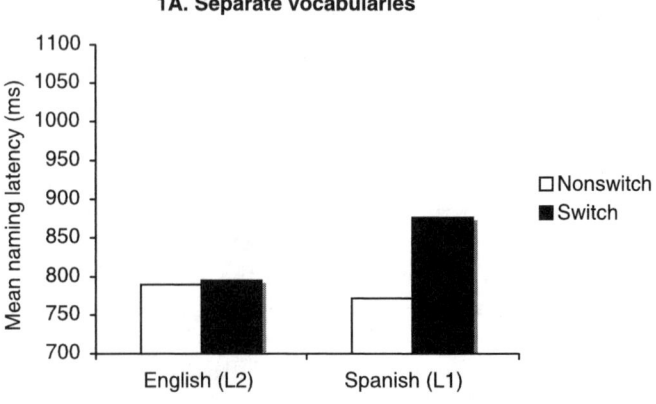

1B. Overlapping vocabularies

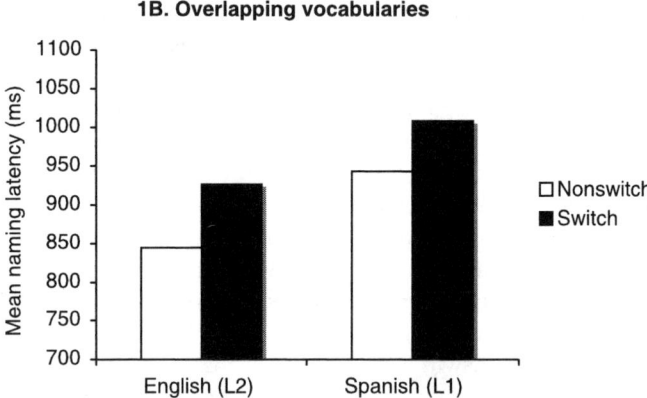

Figure 3.1 Mean naming latencies for pictures named in English (L2) and Spanish (L1)
on nonswitch or switch trials in the separate vocabularies (1A) and overlapping vocabularies (1B) conditions of experiment 3 (between groups).

Spanish) and switch condition (nonswitch faster overall than switch) in this
group, the interaction between language and switch condition did not begin
to approach significance.

Bilinguals in the overlapping vocabularies condition of experiment 3
were required to name pictures in Spanish which they had previously
named on more than one occasion in the same block in English. We
hypothesize that under those circumstances, the English object names
began to compete with the Spanish names for selection, inducing a cost for
switching from L1 into L2. The design of the overlapping vocabularies
version of experiment 3 meant, however, that all the pictures were named
in both languages on multiple occasions. We cannot therefore discern from
the results whether what was inhibited when L2 words began to compete
with their L1 counterparts was the particular words that were proving

troublesome, or the entire L2 vocabulary. If the former, then the cost of switching from L1 to L2 should apply only to the multiply repeated items. If the latter, the cost should generalize to other items experienced in the same context. These alternative possibilities were considered in experiment 4.

Experiment 4: When L2 words are primed to the point where they compete for selection with L1 words, is inhibition applied only to the primed items or to the entire L2 lexicon?

Participants in experiment 4 were exposed to both separate and overlapping vocabularies conditions within the same experiment. Sequences of triplets were presented as before. This time, there were two blocks of 72 triplets each, one block in which the first two items of each triplet were always named in English, with the third item being named in English (nonswitch) or Spanish (switch), and another block in which the first two items of each triplet were always named in Spanish, with the third item being named in Spanish (nonswitch) or English (switch). Both blocks contained within them both separate and overlapping vocabulary items. Only 24 pictures were used in the entire experiment. The 24 pictures were divided into four sets of six. For each participant, the separate vocabularies conditions were made up of six pictures that were only ever named in English and another six pictures that were only ever named in Spanish. The overlapping vocabularies conditions involved 12 pictures that were presented a total of 18 times each, nine times for naming in Spanish and nine times for naming in English. Sets of six pictures were rotated around participants so that each set occurred equally often in each condition. Pictures were repeated across, but not within, triplets. Blocks beginning with two English items followed by another English item (nonswitch) or a Spanish item (switch), or two Spanish items followed by another Spanish item (nonswitch) or an English item (switch) were presented to 24 bilingual participants in a counterbalanced order. The important point to note is that within each block there were items that were only ever named in English or Spanish (separate vocabularies), and other items that were sometimes named in English and sometimes in Spanish (overlapping vocabularies).

The results are shown in Table 3.4 and Figure 3.2. Overall, naming latencies were slower when names were produced in Spanish (L1) than when they were produced in English (L2). Switch trials were slower than nonswitch trials, and naming times to pictures in the separate vocabularies conditions were faster than to pictures in the overlapping vocabularies conditions.

Numerically speaking, the costs of switching from L2 into L1 were higher than the cost of switching from L1 into L2. Thus, in the separate vocabularies condition, the cost of switching into L1 was 73 ms (switch = 824 ms; nonswitch = 751 ms), while the cost of switching into L2 was 50 ms (switch = 784 ms; nonswitch = 734 ms). Similarly, in the overlapping vocabularies

Table 3.4 Mean RT, S.D., and percentage of errors for picture naming in English and Spanish in the nonswitch and switch trials of the separate and overlapping conditions in experiment 4 (within-subjects comparison of separate and overlapping conditions)

	English (L2)		Spanish (L1)	
	Nonswitch	Switch	Nonswitch	Switch
Separate vocabularies				
Mean	734	784	751	824
S.D.	84	117	115	170
% error	2.5	3.0	3.9	3.2
Overlapping vocabularies				
Mean	790	854	845	946
S.D.	129	86	155	174
% error	2.5	6.5	2.5	6.5

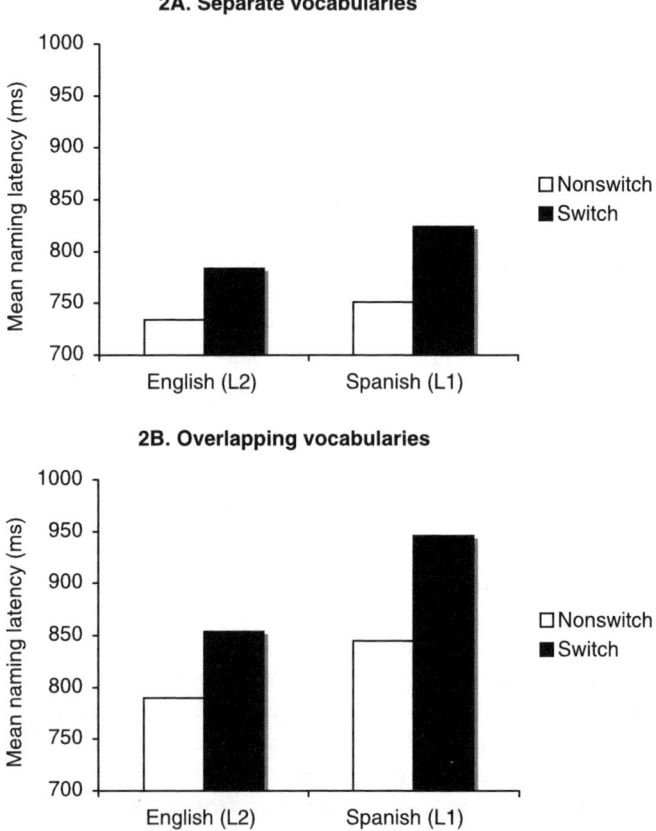

Figure 3.2 Mean naming latencies for pictures named in English (L2) and Spanish (L1) on nonswitch or switch trials in the separate vocabularies (2A) and overlapping vocabularies (2B) conditions of experiment 4 (within subjects).

condition, the cost of switching into L1 was 101 ms (switch = 946 ms; nonswitch = 845 ms), while the cost of switching into L2 was 64 ms (switch = 854 ms; nonswitch = 790 ms). Nevertheless, the interactions that would have indicated that language switching costs were different between Spanish and English, and between separate and overlapping vocabularies, were all nonsignificant. Experiment 4 replicated the induction of a cost of switching from L1 to L2 under conditions where L2 items were heavily primed. In addition, it showed that when some L2 words are primed to the extent that they compete for selection with L1 words, the system responds by inhibiting the entire L2 vocabulary, not just those particular items that have shown a competitive streak.

Discussion

All four of the present experiments used the same general paradigm. Pictures of familiar objects were presented in triplets. Each picture was accompanied by a high or a low tone. With the exception of the "pure" blocks of experiment 1 (where the tones were ignored and every picture was named in the same language), the first two pictures in a triplet were named in one language, and the third picture was named in the same language (nonswitch) or the other language (switch).

Experiment 1 replicated the asymmetrical switching costs reported by Kroll and Peck (1998) and Meuter and Allport (1999): switching from L2 to L1 incurred substantial switching costs compared to both naming in pure blocks and nonswitch trials, while switching from L1 to L2 incurred no significant switching costs. That result is wholly compatible with the proposition that under normal circumstances, bilinguals with one dominant and one subordinate language must inhibit the dominant language in order to speak the subordinate one, but need not inhibit the subordinate language when speaking the dominant one.

Experiments 2 to 4 were all attempts to induce costs for switching from L1 to L2 by boosting the activation levels of L2 words to the point where they might compete with L1 words and therefore need to be inhibited. Experiment 2 attempted to do this by repeating pictures in some triplets between positions 1 and 3. In particular, it was hoped that naming a picture in L2 when it appeared in position 1 of a triplet might cause the English name to compete with the Spanish name if the same picture had to be named in Spanish in position 3 (on a switch trial), and that this might induce inhibition of the English lexicon, causing a switch cost when moving into English. The results were very much in the predicted direction: introducing picture repetitions into the blocks of triplets increased the already substantial cost of switching into L1 (Spanish) but also increased the cost of switching into L2 (English) from 17 to 82 ms. Unfortunately, the statistical comparisons required to underpin any strong empirical claim were not all significant, so a different (but related) method was tried in experiments 3 and 4 that involved multiple repetitions of pictures rather than just single repetitions as in experiment 2.

When items were repeatedly presented in both languages, as in experiments 3 and 4, the costs of switching into L2 became apparent. In one version of experiment 3, pictures were repeated, but each picture only ever had to be named in one language. That was the separate vocabularies condition. In another version, pictures were repeated and had to be named in Spanish on some trials and in English on others. That was the overlapping vocabularies condition. Different groups of participants experienced the two versions. The separate vocabulary group showed costs of switching into Spanish (L1) but no cost of switching into English (L2), but that group would never have experienced enhanced competition from an English word when attempting to retrieve a Spanish word (because none of the pictures to be named in Spanish ever had to be named in English). In contrast, when participants in the overlapping vocabularies group were trying to name pictures in Spanish, they would often have named the same pictures in English, sometimes several times previously. Under those circumstances, English names would compete with Spanish names, and it would become necessary or efficient to inhibit the English names in order to be able to produce the Spanish ones fluently. So it was that in the overlapping vocabularies version of experiment 3 an 81-ms cost of switching from Spanish into English was observed—the first occasion we are aware of when a cost of switching from L1 to L2 has been observed.

A feature of experiment 3 was that for participants in the overlapping vocabularies group, every picture appeared on multiple occasions to be named sometimes in one language and sometimes in the other. It is therefore not possible to tell from the results whether the inhibition of L2 that was observed in that condition applied to all L2 words or only to the multiply repeated L2 words that were making a nuisance of themselves when the speaker was attempting to name in L1. Experiment 4 addressed that issue by exposing the same participants to both overlapping and separate vocabularies conditions. Thus, there were some pictures that appeared on several occasions, sometimes to be named in Spanish and sometimes in English, but there were other pictures that appeared several times, but only for naming in one or other language. If inhibition of L2 was induced by the experience of competition when attempting to name certain items in L1 and was only applied to the competing items, then no generalization of the inhibition to pictures in the separate vocabularies condition should have been observed. But it was: in fact, the costs of switching into L2 were roughly the same for items in the separate vocabularies condition that were only ever named in English as they were for items in the overlapping vocabularies condition that were named sometimes in English and sometimes in Spanish. The results imply that when *some* L2 words are activated to the point when they begin to compete for selection with L1 words, the *entire* L2 lexicon is inhibited (though in truth we have tested only for generalization to other object names:

future studies should look for wider generalization). They also imply that inhibition can be deployed strategically; in this case, it was applied to the L2 lexicon when necessary, even though that lexicon does not normally need to be inhibited.

The switching costs envisaged here are due to what Rogers and Monsell (1995) called "task-set reconfiguration", where stimulus-response mappings are enabled or disabled by a switch mechanism, much like a rail track operator directing trains down one track or another. This may be simplistic, however, because a range of studies suggest that language sets are not switched on or off, but are raised or lowered in activation in a more continuous way (Costa, Miozzo, & Caramazza, 1999; Hermans, Bongaertes, De Bot, & Schreuder, 1998; Kroll & Peck, 1998).

As Meuter and Allport (1999) noted, these findings are compatible with models of bilingual language processing in which language "nodes" exert a broad influence on levels of activation in the different lexicons of a bilingual speaker (e.g., De Bot, 1992; Dijkstra & Van Heuven, 1998; Grainger & Dijkstra, 1992; Green, 1998). For example, in the Green (1998) model, inhibition is proportional to the level of activation of the words that are to be inhibited. When a bilingual is speaking in L1, it is assumed that little or no inhibition of L2 is required because the baseline level of activation of L2 lexical items is low. But when L2 is being spoken, inhibition is required to drive the activation levels to L1 words below their normally high resting level. Switching into L1 from L2 requires release of that inhibition with a resulting processing delay. That would explain the findings of Meuter and Allport (1999) and our experiment 1.

Inhibition in the Green (1998) model is also reactive: if the activation levels of L2 items become sufficiently high (e.g., through priming of the sort seen in the present experiments 2, 3, and 4), then inhibition will be applied to the L2 lexicon when retrieval of L1 words is required. That is precisely what was observed in experiment 2 and, more emphatically, in experiments 3 and 4. We note that in experiment 3, the cost of switching from English into Spanish actually fell from 104 ms in the separate vocabularies version to 65 ms in the overlapping vocabularies version. That may reflect the changed balance of activation between the two lexicons in the two conditions, although it could also imply that there is a finite amount of resource available for the inhibition of lexicons.

The general theory we have outlined provides a satisfactory account of language-switching experiments involving "unbalanced" bilinguals in whom one language was dominant and the other subordinate. What, though, of proficient bilinguals who are more balanced because, for example, they have grown up speaking two languages, both of which they continue to use in daily life? Costa and Santesteban (2004) compared switching costs in unbalanced and balanced bilinguals. They found asymmetrical language switching costs in unbalanced bilinguals like those seen in our experiments and in Meuter and Allport (1999). But when they tested proficient bilinguals, they observed much more symmetrical switching costs. This is compatible with the results of our experiment 4 if we argue that by repeatedly priming some words in L2 we temporarily raised the activation levels of those lexical items to the point where they competed with those of L1 words, so that our participants became proficient bilinguals (if only for those lexical items) and needed to apply mutual inhibition to each of their two languages when responding in the other. That in turn suggests that fluent bilinguals may need to maintain a level of inhibition of one or other language at all times.

There is, however, evidence to suggest that at least in some tasks it is impossible to inhibit one language completely when processing another, and that all that may be possible is to raise or lower activation levels within a certain range (e.g., Colomé, 2001). Furthermore, the findings of Magiste (1979, 1986) indicate that even when bilinguals are operating in only one language, their responses are slower than those of monolinguals operating in the same language, and that trilinguals are slower still. Multilingual speakers operating in Grosjean's "bilingual mode" may be unable to inhibit nonselected languages completely, so that words from other languages exert varying degrees of interference that interfere with the process of lexical retrieval in any of their languages. The benefits of multilingualism are manifest, but there may be a small price to be paid for the privilege of maintaining and managing more than one language within a single mind and brain.

References

Allport, A., Styles, E. A., & Hsieh, S. (1994). Shifting intentional set: Exploring the dynamic control of tasks. In C. Umilta & M. Moscovitch (Eds.), *Attention and performance XV: Conscious and nonconscious information processing* (pp. 421–452). Cambridge, MA: MIT Press.

Allport, A., & Wylie, G. (2000a). Task-switching, stimulus-response bindings and negative priming. In S. Monsell & J. Driver (Eds.), *Control of cognitive processes: Attention and performance XVIII* (pp. 35–70). Cambridge, MA: MIT Press.

Allport, A., & Wylie, G. (2000b). Task-switching: Positive and negative priming of task set. In G. W. Humphreys, J. Duncan, & A. Triesman (Eds.), *Attention, space and action: Studies in cognitive neuroscience* (pp. 273–297). Oxford: Oxford University Press.

Clyne, M. G. (1980). Triggering and language processing. *Canadian Journal of Psychology, 34*, 400–406.

Colomé, A. (2001). Lexical activation in bilinguals' speech production: Language-specific or language-independent? *Journal of Memory and Language, 45*, 721–736.

Costa, A., Miozzo, M., & Caramazza, A. (1999). Lexical selection in bilinguals: Do words in the bilingual's two lexicons compete for selection? *Journal of Memory and Language, 41*, 381–391.

Costa, A., & Santesteban, M. (2004). Lexical access in bilingual speech production: Evidence from language switching in highly proficient bilinguals and L2 learners. *Journal of Memory and Language, 50*, 491–511.

Dalrymple-Alford, E. C. (1985). Language switching during bilingual reading. *British Journal of Psychology, 76*, 111–122.

De Bot, K. (1992). A bilingual production model: Levelt's speaking model adapted. *Applied Linguistics, 13*, 1–24.

De Jong, R. (1995). Strategic determinants of compatibility effects with task uncertainty. *Acta Psychologica, 88*, 187–207.

Dijkstra, A., & Van Heuven, W. J. B. (1998). The BIA model and bilingual word recognition. In J. Grainger & A. Jacobs (Eds.), *Localist connectionist approaches to human cognition* (pp. 189–225). Hove, UK: Lawrence Erlbaum Associates Ltd.

Ellis, A. W., Flude, B. M., Young, A. W., & Burton, A. M. (1996). Two components of repetition priming in the recognition of familiar faces. *Journal of Experimental Psychology: Learning, Memory, and Cognition, 22*, 295–308.

Grainger, J., & Dijkstra, T. (1992). On the representation and use of language information in bilinguals. In R. Harris (Ed.), *Cognitive processing in bilinguals* (pp. 207–220). Amsterdam: Elsevier.

Green, D. W. (1998). Mental control of the bilingual lexico-semantic system. *Bilingualism: Language and Cognition, 1*, 67–81.

Grosjean, F. (1997). Processing mixed languages: Issues, findings and models. In A. M. de Groot & J. F. Kroll (Eds.), *Tutorials in bilingualism: Psycholinguistic perspectives* (pp. 225–254). Mahwah, NJ: Lawrence Erlbaum Associates, Inc.

Grosjean, F. (2001). The bilingual's language modes. In J. Nicol (Ed.), *One mind, two languages: Bilingual language processing* (pp. 1–22). Oxford: Blackwell.

Harvey, N. (1984). The Stroop effect: Failure to focus attention or failure to maintain focusing? *Quarterly Journal of Experimental Psychology, 36A*, 89–115.

Hermans, D., Bongaerts, T., De Bot, K., & Schreuder, R. (1998). Producing words in a foreign language: Can speakers prevent interference from their first language? *Bilingualism: Language and Cognition, 1*, 213–229.

Kolers, P. A. (1966). Reading and talking bilingually. *American Journal of Psychology, 3*, 357–376.

Kroll, J. F., & Peck, A. (1998). *Competing activation across a bilingual's two languages: Evidence from picture naming.* Paper presented at the 43rd Annual Meeting of the International Linguistics Association, New York University, New York.

Macnamara, J., Krauthammer, M., & Bolgar, M. (1968). Language switching in bilinguals as a function of stimulus and response uncertainty. *Journal of Experimental Psychology, 78*, 208–215.

Magiste, E. (1979). The competing language systems of the multilingual: A developmental study of decoding and encoding processes. *Journal of Verbal Learning and Verbal Behavior, 18*, 79–89.

Magiste, E. (1986). Selected issues in second and third language learning. In J. Vaid (Ed.), *Language processing in bilinguals: Psycholinguistic and neurolinguistic perspectives* (pp. 97–122). Hillsdale, NJ: Lawrence Erlbaum Associates, Inc.

Meuter, R. F., & Allport, D. A. (1999). Bilingual language switching in naming: Asymmetrical costs of language selection. *Journal of Memory and Language, 40*, 25–40.

Monsell, S. (2003). Task switching. *Trends in Cognitive Sciences, 7*, 134–139.

Penfield, W., & Roberts, R. (1959). *Speech and brain mechanisms.* Princeton, NJ: Princeton University Press.

Poplack, S. (1980). Sometimes I'll start a sentence in Spanish y termino en Espanol: Toward a typology of code-switching. *Linguistics, 18*, 581–618.

Rayner, J. (2004). *A study to investigate bilingual switching costs in a series of picture naming tasks.* Unpublished PhD thesis, University of York, UK.

Rogers, R. D., & Monsell, S. (1995). Cost of a predictable switch between simple cognitive tasks. *Journal of Experimental Psychology: General, 124*, 207–231.

Snodgrass, J. G., & Vanderwart, M. (1980). A standardized set of 260 pictures: Norms for name agreement, image agreement, familiarity, and visual complexity. *Journal of Experimental Psychology: Human Learning and Memory, 6*, 174–215.

Wheeldon, L. R., & Monsell, S. (1992). The locus of repetition priming of spoken word production. *Quarterly Journal of Experimental Psychology, 44A*, 723–761.

Wheeldon, L. R., & Monsell, S. (1994). Inhibition of spoken word production by priming a semantic competitor. *Journal of Memory and Language, 33*, 332–356.

4 How are speakers' linguistic choices affected by ambiguity?

Victor S. Ferreira
University of California, San Diego, USA

Speakers produce utterances to accomplish goals. For example, a speaker might produce an utterance to assert a belief, make a request, or direct an action (Clark, 1996; Levelt, 1989; Searle, 1969). For speakers to accomplish these goals with their productions, they must succeed in transmitting information from their own minds to the minds of their addressees—addressees cannot understand speakers' beliefs, consider their requests, or obey their directions unless they understand the information that speakers are trying to get across in the first place. Therefore, anything that interferes with this process of information transmission will hinder speakers' attempts to carry out the goal-directed behaviour that is producing linguistic expressions.

One fundamental challenge—arguably *the* fundamental challenge—to this process of information transmission is *ambiguity*. Ambiguity arises when a linguistic expression can be interpreted to have more than one meaning. This implies that when speakers produce ambiguous utterances, their addressees cannot know (at least in principle) the meanings speakers intend, and speakers cannot know (at least in principle) that they have conveyed their intended meanings to their addressees. Therefore, although the goal of any individual act of production may be to assert, request, or direct, it is a goal of the linguistic system as a whole—speakers' production systems, addressees' comprehension systems, and the grammar that those systems use to structure language—to overcome ambiguity.

The objective of this chapter is to analyse how this goal of ambiguity avoidance is accomplished. I approach this objective from a most obvious starting point: If ambiguity is avoided, it seems likely to be because *speakers* somehow avoid it. After all, it is speakers who produce utterances in the first place. By this analysis, ambiguity avoidance is itself a goal-directed action—that to optimize the effectiveness of their utterances, speakers aim to avoid ambiguity, just as they aim to (for example) avoid errors. In turn, I couch the analysis of speakers' possible avoidance of ambiguity in terms of the familiar executive-automatic distinction in cognitive psychology. The idea is that if speakers avoid ambiguity, it must be either because they choose to—because executive processing mechanisms choose unambiguous forms rather than ambiguous ones—or because speakers' language-production systems choose unambiguous forms automatically, without any executive involvement. To present this analysis, the chapter describes the nature of ambiguity and then the nature of the executive and automatic mechanisms that select linguistic forms; together, these suggest specific ways that different forms of ambiguity can be avoided in an executive or automatic way. I then review evidence that informs whether speakers in fact do avoid different forms of ambiguities in these executive and automatic ways. This evidence will lead to a different approach to the problem of ambiguity avoidance that will be described along with some supporting evidence. I conclude by discussing how ambiguity avoidance as a specific problem can provide informative insights into the nature of goal-directed behaviour in general.

A taxonomy of ambiguity

As described above, ambiguity arises when a linguistic expression can carry more than one meaning. But ambiguity can be characterized more precisely. Two orthogonal dimensions of ambiguity are whether it is *full* or *temporary*, and whether it is *conceptual* or *linguistic*.

In everyday settings, ambiguity is usually thought of in its full form. The news headline "Iraqi head seeks arms" is fully ambiguous, because the utterance itself does not determine whether it means that a leader of a country is seeking weapons, or one part of a body is seeking another. Of course in this example, as in most, pragmatic considerations point to a particular interpretation. Nevertheless, either interpretation is at least logically possible, and it is this in-principle possibility of multiple meanings of complete utterances that constitutes full ambiguity.

Temporary ambiguities, or *garden paths*, are in some ways more interesting than full ambiguities. Temporary ambiguities arise because the serial nature of language comprehension leads to momentary ambiguities that are then resolved by subsequent material. For example, a well-studied temporary ambiguity arises in the sentence, "The weary traveller claimed the luggage had been stolen in Rome" (Garnsey, Pearlmutter, Myers, & Lotocky, 1997). Specifically, upon comprehending the phrase "the luggage", a comprehender cannot know whether the sentence constitutes a subject-verb-direct object sequence ("The weary traveller claimed the luggage with relief") or a subject-verb-embedded subject sequence (which is what the sentence actually is). The direct-object interpretation is simpler and more common, and hence is generally preferred and so (at least usually) adopted as soon as the ambiguous noun-phrase is comprehended. However, because the sentence ends with the embedded subject interpretation, the preferred direct-object interpretation must be relinquished in favour of the less preferred embedded-subject interpretation. What makes the ambiguity temporary is that in the course of a single utterance or grammatical unit, it is eventually definitively resolved. In turn, what makes temporary ambiguity interesting is that it provides a controlled and compact way to introduce ambiguity and force its resolution in a single phrase, clause, or sentence.

Full and temporary ambiguity can arise either linguistically or conceptually. Psycholinguistic research has focused mostly on linguistic ambiguity. Linguistic ambiguity arises because accidents or encoding limitations of the language cause expressions to carry more than one meaning. Take, for example, the word "bat". It may mean either a kind of flying animal, or an instrument for hitting baseballs or cricket balls. The cause of this ambiguity is entirely linguistic, in that it is an accident of the vocabulary of English that two fully distinct concepts happen to be expressed with the same word—an instance of *homophony* (note that if different concepts are related in meaning or are *polysemous*, then the similarity of meaning suggests that the ambiguity is probably conceptual, like those outlined below). "Iraqi head seeks arms" is another case where homophony causes ambiguity (twice), this time in a sentence context. Other forms of linguistic ambiguity include syntactic ambiguity (e.g., "Stolen painting found by trees") or segmentation ambiguity ("a back" vs. "aback"). Each of these is an example of a full ambiguity. Examples of temporary linguistic ambiguities include the above-described garden-path effects, in which a syntactic ambiguity is resolved by subsequent syntactic information.

In contrast to linguistic ambiguity, conceptual ambiguity arises because of the way the conceptual world is divided up by language. Most relevantly, natural language describes categories of objects with individual words. This means that if more than one specific instance of a category is available, an individual word can apply to all of those instances and will therefore be ambiguous. For example, imagine a situation where a speaker wishes to individuate a cantaloupe in the context of another smaller cantaloupe. Here, the label "cantaloupe" is ambiguous, because the two ambiguous referents—the two cantaloupes—share meaning, and therefore share a potential label. This represents conceptual ambiguity. Like linguistic ambiguity, conceptual ambiguity may be either full or temporary. Naming a cantaloupe "cantaloupe" in the context of a smaller cantaloupe is fully ambiguous; naming it "a cantaloupe that is larger" is temporarily ambiguous, with the critical point of ambiguity beginning immediately after the word "cantaloupe".

The distinction between conceptual and linguistic ambiguities can also be described representationally. Conceptual ambiguity arises representationally at the level of meaning. For example, the representations of the meanings of "larger cantaloupe" and "smaller cantaloupe" converge on a single representation of the meaning of cantaloupe-in-general, and this convergence at the level of meaning corresponds to the ambiguity. Linguistic ambiguity, in contrast, arises not at the level of meaning but instead at the level of linguistic form. Flying mammals and instruments for hitting balls are as distinct in meaning as any two meanings in the language. The only place these meanings converge is at the phonological representation /bæt/. A similar analysis applies to "Stolen painting found by trees", "/əbæk/", or "The weary traveller claimed the luggage . . .".

I define full and temporary ambiguity here largely to convey the important similarities between these two distinct phenomena with respect to the problem of ambiguity avoidance. In both cases, a linguistic expression can carry more than one meaning, even if with temporary ambiguity, the indeterminacy is subsequently eliminated. I collapse full and temporary ambiguity under the term *ambiguity* for the remainder of this chapter. The distinction between conceptual and linguistic ambiguity is especially relevant to the mechanisms of linguistic choice to be described next. This distinction will figure prominently in the analysis of what kinds of ambiguities speakers can and cannot avoid.

How do linguistic choices get made?

If speakers are to avoid these different forms of ambiguity, they must choose to, or the psycholinguistic mechanisms of language production must choose for them. A number of different models of the language-production process have been proposed. Many focus on the nature of the conceptual and linguistic structures speakers use when they formulate utterances, and how those structures interact with one another (e.g., Dell, 1986; Garrett, 1975; Levelt, Roelofs, & Meyer, 1999). Important for the question of ambiguity avoidance are accounts that relate the processes of language production to the mechanisms that are responsible for cognitive processing more generally. Most especially, models proposed by Bock (1982) and Levelt (1989) provide explicit ideas not only of what language-production processes are like, but of how those processes interface with other cognitive systems. Although these two accounts differ in some theoretical and terminological ways, they also converge to an important degree. In what follows, I pick ideas from these two models and mix them with some of my own, to arrive at an explicit account of how speakers make linguistic choices.

Language production begins with a set of processes that determine what specific meanings a speaker will express. Levelt (1989) called this the *conceptualizer*, whereas Bock (1982) called it the *referential arena*. Levelt breaks conceptualizer processing down into two stages, namely, macroplanning and microplanning. During macroplanning, speakers decide their goals for producing an utterance, and they choose the information they need to express to achieve those goals. During microplanning, speakers impose a perspective on a to-be-expressed idea and determine the information structure (the foreground and background status) of the elements of that idea. Processing within Bock's referential arena operates similarly, though without the explicit distinction between macro- and microplanning. I refer to the general class of processes included in the conceptualizer and the referential arena as *message encoding*.

In his account, Levelt makes the especially relevant observation that during macroplanning, speakers must select what information they need to include in their utterance to achieve their communicative goal. Largely, this depends on the linguistic and nonlinguistic context in which the utterance is to be produced. So, consider again the above example where the goal of the speaker is to individuate a cantaloupe in the context of another smaller cantaloupe. As noted, the label "cantaloupe" here is ambiguous. To avoid the ambiguity, the speaker must select information to express that relates the size of the cantaloupe ("large cantaloupe"), to disambiguate the to-be-individuated object in its context. I term this aspect of macroplanning *information selection*.

The goal of message encoding is to construct what Levelt terms the *preverbal message* and what Bock terms the *interfacing representation*; I'll use the term *preverbal message*. This representation forms the basis of the production system's leap from the nonlinguistic to the linguistic. The preverbal message feeds into a process that Levelt terms the *formulator*, consisting of *grammatical encoding* and *phonological encoding*, and that Bock breaks down into *syntactic processing, semantic processing*, and *phonological processing*. I subsume these constructs under the term *linguistic encoding* (the distinctions among the subprocesses of linguistic encoding are generally unimportant for the issues at hand). Linguistic encoding processes select the specific linguistic features that will express the meaning that was encoded into the preverbal message, including a set of grammatical functions (subjects, verbs, direct objects), constituent structures, lexical items (including their syntactic, morphological, and segmental content), prosodic characteristics, and so forth.

Linguistic encoding is then followed by phonetic processing, motor programming, and articulation, eventually leading to the speech sounds (or manual signs) that are presented to a comprehender. The two models share one more feature that is important for present purposes, which is that both include a *monitoring* process—a connection from a phonetic level of representation back to message encoding that is mediated by the language-comprehension system. Through this processing path, speakers evaluate their inner speech for adequacy, accuracy, appropriateness, and so forth. The fruits of speakers' monitoring labour are then fed back to message encoding so that speakers can modify their preverbal message accordingly. (Later work by Wheeldon and Levelt (1995) and Wheeldon and Morgan (2002) suggested that a phonological rather than phonetic representation may be the source of inner speech monitoring; this distinction is not especially critical here.)

Very importantly for the questions at hand, Bock (1982) includes *working memory* as a construct in her model. Working memory is meant to stand for the mechanisms that speakers use to exert control over their linguistic performance, and so what is especially relevant is the executive-function component of working memory (henceforth, when I refer to *working memory*, I specifically intend the executive-function component of working memory). According to this account, working memory interfaces with language production mechanisms at only two points: at phonetic coding and at the referential arena (here, message encoding). Therefore, executive control can be exerted over production at only these two levels of representation. The interface with phonetic coding reflects the above-mentioned monitoring function as well as speakers' ability to control directly some of the superficial aspects of their utterances (e.g., amplitude or enunciation). The interface with message encoding reflects the obvious idea that speakers can exert control over which ideas they will express, what perspective they will take on that expression, and (presumably) all other functions implemented at message encoding. This control over the preverbal message thus constitutes the first locus of linguistic choice: Via a process of executive control, speakers determine the details of the meanings that they wish to express, thereby determining the linguistic forms of their utterances.

In the Bock (1982) account, what is at least as important as where working memory interfaces with the language-production process is where working memory does *not* interface with the language-production process. Specifically, Bock assumes that working memory does not exert direct control over linguistic encoding, and this assumption is endorsed here. This implies that speakers have no executive control over the linguistic features they use to express the meaning encoded in the preverbal message. Rather, speakers can executively control what they say *only* by how they encode the meaning they wish to express. (Note that this sets aside that speakers can also control late-stage phonetic features of their utterances. Because this aspect of control is not especially relevant to the issues addressed in this chapter, I will not discuss it further. Moreover, Bock hedges by noting that, under unusual circumstances, speakers may be able to control directly linguistic-feature selection. For example, a copy-editor or a psycholinguist can intentionally choose to express an idea with an active structure instead of a passive. This hedge will become relevant for only one analysis below.)

Still, just because speakers cannot exert executive control over linguistic encoding does not mean that no linguistic choices happen at linguistic encoding. Indeed, language is rife with what can be termed *optionality*. This refers to the possibility of expressing a given preverbal message in more than one way. To choose an example that will figure prominently, a speaker can say, "I knew *that* I would enjoy the single malt" or "I knew I would enjoy the single malt". These are examples of *sentence-complement structures*—structures in which a main verb takes an embedded-clause complement, between which a speaker can mention or omit a complementizer *that*. It is likely that sentence-complement structures with vs. without the *that* arise from the same preverbal message. If so, then linguistic-encoding processes themselves must determine which form to use. The implication is that the choice between some linguistic alternatives is not an executive one, but rather is made automatically by the information-processing mechanisms of linguistic encoding.

Bringing all of this together yields the following analysis: Linguistic choices are made in two ways. One way is executive, whereby working memory can exert direct control over message-encoding processes to formulate a preverbal message that is then linguistically encoded with a particular set of linguistic features. An important aspect of this message-encoding process is information selection, where specific features of meaning are encoded into the preverbal message. The other way linguistic choices are made is automatic, whereby linguistic encoding processes choose one optional linguistic form over another without the intervention of executive processes.

Of course, there is the additional process of monitoring, which is a way that indirect control can be exerted over the choice of linguistic form. Specifically, monitoring processes can take an expression that linguistic encoding processes have formulated, comprehend it, and inject the products of comprehension back into message encoding, so that the preverbal message can be modified or created anew. However, the influence of monitoring upon linguistic choice is restricted in two ways. The first is at the input end, because monitoring is assumed to operate at a phonetic (e.g., Bock, 1982; Levelt, 1989) or phonological (Wheeldon & Levelt, 1995; Wheeldon & Morgan, 2002) level of analysis. This means that monitoring processes cannot assess linguistic features directly, but can assess linguistic features only once phonetically or phonologically encoded. The second restriction is at the output end, because monitoring can direct linguistic encoding only through the already described message-encoding process. Overall, then, monitoring can neither comprehend linguistic features directly nor select linguistic features directly. Together, these restrictions greatly limit the degree to which monitoring can exert control over linguistic encoding (for alternative views of monitoring, see Postma, 2000).

Placing this analysis of linguistic choice against the analysis of ambiguity described above suggests specific ways that ambiguity might be avoided. Recall that conceptual ambiguity is represented at the level of meaning. In the current model, this means conceptual ambiguity is represented within the level of message encoding—a process subject to executive control. This suggests that if speakers can detect the meaning-level convergence that corresponds to conceptual ambiguity (i.e., that two potential meanings are similar), they ought executively to avoid conceptual ambiguities. In contrast, linguistic ambiguity is not represented at message encoding, but is instead represented at the level of linguistic encoding—a process that is not subject to executive control. This suggests that if speakers are going to avoid linguistic ambiguity, it may be automatically, if the representations or processing strategies at linguistic encoding work such that when linguistic ambiguity is a threat, an unambiguous linguistic option is automatically selected. It also might be that speakers avoid linguistic ambiguity executively, but if so, then the means of that executive avoidance of linguistic ambiguity must be indirect. Two such indirect means of executive avoidance of linguistic ambiguity are possible. One comes from the fact that even though linguistic ambiguities do not arise until linguistic encoding, they may have correlates at the level of message encoding (examples will be discussed below). If so, perhaps some forms of linguistic ambiguity might be avoided via executive influences at the level of message encoding, if those message-encoding processes are sensitive to the conceptual-level correlates of linguistic ambiguity. Additionally, some linguistic ambiguities might be avoided executively via monitoring, whereby a linguistically ambiguous expression, once phonologically or phonetically encoded, might be comprehended and fed back to message encoding, which could then use information selection (and possibly other message-encoding processes) to avoid linguistic ambiguity again in an executive manner.

Ambiguity and linguistic choice

Executive control at message encoding

The first study I review explored the basic question of whether speakers can intentionally avoid conceptual ambiguities, linguistic ambiguities, or both. In experiments reported in Ferreira, Slevc, and Rogers (2005), speakers were shown displays of line-drawn pictures and were asked to describe them "with enough information so that someone else who was looking at the same display ... could figure out exactly which picture you are trying to describe"—in other words, unambiguously. In an experiment not formally described in that report, speakers saw displays like those in Figure 4.1. The display included a *target* object (at the left in each display in Figure 4.1, the flying-animal bat), descriptions of which were elicited and analysed. The display also included a *foil* object (at the top of each display in Figure 4.1), which sometimes caused different forms of ambiguity. Finally, the display included two filler objects, which complicated the displays and thereby discouraged the use of task-specific strategies.

The nature of the foil object was manipulated to create three ambiguity conditions. On one third of critical trials, the foil depicted an object that came from the same conceptual category as the target object but differed in some describable way, thereby creating conceptual ambiguity (e.g., the left sample display in Figure 4.1, including a larger flying-animal bat). On another third of critical trials, the foil depicted an object that had a name that was a

Figure 4.1 Sample displays from V. S. Ferreira, Slevc, and Rogers (2005).

homophone of the name of the target object, thereby creating linguistic ambiguity (e.g., the middle sample display in Figure 4.1, including a baseball bat). On the final third of critical trials, the foil object depicted an object that was semantically and lexically distinct from the foil object, thereby creating no ambiguity at all (e.g., the right sample display in Figure 4.1, including the goat). Speakers were shown an arrow that pointed at the target object, and were asked to describe it uniquely (i.e., unambiguously), and we measured how often speakers used a potentially ambiguous, bare-homophone label like "bat". If speakers used bare-homophone labels less often in either ambiguous condition (e.g., by saying "larger bat" or "flying bat") than in the unambiguous control condition, it indicated that they chose to include additional information in their utterance specifically to disambiguate the target object from the ambiguity-causing foil.

The experiment also included a manipulation of *preview*. Either the arrow that indicated the target appeared at the same time as the onset of the four pictures, or it appeared 5 s after the onset of the four pictures (a period long enough to allow full evaluation of all four pictures). Speakers were instructed to start their descriptions as soon as the arrow appeared. Therefore, speakers had either no time or 5 s to preview objects before they had to describe the target object (or before they even knew which object was the target).

Figure 4.2 shows the percentage of bare homophones speakers produced as a function of ambiguity condition and preview. For the moment, consider the no-preview condition (the three bars on the left), because it directly illustrates the first-pass operation of the language-production process (I return to the preview condition below, when monitoring is discussed). Compared to

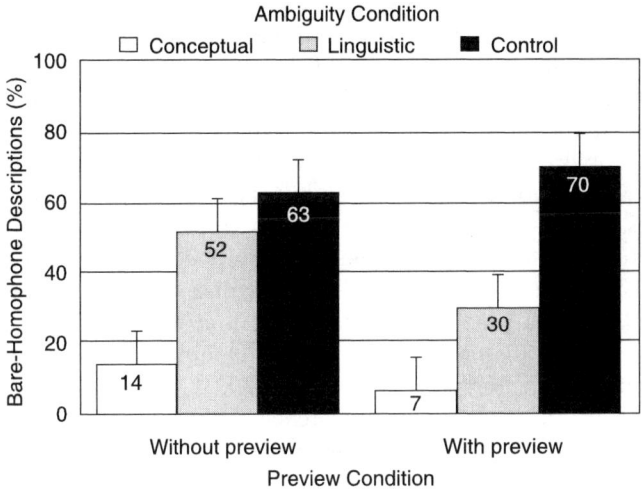

Figure 4.2 Results from V. S. Ferreira, Slevc, and Rogers (2005). Error bars illustrate 95% confidence intervals of the difference.

the level of bare-homophone production in the unambiguous control condition (black bar, 63%), speakers produced bare homophones much less often in the conceptual-ambiguity condition (white bar, 14%), but they produced bare homophones only a little less often (though significantly so) in the linguistic-ambiguity condition (grey bar, 52%). Thus, speakers disambiguated target and foil objects much more for conceptual ambiguities than for linguistic ambiguities.

Of course, the idea that speakers effectively avoid conceptual ambiguities is not new (even if, often, it has not been phrased in terms of ambiguity avoidance). For example, Nadig and Sedivy (2002) showed that in an elicited-production task, children distinguish conceptually ambiguous referents (see also Horton & Keysar, 1996), and Brennan and Clark (1996) showed that when presented with two objects from the same basic-level category, speakers use a subordinate-level label to distinguish them (e.g., speakers will use the label "loafer" to describe a shoe in the context of a loafer and a pump). Further back, Pechmann (1984, as described by Levelt, 1989) showed that speakers distinguish conceptually ambiguous items, and that they even erred on the side of providing redundant information—being hyper-unambiguous, if you will.

Given the above analysis, the explanation for speakers' successful avoidance of conceptual ambiguity is that conceptual ambiguities involve a convergence of representations at message encoding, and message encoding is subject to executive control. If this is so, then, because executive control is involved, speakers should be able to *not* avoid conceptual ambiguities when they need not or should not. Relevant evidence comes from Wardlow and Ferreira (2003). Naive speakers and addressees were shown cards with objects on them. On critical trials, two size-contrasting (i.e., conceptually ambiguous) objects were presented to speakers, such as a larger and a smaller circle. However, one of these objects was obscured from the addressee, so that, for example, the small circle was blocked from the addressee's view. This meant that, to speakers, the display included a conceptual ambiguity, but, to addressees, it did not. Speakers were asked to describe the shared size-contrasting object so that the addressee could pick it out. Note that with this setup, speakers should *not* avoid ambiguity, as from the perspective of addressees, "large circle" is a confusing description of the only circle they can see. Results showed that speakers used size-contrasting adjectives (i.e., they named the target "large circle", thereby disambiguating it with respect to the ambiguity-causing but privileged small circle) 10–40% of the time, depending on various task conditions (for complementary evidence from comprehension, see Keysar, Lin, & Barr, 2003). These were significantly higher rates of adjective use than in matched control conditions, in which the obscured object did not contrast in size with the target object (and therefore, no conceptual ambiguity existed).

From the perspective of executive control over conceptual-ambiguity avoidance, this result can be interpreted as either "half-empty" or "half-full".

On the half-empty side, the fact that speakers sometimes disambiguated targets even though they were unambiguous to addressees shows that the impulse to disambiguate conceptually ambiguous objects is powerful enough that speakers sometimes do so even when they should not. This shows that the process of conceptual ambiguity avoidance is not completely under executive control, but instead is sensitive to certain properties of the context that affect speakers' assessments that the displays are unambiguous to addressees (current work in the project is exploring those properties). This result may also help to explain speakers' tendency to provide redundant information in their descriptions (Pechmann, 1984). On the half-full side, speakers nonetheless disambiguated targets far less than 100% of the time, and far less than the 86% of the time they disambiguated targets in the experiment reported in Figure 4.2 (note that speakers produced ambiguous utterances 14% of the time in the conceptually ambiguous condition). This illustrates that even if executive control cannot fully regulate the impulse to avoid conceptual ambiguities, its influence is yet substantial. Thus, on balance, the reason that speakers can avoid conceptual ambiguities is evidently that conceptual ambiguities are represented at the level of message encoding, allowing speakers to use executive mechanisms to determine the production of a linguistic form that circumvents the conceptual ambiguity (specifically, through the process of information selection).

To return to the results in Figure 4.2, the other implication is that without preview, speakers only barely avoided linguistic ambiguities. Recall that without monitoring, speakers can avoid linguistic ambiguity two ways: either automatically, if linguistic encoding processes use (tacit) strategies that choose an unambiguous optional form over an ambiguous one, or executively, if message encoding processes are sensitive to conceptual-level correlates of a linguistic ambiguity. Concerning the automatic possibility, linguistic encoding processes might have distinguished a flying-animal bat from a baseball bat in the following (admittedly complex) way: Assume that meanings activate corresponding lexical representations (the "flying mammal" meaning activates the word "bat"), that lexical representations activate phonological representations ("bat" activates /bæt/), and that phonological representations then feedback to activate all connected lexical representations (/æt/ activates all words that sound like "bat"). This would activate both words for "bat". This could have induced competition between the two forms, which might allow an alternative form, say, "animal", to overtake these ambiguous forms and become selected. Of course, this seems a rather intricate processing sequence, and so it is not too surprising that the production system does not implement it.

Concerning the executive possibility, it is in principle possible that linguistically ambiguous referents might be tagged as ambiguous at the level of message encoding. In fact, this may be true for meanings that speakers come to learn are commonly described in linguistically ambiguous ways. For example, when discussing the work of a Sternberg, most cognitive psychologists know to encode in their preverbal message information that distinguishes Saul from Robert, even though the ambiguity of the last names of these researchers is wholly linguistic (because, presumably, Saul and Robert are no more conceptually similar than any two cognitive psychologists). (Note that if the two Sternbergs were known to be related, any analogous impulse to disambiguate them may derive from that conceptual-level characteristic even without any special tagging.) However, this, of course, is an unwieldy strategy for avoiding linguistic ambiguity in general (every homophone is unlikely to be tagged at the level of message encoding for its potential to be ambiguous), and the results in Figure 4.2 suggest that speakers do not commonly use it.

Of course, homophony is only one form of linguistic ambiguity. A more commonly investigated (and probably more prevalent) form of ambiguity is syntactic ambiguity. Is syntactic ambiguity avoided via automatic or executive processes? Next, I describe evidence that assesses the automatic possibility.

Does linguistic encoding automatically avoid syntactic ambiguity?

As noted, it seems implausible that linguistic encoding processes might automatically avoid the form of linguistic ambiguity that arises with homophony. However, it is more reasonable that linguistic encoding processes might automatically avoid forms of linguistic ambiguity that arise with syntactic ambiguity, for two reasons. First, linguistic encoding processes have ready access to optional linguistic features that can disambiguate otherwise ambiguous syntactic structures (so that avoidance mechanisms need not rely on information selection for disambiguation to occur). Specifically, consider the statement, "The weary traveller claimed the luggage had been stolen in Rome", in which "the luggage" is ambiguous between a direct-object versus an embedded-clause interpretation. As already noted, these sentence-complement structures can include an optional *complementizer* "that" after the verb but before the embedded clause ("The weary traveller claimed *that* the luggage had been stolen in Rome."). This is important, because complementizers provide a reliable (though not perfect) cue that the following material constitutes an embedded clause (Juliano & Tanenhaus, 1994). Therefore, linguistic encoding processes can easily and quite effectively avoid the form of syntactic ambiguity that arises with sentence-complement structures simply by mentioning the optional complementizer "that" in sentences that would otherwise permit or encourage a direct-object interpretation.

Second, it is reasonable that linguistic encoding might employ a (tacit) processing strategy by which an unambiguous form is automatically chosen over an ambiguous form. Assume that a speaker has formulated the incremental sentence fragment, "The weary traveller claimed . . .", and is preparing to use the noun "luggage" (without the "that"). A number of theories of syntactic encoding (e.g., F. Ferreira, 2000; V. S. Ferreira, 1996; Levelt, 1989;

Pickering & Branigan, 1998) claim that activated lexical representations make available the syntactic structures they can be used in. So, the noun "luggage" (without the "that") could activate both an embedded-subject structure and a direct-object structure. These two structures might then compete, interfering with each other's selection. In contrast, the structure with the "that" is not compatible with a direct-object interpretation, and so it should not suffer comparable interference. In short, it could be that because of their ambiguity, ambiguous forms might cause linguistic encoding processes to select unambiguous forms instead, even without the involvement of executive-control processes.

V. S. Ferreira and Dell (2000) tested the possibility that linguistic encoding processes might automatically select unambiguous rather than ambiguous syntactic structures. Along with one or two filler sentences, speakers encoded into memory sentences like "The coach knew (that) you missed practice", which (without the "that") include the direct-object versus embedded-subject ambiguity. They then produced the sentence back from memory when presented with a cue consisting of its main subject and verb ("coach knew"), and we measured whether speakers produced sentences back with the optional "that" or not. (Half of the sentences that speakers originally encoded included the "that" and half did not. This factor influenced "that"-mention—speakers mentioned the "that" when it was in the originally encoded sentence and omitted it when it was not, 65% of the time. However, though well above chance, this rate is far enough from 100% that other factors can easily influence "that"-mention as well.)

In six experiments, we contrasted sentences that would vs. would not be ambiguous even without the "that". In five of these experiments, unambiguous forms were constructed by replacing the ambiguous noun phrase "you" with an unambiguous form like "I", "she", or "he". These latter forms are unambiguous because they are explicitly marked with their nominative case, and so they can only be subjects (i.e., "The coach knew I . . ." would have to be "The coach knew me" under a direct-object interpretation). Therefore, if the production system automatically avoids ambiguous productions, it should include a "that" more in a sentence that would otherwise be "The coach knew you missed practice", which includes an ambiguity, than in a sentence that would otherwise be "The coach knew I missed practice", which does not.

This prediction was disconfirmed. In all five experiments, speakers never produced "thats" significantly more in sentences that would be disambiguated by their mention. The other experiment tested a different syntactic ambiguity, namely, the notorious main-clause vs. reduced-relative ambiguity (the one made famous with the example "The horse raced past the barn fell" (Bever, 1970)). Here, a form like "The astronauts selected for the missions made history" is ambiguous, because "The astronauts selected . . ." can be interpreted either as a subject-main verb sequence ("The astronauts selected their spacesuits"—the preferred interpretation) or as a subject-passive relative clause sequence (which is the eventual but less pre-ferred interpretation). However, speakers can circumvent the ambiguity by producing an optional full passive-relative clause like "The astronauts *who were* selected for the mission made history". We contrasted sentences like these that required disambiguation against sentences that included an unambiguous past-participle form and so were unambiguous regardless, like "The astronauts chosen for the mission made history" ("The astronauts chosen . . ." cannot be a main-clause fragment). Again, speakers showed no tendency toward producing disambiguating "who weres" (etc.) more in sen-tences that would be disambiguated by their mention. (It is worth noting that the lack of any effect of ambiguity was unlikely to be due to a statistical null-effects problem. Though ambiguity failed to affect "that"-mention, another factor discussed briefly below, namely, the *accessibility* of the material after the "that", consistently affected "that"-mention. Thus, the experiment was sensitive enough to detect the effect of factors that affect the selection of linguistic form.)

   This evidence suggests that linguistic encoding processes do not auto-matically choose expressions that are unambiguous over expressions that are ambiguous. However, the nature of the manipulations assessed by V. S. Ferreira and Dell (2000) limit how far this conclusion can be taken. Specific-ally, it may be that speakers are sensitive to ambiguity-relevant factors other than pronoun case ("I" vs. "you") or verb inflection ("selected" vs. "chosen"). Furthermore, the evidence thus far does not address whether speakers avoid linguistic ambiguity with strategies that operate at message encoding, by tap-ping into conceptual-level correlates of linguistically ambiguous structures (so that if linguistically ambiguous alternatives are accompanied by some systematic message-level pattern, speakers might detect that message-level pattern, and then avoid ambiguity in some executively controlled fashion). The experiments reviewed next addressed these questions.

Avoiding syntactic ambiguity at linguistic encoding revisited, and avoiding syntactic ambiguity at message encoding

In a current project, I am investigating two factors that might affect ambigu-ity avoidance, one that could operate at message encoding and one at lin-guistic encoding. These two factors, originally explored in comprehension work by Garnsey et al. (1997), are *verb bias* and *direct-object plausibility*. Verb bias here refers to the degree to which the verb in a sentence tends to occur with direct objects, embedded clauses, or any other syntactic form. For example, the verb "accept" commonly occurs with direct objects (henceforth *direct-object biased*), "claim" commonly occurs with embedded clauses (*embedded-clause biased*), and "announced" is in between (*equibiased*). Given a sentence-complement structure, the more a verb tends to occur with a direct object, the greater the threat of the ambiguity. Direct-object plausibility refers to how plausible the post-verbal noun phrase is as a direct object. In

"The weary traveller claimed the luggage . . .", "luggage" is a very plausible direct object—it is something that travellers claim. But in "The weary traveller claimed the attendant . . .", "attendant" is an implausible direct object—it is not something that travellers (plausibly) claim. As with verb bias, given a sentence-complement structure, the more the postverbal noun phrase seems plausible as a direct object, the greater the threat of ambiguity.

Note that plausibility is a message-encoding factor. It is at the level of meaning that "luggage" seems like a claimable thing and "attendant" does not. This means that by testing whether plausibility affects ambiguity avoidance, we are testing whether message-encoding processes can recognize the potential for ambiguity and thereby cause the selection of a syntactic structure that avoids it. In contrast, verb bias is a linguistic encoding factor. That "accept" commonly takes a direct object but "claim" commonly takes an embedded subject must be represented at a point in the system where these particular words are represented, namely, in the lexicon, which is represented at the level of linguistic encoding. Thus, by investigating whether verb bias affects ambiguity avoidance, we provide another test of the V. S. Ferreira and Dell (2000) claim that linguistic encoding processes do not automatically choose unambiguous expressions over ambiguous ones.

So far, two experiments have explored the effects of plausibility and verb bias. In one, speakers produced sentences from memory, as in V. S. Ferreira and Dell (2000). In the second, speakers participated in what Bradley, Fernandez, and Taylor (2003) called the *"New York Post* to *New York Times"* task, where speakers are given two simple sentences and are asked to combine them into a single, more complex sentence (e.g., speakers are given "The weary traveller claimed something" and "The luggage had been stolen in Rome", and asked to combine them; the overwhelmingly most common product is, "The weary traveller claimed (that) the luggage had been stolen in Rome"). Plausibility and verb bias were factorially manipulated (following Garnsey et al., 1997), and the likelihood of producing a "that" was measured. The results were clear: Plausibility exerted no consistent effect on "that"-mention. The two experiments showed opposite differences in "that"-mention due to direct-object plausibility, but in neither case was the difference significant. In contrast, verb bias exerted a robust effect on "that"-mention. As predicted by an ambiguity-avoidance account, speakers produced "thats" most in sentences that included direct-object biased verbs, and least in sentences that included embedded-subject-biased verbs, and equibiased verbs (which were tested only in the first experiment) were in between.

The absence of a plausibility effect is important, because it shows that a conceptual correlate of a linguistic ambiguity is not enough to allow message-encoding processes to choose unambiguous over ambiguous linguistic structures. This extends the implications of the evidence in Figure 4.2 regarding the (nearly total) nonavoidance of ambiguity caused by homophony.

However, what about the effect of verb bias—does it indicate that linguistic encoding processes automatically choose unambiguous rather than ambiguous forms? Actually, the current evidence is not definitive, because there are two ways to explain this effect. One is as ambiguity avoidance: Speakers' grammatical knowledge might represent that some verbs tend to be interpreted as occurring with direct objects more, and so those verbs' "that"-preferences—the degree to which each is produced with the optional "that" in a sentence-complement structure—is increased accordingly. It is important to note, however, that this was entirely unaffected by plausibility. This means that if this explanation is correct, it is not a dynamically deployed automatic ambiguity-avoidance effect. Rather, it is a static strategy that might be "built in" to speakers' grammatical knowledge. If this explanation holds, building ambiguity avoidance into the grammar may be a brute force way that linguistic encoding processes can automatically circumvent ambiguity.

There is, however, another interpretation of the effect of verb bias, one that does not attribute it to ambiguity avoidance at all. The ambiguity-avoidance interpretation emphasizes the fact that some verbs are used with direct objects more than others. However, one could instead emphasize the claim that some verbs are used with embedded clauses more than others. And of course, these factors trade off—verbs that are used more with direct objects are used less with embedded subjects, and vice versa. Thus, it may be that the reason that sentences with direct-object-biased verbs are often produced with "thats" is not because such verbs commonly occur with direct objects, but rather because such verbs rarely occur with embedded subjects (and vice versa for sentences with embedded-clause-biased verbs). This may be because, if a verb is rarely used with an embedded subject structure, it may be a little harder to produce that embedded subject structure, and this in turn may cause speakers to say the "that" more (for evidence that speakers say "thats" more in hard-to-produce sentences, see V. S. Ferreira & Dell, 2000; V. S. Ferreira & Firato, 2002). Thus, based on existing evidence at least, it is not clear whether these influences of verb bias on "that"-mention are due to some kind of ambiguity-avoidance influence.

Thus far, then, there seems to be little knockdown evidence to suggest that speakers avoid linguistic ambiguity either executively at message encoding or automatically at linguistic encoding. However, a concern with the evidence described thus far is that speakers always produced sentences in some kind of isolated production task, either recalling sentences from memory or combining simple sentences into more complex sentences. Perhaps if speakers produced sentences in a more communicative setting, ambiguity avoidance would be observed.

Speaking to real addressees

In a key experiment in V. S. Ferreira and Dell (2000), speakers produced from memory one of four kinds of sentences:

(1)   I knew (that) I had booked a flight for tomorrow.

(2) I knew (that) you had booked a flight for tomorrow.
(3) You knew (that) I had booked a flight for tomorrow.
(4) You knew (that) you had booked a flight for tomorrow.

Of these four options, only sentence (2) contains a temporary ambiguity. Sentences (1) and (3) do not, because the embedded subject is the unambiguous pronoun "I". Sentence (4) does not, because "you" cannot be a direct object in the same clause that "you" is the main subject (it would have to be "you knew yourself"). If linguistic encoding processes avoid ambiguity, speakers should produce "thats" more in sentence (2) than in the other sentences. Instead, the experiment found that speakers said "thats" more often both in sentence (2) and in sentence (3). This was interpreted as an accessibility effect. In sentences (1) and (4), because the embedded subject pronoun is identical to the main subject pronoun, it should be relatively more accessible, meaning it should be mentioned sooner, which speakers can do by omitting the "that".

In an ongoing project, Melanie Hudson and I have looked at sentences like (1)–(4) in naturalistic dialogue. In five experiments (so far), two experimentally naive speakers described scenarios to each other whereby one of them observed the other performing a behaviour, and then asked for a statement about what emotion the observer would infer about the behaver. For example, one speaker asked the other, "I notice you are stamping your feet. What do I believe about you?" To this, the answer might be, "You believe (that) I am angry." Then, by manipulating who observes the behaviour and who performs the behaviour, all four sentences like (1)–(4) above can be elicited.

If speakers avoid ambiguous utterances in naturalistic dialogues like this, they should say "thats" most in sentences like (2)—"I believe (that) you are angry". In contrast, all five experiments found that speakers said "thats" *least* in sentences like (2), compared to the other three sentences (see Figure 4.3 for representative results). Speakers said "thats" most in sentences like

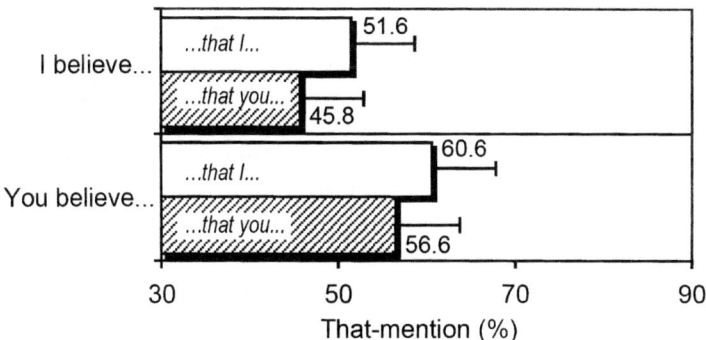

Figure 4.3 Results from V. S. Ferreira and Hudson (2005).

(3)—"You believe (that) I am angry"—and the other two sentences (where the pronouns were the same) were in between. Our experiments are exploring whether, in the context of this task, sentences like (2) are easiest for speakers to determine the content of because of the influence of social-cognitive factors. Specifically, to answer, "I believe (that) you are angry", a speaker must (a) take his or her own perspective ("I believe . . .") and (b) attribute an emotion to another person ("you are angry"). Doing both of these things should be easy. In contrast, a sentence like (3)—"You believe (that) I am angry"—is the hardest to determine the content of, because a speaker must (a) take the perspective of another person ("You believe . . .") and (b) attribute an emotion to oneself ("I am angry"; from the actor-observer discrepancy in social psychology, we know that people more readily use behaviours to attribute emotions to others than to themselves). If we assume that "that"-mention is linked to the difficulty with which a sentence is produced (as already suggested), "I believe (that) you are angry" should have the fewest "thats", "you believe (that) I am angry" the most, and the other two conditions should be in between. In any case, what is most important for present purposes is that speakers did not use "thats" most in ambiguous sentences.

Other evidence converges with this claim. Elsness (1984) found that in the Brown corpus—real sentences written for real people to read—the same kind of contrast that was tested by V. S. Ferreira and Dell (2000) and V. S. Ferreira and Hudson (2005) also did not yield evidence of ambiguity avoidance. More recently, Arnold, Wasow, Asudeh, and Alrenga (2004) revealed that in a dialogue task, speakers used neither different forms of dative sentences nor different prosody to avoid what would otherwise be ambiguous structures. Kraljic and Brennan (2005) showed that in a task where subjects directed each other to perform actions, speakers used neither the mention of optional words nor particular patterns of prosody selectively to avoid ambiguous structures. Schafer, Speer, Warren, and White (2000) observed the same absence of disambiguating prosody in a game-playing task, as did Albritton, McKoon, and Ratcliff (1996) in a sentence-reading task. On balance then, the bulk of evidence suggests that speakers do not take special steps to avoid linguistic ambiguities (with a few exceptions to be taken up below).

Up until now, we have set aside monitoring. But monitoring may be the best candidate for a process that will avoid ambiguity. The evidence reviewed thus far suggests that speakers cannot foresee linguistic ambiguities during message encoding, and they cannot avoid ambiguities automatically during linguistic encoding (except, perhaps, if the grammar encodes the effect of verb bias). But once speakers have formulated an ambiguous utterance, it may be that they can monitor it and detect its ambiguity, abort its articulation, and reconduct message encoding and linguistic encoding until it is no longer ambiguous.

Monitoring

As described above, the experiment reported in Figure 4.2 suggests that without preview, speakers produced ambiguous descriptions of linguistically ambiguous targets almost as often as they produced "ambiguous" descriptions of unambiguous targets. With preview, however, speakers' rate of linguistically ambiguous description drops from 52% to 30%. It turns out that other evidence from the experiment suggests that this with-preview level of ambiguous production (30%) is probably maximally unambiguous (because the pictures did not perfectly cause ambiguity—if speakers do not think that a baseball bat ought to be called "bat", "bat" as a description of the flying animal is unambiguous). Why is it that with preview, speakers avoided linguistic ambiguity so much better—maximally, even?

The remaining experiments reported in V. S. Ferreira, Slevc, and Rogers (2005) suggest that the linguistic ambiguity caused by homophony can be avoided via inner-speech monitoring. However, the way that monitoring can most effectively detect ambiguity is complex and revealing. In three more experiments, speakers described pictures in displays like those in Figure 4.1, except that instead of just the target object being indicated with an arrow, a dot bounced from picture to picture. On critical trials, the dot always indicated both the target picture and the ambiguity-causing foil. Initially, the point of using this dot was to require that speakers at least look at the ambiguity-causing foil before they formulated a description of the target. It turned out, however, that to get maximal ambiguity avoidance (as observed with preview in Figure 4.2), speakers not only had to *look* at the ambiguity-causing foil before they described the target, but they also had to *describe* the ambiguity-causing foil before they described the target.

Specifically, in two experiments, speakers had to describe every picture indicated by the bouncing dot. On critical trials, the dot either bounced from the target to the foil (e.g., the flying mammal and then the baseball bat), or it bounced from the foil to the target (e.g., the baseball bat and then the flying mammal; the dot also bounced to fillers before or after the target and foil). When the dot bounced from target to foil, speakers still described the target with a (potentially ambiguous) bare-homophone label about 47% of the time (which is close to the 52% level observed without preview in Figure 4.2). In fact, speakers used utterances like "the bat and the baseball bat", implying that they failed to determine that the description "bat" would ambiguously describe the flying mammal, even when the very next description they were about to utter was of the object that caused the ambiguity. When speakers described targets after foils, however, they described targets with bare homophones much less—25% of the time, right around the 30% level observed with preview in Figure 4.2. In this case, a speaker's typical utterance was "bat and flying bat", suggesting that they again failed to anticipate the ambiguity of the first-described object (the foil), but then detected the ambiguity in time to avoid an ambiguous description of the second-described object (the target).

When speakers described targets before foils, why did they tend to produce "bat and baseball bat", rather than (for example) "flying bat and baseball bat"? The most straightforward explanation is that speakers can detect ambiguity, but only when they retrieve for production the same description for two distinct objects. The idea is that when speakers said "bat and animal bat", they first retrieved the description "bat" for the flying mammal, and they articulated that description, unaware that it would ultimately be ambiguous. Then they retrieved the description "bat" again, but this time for the baseball bat. Presumably, before speakers articulated the second description "bat", monitoring processes detected in the phonological or phonetic stream that the second description was the same as a previous description that was applied to a different object. This permitted speakers to stop and do the message-encoding process again so that distinguishing information about the second object could be incorporated into speakers' preverbal messages. Of course, this account can also explain performance in Figure 4.2 with preview—when given 5 s to view pictures before the target had to be described, speakers probably named each object covertly, thereby naming two objects with the same description and allowing their monitoring process to detect the threat of linguistic ambiguity.

What is revealing about this explanation is that it implies that monitoring is able to engage in very little looking ahead. Presumably, if production worked such that monitoring processes could detect the two uses of the word "bat" before the first use was articulated, speakers would have avoided that first description. (Indeed, in the conceptual-ambiguity condition, in which speakers could foresee the threat of ambiguity based on conceptual information, they nearly always disambiguated both the first-described and the second-described object, as for example, by saying "small bat and large bat"). In the linguistic ambiguity condition, to avoid the first "bat", speakers would have to have formulated all of "the bat and the bat" as a proto-utterance *before* the first mention of "bat" was articulated, so that the use of the two "bats" could be detected. Evidently, production is more incremental than this, in that speakers do not plan that much material before articulating it (for compelling evidence on this front, see Griffin, 2001).

Note that if this analysis of how monitoring can help speakers avoid ambiguity is correct, it does not bode well for the avoidance of syntactic ambiguity. If monitoring can detect ambiguity only after the fact, by determining that a current description is somehow similar to a previous description, this would mean that speakers would have to formulate both interpretations of a potentially ambiguous syntactic sequence to detect the ambiguity. With individual words that map onto distinct concepts, this is relatively manageable. With a string of words that map onto distinct syntactic structures, it would be more difficult.

Indeed, results of an unpublished study from my laboratory do not give reason to be optimistic that monitoring processes can readily detect syntactic ambiguity. In this task, speakers were shown relative-clause sentences like the following:

(5) The *winning team* (that was) *defeated* in the Super Bowl vowed revenge the next season.
(6) The *losing team* (that was) *defeated* in the Super Bowl vowed revenge the next season.
(7) The *winning team* (that was) *beaten* in the Super Bowl vowed revenge the next season.
(8) The *losing team* (that was) *beaten* in the Super Bowl vowed revenge the next season.

Sentence (5) is the most ambiguous of the set. Here, a fragment without the optional material ("that was") is "The winning team defeated . . .", which seems extremely likely to continue with "defeated" as a main verb (e.g., "The winning team defeated the losing team"), which it does not. Sentence (6) includes a structural ambiguity, but it is rendered less likely by the pragmatics of "losing team" (it is relatively unlikely that "the losing team defeated" anything). Sentences (7) and (8) are unambiguous, because of the unambiguous inflection on the verb "beaten". Therefore, if speakers are sensitive to ambiguity, they should produce the disambiguating "that was" (or "that were", "who were", and so forth) more in sentences like (5) than in the other three.

These materials were tested in what I term a *copy-editor* task. Subjects ($n = 48$) were shown printed sentences like (5) through (8) above (half the time with the optional material and half the time without). The optional material, when present, was underlined (no material was italicized). Subjects were instructed:

> Look at each sentence, and rewrite it with or without the *that was* (or *that were*, or whatever), depending on which would be easier to understand. If the sentence would be easier to understand with the *that was*, make sure that it's there, but if it would be easier to understand without the *that was*, make sure that it's not.

In other words, speakers were to read the sentence for its comprehensibility and include or omit the optional material to enhance that comprehensibility. The percentages of sentences speakers wrote with the disambiguating material as a function of the plausibility of the main subject argument and the ambiguity of the verb are shown in Figure 4.4. Speakers wrote in the disambiguating material more when the plausibility of the main subject especially exacerbated the ambiguity, but only when the verb already made the sentence unambiguous. Statistically, the only effect that approached significance was the main effect of plausibility ($p < .08$). Thus, if speakers only

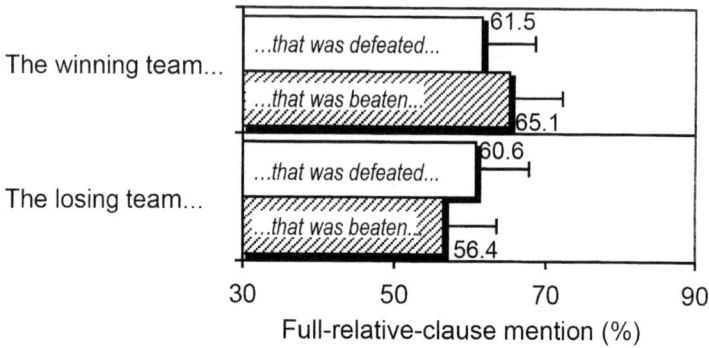

Figure 4.4 Results from copy-editor task.

very weakly (if at all) detected ambiguity even when they were shown sentences and asked to judge how easy or hard they are to understand, it is unlikely that their monitoring processes will be able to detect and circumvent that ambiguity in the more pressured circumstances of naturalistic production.

To summarize the whole story: Speakers can make choices that influence the forms of their linguistic utterances at two stages: at message encoding, by choosing to express information that distinguishes an intended meaning from an unintended meaning, and at linguistic encoding, by automatically choosing one optional form rather than another. As shown in Figure 4.2 and in many studies before, message-encoding processes do seem to avoid conceptual ambiguities effectively, and as suggested by the evidence from Wardlow and V. S. Ferreira (2003), this process is subject to executive control. This makes sense, because conceptual ambiguities are represented at the level that message encoding operates, and because message-encoding processes themselves, through the executively controlled information-selection process, can disambiguate conceptual ambiguities. In contrast, message-encoding processes seem unable to avoid linguistic ambiguities. This was revealed both by the observation that speakers did not avoid bare-homophone descriptions when the homophonous counterpart object was present in displays (without preview), and by the observation that the plausibility of a garden-path analysis had no effect on speakers' use of a disambiguating "that". Moreover, linguistic encoding processes do not seem automatically to avoid linguistic ambiguity, because speakers did not use disambiguating material more in sentences that were ambiguous due to the ambiguity of a pronoun or a verbal inflection. This was true regardless of whether speakers participated in a memory-based sentence-production task or in an interactive dialogue. Speakers did produce disambiguating "thats" more often in sentence-complement structures with verbs that tend to often take direct objects, and this might be an automatic ambiguity-avoidance effect. However, there is an alternative explanation for this effect that has nothing to do with ambiguity avoidance. Finally, monitoring processes were sensitive to linguistic ambiguities caused by homophony, in that they could detect that speakers were about to use the same description for two different meanings. However, monitoring seemed unable to detect syntactic ambiguity, as revealed by speakers' insensitivity to ambiguity when they were shown sentences and asked to include or omit material in order to make them as comprehensible as possible.

In short, conceptual ambiguities are avoided, but linguistic ambiguities are not, at least most of the time. However, others have reported evidence of linguistic ambiguity avoidance. How does that evidence square with the present analysis?

Other observations of ambiguity avoidance

In an analysis of the Brown corpus, Elsness (1984) showed, like V. S. Ferreira and Dell (2000), that speakers did not use disambiguating "thats" more in sentences that had ambiguous pronouns compared to unambiguous pronouns. However, he did report one case of "that"-mention that did seem to reflect ambiguity avoidance. Specifically, he examined sentences like "The weary traveller claimed yesterday (that) the luggage had been stolen in Rome", or "The weary traveller claimed (that) yesterday the luggage had been stolen in Rome." Without the "that", such sentences are (fully) ambiguous, in that the adverbial might modify the main-clause content (when the claim happened) or it might modify the embedded-clause content (when the luggage got stolen). The "that", however, forces the adverbial to modify one clause's content or the other. This seems like a natural situation where a "that" might be used to avoid a (fully) ambiguous utterance.

However, it is worth noting that Elsness did not show that speakers' use of "thats" in sentence-complement structures with these kinds of adverbials is sensitive *specifically* to ambiguity. In fact, it may be that any time additional material is mentioned near the location of an optional "that" (such as the adverbial in the above examples), speakers mention "thats" more often, independent of ambiguity. For example, compare "Today, the weary traveller claimed (that) yesterday the luggage had been stolen in Rome" and "Angrily, the weary traveller claimed (that) yesterday the luggage had been stolen in Rome". If speakers mention "thats" to avoid ambiguity, they should freely omit "thats" from the first sentence, because "yesterday" cannot be misinterpreted (the preposed "today" blocks the interpretation where "yesterday" modifies the main clause). If not, and if speakers mention "thats" equally in these two kinds of sentences, then it cannot be ambiguity per se that is driving the "that"-mention in sentences like these.

Another corpus analysis that pointed to ambiguity avoidance comes from Temperley (2003). He investigated the use of object-relative clauses, which also can include optional "thats", in a subset of the parsed *Wall Street Journal* corpus. His analysis revealed that object-relative structures in the analysed subset of the *Journal* included "thats" most often when the material that followed the optional "that" was a plural noun or a name, as in "The lawyer (that) companies . . ." or "The lawyer (that) Smith . . .". In contrast, object-relative structures included "thats" least often when the material that followed the "that" was a pronoun or a determiner-noun sequence, as in "The lawyer (that) I . . ." or "The lawyer (that) the company . . .". This fits with an ambiguity-avoidance analysis: "The lawyer companies . . ." or "The lawyer Smith . . ." can be interpreted as simple noun phrases with noun-noun compounds, and the "that" blocks that interpretation. In contrast, "The lawyer I . . ." or "The lawyer the company" cannot be interpreted as noun-noun compounds, and so the "that" is not needed for disambiguation.

A different explanation for this same pattern, however, attributes it to accessibility, which V. S. Ferreira and Dell (2000) showed affects "that"-mention in sentence-complement structures. Specifically, pronouns like "I" and determiners like "the" are highly frequent structures that are presumably easy to access for production. In contrast, plural nouns and proper names are far less frequent, and are presumably more difficult to access for production. If the mention of a "that" in an object relative is sensitive to accessibility in the same way that the mention of a "that" in a sentence-complement structure is (for relevant evidence, see Jaeger, 2005), this pattern can be explained without appealing to ambiguity avoidance at all.

A recent observation of ambiguity avoidance that is especially compelling comes from Snedeker and Trueswell (2003). In a directed-action task, they had speakers produce sentences like "tap the frog with the flower", where "with the flower" can be either a modifier of "frog" or an instrument of "tap". Speakers produced this instruction to tell addressees to perform one of these actions or the other. Results showed that speakers who were aware of the potential for ambiguity in these sentences produced them with prosodic structures that distinguished one interpretation from the other. Furthermore, speakers used disambiguating prosody only when the context did not disambiguate the utterance for their addressees (i.e., if only one interpretation of "tap the frog with the flower" was possible).

Given the above analysis, Snedeker and Trueswell's (2003) results may have come about because certain features of their procedure could have created unusual circumstances that allowed for linguistic ambiguity avoidance. In the experiment, speakers repeatedly produced sentences that were ambiguous between attribute and instrument interpretations, and this may have cued speakers to the potential of the ambiguity. Furthermore, speakers were told to produce the utterances by being shown the written utterance on a card, and then over an approximate 10-s interval, the experimenter demonstrated which specific instruction the speaker was to convey by acting on objects. This may not only have cued the potential for ambiguity, but also given speakers ample opportunity to try various forms of utterances covertly before producing them. Finally, the fact that only speakers who were aware of the ambiguity provided disambiguating prosody especially hints that unusual executive control or monitoring (or both) may have been involved. Overall, the Snedeker and Trueswell demonstration is an important illustration that speakers *can* use linguistic devices to avoid linguistic ambiguity. However, it may not reveal how language-production processes typically choose linguistic utterances.

Finally, Haywood, Pickering, and Branigan (2005) recently observed that in a dialogue task where speakers took turns describing actions to be performed on displays, speakers included more disambiguating "that's" in utterances like "put the penguin (that's) in the cup on the star" specifically with displays that would otherwise be ambiguous (i.e., when there was more than one penguin). Haywood et al. speculate that a key difference between their study and previous observations of failures to avoid ambiguity may be that interactive dialogue promotes sensitivity to the potential ambiguity of speakers' own utterances. An alternative to consider is whether speakers were sensitive to *linguistic* ambiguity (because they recognized that "put the penguin in the cup . . ." could mean that the cup is a target location) or *conceptual* ambiguity (because when speakers saw more than one penguin in a display—when it was ambiguous—they used more explicit structures in their instructions, a pattern analogous to that observed by V. S. Ferreira et al. (2005), and supported by evidence in Kraljic and Brennan (2005). The impact of this result on the overall analysis presented here awaits future research.

So, how is ambiguity avoided?

The analysis provided in this chapter is potentially troubling. Speakers do not avoid most forms of linguistic ambiguity, most of the time. Does this mean that language is heavily ambiguous, so that speakers either fail to communicate their meanings or produce utterances that are especially difficult for their addressees to understand? Recent analyses by Roland, Elman, and V. S. Ferreira (2006) suggest that this might not be the case.

This study examined a corpus of over 186,000 automatically parsed sentences from the British National Corpus. All sentences were of the form subject-verb-noun-phrase (e.g., "The traveller claimed the luggage"), where the noun-phrase was either an embedded subject or a direct object. For each sentence, different linguistic properties of the sentence fragments were measured, including which specific verb the fragment included, and the length, frequency, and semantic properties of the main subject and post-verbal-noun-phrase material. Then, these properties of each sentence were entered into a logistic regression model that was designed to predict whether the real sentence included a direct object or an embedded subject. The result was striking: Based on the measured properties, the regression model predicted with nearly 87% accuracy whether a formally ambiguous sentence fragment really included a direct-object or an embedded subject. Furthermore, additional analyses suggested that the best the model could have done was about 90%, because the automatic parsing routine that was used for the

186,000 sentences was imperfect and thus misparsed some direct-object sentences as embedded-subject sentences, and vice versa.

The implication of this analysis is profound. It suggests that, in principle, the utterances that comprehenders encounter include enough information to guess correct syntactic analyses, even when the encountered structures are formally ambiguous. In other words, when all the information available to a comprehender is taken into account, language may not be so ambiguous after all.

The Roland et al. (2006) evidence is critical, as it points to an alternative way that the challenge posed by linguistic ambiguity might be overcome. Specifically, it is likely that the reason the grammar of English can allow the complementizer "that" to be optional at all in sentence-complement (and other related) structures is because almost every time that speakers might omit the "that", addressees can still readily infer speakers' intended interpretations, perhaps even without disrupting the comprehension process (much) at all. This implies that the reason speakers do not generally avoid linguistic ambiguity may be that they need not avoid linguistic ambiguity— the grammar of the language they speak will allow them to (most of the time) produce only utterances that will be unambiguous most of the time.

To illustrate, contrast the optionality of the "that" in sentence-complement structures and the well-known observation from linguistics that languages are of two general types—fixed word-order and free word-order languages. Fixed word-order languages indicate the grammatical functions of subject, direct object, indirect object, and so forth by relative order. For example, in English, the grammatical subject precedes the verb and the direct object follows the verb. Fixed word-order languages typically do not use suffixes (or other explicit *case markers*) to indicate these roles. Free word-order languages manifest the complementary pattern: Grammatical functions (subject, direct object, etc.) are indicated by explicit case markers, and the relative order of grammatical functions is far less constrained (e.g., in Japanese, a direct object is indicated by the suffix "-o", and can, relatively freely, appear before the subject, after the subject, after an indirect object, etc.). Critically for present considerations, it is highly unusual for languages to have very free word-order and not to use explicit case markers to indicate grammatical functions. The reason is obvious: If a language were free word order and did not use case markers, addressees would find it very difficult to determine the grammatical functions in sentences, because speakers' utterances would be profoundly ambiguous in this regard. This illustrates that it is the job of the grammar to ensure that speakers' utterances cannot be systematically ambiguous, and so speakers need not have processing mechanisms—executive or automatic—to avoid ambiguity themselves.

Conclusions

To summarize, the analyses and evidence presented in this chapter suggest that speakers robustly avoid conceptual ambiguities, because their executive mechanisms can. They barely avoid linguistic ambiguities, because their executive mechanisms cannot, and their linguistic encoding processes do not automatically avoid the ambiguities for them. Nonetheless, that speakers fail to avoid many linguistic ambiguities may not be detrimental, because the information comprehenders need to get past most forms of ambiguity might be in the speech signal anyway. Presumably, this is because, in general, the grammars of languages develop so as to prevent speakers from being able to produce rampantly (linguistically) ambiguous utterances in the first place.

This analysis of ambiguity avoidance is informative not just to psycholinguists, but also to researchers interested in behavioural choice more generally. The analysis illustrates that to accomplish its functional goals, a behavioural system can not just use executively controlled processing mechanisms and automatically deployed processing mechanisms, but, at least in some cases, can also sculpt the overall context or environment that the behavioural system operates within, thereby circumventing the need for executive or automatic mechanisms to accomplish certain goals at all. By this view, the important goal of avoiding linguistic ambiguity is essentially accomplished by the language system as a whole, so that the way that language is learned, represented, and used encourages a grammar that avoids ambiguity for speakers, leaving their executive processing mechanisms free to determine what meanings to express, and their automatic processing mechanisms free to select efficiently linguistic forms that express those meanings.

References

Albritton, D. W., McKoon, G., & Ratcliff, R. (1996). Reliability of prosodic cues for resolving syntactic ambiguity. *Journal of Experimental Psychology: Learning, Memory, and Cognition, 22,* 714–735.

Arnold, J. E., Wasow, T., Asudeh, A., & Alrenga, P. (2004). Avoiding attachment ambiguities: The role of constituent ordering. *Journal of Memory and Language, 51,* 55–70.

Bever, T. G. (1970). The cognitive basis for linguistic structures. In J. R. Hayes (Ed.), *Cognition and the development of language.* New York: Wiley.

Bock, J. K. (1982). Toward a cognitive psychology of syntax: Information processing contributions to sentence formulation. *Psychological Review, 89,* 1–47.

Bradley, D., Fernandez, E. M., & Taylor, D. (2003). *Prosodic weight versus information load in the relative clause attachment ambiguity.* Paper presented at the CUNY Conference on Human Sentence Processing, Boston, MA.

Brennan, S. E., & Clark, H. H. (1996). Conceptual pacts and lexical choice in conversation. *Journal of Experimental Psychology: Learning, Memory, and Cognition, 22,* 1482–1493.

Clark, H. H. (1996). *Using language.* Cambridge: Cambridge University Press.

Dell, G. S. (1986). A spreading-activation theory of retrieval in sentence production. *Psychological Review, 93*, 283–321.

Elsness, J. (1984). *That* or zero? A look at the choice of object clause connective in a corpus of American English. *English Studies, 65*, 519–533.

Ferreira, F. (2000). Syntax in language production: An approach using tree-adjoining grammars. In L. Wheeldon (Ed.), *Aspects of language production* (pp. 291–330). Philadelphia: Psychology Press/Taylor & Francis.

Ferreira, V. S. (1996). Is it better to give than to donate? Syntactic flexibility in language production. *Journal of Memory and Language, 35*, 724–755.

Ferreira, V. S., & Dell, G. S. (2000). Effect of ambiguity and lexical availability on syntactic and lexical production. *Cognitive Psychology, 40*, 296–340.

Ferreira, V. S., & Firato, C. E. (2002). Proactive interference effects on sentence production. *Psychonomic Bulletin and Review, 9*, 795–800.

Ferreira, V. S., & Hudson, M. (2005). *An emotion (that) I second: Effects of formulation difficulty and ambiguity on sentence production.* Poster presented at the AMLaP 2005, Ghent, Belgium.

Ferreira, V. S., Slevc, L. R., & Rogers, E. S. (2005). How do speakers avoid ambiguous linguistic expressions? *Cognition, 96*, 263–284.

Garnsey, S. M., Pearlmutter, N. J., Myers, E., & Lotocky, M. A. (1997). The contributions of verb bias and plausibility to the comprehension of temporarily ambiguous sentences. *Journal of Memory and Language, 37*, 58–93.

Garrett, M. F. (1975). The analysis of sentence production. In G. H. Bower (Ed.), *The psychology of learning and motivation* (Vol. 9, pp. 133–177). New York: Academic Press.

Griffin, Z. M. (2001). Gaze durations during speech reflect word selection and phonological encoding. *Cognition, 82*, B1–B14.

Haywood, S. L., Pickering, M. J., & Branigan, H. P. (2005). Do speakers avoid ambiguity during dialogue? *Psychological Science, 16*, 362–366.

Horton, W. S., & Keysar, B. (1996). When do speakers take into account common ground? *Cognition, 59*, 91–117.

Jaeger, T. F. (2005). *"That" indicates anticipated production difficulty: Evidence from disfluencies.* Paper presented at the Disfluency in Spontaneous Speech Workshop, Aix-en-Provence, France.

Juliano, C., & Tanenhaus, M. K. (1994). A constraint-based lexicalist account of the subject/object attachment preference. *Journal of Psycholinguistic Research, 23*, 459–471.

Keysar, B., Lin, S., & Barr, D. J. (2003). Limits on theory of mind use in adults. *Cognition, 89*, 25–41.

Kraljic, T., & Brennan, S. E. (2005). Prosodic disambiguation of syntactic structure: For the speaker or for the addressee? *Cognitive Psychology, 50*, 194–231.

Levelt, W. J. M. (1989). *Speaking: From intention to articulation.* Cambridge, MA: MIT Press.

Levelt, W. J. M., Roelofs, A., & Meyer, A. S. (1999). A theory of lexical access in speech production. *Behavioral and Brain Sciences, 22*, 1–75.

Nadig, A. S., & Sedivy, J. C. (2002). Evidence of perspective-taking constraints in children's on-line reference resolution. *Psychological Science, 13*, 329–336.

Pechmann, T. (1984). *Überspezifizierung und Betonung in referentieller Kommunikation.* Dissertation, Universität Mannheim.

Pickering, M. J., & Branigan, H. P. (1998). The representation of verbs: Evidence from syntactic priming in language production. *Journal of Memory and Language, 39,* 633–651.

Postma, A. (2000). Detection of errors during speech production: A review of speech monitoring models. *Cognition, 77,* 97–131.

Roland, D. W., Elman, J. L., & Ferreira, V. S. (2006). Why is *that?* Structural prediction and ambiguity resolution in a very large corpus of English sentences. *Cognition, 98,* 245–272.

Schafer, A. J., Speer, S. R., Warren, P., & White, S. D. (2000). Intonational disambiguation in sentence production and comprehension. *Journal of Psycholinguistic Research, 29,* 169–182.

Searle, J. R. (1969). *Speech acts.* Cambridge: Cambridge University Press.

Snedeker, J., & Trueswell, J. (2003). Using prosody to avoid ambiguity: Effects of speaker awareness and referential context. *Journal of Memory and Language, 48,* 103–130.

Temperley, D. (2003). Ambiguity avoidance in English relative clauses. *Language, 79,* 464–484.

Wardlow, L., & Ferreira, V. S. (2003). *Finding common ground: How do speakers block privileged information?* Paper presented at the AMLaP 2003, Glasgow, Scotland.

Wheeldon, L. R., & Levelt, W. J. M. (1995). Monitoring the time course of phonological encoding. *Journal of Memory and Language, 34,* 311–334.

Wheeldon, L. R., & Morgan, J. L. (2002). Phoneme monitoring in internal and external speech. *Language and Cognitive Processes, 17,* 503–535.

5 Studies on verbal self-monitoring: The perceptual loop model and beyond

Robert J. Hartsuiker
Ghent University, Belgium

Introduction

In order to interact with our environment, it is necessary to plan actions that we expect to lead to the desired outcomes, but also to *monitor* whether we have planned and have executed these actions in accordance with the outcomes we wished to achieve. If the monitoring processes detect a mistake in planning or in execution, a correction is necessary. In the human-performance literature, monitoring has mostly been studied with two-alternative, forced-choice reaction time tasks. Such studies have led to cognitive models and suggestions about their neural implementation (e.g., Botvinick, Braver, Barch, Carter, & Cohen, 2001). This chapter deals with the question of how we monitor and correct ourselves when performing the more complex task of language production (verbal self-monitoring).

A challenge for verbal self-monitoring theories is to explain the mechanisms responsible for *self-repairs* (1–2).

(1) Then you go to the gold line——, gold mine   (Anderson et al., 1991).
(2) To the left side of the purple disk is a v——,
       a horizontal line   (Levelt, 1989).

In (1), the speaker produced a word in error: He said *line* instead of *mine*. However, he detected this error and produced a *repair* (*gold mine*). In (2), the speaker interrupted after the first phoneme of the error (the error presumably would have come out as *vertical*, had the monitor not interrupted).

In order to produce self-repairs, the monitor needs to do several things. It needs to detect that the utterance being produced violates the speaker's intentions or that it does not conform to linguistic standards. The monitor also needs to initiate a "stop-signal", so that speech is interrupted. Additionally, the monitor needs to initiate the planning of the repair. An influential theory of how the self-monitoring system does these things is Levelt's (1983, 1989) perceptual loop theory (PLT). This theory was extended and implemented as a computational model by Hartsuiker and Kolk (2001). From now on, I will refer to that model as the perceptual loop *model* (PLM). This chapter will first present the PLT and the PLM and then review a number of new studies, which provide directions for further development of PLM.

The perceptual loop theory (PLT)

The PLT (Levelt, 1983, 1989) claims that self-monitoring of language production involves the language comprehension system. As illustrated in Figure 5.1, Levelt proposed that speaking involves a level of *conceptualizing* (which constructs a message to be expressed in language, but which also includes the self-monitor), a level of *formulating* (which includes lexical retrieval and grammatical and phonological encoding), and a level of *articulating* (which includes speech motor programming). The comprehension side includes a level of *auditory processing* (which identifies speech sounds), and a *speech comprehension system*. The end result of speech comprehension, which Levelt called "parsed speech", feeds back into the conceptualizer, where it can be compared with the speaker's intended message.

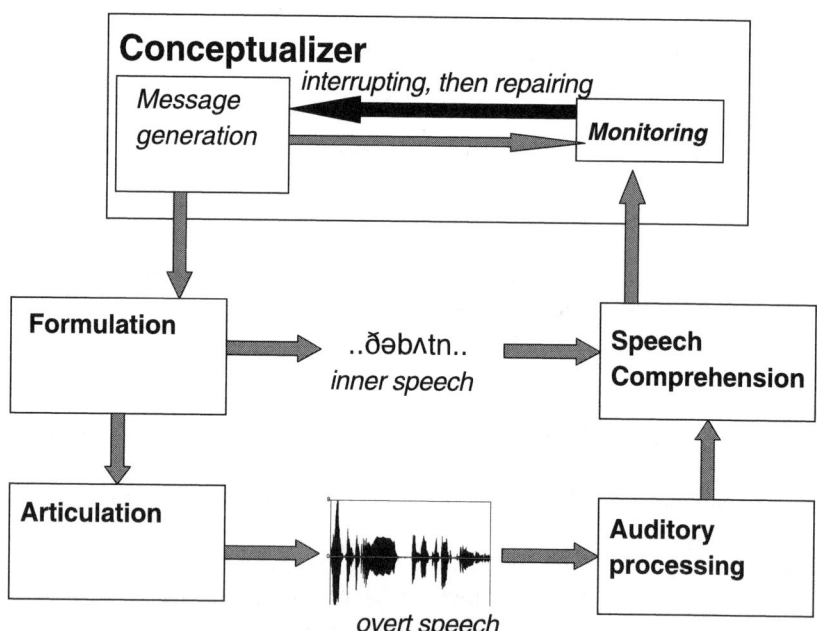

Figure 5.1 Sketch of Levelt's (1983, 1989) perceptual loop theory. The phonological code (corresponding to the fragment, *the button*) is the output of phonological encoding. The sound wave represents the overt production (of a phrase containing *the button*). The internal channel inspects the first code (inner speech), and the external channel inspects the second code (overt speech).

PLT makes four important assumptions. First, it assumes that there are two channels for error detection: an external channel and an internal channel. The external channel involves the speaker's own overt speech, whereas the internal channel involves the inspection of a linguistic code that is not yet articulated (i.e., a phonetic or phonological string; see Wheeldon and Levelt (1995) for the proposal that the code is phonological). As reviewed in Hartsuiker and Kolk (2001), there is plenty of evidence in favour of an internal channel. An example is the occurrence of extremely fast interruptions such as the one in (2). Given constraints on timing, it is very unlikely that the speaker began to interrupt only after hearing that the initial phoneme was wrong; it is much more likely that this error was detected through the internal channel, but that the process of interruption was too slow to prevent part of the error (i.e., the initial phoneme) from being said aloud.

A second assumption of PLT is that both the internal and external channels converge on a single system: language comprehension. Thus, speakers would exploit the same cognitive machinery for monitoring their own speech and for perceiving the speech of other people (with the difference, of course, that listeners do not always know what speakers intended to say!). Although this assumption has the advantage of parsimony (only one analysis system is necessary for two tasks), it is also PLT's most controversial assumption. In contrast to this assumption, neuropsychological studies have reported patients with impairments in monitoring but with spared language comprehension (Marshall, Robson, Pring, & Chiat, 1998), and patients with spared monitoring, but with impaired language comprehension (Schlenk, Huber, & Willmes, 1987). This double dissociation appears to disconfirm the assumption that monitoring is based on language comprehension. However, Hartsuiker and Kolk (2001) argued that the first dissociation (spared comprehension, impaired monitoring) is compatible with PLT, because the impairments might involve monitoring processes that take place after comprehension (e.g., comparing or repairing). The reverse dissociation (impaired comprehension, spared monitoring) is more wounding for the PLT. But the patient studies conducted so far cannot exclude the possibility that only some aspects of comprehension were impaired (e.g., sentence parsing), leaving other aspects of comprehension, and therefore monitoring, intact. In sum, there is no compelling evidence for or against the assumption that self-monitoring uses the language comprehension system.

Third, the PLT assumes that the end result of language comprehension (parsed speech) is input into a comparison process at the level of the conceptualizer. It is at this point that intended speech is compared with perceived actual speech, and if this comparison process detects a mismatch, adjustments (self-interruption and self-repair) will take place. Unfortunately, neither the PLT nor the PLM specifies the details of this comparison process, but a number of testable predictions can be derived from its localization in the conceptualizer. That is, according to Levelt (1989), the component of language production that is most controlled is the conceptualizer, whereas, for example, formulating is considered "a largely automatic process" (p. 21). There are several ways in which more controlled processes differ from more automatic ones, including interruptibility, accessibility to consciousness, and efficiency (see Garrod and Pickering, Chapter 1, this volume, for an overview), but one aspect that Levelt emphasized was that controlled processes, as opposed to automatic ones, make a demand on central working memory resources.[1] Levelt's theory therefore predicts that error detection performance depends on the availability of these resources. Consistent with that prediction, Oomen and Postma (2002) recently showed that speakers who were engaged in a picture-description task repaired fewer errors when they simultaneously executed a secondary task (random finger tapping).

A fourth assumption of the PLT concerns the coordination of the processes subsequent upon the detection of a mismatch. The PLT incorporated the *main interruption rule*, introduced by Nooteboom (1980), on which speech is interrupted immediately after the detection of an error. In particular, an interruption signal would go simultaneously to the conceptualizer, formulator, and articulator. Once interruption has effectively occurred (there is an interruption in the actual flow of overt speech), repair planning would commence. However, studies that measured the time-course of interruptions and repairs (Blackmer & Mitton, 1991; Oomen & Postma, 2001) do not support that proposal, as a considerable proportion of error repairs followed the moment of interruption without delay. Because repair planning necessarily takes some time, these findings argue against interruption and repair proceeding serially.

To summarize, the PLT assumes that (1) speakers monitor both internal and external speech (and this assumption is supported by data); (2) the two monitoring channels converge on the *language comprehension* system (and there is no compelling evidence for or against that assumption); (3) monitoring is a controlled function (and this assumption is supported by secondary-task effects on monitoring); (4) interruption and repair take place sequentially (and this assumption has been disconfirmed).

The perceptual loop model (PLM)

As illustrated in Figure 5.2, the PLM shares the basic architecture with the PLT. In particular, the PLM shares with the PLT the assumptions that there is internal-channel monitoring, that the internal and external channel converge on the language comprehension system, and that the comparison of intended speech with the output of language comprehension takes place at the level of the conceptualizer.

But the PLM differs from the PLT in several other ways. First, the main interruption rule, by which interrupting and repairing take place serially, can not be maintained (see above). The PLM therefore includes the *modified* main

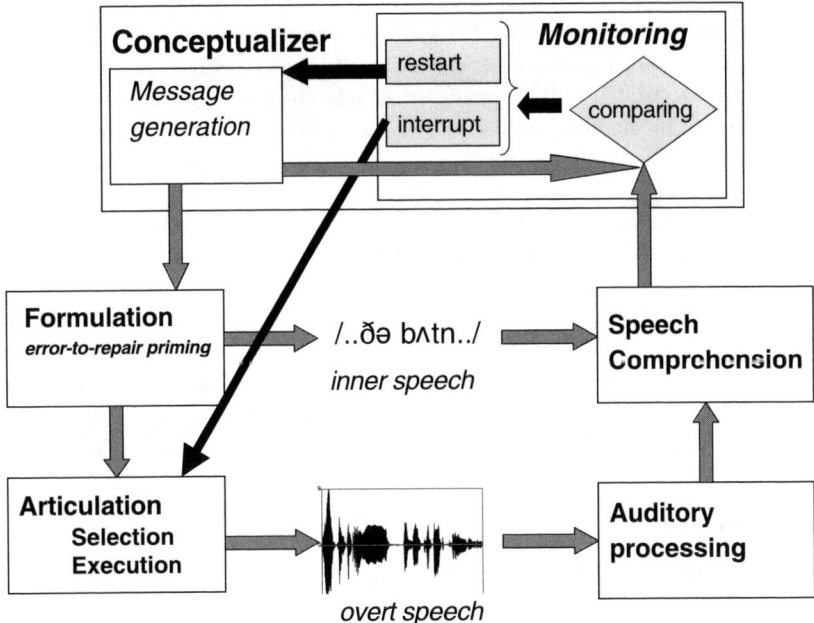

Figure 5.2 Sketch of the PLM, based on Hartsuiker and Kolk (2001). Note that the processes of interruption and repair proceed in parallel in this model, as opposed to the PLT.

interruption rule, which differs from the main interruption rule in that the processes of interruption and repair planning proceed in parallel, and that both of these processes begin as soon as the error is detected. Following a proposal by Ladefoged, Silverstein, and Papçun (1973), the modified interruption rule assumes that interruption bypasses the formulator (the "speech organization system" in Ladefoged et al.'s terminology) and halts the articulator directly.

A second assumption of the PLM is that repairing can be considered to be a *restart* (also see Postma & Kolk, 1993). When a word is spoken in error, it is planned afresh, requiring that it is retrieved from the lexicon, phonologically encoded, and articulated once again. This is the simplest view of repair, because the monitor does not have to make a detailed analysis of what was wrong about the utterance. An alternative to this view is the *revision* hypothesis, by which speakers can maintain what was right about the original utterance and change only what was wrong. Below, under the heading, "New findings", I report on a study designed to arbitrate between those hypotheses.

A third assumption of the PLM concerns error-to-repair priming. Repairing would be facilitated (relative to the production of a word that is not a repair) because of the representations that the error and repair have in common. These common representations will have residual activation, making it easier to retrieve them again. For example, if I say *door* instead of *bore*, I may have selected the correct conceptual and lexical representations for *bore* and made an error in retrieving the speech sounds (Dell, 1986). But on my second attempt (the repair), it will be easier to retrieve the lexical representation *bore* again, due to its residual activation. This assumption is incorporated in a parameter of the PLM, so that repairs will be produced somewhat more quickly than other words. So far, manipulations of this parameter in simulations have not been explored (and the parameter was held constant). But note that it is conceivable that the magnitude of priming varies with error type (semantic errors or phonological errors). Below, under "New findings", I report on a study that tested this hypothesis.

The next three sections explain the PLM in some more detail. The first two sections will describe the model's input and the way processing times are computed. The third section will briefly review Hartsuiker and Kolk's (2001) simulations with the PLM.

Input to the model

The main unit of production in the model is the phonological *phrase*, consisting of a lexical head and all preceding or following function words (Booij, 1995). This unit is composed of phonological *words*, which are lexical words with one or more cliticized function words. The smallest unit of production in the model is the *syllable*. An example of a Dutch phonological phrase is *naar een blauwe tafel* ("to a blue table"), which contains three phonological words of two syllables each: na rən blɑu və ta fəl. All three relevant units (the phonological phrase, the phonological word, and the syllable) have been argued to be relevant to speech production, but it should be acknowledged that the field has not reached consensus about the exact definition of these units or of their role in speech production. Although the PLM thus simplifies these issues, simulations showed that model predictions did not critically depend on the composition of production units (Hartsuiker & Kolk, 2001).

To "tell" the PLM to determine the time course of monitoring for a phrase of a given length and composition, a simple coding scheme is used, such as the string "2 2 2 1". The first three digits indicate that there is a phonological phrase of three phonological words with two syllables each. The last digit indicates that there is an error in the first word. In a typical simulation, the model will determine the time course of monitoring for a large number of phonological phrases (typically, 100 or 1000). On each trial, the model will calculate the onset time of the word containing an error, the moment at which speech is halted, and the moment speech is resumed (repaired), for both internal-channel and external-channel detections. The model is a simplification of monitoring in that it does not code for the position of the error in the word or for the type of error. It also does not take into account the production of editing terms (e.g., *um, I mean*) or repairs with retracing (where the repair repeats words said before the error, as in *the man with the hat,—with the beret*).

Processing in the model

The goal of the PLM is to simulate the time course of speech error detection and repair. Specifically, the model predicts the time intervals between the onset of error, the onset of interruption, and the onset of repair, as a function of variables such as speech rate. The distribution of these intervals is then compared to those in actual data. The PLM simulates these intervals by adding estimated processing durations at each level, while compensating for "traffic jams" in the system. Estimates for these processing durations come from a variety of sources in the literature, and these estimates are the most important model parameters. There are eight time-course parameters (Table 5.1), namely, parameters for the durations of *phonological encoding*, for two stages of articulation (*motor program selection* and *motor program execution*), for two stages of perception (*audition* and *speech parsing*), and for the monitoring processes of *comparing*, *interrupting*, and *restart planning* (to reduce the number of parameters, restart planning combines the duration of repeated lexical selection minus the time benefit of priming). Finally, a ninth parameter is the amount of *noise* (from a normal distribution) added to the other parameters on each trial. This parameter reflects variability in processing times.

To illustrate model processing, consider an example with the noise parameter set at 0 (i.e., no noise). If a disyllabic, phrase-initial phonological word (which contains an error) begins phonological encoding at moment $t = 0$ ms, this stage will be completed at $t = 220$ ms (110 ms per syllable) (Table 5.1). At this point, the word's phonological code becomes available for inspection by the internal channel, and at the same moment, the word can begin the stage of motor program selection (provided that the articulator is not busy with the selection or execution stage of the previous word).

Table 5.1 Basic duration of each time interval in the model

Stage	Duration (ms)	Per unit
Phonological encoding	110	Syllable
Selection	100	Phonological word
Execution	100	Syllable
Audition	50	Phonological word
Parsing	100	Phonological word
Comparing	50	Phonological word
Interrupting	150	Phonological word
Restart planning	50	Phonological word

The selection stage takes 100 ms per word, so that overt speech begins at $t =$ 320 ms. At this moment, speech becomes available for inspection by the external channel. Because the internal channel began at 220 ms, and the stages of parsing, comparing, and interrupting take 300 ms altogether, after internal-channel error detection, speech is halted at $t = 520$ ms (an error to cut-off interval of 200 ms). And because the external channel began at $t =$ 320 ms, and the stages of audition, parsing, comparing, and interrupting take 350 ms together, after external-channel error detection, speech is halted at $t =$ 670 ms (an error to cut-off interval of 340 ms). The times for cut-off to repair intervals are computed in a similar way.

Importantly, the time course is affected by "traffic jams" in the system. For example, assume that the error is in the *second* word of the same phonological phrase as before. The error word will undergo phonological encoding at $t = 220$ ms, and the phonological code will be ready at 440 ms. However, at this moment, the articulator is still engaged with the first word (the motor execution phase of that word starts at $t = 320$ ms and ends at $t = 520$ ms). Thus, the phonological code needs to be buffered for 80 ms, until the articulator becomes available for new input. This gives the internal channel a "head start" of 80 ms, so that the error to cut-off interval is now only 120 ms instead of the 200 ms in the previous example (note that the external-channel prediction is unaffected by traffic jams).

PLM simulations

The target data of the simulations were the distributions of error to cut-off and cut-off to repair intervals collected by Oomen and Postma (2001). These authors had participants describe networks of coloured line drawings while speech rate was paced by means of a moving marker (a red dot) that indicated which object to describe at which moment. A typical utterance would be the Dutch equivalent of *then follow the horizontal line to the left to a blue table*. This task elicits many errors and repairs, and the time intervals between errors and cut-offs, and between cut-offs and repairs were determined from speech recordings by phonetic software. From this data set, Hartsuiker and Kolk (2001) selected 98 incidents that were unambiguously repairs of errors and that contained only a single error and repair.

Is the internal channel necessary?

In one set of simulations, error to cut-off times were generated for 99 three-word phrases, with the location of the error balanced over the three possible positions. Two parameters were varied: time-to-interrupt (four levels) and noise (nine levels). The other parameters were held constant (Table 5.1). To test whether it is necessary to postulate an internal channel, a first simulation was run using a model version *without* an internal channel. To assess the fit of the empirically obtained time intervals with the simulated time intervals for each of the 36 combinations of parameters, goodness-of-fit tests were conducted which compared these distributions. These tests are not only sensitive to central tendency, but also to the dispersion and skewness of distributions. For all parameter combinations, the observed and simulated distributions were significantly different from each other. In almost all cases, the model without an internal channel overestimated the mean error to cut-off time. Thus, the model without an internal channel did not account for the empirical data.

The second simulation was identical to the first, except that now the internal channel was included. This of course raises the issue of how the two channels should be combined: What proportion of cut-offs was triggered by internal-channel monitoring and by external-channel monitoring? Hartsuiker and Kolk (2001) proposed a mathematical method of estimating this "division of labour", which was based on the distribution of "covert repairs" (i.e., disfluencies, assumed to result from internal-channel monitoring), overt repairs (assumed to result from either internal- or external-channel monitoring), and uncorrected errors (assumed to reflect "misses" by both channels). On the assumption that both channels have equal detection accuracies (see below, under the heading, "New findings"), the estimated contribution of the internal channel to overt repairs was around 30%. For practical reasons, one simulation approximated this contribution (33%). Another simulation used a larger internal-channel contribution (50%). For both divisions of labour, about 1/3 of the parameter combinations yielded distributions that did not differ significantly from the observed distributions, especially when the interruption time was 150 ± 50 ms and with moderate noise levels. This value of 150 ms is very close to Logan and Cowan's (1984) estimate of 200 ms minus a value of 0–100 ms for signal perception. Subsequent control simulations generalized the good fit between empirical and simulated distributions to other values of the parameters now held constant.

In conjunction, these simulations provided further support for the assumption of the PLT and the PLM that we monitor internal speech. Most importantly, they showed that given reasonable estimated durations for each language production and perception process, perceptual monitoring is fast enough to account for the time course of monitoring. These results can be considered an "existence proof" that monitoring by speech perception is possible.

The modified main interruption rule

Another simulation with the PLM showed that the predicted distribution of cut-off to repair times was not different from the empirical distribution. Additionally, the percentage "repairs-on-the-fly" (i.e., repairs without a time interval between cut-off and repair) was of very similar magnitude in the data (11.3%) and the simulation (11.1%). Thus, this simulation yielded support for the PLM's modified main interruption rule.

Speech rate effects

The next simulation considered the effect of speech rate on the timing of monitoring processes. Oomen and Postma (2001) found that both error to cut-off and cut-off to repair intervals became shorter when speech was faster, and they interpreted this as evidence against the PLT. They argued that in faster speech, the asynchrony between the phonological encoding of a given word and the articulation of the previous word will be reduced, so that the phonological plan is buffered for a shorter time. Specifically, buffering is necessary when phonological encoding of word *n* is completed before articulation of word *n-1*. If articulation time becomes shorter (and phonological encoding time remains the same), word *n* needs to be buffered for a shorter time. This reduction in buffer time reduces the "head start" of the inner monitor relative to articulation (see above, under the heading, "Processing the model"), from which it follows that the error to cut-off interval should be *longer* in faster speech.

However, Oomen and Postma tacitly assumed that the only process that speeds up in fast speech is articulation. In contrast, there are reasons to believe that other stages also speed up. For example, Dell (1986) assumed that phonological encoding speeds up in faster speech, and under this assumption his model accounted for speech rate effects on the number of phonological errors. Under the assumption that *all* production and perception stages are executed more quickly in faster speech, the PLM correctly predicted that error to cut-off intervals (and cut-off to repair intervals) are shorter in fast speech. In that situation, buffer time is not affected by speech rate and inner-channel repairs will therefore produce almost identical cut-off times in normal and fast speech. However, due to the speed-up in perception, external-channel repairs will produce faster cut-off times in fast speech, and this translates to faster cut-off times on average in fast speech.

Positional effects

Finally, the model made new predictions about the effects of the position of the error word in the phrase. Because of the asynchrony between phonological encoding and articulation (see above, "Processing in the model"), the phonological plan needs to be buffered longer for words that appear later in the phrase. Therefore, the internal channel has more look-ahead time for later words, and this implies that the error to cut-off time for these words should be shorter than for earlier words. Additionally, the monitor should be able to interrupt speech *before the onset of the error* (i.e., covert repairs) more often in the case of later words. As mentioned above, we assume that such covert repairs will interrupt the flow of speech and therefore lead to disfluencies (see Postma & Kolk, 1993). The PLM therefore predicts that the proportion of covert repairs (disfluencies) out of overt and covert repairs should be larger at later word positions. Both of these predictions remain to be tested.

Summary and interim conclusion

In sum, simulation studies with the PLM confirmed that monitoring via a perceptual channel is possible, but only if both the internal and external channel are included. Additionally, simulations showed that with the modified main interruption rule, on which interruption and restart proceed in parallel, the model accounted for the distribution of cut-off to repair intervals, including "intervals" of 0 ms. The simulations also showed that the reduction in mean error to cut-off times in fast speech, which Oomen and Postma (2001) took as evidence against the PLT, is compatible with the PLM, but only under the assumption that in fast speech, *every* stage of production and perception is sped up. Thus, the PLM gave a precise account of the time course of self-monitoring and made new predictions about this time course. The model can thus be considered a promising first step toward understanding monitoring.

New findings

I will now review the results of new studies on self-monitoring. The next section considers studies on error detection. These studies confirmed that monitoring is a *controlled* function, as assumed by the PLT/PLM. The section following "Error detection" considers studies on self-interrupting and self-repairing. The findings illustrate that the PLT and the PLM fail to do full justice to the complexity of these processes.

Error detection: Adaptation and selective attention

As mentioned above, under the heading "The perceptual loop theory", the locus of the monitor in the PLT and the PLM is the conceptualizer, and according to Levelt (1989), this is the only component of the language production system that is "controlled". Controlled processes are "flexible and adaptable to the requirements of the task" (Levelt, 1989, p. 21). This view predicts that the monitor can adaptively respond to the context (i.e., the speaking situation at hand). For example, if we address a queen, we need to speak differently than if we chat with a friend in a bar, and if we reprimand a child, we should speak in a way that is different from both of the former situations. A context-sensitive monitor would set its criteria accordingly.

The seminal study of Baars, Motley, and MacKay (1975) provided some evidence for such an adaptive monitor. These authors argued that in most situations, a functional monitoring criterion is lexicality (if I am about to say a nonword, I am about to make an error). As a result, errors resulting in nonwords (nonword errors) are usually intercepted and corrected more often than errors resulting in words (word errors); therefore, word errors will become overt more often. This *lexical bias effect* has indeed been widely attested (e.g., Dell & Reich, 1981; Hartsuiker, Anton-Mendez, Roelstrate, &

Costa, 2006; Nooteboom, 2005a, 2005b). However, if the monitor is really context-sensitive, it would not apply the lexicality criterion in situations where it is no longer functional. To test this hypothesis, Baars et al. (1975) presented target pairs of nonwords in a speech-error elicitation experiment that varied the context. In one context, all items were nonwords (nonword context), and in another context, some items were words and others were nonwords (mixed context). There was a lexical bias effect in the mixed context, but not in the nonword context, and Baars et al. (1975) attributed this to the adaptiveness of the monitor: If every item is a nonword, it is no longer functional to use the lexicality criterion, but even if only a few items are words (mixed context), the lexicality criterion remains in place.

However, a recent study by Hartsuiker, Corley, and Martensen (2005) challenged this logic. Our replication solved several methodological problems with the original study (i.e., Baars et al. (1975) used different items in the different contexts and did not statistically test for an interaction). With an improved (within-items) design, we found that the lexical bias effect was indeed restricted to the mixed context. But, importantly, the interaction between context and elicited error type (word error or nonword error) had a different form from that of Baars et al. (1975) (Figure 5.3).

Whereas Baars et al.'s (1975) data suggest that nonword errors are suppressed in the mixed context (consistent with a lexicality criterion restricted to the mixed context), the data from our (improved) experiment suggest that word errors are suppressed in the nonword context (suggesting an *anti-lexicality* criterion restricted to the nonword context). Our findings make sense if we assume that the monitor is *truly* adaptive. Consider the mixed context of words and nonwords. If the monitor detects that an upcoming utterance is a nonword, this is uninformative: Because there are nonwords in the context, a nonword could be either right or wrong. And if the monitor detects that an upcoming utterance is a *word*, this is equally uninformative, because the context also contains words. However, in a context with only nonwords, it is highly informative that an upcoming utterance is a word: Because this context does not contain words, an upcoming word is a sure sign of error. Thus, if the task is to speak deviantly (i.e., read aloud nonwords), the monitor adapts its criteria so as to maintain deviance.

In sum, both Baars et al. (1975) and Hartsuiker et al. (2005) found evidence for the monitor being able to set context-sensitive criteria, but Baars et al. (1975) gave the monitor too little credit. On their account, the monitor is half-adaptive: It persists in using a monitoring criterion that is no longer functional, while ignoring potentially relevant information. On our account, the monitor is truly adaptive: It ignores information that is irrelevant for the task at hand, while exploiting relevant information.

Another consequence of considering the monitor as a controlled function is that it is constrained by attentional resources. It follows that monitoring behaviour should be affected in situations of divided attention, such as speaking while engaging in a demanding secondary task (e.g., Oomen &

A) Baarset al. (1975; Experiment 2)

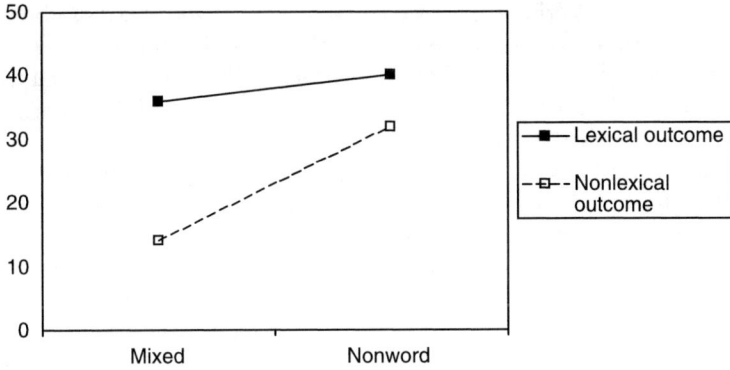

B) Hartsuiker, Corley et al. (2005; Experiment 2)

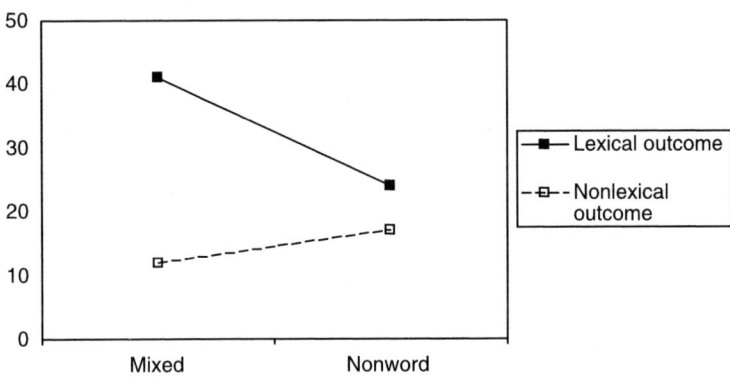

Figure 5.3 Number of errors with lexical outcome and nonlexical outcome in the mixed context and nonword context of (A) Baars et al. (1975; experiment 2) and (B) Hartsuiker, Corley et al. (2005; experiment 2).

Postma, 2002; Vasić & Wijnen, 2005). But more fundamentally, monitoring *itself* can be considered a divided-attention task, because the monitor has to attend to two channels for error detection (an internal and an external channel). This raises an important issue: Can the monitor selectively attend to one channel more than the other? Do we primarily monitor the internal channel, perhaps so as to prevent errors from being said, rather than having to repair them overtly (which may disrupt the flow of communication and lead to embarrassment)? Or do we invest equal amounts of attention in monitoring the two channels?

Given the architecture of the PLT and the PLM, by which both channels converge into the same analysis system (speech perception), the hypothesis that attention is distributed equally predicts that the probability of error detection (the detection rate) is equal for internal-channel and external-channel monitoring.[2] That is, the same analysis system would invest the same amount of effort in the inspection of each channel and therefore be equally likely to note an error. As described above, under the heading, "Is the internal channel necessary?", Hartsuiker and Kolk (2001) estimated the proportions of overt repairs triggered by the internal and external channel respectively under that assumption. A recent mathematical modelling study (Hartsuiker, Kolk, & Martensen, 2005) evaluated that assumption with so-called multinomial models. These models work with a probability tree that has parameters for certain "outcome probabilities". For example, there would be a parameter for the probability that the internal channel detects an error, and there would be another parameter for the conditional probability that an error is still partially said, *given* that the internal channel had detected the error. These parameters were estimated from empirical outcome frequencies, determined for both control speakers and speakers with aphasia (Oomen, Postma, & Kolk, 2001). The goodness of fit was calculated for models in which (1) the parameters for internal and external channel detection rates were equal and (2) these parameters were allowed to vary freely. It turned out that the unconstrained models provided a significantly better fit to the data than the ones with equal detection accuracy. Importantly, in these latter models, the estimated internal-channel detection accuracy was considerably higher than the external-channel detection accuracy (Figure 5.4). This difference was even larger in the speakers with aphasia, consistent with the suggestion that these speakers have impairments in monitoring external speech (Schlenk et al., 1987).

Thus, these findings supported the view that the monitor invests more effort in internal-channel monitoring than external-channel monitoring. This

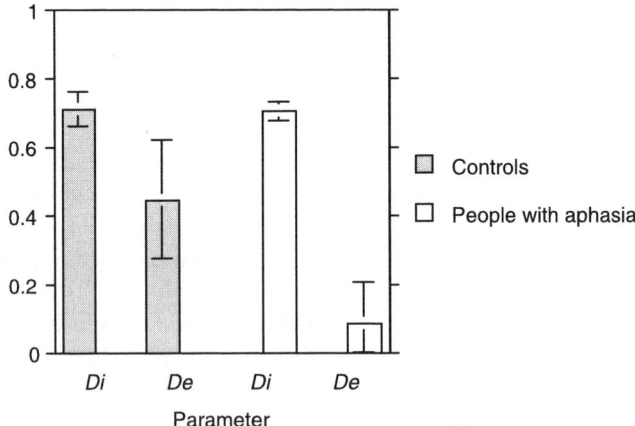

Figure 5.4 Estimates of the detection rate for the internal channel (*Di*) and external channel (*De*) for control speakers and speakers with aphasia from the multinomial analysis in Hartsuiker, Kolk et al. (2005).

makes sense, because in order to optimize success in conversation, it may be more functional to prevent errors from occurring than to let them slip through and then repair them overtly (Hartsuiker, Kolk, & Martensen, 2005). As pointed out by Roelofs (2004), the assumption that the monitor invests more effort in the internal channel might also account for a puzzling finding reported by Nooteboom (2005b). In a corpus study, Nooteboom found a lexical bias in speech errors (consistent with a lexicality criterion in internal-channel repair), but there was no lexical bias in the correction rates of overt errors (at least partly external-channel repairs): Lexical errors were corrected as often as nonlexical errors. If there is a trade-off in attention between the two channels, "monitoring internal speech (yielding the error bias) may have as a result that external speech can be monitored less well (causing the absence of a repair bias)" (Roelofs, 2004, p. 564). Note that this account assumes that a quantitative decline in attention can lead to a qualitatively different performance pattern; it still remains to be seen whether that assumption is valid.

In summary, the studies reviewed in this section provide evidence for an adaptive monitoring system that is constrained by attentional capacity, consistent with the assumption of the PLT and the PLM that monitoring is located in a controlled system (the conceptualizer).

The aftermath of error detection: Interruption and repair

After error detection, the monitor will trigger an interruption and will initiate the planning of the repair. Two new studies have addressed the question of *how* we repair. As described above, under "The perceptual loop theory", the PLM makes minimal assumptions about these processes: Repairing consists of a fresh start. This restart is facilitated by residual activation of the representations that are common to error and repair. For example, if the monitor detects the error *door* (when the intended word was *bore*), it will simultaneously start interrupting ongoing speech and start a new attempt at producing the word *bore*. This will be somewhat easier than saying a word that is not a repair, because some of the correct representations are primed by the error (e.g., the final sounds in this example).

An alternative to the restart hypothesis is that speakers can *revise* a stored representation (Van Wijk & Kempen, 1987). A study by Boland, Hartsuiker, Pickering, and Postma (2005) tested for this possibility. They experimentally elicited so-called appropriateness repairs, as in (3–4).

(3) the blue square . . . the dark blue square
(4) the dark blue square . . . the blue square.

In (3), the speaker repaired an underspecified utterance by adding a word, and in (4) she repaired an overspecified utterance by deleting a word. It is possible that these repairs are implemented by completely starting anew with the planning of the entire phrase, but on the revision hypothesis the speaker would retain a representation of the phrase and just add what was missing (3) or delete what was superfluous (4).

To test this, Boland et al. (2005) exploited the fact that the difference between the original utterances and their repairs (3–4) is one of context. In the context of a blue square and a green square, the description *blue square* is fine. But in the context of a dark blue square and a light blue square, an informative description mentions the shade term "dark". In two experiments, speakers named coloured geometrical objects that were accompanied by context objects. A line underneath one of the objects indicated which one was to be selected. Within pairs of trials, the selected object always remained the same, but in one condition the context object changed (incongruent trials) from the first trial (the prime) to the second trial (the target), so that the description of the prime became an underspecific (3) or overspecific (4) description for the target. Figure 5.5 illustrates the prime and target pictures for each of the four conditions.

In both experiments, the participants were told to describe the selected object in such a way that someone else, who did not know which object was selected, could pick it out. Each picture was displayed for 2000 ms, with an interval of 1000 ms between pictures. The pictures were organized in prime-target pairs. In 90% of these pairs, the prime and target pictures were completely identical (80% filler items and 10% congruent experimental items). In the remaining 10% of pairs, the target was different from the prime (Figure 5.5) in that its description either required one word more or one word less.

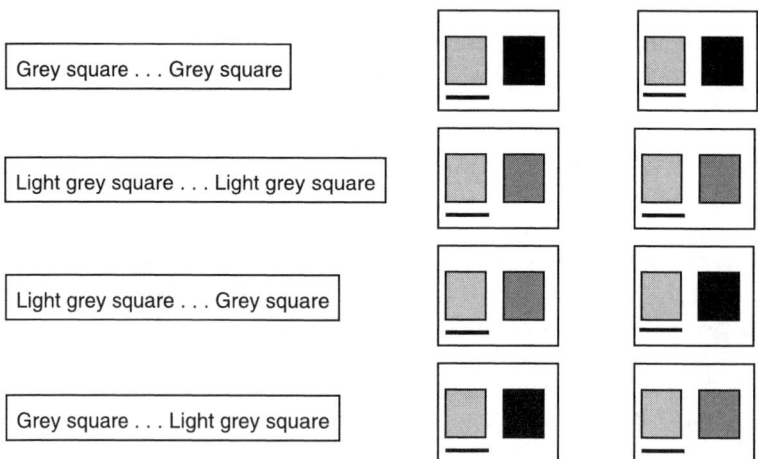

Figure 5.5 Example of the stimuli used by Boland et al. (2005). Note that in the actual experiment, the objects were coloured. The example uses (light and dark) grey and black for practical purposes.

The two experiments were identical in every respect of the procedure and materials with one exception. In experiment 1, participants were instructed to name each picture (both prime and target), and they were told that subsequent pictures would be usually identical. But in experiment 2, they were instructed to alternate between preparing (but not saying) the name of a picture on one trial (i.e., the prime) and actually naming the picture on the next trial (i.e., the target). We reasoned that in experiment 1, speakers restart upon naming the target picture; it is a situation in which they name one picture, and then name the next one, and so on. Of course, there may be priming here, because prime and target share two words (e.g., *blue, square*). If so, one might expect more priming when deleting a word, because adding a word introduces a new word that has not been primed. In contrast, response latencies for the targets were of similar magnitude in the case of adding and deleting. In experiment 2, participants prepared the name of the prime and then named the target. According to the restart hypothesis, this situation is analogous to experiment 1, because both situations require a restart. But on the revision hypothesis, speakers can revise a prepared representation. Because an addition repair requires the retrieval of an additional word from the lexicon, one can expect adding to take longer than deleting. Consistent with the revision hypothesis, experiment 2 showed a large advantage of deleting words compared to adding words (of roughly 100 ms) (see Figure 5.6). This finding suggests that the PLM's assumption of repairing by restarting is too simple.

A further question about repairing concerns the extent to which the production of the repair is influenced by its relationship with the error. For example, after a phonological error (5), repair planning might be affected by the phonological overlap with the error, and after a semantic error (6), there may be an influence of the semantic overlap.

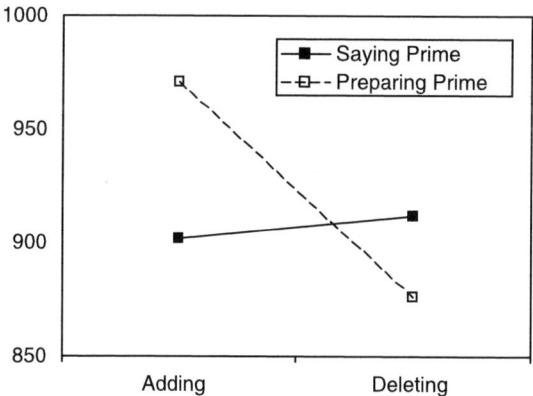

Figure 5.6 Reaction times (ms) for the addition and deletion conditions in the two experiments reported by Boland et al. (2005).

(5) mountain,–mouse
(6) artichoke,–corn.

On the other hand, the monitoring system might assign a special status to the representations of errors, in order to prevent them from being produced again and again. On such a view, the activation of these representations might be "wiped clean" (e.g., reset to the resting activation level).

A recent study tested this with a picture-naming paradigm (Hartsuiker, Pickering, & De Jong, 2005), which aimed to simulate speech error repair under controlled laboratory conditions (cf. Van Wijk & Kempen, 1987). Note that similar "probe" paradigms have also been used for other purposes. For example, Kambe, Duffy, Clifton, and Rayner (2003) presented "probe words" for naming out loud that replaced the word people were reading. These probe words were named faster when they were semantically related to the target words they replaced. Additionally, Levelt, Schriefers, Vorberg, Meyer, Pechmann, and Havinga (1991) had participants name pictures, but occasionally presented an auditory probe word for lexical decision. Effects of semantic and phonological relatedness between picture name and probe word were obtained on lexical decision times (also see Peterson & Savoy, 1998).

In our experiments, the participants were instructed to name pictures of single objects as quickly and as accurately as possible, but on a minority of trials the picture was replaced by another picture 300 ms later (Figure 5.7).

When the picture changed, the participants had to abandon naming the first (context) picture and name the second (target) picture instead. The name of the context picture was thus regarded as an "error" and that of the target as a "repair". The dependent variable was the naming latency of the second picture.

The picture names were related in form (5), related in meaning (6), or were unrelated. If the error's representations in the lexicon are "wiped clean",

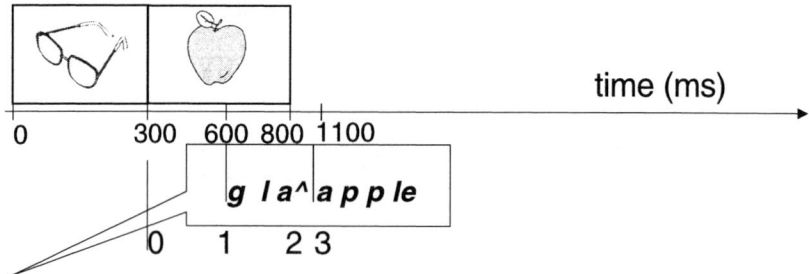

Figure 5.7 Overview of the interruption paradigm used in Hartsuiker, Pickering et al. (2005). The time line indicates the presentation of the context picture (glasses), target picture (apple), the speaker's initial naming of the context ("glass"), and the repair ("apple"), with representative timing of the responses.

relatedness should not matter. But if residual activation of the error's representations influences repair time, there should be an effect of the related context pictures relative to the unrelated baseline. Additionally, sometimes the participants will interrupt early (7), so that the context name is only partially said, but at other times (5, repeated as 8) interruption will be so slow that the context name is said completely. Because residual activation will vary with time, it is conceivable that this time course mediates relatedness effects.

(7) mount,–mouse
(8) mountain,–mouse.

Consistent with the residual activation hypothesis, naming latencies of the target pictures indeed varied with context. The direction of the effects was a function of whether or not speakers interrupted word-internally (Figure 5.8). There were significant interactions between context name completion and semantic relatedness (experiment 1) and context name completion and phonological relatedness (experiment 2). In the case of word-internal interruptions, (7), speakers produced the target name more quickly when the names were phonologically related than when they were unrelated (phonological facilitation), but they were slower when the names were semantically related than unrelated (semantic interference). In contrast, when the context name was said completely (8), there was semantic facilitation and phonological interference (all simple effects were significant, with the exception of the phonological facilitation for word-internal interruptions, which was marginally significant).

This study therefore provided strong evidence against a "wipe-clean" hypothesis: Both the relation between error and repair and the time course

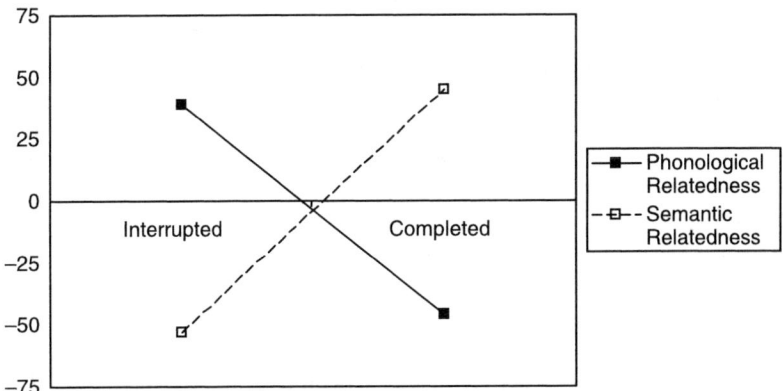

Figure 5.8 Reaction time difference scores (unrelated condition minus related condition) in the Hartsuiker, Pickering et al. (2005) data. Values below 0 indicate interference, and values above 0 indicate facilitation.

of interrupting influence the time it takes to say the repair. Interestingly, relatedness can both help and hinder repairing. It is important to point out that reversals of the polarity of context effects have also been noted in the word production literature. For example, Bloem and La Heij (2003) note that the direction of semantic effects in Stroop-like paradigms (naming one stimulus while ignoring a competitor stimulus) varies with the time interval between these stimuli. Similarly, Wheeldon (2003) notes that phonological effects are facilitatory under some conditions and inhibitory under other conditions. We therefore argued that repairing single-word errors is similarly affected by residual activation of representations in the lexicon, as is naming stimuli in the context of distractors.

In summary, the studies reported in this section suggest that the process of repairing is more complex than the PLM assumed. The study of Boland et al. (2005) fits much better with the notion of repairing by revising a stored representation than with the PLM's assumption of repairing by restart. The results of Hartsuiker, Pickering et al. (2005) suggest that the PLM's assumption of error-to-repair priming can be maintained, but that the direction of priming depends on two variables that the model does not take into account: the type of relatedness between error and repair, and whether or not the error is interrupted.

Discussion

This chapter presented the perceptual loop theory and model, summarized the results of simulations with the model, and reviewed four new studies on verbal self-monitoring (Boland et al., 2005; Hartsuiker, Corley et al., 2005; Hartsuiker, Kolk et al., 2005; Hartsuiker, Pickering et al., 2005). These studies have repercussions for the assumptions of the PLT and the PLM, and further raise a number of new issues. I will first discuss these repercussions and new issues below, and then briefly discuss alternatives to perceptual monitoring.

First, the simulations discussed above, under the heading, "PLM simulations", yielded results that are consistent with the assumptions of the PLT and the PLM. One set of simulations showed that the PLM can fit the time course of empirical chronometric data on error repair, provided the model has both the internal and the external channel available. These simulations constitute an existence proof that perceptual monitoring is at least a possibility. Another simulation showed that with the PLM's (as opposed to PLT's) assumption about the coordination between interruption and repair, a good fit is obtained with the empirical data on cut-off to repair intervals. Thus, the existence of extremely short time intervals between interruption and repair does not constitute evidence against perceptual monitoring (although these intervals do provide evidence against the specific interruption rule of PLT).

Second, the data reviewed above, under the heading, "Error detection", showed that self-monitoring can be considered a controlled process. For example, the monitor can set its criteria adaptively as a function of task demands (Hartsuiker, Corley et al., 2005). In the context of our experiments, this means that if the task is to speak in a deviant way (i.e., name nonwords), the monitor sets its criteria so as to maintain deviance. Paradoxically, in that case, lexical status is a sign that something went wrong in planning. Another aspect of monitoring as a controlled process is that monitoring performance should be constrained by resource limitations. Consistent with that prediction, a number of studies have found secondary-task effects on the quality of monitoring (Oomen & Postma, 2002; Vasic & Wijnen, 2005).

But additionally, it appears as if the limited monitoring capacity is allocated in a *functional* way, so that more effort is invested in the monitoring of internal than external speech (Hartsuiker, Kolk et al., 2005; Roelofs, 2004). This may be functional, because focusing on the internal channel would prevent errors from being said, thereby minimizing any disruption in communication or embarrassment to the speaker. The latter conclusion has a direct implication for the PLM, because it puts constraints on the division of labour between internal- and external-channel monitoring. This is important for predictions about the time course of monitoring because internal-channel monitoring is faster than external-channel monitoring (the internal channel bypasses the levels of articulation and auditory processing). It is important to note that the PLM simulations with 33% of overt repairs triggered by the internal channel (consistent with equal detection rates of each channel) fit the empirical data on error to cut-off intervals, but that an equally good fit was obtained in a simulation with more internal-channel involvement (i.e., 50%). In sum, the findings are consistent with the monitor being a controlled process, which in turn is consistent with the localization of the monitor at the level of the conceptualizer (but see below).

Third, the PLM's assumption about the aftermath of error detection does not do full justice to the complexity of these processes. Thus, the study by Boland et al. (2005) suggested that speakers can sometimes repair by *revising* a stored representation instead of always starting afresh. Of course, this does not mean that speakers *always* repair by revising: It is conceivable that it is more efficient to revise some errors but to restart others (see Postma & Kolk, 1993; Van Wijk & Kempen, 1987). Two further observations are compatible with the revision hypothesis. Not all error-repair sequences are "grammatical" (Levelt, 1983; Van Wijk & Kempen, 1987). In particular, Levelt (1983) proposed a rule that specified what kind of concatenation of original utterance (including the error) and repair (including possible retracing of words already said) is "grammatical". However, if the form of the original utterance determines what kind of repairs can follow it, this suggests that speakers retain the original utterance and add the repair onto it. Additionally, some repairs use a pronoun to refer back to a noun in the error. This suggests that a representation of the noun must be retained (otherwise the pronoun could not be specified for grammatical features like gender).

The assumption that representations of errors in the lexicon retain some of their activation and that this affects the planning of repairs can be maintained (Hartsuiker, Pickering et al., 2005). This clearly argues against a wipe-clean hypothesis, by which the representations for the error are set back to the level of resting activation. But, importantly, the polarity of these effects varied with the type of relation between error and repair, and it also depended on whether the error was interrupted or not. This suggests that the PLM's assumption of a time benefit in repairing does not always hold; sometimes residual activation of the error's representations might actually *hinder* the repair.

In sum, the studies reviewed in this chapter provide evidence that is mostly compatible with the main assumptions of the PLM, but the model's assumption about the details of repairing are in need of elaboration. Additionally, these studies raise a number of issues for further investigation, and these will be discussed next.

Directions for future research

The studies reviewed in this chapter suggest a number of issues that await investigation. For example, several new predictions about the time course of monitoring follow straightforwardly from the PLM. As described above under the heading, "Positional effects", the model makes clear predictions about the effects of word position (in the phrase) on the error to cut-off times for those words (i.e., shorter times for later words) and on the proportion of "covert repairs" (assumed to be disfluencies) relative to all repairs (i.e., disfluencies and overt error repairs). Note that is conceivable that the probability of making an error in the first place varies with position. Therefore, the PLM does not necessarily predict that there are more covert repairs in later positions, but rather that the proportion of covert repairs out of all repairs is higher in later positions. Similarly, the PLM predicts shorter error to cut-off times and larger proportions of covert repairs for short words (in syllables) that follow longer words as opposed to long words that follow short words. This is so because the articulation time of a long word will be longer than the planning time of a short word. Thus, if the short word comes second, the monitor has more look-ahead time and can produce the cut-off relatively early.[3]

Additionally, the PLM assumes that interrupting directly halts the articulator and bypasses the formulator. This predicts that, all other things being equal, the time to interrupt should be independent of the content the formulator is generating and of the speed of formulator processes. Interrupting speech is an instance of the broader question of interrupting continuous *actions*. Although there is a literature on action inhibition (e.g., Logan & Cowan, 1984), no recent studies have considered such questions in the domain of language production.

A related prediction comes from the PLM's assumptions about *speech rate*, which were necessary in order to account for Oomen and Postma's (2001) finding of shorter error to cut-off intervals in faster speech. The PLM assumed a speed-up in processing across the board (for each production and perception stage) in fast speech. To make the model as parsimonious as possible, this was done by introducing only a single parameter, namely, a fixed proportion by which every time-course parameter was shortened (with the exception of interrupting, which was assumed to be independent of speech rate; see above). Clearly, these assumptions about speech rate are in need of empirical verification. This situation is a good example of how a modelling study—which forces one to make extremely explicit assumptions—can raise basic theoretical problems that the field has so far not addressed (i.e., "What changes in language production when speakers talk quickly rather than slowly?").

A further open issue concerns the process of *comparison*. The studies reviewed above, under the heading, "Error detection", are compatible with monitoring as a controlled process, and thus with the monitor's localization in the conceptualizer (following Levelt's 1989 assumption that this component is more controlled than the formulator). But this does not answer the question of *how* a comparison takes place between the thing the speaker wanted to say and the speech she generated. Given the monitor's localization in the conceptualizer, the most simple view would be that the monitor compared the concept intended for production with the concept extracted from perception. Thus, if a speaker intends to say *dog* but makes the semantic error *cat*, a comparison of the concepts of *dog* and *cat* allows error detection. However, it is unclear how such an architecture could account for the detection of nonword errors. If the speaker says a nonword, this means by definition that no word will be recognized and hence no concept will be extracted in perception. How then could conceptual comparison take place?

The latter question clearly merits consideration. One recent proposal (Nooteboom, 2005b) is that the monitor has access to intermediate representations of language production such as the word form "intended" in production. The monitor would be able to make a comparison of this intended word form with the word form that is actually phonologically encoded (or said out loud) and then perceived, and thus detect the mismatch at the phonological level. In support of this hypothesis, Nooteboom's corpus study showed that phonological errors resulting in words (*cat* → *sat*) and phonological errors resulting in nonwords (*cat* → *zat*) were extremely similar in the characteristics of their repairs (e.g., how many words were spoken before the interruption). But lexical errors (*cat* → *dog*) were clearly different from the phonological word errors (*cat* → *sat*) in those characteristics, even though both types of error have lexical status. This can be taken as evidence that the monitor has access to the intended word form in production; for both word and nonword phonological errors, the intended word form (*cat*) and realized (*sat* or *zat*) word form are different. But for lexical errors, the "intended" word form (*dog*) and realized word form (*dog*) are the same, because a lexical error (which takes place at the lemma or conceptual level) implies that the wrong lemma activates its corresponding word form, which is then correctly phonologically realized.

A final "open issue" raised by the current results concerns the nature of repairing. Boland et al. (2005) provided some evidence that repair can involve a revision to a stored representation, but this of course raises the question of how such revision mechanisms would work (and when they would be used). In contrast to the much simpler restart hypothesis, revision requires that (1) some representation of the error be stored; (2) that the monitor analyse exactly what went wrong; and (3) that the required changes be made to the stored representation. But what would be the nature of the stored representation? For the types of repairs Boland et al. (2005) considered (i.e., deletions and additions of words), a plausible candidate might be the structure that results from grammatical encoding (i.e., a syntactic structure with words inserted in the appropriate places; e.g., Bock & Levelt, 1994). Revision would then entail that a branch of the syntactic tree be removed (deletion) or that a branch be added and that a new word be inserted (addition). It seems that similar revisions might also underlie syntactic repairs. For example, Levelt and Maassen (1981) had participants describe animations, with sentences like "the square and the circle went up". Although the participants clearly chose this structure more often than the alternative "the square went up and the circle went up", the latter option was sometimes chosen, especially when the second noun was hard to retrieve (e.g., *octagon* instead of *circle*). Importantly, production latencies for the second type of sentence were about 85 ms longer than for the first type. This can be interpreted as reflecting a syntactic revision process, by which the initial structure is abandoned in favour of the eventual structure because it is easier to retrieve the verb (*went*) than the noun (*octagon*).

An obvious challenge for future research is to specify the mechanisms of revision, and to determine which kinds of repairs can and cannot be accounted for by revision. For example, if semantic or phonological errors could be revised, this has further implications for which representations in speech can be edited (e.g., this might then include the phonological code).

Limitations and theoretical alternatives

An important limitation of the studies reviewed so far concerns the central assumption of the PLT and the PLM that the internal monitoring channel uses the perception system. Although the PLM simulations provide an "existence proof" of perceptual monitoring, they cannot exclude the possibility that other monitoring architectures are also compatible with the data. Specifically, on some accounts, there are monitoring mechanisms based within the production system itself (e.g., Nickels & Howard, 1995; Oomen, Postma, & Kolk, 2005; Postma, 2000). For example, Postma (2000) suggested a hybrid model which included the monitoring loops in perception in addition to several production-monitoring devices that target specific operations in production (e.g., a syntactic monitor). Recent work provides some evidence that can be interpreted as supporting a production-based monitor. For example, Oomen et al. (2005) presented the case of G, a patient with Broca's aphasia, whose monitoring deficits mimic his production deficits, suggesting a deficit at a level subserving both production and perception monitoring.

An often-heard criticism of such proposals is that such a system would need to reduplicate knowledge (e.g., Levelt, 1989): The same production processes would be responsible for generating an utterance *and* for generating a target to which the utterance is compared. Additionally, a system with many monitors is far from parsimonious. However, these criticisms no longer hold when one considers connectionist theories of monitoring (see Vigliocco & Hartsuiker, 2005, for a discussion of such theories). Such theories would exploit the activational dynamics of error processing. For example, if an error occurs at the level of phoneme selection (e.g., the /b/ is erroneously selected as the first phoneme of *door*), less activation than is to be expected will feed back to the lexical representation (i.e., there is no feedback from /d/). If the encoding had gone well, there would have been feedback from three segments (the onset, nucleus, and coda of door); instead, there is only feedback from two segments. In this view, a monitoring device at each level compares the amount of outgoing activation from the target unit with the amount of incoming activation (through feedback) to that unit. This view does not require reduplication of information, and it has the advantage that the same monitoring mechanism is used at each level, namely, a comparison of output and input via feedback.

Interestingly, there is a connectionist alternative that does not require the postulation of feedback connections. Mattson and Baars (1992) proposed that a connectionist system might implement the monitoring function, if it were sensitive to the global activation dynamics of an output (or response) layer.[4] In many connectionist systems, there is a winner-take-all system, so that only a unit corresponding to the correct response (say, the correct word) is active, whereas the activation of competitors has died down. But in the case of an error, multiple units would be active: the one corresponding to the error, but also the one corresponding to the correct response, because the latter representation would also receive top-down input (e.g., the concept corresponding to the word). For example, if I say the word *door* correctly, the phoneme /b/ is probably not very active. But if I make the error of saying *bore*, one can expect both the /b/ and the /d/ to be active (the former somewhat more than the latter). Thus, on this view, there would also be a production-monitoring device at each level, but one that raises the alarm whenever there is too much activation at its level.

This mechanism has commonalities to the model of conflict monitoring proposed by Botvinick et al. (2001), although this model is restricted to response conflicts within extremely small response sets (e.g., pushing the left or right button). In this model, there is a unit for responding "left" and one for responding "right". The activation of those units is combined by multiplication. This means that a large amount of activation is sent to a "monitor unit" only when both the left and the right unit are highly active (otherwise, multiplication with a value close to 0 will lead to very low output). When the monitor unit receives a large amount of activation, it will in its turn send activation to the input units, facilitating the possibility that the correct unit will be selected eventually. Of course, it still remains to be seen where such mechanisms can be adapted to account for the much more complex task of monitoring language production.

Conclusions

The research discussed in this chapter shows that many of the PLM's assumptions can be maintained. The results are consistent with the view that monitoring has access to an internal channel, both the internal and external channel converge onto perception, repairing and interrupting start simultaneously, and monitoring is a controlled function. At the same time, the studies pinpoint many issues that await further investigation. These include several predictions that follow straightforwardly from the PLM, but also the following issues: the way in which comparison takes place, the way in which repairs are affected by the representations of the error, and, perhaps most crucially, whether there are production-monitoring devices, instead of or in addition to the perceptual loop.

Summary

This chapter described the perceptual loop theory of verbal self-monitoring (PLT) and the perceptual loop model (PLM) that implemented and extended this theory. The model assumes that speakers can monitor their speech for errors through two channels (internal and external speech) that both converge on the speech perception system. In the model, monitoring is a controlled function. After error detection, two processes (self-interrupting and restarting) begin simultaneously, and restarting benefits from residual activation of the error's representations. A number of new empirical studies help elaborate that proposal; they suggest that (1) the monitoring system is a controlled process that adaptively allocates selective attention; (2) speakers can repair by making revisions to a stored plan; and (3) repair planning is affected by residual activation of the error's representations in the lexicon. The chapter concluded with a discussion of new issues raised by these studies and with a brief discussion of alternatives to perceptual monitoring.

References

Anderson, A. H., Bader, M., Bard, E. G., Boyle, E., Doherty, G., Garrod, S., Isard, S., Kowtko, J., McAllister, J., Miller, J., Sotillo, C., Thompson, H. S., & Weinert, R. (1991). The HCRC Map Task Corpus. *Language and Speech, 34*, 351–366.

Baars, B. J., Motley, M. T., MacKay, D. G. (1975). Output editing for lexical status in artificially elicited slips of the tongue. *Journal of Verbal Learning and Verbal Behavior, 14,* 382–391.

Blackmer, E. R., & Mitton, J. L. (1991). Theories of monitoring and the timing of repairs in spontaneous speech. *Cognition, 39,* 173–194.

Bloem, I., & La Heij, W. (2003). Semantic facilitation and semantic interference in word translation: Implications for models of lexical access in language production. *Journal of Memory and Language, 48,* 468–488.

Bock, J. K., & Levelt, W. J. (1994). Language production. Grammatical encoding. In M. A. Gernsbacher (Ed.), *Handbook of psycholinguistics* (pp. 945–984). San Diego, CA: Academic Press.

Boland, H. T., Hartsuiker, R. J., Pickering, M. J., & Postma, A. (2005). Repairing inappropriately specified utterances: Revision or restart? *Psychonomic Bulletin and Review, 12,* 472–477.

Booij, G. (1995). *The phonology of Dutch.* Oxford: Clarendon Press.

Botvinick, M. M., Braver, T. S., Barch, D. M., Carter, C. S., & Cohen, J. D. (2001). Conflict monitoring and cognitive control. *Psychological Review, 108,* 624–652.

Dell, G. S. (1986). A spreading-activation theory of retrieval in sentence production. *Psychological Review, 93,* 283–321.

Dell, G. S., & Reich, P. A. (1981). Stages in sentence production: An analysis of speech error data. *Journal of Verbal Learning and Verbal Behavior, 20,* 611–629.

Ferreira, V. S., & Pashler, H. (2002). Central bottleneck influences on the processing stages of word production. *Journal of Experimental Psychology: Learning, Memory, and Cognition, 28,* 1187–1199.

Hartsuiker, R. J., Anton-Mendez, I., Roelstrate, B., & Costa, A. (2006). Spoonish Spanerisms: A lexical bias effect in Spanish. *Journal of Experimental Psychology: Learning, Memory, and Cognition, 32,* 949–953.

Hartsuiker, R. J., & Barkhuysen, P. N. (2006). Language production and working memory: The case of subject–verb agreement. *Language and Cognitive Processes, 21,* 181–204.

Hartsuiker, R. J., Corley, M., & Martensen, H. (2005). The lexical bias effect is modulated by context, but the standard monitoring account doesn't fly: Related Beply to Baars, Motley, and MacKay (1975). *Journal of Memory and Language, 52,* 58–70.

Hartsuiker, R. J., & Kolk, H. H. J. (2001). Error monitoring in speech production: A computational test of the perceptual loop theory. *Cognitive Psychology, 42,* 113–157.

Hartsuiker, R. J., & Kolk, H. H. J., & Lickley, R. J. (2005). Stuttering on function words and content words: A computational test of the covert repair hypothesis. In R. J. Hartsuiker, R. Bastiaanse, A. Postma, & F. Wijnen (Eds.), *Phonological encoding and monitoring in normal and pathological speech* (pp. 261–280). Hove, UK: Psychology Press.

Hartsuiker, R. J., & Kolk, H. H. J., & Martensen, H. (2005). The division of labour between internal and external speech monitoring. In R. J. Hartsuiker, R. Bastiaanse, A. Postma, & F. Wijnen (Eds.), *Phonological encoding and monitoring in normal and pathological speech* (pp. 187–205). Hove, UK: Psychology Press.

Hartsuiker, R. J., Pickering, M. J., & De Jong, N. H. (2005). Semantic and phonological context effects in speech error repair. *Journal of Experimental Psychology: Learning, Memory, and Cognition, 31,* 921–932.

Kambe, G., Duffy, S. A., Clifton, C., & Rayner, K. (2003). An eye-movement-contingent probe paradigm. *Psychonomic Bulletin and Review, 10*, 661–666.

Ladefoged, P., Silverstein, R., & Papçun, G. (1973). Interruptibility of speech. *Journal of the Acoustical Society of America, 54*, 1105–1108.

Levelt, W. J. M. (1983). Monitoring and self-repair in speech. *Cognition, 14*, 41–104.

Levelt, W. J. M. (1989). *Speaking: From intention to articulation.* Cambridge, MA: MIT Press.

Levelt, W. J. M., & Maassen, B. (1981). Lexical search and order of mention in sentence production. In W. Klein & W. J. M. Levelt (Eds.), *Crossing the boundaries in linguistics: Studies presented to Manfred Bierwisch* (pp. 221–252). Dordrecht, The Netherlands: Reidel.

Levelt, W. J. M., Schriefers, H., Vorberg, D., Meyer, A. S., Pechmann, T., & Havinga, J. (1991). The time course of lexical access in speech production: A study of picture naming. *Psychological Review, 98*, 122–142.

Logan, G. D., & Cowan, W. B. (1984). On the ability to inhibit thought and action: A theory of an act of control. *Psychological Review, 91*, 295–327.

Marshall, J., Robson, J., Pring, T., & Chiat, S. (1998). Why does monitoring fail in jargon aphasia? Comprehension, judgment, and therapy evidence. *Brain and Language, 63*, 79–107.

Mattson, M. E., & Baars, B. J. (1992). Error-minimizing mechanisms: Boosting or editing? In B. J. Baars (Ed.), *Experimental slips and human error: Exploring the architecture of volition* (pp. 263–287). New York: Plenum.

Nickels, L., & Howard, D. (1995). Phonological errors in aphasic naming: Comprehension, monitoring, and lexicality. *Cortex, 31*, 209–237.

Nooteboom, S. G. (1980). Speaking and unspeaking: Detection and correction of phonological and lexical errors in spontaneous speech. In V. A. Fromkin (Ed.), *Errors in linguistic performance: Slips of the tongue, ear, pen, and hand* (pp. 87–95). New York: Academic Press.

Nooteboom, S. G. (2005a). Lexical bias revisited: Detecting, rejecting and repairing speech errors in inner speech. *Speech Communication, 47*, 43–58.

Nooteboom, S. G. (2005b). Listening to oneself: Monitoring speech production. In R. J. Hartsuiker, R. Bastiaanse, A. Postma, & F. Wijnen (Eds.), *Phonological encoding and monitoring in normal and pathological speech* (pp. 167–186). Hove, UK: Psychology Press.

Oomen, C. C. E., & Postma, A. (2001). Effects of time pressure on mechanisms of speech production and self-monitoring. *Journal of Psycholinguistic Research, 30*, 163–184.

Oomen, C. C. E., & Postma, A. (2002). Limitations in processing resources and speech monitoring. *Language and Cognitive Processes, 17*, 163–184.

Oomen, C. C. E., Postma, A., & Kolk, H. H. J. (2001). Prearticulatory and postarticulatory self-monitoring in Broca's aphasia. *Cortex, 37*, 627–641.

Oomen, C. C. E., Postma, A., & Kolk, H. H. J. (2005). Speech monitoring in aphasia: Error detection and repair behaviour in a patient with Broca's aphasia. In R. Hartsuiker, R. Bastiaanse, A. Postma, & F. Wijnen (Eds.), *Phonological encoding and monitoring in normal and pathological speech* (pp. 209–225). Hove, UK: Psychology Press.

Peterson, R. R., & Savoy, P. (1998). Lexical selection and phonological encoding during language production: Evidence for cascaded processing. *Journal of Experimental Psychology: Learning, Memory, and Cognition, 24*, 539–557.

Postma, A. (2000). Detection of errors during speech production: A review of speech monitoring models. *Cognition, 77*, 97–131.

Postma, A., & Kolk, H. H. J. (1993). The covert repair hypothesis: Prearticulatory repair processes in normal and stuttered disfluencies. *Journal of Speech and Hearing Research, 36*, 472–487.

Roelofs, A. (2004). Error biases in spoken word planning and monitoring by aphasic and nonaphasic speakers: Comment on Rapp and Goldrick (2000). *Psychological Review, 111*, 561–572.

Schlenk, K. J., Huber, W., & Willmes, K. (1987). "Prepairs" and repairs: Different monitoring functions in aphasic language production. *Brain and Language, 30*, 226–244.

Van Wijk, C., & Kempen, G. (1987). A dual system for producing self-repairs in spontaneous speech: Evidence from experimentally elicited corrections. *Cognitive Psychology, 19*, 403–440.

Vasić, N., & Wijnen, F. (2005). Stuttering as a monitoring deficit. In R. Hartsuiker, R. Bastiaanse, A. Postma, & F. Wijnen (Eds.), *Phonological encoding and monitoring in normal and pathological speech* (pp. 226–247). Hove, UK: Psychology Press.

Vigliocco, G., & Hartsuiker, R. J. (2005). Maximal input and feedback in production and comprehension. In A. Cutler (Ed.), *Twenty-first century psycholinguistics: Four cornerstones* (pp. 209–228). Mahwah, NJ: Lawrence Erlbaum Associates, Inc.

Wheeldon, L. R. (2003). Inhibitory form priming of spoken word production. *Language and Cognitive Processes, 18*, 81–109.

Wheeldon, L. R., & Levelt, W. J. M. (1995). Monitoring the time-course of phonological encoding. *Journal of Memory and Language, 34*, 311–334.

Notes

1 However, several recent studies provide evidence for stages of formulating demanding working memory. This includes lexical retrieval (Ferreira & Pashler, 2002) and grammatical encoding (Hartsuiker & Barkhuysen, 2006). Note that these findings, of course, do not run counter to the claim that conceptualizing is working-memory demanding.

2 Except for errors at the acoustic level (e.g., errors in pitch or loudness).

3 As pointed out by Hartsuiker, Kolk, and Lickley (2005), these predictions are complicated by the possibility that covert repairs do not always lead to disfluencies (i.e., when the look-ahead time of the internal channel is extremely long, the error might be filtered out without observable consequences).

4 Note that the WEAVER++ model is also sensitive to the global activation of certain levels (for example, the lemma level), because that is a parameter that enters into the "Luce-ratio", which in turn determines the time for selection.

6   Modelling the control of visual attention in Stroop-like tasks

Ardi Roelofs[1,2,3] and Martijn Lamers[3]
[1]Max Planck Institute for Psycholinguistics, The Netherlands
[2]F. C. Donders Centre for Cognitive Neuroimaging, The Netherlands
[3]Nijmegen Institute for Cognition and Information, The Netherlands

Introduction

In naming one of several objects in a visual scene or in reading aloud one of several words in a text, a speaker has to perform a number of interrelated attentional tasks. The first major task is to select one particular object or word for further processing. This usually involves moving the gaze to the spatial location of the relevant object or word. Objects and words are multi-dimensional entities. For example, they usually have a colour and shape, and they consist of several parts (i.e., written words are made up of letters). The second major task is therefore to select the action-relevant dimension, such as the shape of the objects and words rather than their colour. For words, responding to the shape rather than their colour is the default. Finally, if the objects and words are spatially close together, the speaker has to plan and execute the appropriate action in the face of distraction by the other objects and words. This constitutes the third major task.

In a number of influential publications, Posner and colleagues (e.g., Posner, 1994; Posner & Peterson, 1990; Posner & Raichle, 1994) argued that the three major tasks described above are achieved by two different attentional systems. They postulated a perceptual attention system that controls the orienting of attention and gaze in order to select the appropriate input (the first major task). Moreover, they postulated an executive attention system that helps to achieve selective perceptual processing of the target dimension (the second major task) and that controls the selection of appropriate actions (the third major task). It was hypothesized that the executive system also controls the orienting of attention.

According to Posner and colleagues, directing attention from one location to another involves disengaging attention from the current location, moving attention to the new location of interest, and engaging it there. The disengage, move, and engage operations were associated with, respectively, the posterior parietal cortex of the human brain, the superior colliculus in the midbrain, and the pulvinar nucleus of the thalamus. Executive attention was associated with the lateral prefrontal and anterior cingulate cortices. It was assumed that the allocation of attention to a spatial location causes modulatory changes in extrastriate visual areas involved in the analysis of stimulus features. Selection of a dimension is less specified than the allocation of spatial attention in Posner's framework, but one presumes it is achieved through interactions between the anterior and posterior attentional networks (e.g., Posner & Raichle, 1994).

In this chapter, we provide an overview of recent work that examined these attentional systems in object-naming and word-reading tasks. We restrict ourselves to the visual domain and to vocal responding, in particular, the interplay between visual attention and vocal responding in Stroop-like tasks such as the classic colour-word Stroop task (MacLeod, 1991; Stroop, 1935) and various picture-word versions of it (e.g., Glaser & Düngelhoff, 1984; Glaser & Glaser, 1989; Lupker, 1979; Smith & Magee, 1980). A major way to study attention is to introduce conflict. In the classic colour-word Stroop task (Stroop, 1935), participants are asked to name the ink colour of written colour words, such as the word RED in blue ink. Results have consistently shown that people are much slower in naming the ink colour of incongruent colour words than in naming the ink colour of a row of neutral Xs, an effect called Stroop interference, and people are fastest when colour and word are congruent (e.g., BLUE in blue ink), an effect called Stroop facilitation. The literature documents numerous manipulations of the basic Stroop interference and facilitation effects (reviewed by MacLeod, 1991), providing evidence on the nature of the attentional control systems.

A theory of attentional control is limited by the theories of the processes that are controlled. To know what attentional control does in Stroop-like tasks, it is essential to know what the subordinate processes of perception and vocal response planning do in these tasks. In the first section, we provide a short overview of a computationally implemented theory for vocal responding and its attentional control. The theory provides an account of the various processes underlying spoken word production and its relation with word and object/colour recognition (Levelt, Roelofs, & Meyer, 1999; Roelofs, 1992, 1997) and an account of how attention controls word production and perception (Roelofs, 2003). The theory has been computationally implemented in the WEAVER++ model. In the next section, we address the issue of how visual orienting, selective stimulus processing, and vocal response planning are related. In particular, is visual orienting dependent only on visual processing (e.g., D. E. Meyer & Kieras, 1997; Sanders, 1998) or also on verbal response planning? We describe recent work that suggests that visual orienting in Stroop-like tasks is jointly determined by visual processing and response planning. In the third section, we address the issue of selective perceptual processing in Stroop-like tasks. We review the literature on the role of space-based and object-based attention and on dimensional selection in the Stroop task. Moreover, we report on computer simulations of a paradoxical finding using WEAVER++. In the final section, we briefly discuss evidence on the neural correlates of executive attention in Stroop-like tasks.

An outline of WEAVER++

WEAVER++ is a computational model designed to explain how speakers plan and control the production of spoken words. The model falls into the general class of "hybrid" models of cognition in that it combines a symbolic associative network and condition-action rule system with spreading activation and activation-based rule triggering. The model plans spoken words by activating, selecting, and connecting (weaving together) types of verbal information. The model gives detailed accounts of chronometric findings on spoken word production (e.g., Levelt et al., 1999; Roelofs, 1992, 1997). Recently, WEAVER++ has also been applied to neuroimaging data (Roelofs & Hagoort, 2002).

In a classic paper, Norman and Shallice (1986) made a distinction between "horizontal threads" and "vertical threads" in the control of behaviour. Horizontal threads are strands of processing that map perceptions onto actions, and vertical threads are attentional influences on these mappings. Behaviour arises from interactions between horizontal and vertical threads. WEAVER++ implements specific theoretical claims about how the horizontal and vertical threads are woven together in planning verbal actions (Roelofs, 2003). A central claim embodied by WEAVER++ is that the control of verbal perception and action is achieved symbolically by condition-action rules rather than purely associatively (cf. Deacon, 1997; Logan, 1995).

Until the beginning of the twentieth century, the problem of the directedness of thought, perception, and action was largely ignored. Starting with Aristotle and revitalized by Locke, the prevailing theorizing was largely associationistic. A major credit for introducing a directional notion into theorizing goes to Ach and Watt of the Würzburg school (Ach, 1905; Watt, 1905), who experimentally investigated the effects of the task, or *Aufgabe*, and they demonstrated its vital importance in determining the course of associations (e.g., Mandler & Mandler, 1964). We refer to Humphrey (1951) for a thorough and sustained treatment of what the Würzburgers did, why they did it, and how they interpreted it.

Watt (1905) presented participants with written nouns and asked them to produce partially constrained associations, like producing a superordinate term (e.g., say the hyperonym "animal" in response to the word DOG) or a name for a part (e.g., say "tail" in response to DOG). Response times were measured. Watt observed that the speed of responding was determined independently by the type of task instruction (e.g., naming a superordinate vs. naming a part) and the strength of the association between stimulus and response given a particular task. For example, if in free word associations, "tail" was more frequently given than "neck" in response to DOG, the production latency was smaller for "tail" than for "neck" in producing a name of a part in response to DOG. These findings led Watt to propose that the direction of our thoughts and actions is determined by associations among stimuli and goals (*Aufgaben*), on the one hand, and responses, on the other. In the 1910s, this view was firmly integrated within an associationist framework and fiercely defended by Müller (1913), whereas Selz (1913) held that mental rules rather than associations are critical in mediating between stimuli/goals and responses. All current theories are descendants of these ideas.

In the view that currently dominates the attention and performance literature (e.g., computationally implemented in GRAIN by Botvinick, Braver, Barch, Carter, & Cohen, 2001), goals associatively bias the activation of one type of response (e.g., colour naming in the Stroop task) rather than another (e.g., oral reading), following Müller (1913). WEAVER++ implements a third theoretical alternative (considered but rejected by Selz, 1913), in which both rules and associations play a critical role. WEAVER++'s lexical network is accessed by spreading activation while the condition-action rules determine what is done with the activated lexical information depending on the task. When a goal symbol is placed in working memory, the attention of the system is focused on those rules that include the goal among their conditions. These rules ensure that colour naming rather than word reading is performed and that the irrelevant perceptual input is suppressed (Roelofs, 2003). Both GRAIN (Botvinick et al., 2001) and WEAVER++ have been applied to the colour-word Stroop task. Elsewhere (Roelofs, 2003; Roelofs & Hagoort, 2002), WEAVER++ is compared in great detail with GRAIN and other implemented models of attentional control in the Stroop task. However, to provide such detailed model comparisons for the modelling of visual attention in Stroop-like tasks is outside the scope of the present chapter.

As indicated, to know what attentional control does, it is essential to know what the subordinate processes of perception and vocal response planning do. As concerns conceptually driven naming (e.g., object naming), the WEAVER++ model distinguishes between conceptual preparation, lemma retrieval, and word-form encoding, with the encoding of forms further divided into morphological, phonological, and phonetic encoding (Levelt et al., 1999). The model assumes that memory is an associative network that is accessed by spreading activation. Figure 6.1 illustrates the structure of the network. During conceptual preparation, concepts are retrieved from memory and flagged as goal concepts. In lemma retrieval, a goal concept is used to retrieve a lemma from memory, which is a representation of the syntactic properties of a word, crucial for its use in sentences. For example, the lemma of the word *blue* says that it can be used as an adjective. Lemma retrieval

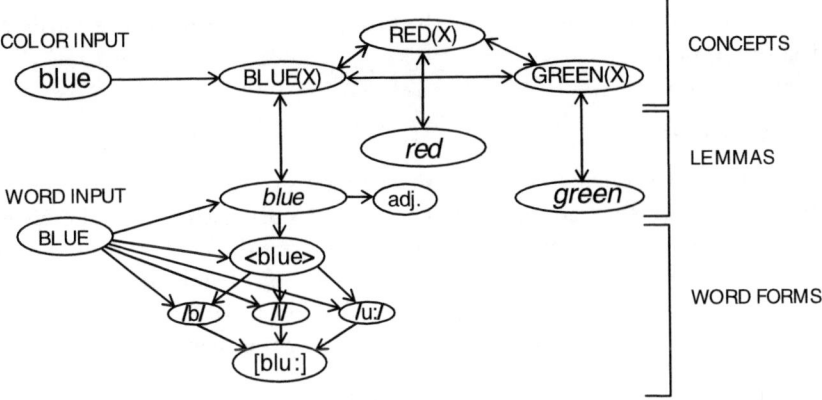

Figure 6.1 Fragment of the lexical network of WEAVER++ for colour terms (cf. Roelofs, 2003); adj. = adjective.

makes these properties available for syntactic encoding processes. In word-form encoding, the lemma is used to retrieve the morphophonological properties of the word from memory in order to construct an appropriate articulatory program. For example, for *blue*, the morpheme <blue> and the speech segments /b/, /l/, and /u:/ are retrieved, and a phonetic plan for [blu:] is generated. Finally, articulation processes execute the motor program, which yields overt speech. Perceived words (e.g., BLUE) may be read aloud by selecting a lemma (*blue*) and then encoding the corresponding word form (i.e., [blu:]) or by directly encoding a word form without first selecting a lemma (see Figure 6.1).

Let us assume that a participant in a colour-word Stroop experiment has to name the ink colour of the word RED in blue ink. This involves the conceptual identification of the colour based on the perceptual input and its designation as goal concept (i.e., BLUE(X)), the retrieval of the lemma of the corresponding word (i.e., *blue*), and the encoding of the form of the word (i.e., [blu:]). The final result is a motor program for the word "blue", which can be articulated. Perceived words activate their lemmas and word forms in parallel.

It has been shown that WEAVER++ successfully simulates several classic data sets on Stroop, mostly taken from the review by MacLeod (1991), including response set, semantic gradient, stimulus, spatial, multiple task, manual, bilingual, training, age, and pathological effects (Roelofs, 2003). With only three free parameters taking two values each to accommodate task differences (colour naming, picture naming, word reading, and manual responding), the model accounted for 96% of the variance of 16 classic studies (250 data points). Moreover, WEAVER++ successfully simulated the human brain's blood-flow response during Stroop task performance in neuroimaging studies; in particular, the functional magnetic resonance imaging (fMRI) BOLD response in the anterior cingulate cortex, one of the classic brain areas involved with Stroop task performance (Roelofs & Hagoort, 2002).

Visual orienting

Visual acuity is best at the centre of eye fixation. By 5° from the centre, acuity has diminished about 50%. Therefore, to bring aspects of the visual world into the focus of attention, eye fixations are directed to those visual aspects that are of most interest. This makes a shift of gaze an overt sign of the allocation of attention (e.g., Kustov & Robinson, 1996), although attention and eye movements can be dissociated in simple signal detection tasks (e.g., Posner, 1980).

Over the past few decades, the control of eye movements has been intensively investigated for visual search and other cognitive tasks, such as problem solving, typing, and reading for comprehension. We refer to Rayner (1998) for an extensive review of the literature. However, the control of eye movements during the production of spoken words has only recently become a topic of interest. Whereas it has long been assumed that we look at aspects of the visual world just as long as is needed to identify them and that response factors play no role (D. E. Meyer & Kieras, 1997; Sanders, 1998), recent research suggests that when we want to respond vocally to the visual aspects, the gaze durations depend on the time to plan the corresponding words (e.g., Griffin, 2001; A. S. Meyer, Sleiderink, & Levelt, 1998). For example, when speakers are asked to name two objects in a row, they look longer at first-to-be-named objects with two- than with one-syllable names even when the object-recognition times do not differ (A. S. Meyer, Roelofs, & Levelt, 2003). The effect of the number of syllables suggests that the shift of gaze from one object to another is initiated only after the phonological form of the object name has been encoded.

In terms of the theory of Posner and colleagues, the effect of the number of syllables suggests that the endogenous visual orienting of attention is determined by response factors. This does not exclude, however, a role for factors related to visual processing. In order to examine the interplay between visual orienting, selective visual processing, and vocal response selection, we performed a series of Stroop-like experiments (Roelofs, submitted). The experiments examined what the trigger is for moving the eyes from fixated stimuli that cause more vs. less interference for vocal responding. In all experiments, picture-word versions of the Stroop task were used. Instead of naming colour patches with superimposed colour words, participants responded to pictured objects with superimposed distractor words.

Earlier research demonstrated that reading the word or naming the picture of a picture-word stimulus replicates the response time patterns known from colour-word Stroop experiments (e.g., Glaser & Düngelhoff, 1984; Glaser &

Glaser, 1989; see Roelofs, 2003, for a review). This suggests that the colour of a colour-word Stroop stimulus is the limiting case of a picture. As with colour-word stimuli, WEAVER++ assumes that pictures have direct access to concepts, whereas words have direct access to lemmas and word forms (see Figure 6.1).

In the eye-tracking experiments, speakers were presented with picture-word stimuli displayed on the left side of a computer screen and left- or right-pointing arrows (flanked by Xs on each side: XX<XX or XX>XX) displayed on the right side of the screen. Figure 6.2 illustrates the visual displays that were used in the experiments. The picture-word stimuli and the arrow were presented simultaneously on the screen. The participants' task was to respond vocally to the picture-word stimulus, and to shift their gaze to the arrow stimulus in order to indicate the direction in which the arrow was pointing by pressing a left or right button. Eye movements were recorded. In particular, it was measured how long participants looked at a picture-word stimulus before they moved their gaze to the arrow. The manual task involving the arrow stimuli was given in order to be able to assess the gaze durations for the picture-word stimuli. Moreover, it is possible that the eyes remain fixated on the left picture-word stimulus while attention is covertly moved to the right side of the screen to allow processing of the arrows before a gaze shift. If this were the case, the gaze durations would not reflect the attention given to the left object. However, when the manual response latencies parallel the gaze durations (i.e., when the differences among the gaze durations are preserved by the manual response latencies), this would be evidence that preprocessing of the arrow has not taken place and that the shift of gaze corresponds to a shift of attention.

The experiments were run with three basic tasks used within the picture-word interference paradigm (e.g., Glaser & Düngelhoff, 1984; Glaser & Glaser, 1989; Lupker, 1979; Smith & Magee, 1980): picture naming, word reading, and word categorizing. These tasks were performed in the context of written distractor words (picture naming) or distractor pictures (word reading and categorizing). In all experiments, vocal response latencies, gaze durations, and manual response latencies were measured. The picture-word

Figure 6.2 Illustration of the visual displays used in the eye-tracking experiments.

stimuli had varying types of relatedness between picture and word: semantic, unrelated, identical, and control. For example, participants said "swan" in response to a pictured swan (picture naming), while trying to ignore the word DOG (the semantic condition), the word VEST (the unrelated condition), the word SWAN (the identical condition), or a series of Xs (the control condition). The word-reading experiment used displays that were identical to those used for picture naming except for the control condition. The string of Xs of the control condition in picture naming was replaced by an empty rectangle (cf. Glaser & Düngelhoff, 1984). The task for the participants was to read aloud the word while ignoring the picture and then to respond to the arrows, as in the picture-naming experiment. Finally, the word-categorizing experiment used the same displays as the word-reading experiment, while the vocal task was changed from word naming to word categorizing. That is, participants responded to the written words by categorizing them (i.e., producing hyperonyms) while trying to ignore the picture distractors. For example, they said "animal" in response to the word DOG, while trying to ignore the pictured swan (semantic), the pictured vest (unrelated), the pictured dog (identical), or the empty rectangle (control).

Previous research (e.g., Glaser & Düngelhoff, 1984; Glaser & Glaser, 1989; Lupker, 1979; Smith & Magee, 1980) showed that participants are slower in naming a picture with an incongruent word superimposed (e.g., saying "swan" to a pictured swan with the written word DOG superimposed) than in naming the picture with a series of Xs superimposed in the control condition. Furthermore, participants are faster than control when picture and word agree in the congruent condition (e.g., saying "swan" to a pictured swan with the identical word SWAN superimposed). This corresponds to what is obtained with the colour-word Stroop task (e.g., MacLeod, 1991), where speakers are slower in naming a colour patch with an incongruent colour word superimposed (e.g., the word RED superimposed onto a blue patch of colour) than in naming a colour patch with a row of neutral Xs, and speakers are fastest when colour patch and word are congruent (e.g., the word BLUE superimposed onto a blue colour patch). In addition, a semantic effect is obtained with picture-word stimuli. Participants are slower in naming a picture (e.g., saying "swan" to a pictured swan) with a semantically related word superimposed (e.g., DOG) than with an unrelated word (e.g., VEST). When the task is to read aloud the words and to ignore the pictures, there is no interference from incongruent pictures or facilitation from congruent pictures relative to control, and there is also no semantic effect (e.g., Glaser & Düngelhoff, 1984). However, when the words have to be categorized (e.g., saying "animal" to the word DOG), the response latencies with picture distractors are shorter in the semantic than in the unrelated condition, whereas the latencies in the semantic, identical, and control conditions do not differ (e.g., Glaser & Düngelhoff, 1984). The semantic, incongruency, and congruency effects were computationally modelled with WEAVER++ by Roelofs (Levelt et al., 1999; Roelofs, 1992, 2003).

The results for the vocal response latencies in our eye-tracking experiments replicated earlier findings in the literature (e.g., Glaser & Düngelhoff, 1984; Lupker, 1979; Roelofs, 2003; Smith & Magee, 1980). The gaze durations generally paralleled the vocal response latencies, but not always. This indicates that the signal to move the eyes is not simply the completion of the planning of the vocal response. The manual response latencies always paralleled the gaze durations, suggesting that the gaze shifts indexed attention shifts in the experiments.

Picture naming was slowed by semantically related compared to unrelated word distractors, whereas naming was facilitated by identical relative to control distractors. The gaze durations and the manual response latencies closely followed this pattern. These results suggest that the response planning latency is a major determinant of gaze shift, unlike what has been previously suggested (D. E. Meyer & Kieras, 1997; Sanders, 1998). Why do the results implicate response planning (i.e., word planning including phonological encoding), as opposed to lemma retrieval or any other stage? It is generally assumed that Stroop-like effects reflect response selection processes (e.g., MacLeod, 1991; Roelofs, 2003). Thus, given that the distractor effects on the naming latencies were reflected in the gaze durations for the pictures, gaze shifts must have been triggered after response selection (i.e., lemma retrieval in WEAVER++). Moreover, earlier research (e.g., A. S. Meyer et al., 2003) and (yet) unpublished picture-word interference experiments with written distractor words from our own laboratory showed that phonological effects in picture naming are reflected in the gaze durations. This suggests that gaze shifts are dependent on the completion of phonological encoding. To conclude, the results suggest that response-planning latencies are a major determinant of gaze shifts in picture naming.

In reading aloud the words while ignoring the pictures, participants moved their eyes from words with rectangles around them sooner than they moved their eyes from words with actual pictures around them, even though the vocal response latencies did not differ among conditions (see upper panel of Figure 6.3). This suggests an independent role for lower-level stimulus-related factors in determining the gaze shift. The data suggest that the actual pictures held the attention of the participants longer (in spite of their task irrelevance) than the rectangles, and so speakers could move their eyes away sooner with the rectangles. To conclude, Stroop-like stimuli appear to have attentional effects on reading that are reflected in the eye fixation durations but not in the vocal reading latencies.

In categorizing the word while ignoring the pictures (e.g., saying "animal" to the word DOG), vocal responding was slowed by unrelated picture distractors relative to the other distractors, and the gaze durations followed this pattern. Relative to the control condition, the effect of response-incongruent distractors (e.g., the unrelated picture of a vest activating the incongruent response "clothing") and congruent distractors (e.g., the picture of a dog activating the response "animal") was now the same for the vocal

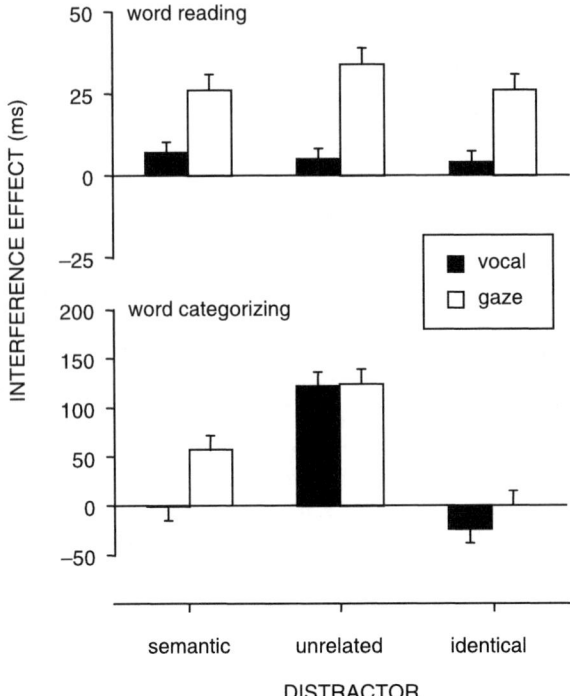

Figure 6.3 Mean effect sizes of the semantic, unrelated, and identical distractors relative to the control stimuli for the vocal responses and gaze shifts in word reading (upper panel) and word categorizing (lower panel) obtained by Roelofs (submitted). The error bars indicate the standard error of the mean.

responses and the gaze durations. This is different from what was observed for reading the words. It seems that when the attentional demands of the task are high, as with word categorizing compared with word reading, the difference in effect between actual pictures and rectangles in determining the shift of gaze disappears. However, with word categorizing, the difference in effect between semantically related and unrelated pictures was much smaller for the gaze shifts than for the vocal responses (see the lower panel of Figure 6.3). Participants fixated the picture-word stimuli in the semantic condition much longer than to be expected on the basis of the vocal categorizing latencies. The difference in semantic effect between the gaze shifts and vocal responses again suggests that the signal to move the eyes is not simply a flag that the planning of the vocal response is completed. Rather, the dissociation implies an independent role for semantic factors. The data suggest that the picture-word stimuli held the attention of the participants longer in the semantic than in the unrelated condition, and so speakers could move their eyes away only later in the semantic condition. To conclude, Stroop-like stimuli appear to have attentional effects on word categorizing that are reflected in the eye fixation durations, but not in the vocal categorizing latencies.

The findings from the experiments support the following model of the orienting of attention and gaze in Stroop-like tasks (Figure 6.4). The model assumes that gaze shifts and attention shifts are closely related in Stroop-like tasks. An attention shift issues a gaze shift command to the saccadic gaze control system, which executes the saccade (e.g., Van Opstal, 2002). The critical assumption for explaining the described findings is that the decision to shift attention is based on input from both perception/conceptualizing and response planning, whereby the former biases only for an attention shift (i.e., lowers or heightens the threshold) and the latter actually triggers the shift (i.e., leads to an actual exceeding of the threshold). The findings suggest that a rectangle lowers the threshold for an attention shift relative to actual pictures in reading words. Consequently, gaze durations are shorter for

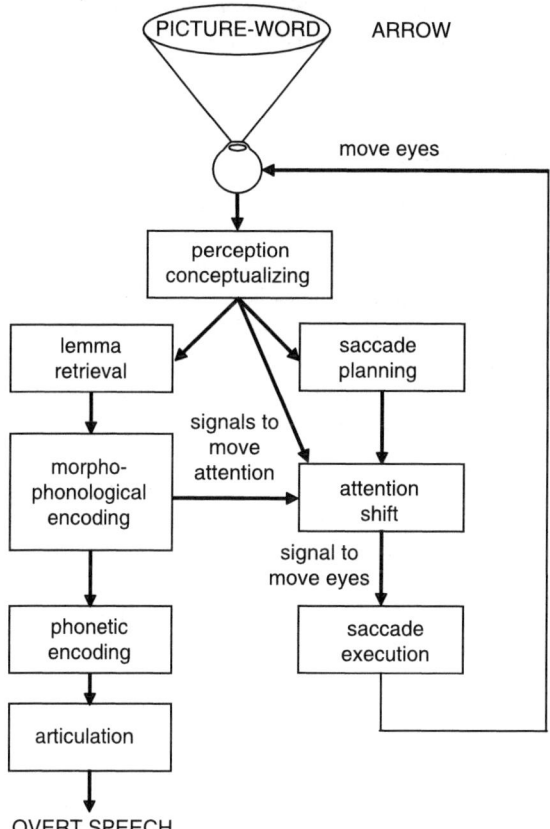

Figure 6.4 A model for the orienting of attention and gaze in the picture-word interference paradigm.

rectangles than actual pictures, even when the word-reading latencies do not differ. The findings also suggest that semantically related pictures as distractors may heighten the threshold relative to other pictures and rectangles in word categorizing. Consequently, semantically related pictures are looked at longer than is to be expected on the basis of the vocal categorizing latencies. Therefore, the difference in effect between semantically related and unrelated pictures is smaller for the gaze shifts than for the vocal responses. Moreover, gaze durations are longer for semantically related than identical pictures and rectangles, even though the word-categorizing latencies do not differ.

To conclude, our findings suggest that the time it takes to prepare a vocal response is a major determinant of gaze shifts in Stroop-like tasks. However, the finding that the distractor effects on the gaze shifts and the vocal responding may dissociate suggests that the signal to move the eyes is not simply the completion of the planning of the vocal response. Instead, the shift of gaze is independently determined by stimulus-related factors. In all experiments, the distractor effects on the gaze shifts were propagated into the manual responses, indicating that gaze shifts index attention shifts in Stroop-like tasks.

Selective stimulus processing

In visual orienting, preattentive processes provide a map of spatial locations through which attention moves (i.e., from the location of the picture-word stimulus to the location of the arrow). In naming one of several objects in a visual scene or in reading aloud one of several words in a text, visual orienting may help to separate the target in one location from irrelevant distractors in other locations. However, selecting a spatial location does not separate the target and distractor in the Stroop task, because the word and colour are spatially integrated in a classic Stroop stimulus. Object-based attention does not help either. In object-based attention, preattentive processes segment the visual scene into figures and ground, whereby attention selects one of the figures for further processing (e.g., Kanwisher & Wojciulik, 2000). Object-based attention does not help to separate the word from the colour word in the Stroop task, because evidence for this type of attention suggests activation enhancement for all information within the spatial boundaries of the object. Rather than separating the word from the colour, space-based and object-based attention lead to a "Trojan horse effect" in the Stroop task (cf. Kahneman & Henik, 1981; Neumann, 1986). According to legend, the Greeks won the Trojan War by hiding in a huge, hollow, wooden horse to sneak into the fortified city of Troy. By attending the ink colour of a Stroop colour-word stimulus, the colour word also receives attention and sneaks into the word-production system. This is also evident from manipulations that increase the spatial distance between a colour patch and colour word and that make the colour and word part of different objects.

It has been shown that increasing the spatial distance between a colour patch and colour word reduces Stroop interference. Gatti and Egeth (1978) increased the spatial distance between colour and word from 1° to 5° and observed that interference diminished from 90 to 40 ms. Merikle and Gorewich (1979) observed no decrease of Stroop interference with increasing distance from 0.5° to 2.5° when letter size was increased to compensate for acuity loss. Brown, Gore, and Carr (2002) presented colour patches and words at different locations. Before stimulus onset, the location of either the colour patch or the word was cued. Manipulation of the locus of attention modulated the magnitude of Stroop interference. Stroop interference was larger when the locations of the colour and word were close together than when they were far apart (e.g., 13°) and attention was drawn to the location of the colour patch. To conclude, the manipulations of the spatial distance between colour and word show that increasing the distance reduces but does not eliminate Stroop interference. This supports the idea that the spatial integration of the colour and word in the classic Stroop stimulus leads to a Trojan horse effect.

It has been observed that making the colour and the word part of different objects also reduces Stroop interference. Kahneman and Henik (1981) presented colour-word Stroop stimuli and coloured colour-neutral words in a circle and square that were about 9° apart on the screen. The task was to name the colour of the word in the circle, which could be the colour word or the neutral word. Stroop interference was much larger when the colour-word Stroop stimulus was part of the relevant object (the circle) than when it was not. Van der Heijden, Hagenaar, and Bloem (1984) replicated this result with a much smaller spatial distance between the objects (about 1°). In the experiments of Kahneman and Henik (1981) and Van der Heijden et al. (1984), object membership and spatial distance are confounded. Wühr and Waszak (2003) controlled for spatial distance by having participants name the colour of one of two partly overlapping objects and ignore colour words that appeared in the relevant object, in the irrelevant object, or in the background. Words produced much larger Stroop interference in the relevant object than in the irrelevant object or background. Irrelevant objects and background did not differ in the magnitude of interference produced. To conclude, the manipulations of object membership suggest that Stroop interference is greater when the colour and incongruent word are part of the same object than when they are not. This supports the idea that the integration of the colour and word into one object in the classic Stroop stimulus leads to a Trojan horse effect.

Space-based and object-based attention lead to the selection of a location or object that contains the relevant information for performing the task, the colour-word stimulus in the Stroop task. Next, attention needs to be engaged to the task-relevant stimulus dimension (the colour) and disengaged from the irrelevant dimension (the word). In WEAVER++, this is achieved by a condition-action rule that blocks out the irrelevant input depending on the task. Consequently, the system receives perceptual input much longer for the relevant than for the irrelevant stimulus dimension.

Whereas the onset of an event (e.g., a flash of light or the appearance of an object or word) often attracts attention, the offset of a significant event may lead to a disengagement of attention. La Heij, Van der Heijden, and Plooij (2001) reported the paradoxical finding that an early removal of the Stroop stimulus from the screen reduces rather than increases Stroop interference. The interference was larger when the colour-word Stroop stimulus stayed on the screen until the response was made (the "continuous" condition) than when the stimulus was presented only briefly (the "short" condition) or the colour was replaced by neutral white colour after 120 ms (the "replaced" condition). This suggests that an early offset helped to disengage the space-based or object-based attention to the Stroop stimulus, thereby reducing Stroop interference. Interestingly, when the colour was replaced by neutral white after 120 ms while the word stayed on the screen until the response (the replaced condition), the Stroop interference was even less than when both colour and word were presented briefly (the short condition). This suggests that a temporal segregation of colour and word helps to disengage attention from the irrelevant dimension.

In order to provide some form of test of this theoretical analysis ("a proof of principle"), we tested the effect of early stimulus offset in computer simulations with the WEAVER++ model. The simulations showed that the model correctly produced the paradoxical result. Reducing the duration of both colour and word input in the model reduced the magnitude of Stroop interference, as shown in Figure 6.5. The simulation of the continuous condition followed Roelofs (2003). Colour input was provided to the lexical network until response, whereas word input was given for 100 ms. The processes of colour and word perception were not included in the simulation. The duration of these processes is estimated to be around 100–125 ms (Roelofs, 2003). This means that attention disengaged around 200–225 ms after stimulus onset in the model. This corresponds to estimates of attention to colour between 150 and 350 ms after stimulus onset (e.g., Hillyard, Mangun, Woldorff, & Luck, 1995). In the replaced condition, the durations of both the colour and word input were set at 75 ms. This implies that attention in this condition disengaged early, namely, around 175–200 ms after stimulus onset.

Neural correlates of executive attention

Neuroimaging studies have revealed that colour-word Stroop performance engages the anterior cingulate and dorsolateral prefrontal cortices for attentional control, the left lingual gyrus for colour processing, the left extrastriate cortex for visual word-form processing, and the left-perisylvian language areas, including the areas of Broca (posterior inferior frontal) and Wernicke (posterior superior temporal), for word planning (see Roelofs and Hagoort

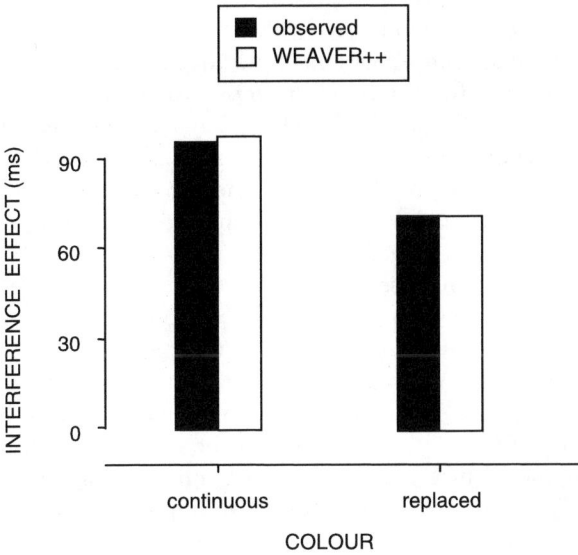

Figure 6.5 The paradoxical colour duration effect in the Stroop task: Real data (means across experiments; La Heij et al., 2001) and WEAVER++ simulation results.

(2002) for a review). Much evidence suggests that the dorsolateral prefrontal cortex serves to maintain the goals in working memory (e.g., Miller, 2000). Anterior cingulate cortex (ACC) involvement in attentional control agrees with the idea that attention is the principal link between cognition and motivation. For action control, it is not enough to have goals in working memory, but one should also be motivated to attain them. Extensive projections from the thalamus and brainstem nuclei to the anterior cingulate suggest a role for drive and arousal. Extensive reciprocal connections between the anterior cingulate and dorsolateral prefrontal cortex suggest a role for working memory. The motor areas of the cingulate sulcus densely project to the spinal cord and motor cortex, which suggests a role of the anterior cingulate in motor control. Paus (2001) argued that the cingulate motor areas contain subregions controlling vocal responses, manual responses, and eye movements. However, based on a meta-analysis of the existing literature and the results from a new neuroimaging experiment, Barch, Braver, Akbudak, Conturo, Ollinger, and Snyder (2001) argued that response conflict activates the rostral cingulate zone regardless of response modality (spoken, manual).

Previous neuroimaging studies showed that the presence of conflicting response alternatives increases ACC activity, indicating that the ACC is involved in attentional control. However, the exact nature of the ACC function is still under debate. The prevailing conflict detection hypothesis maintains that the ACC is involved in performance monitoring (Botvinick et al., 2001). According to this view, ACC activity reflects the detection of response conflict and acts as a signal that engages regulative processes subserved by lateral prefrontal brain regions. According to an alternative view, the ACC plays a role in regulation itself. For example, the ACC may be involved in the top-down regulation of response selection processes (e.g., Holroyd & Coles, 2002; Posner & DiGirolamo, 1998, 2000; Posner & Raichle, 1994). Roelofs and Hagoort (2002) implemented a version of the regulative hypothesis about ACC function in WEAVER++. They showed that the model did a good job in fitting data on ACC activity derived during Stroop task performance.

It should be noted that assumptions about neural correlates (e.g., ACC function) are not a necessary part of functional models like GRAIN and WEAVER++. For example, it is not critical to the operation of WEAVER++ that the ACC be involved in regulation, and not in conflict detection. In order to apply a functional model like WEAVER++ to neuro-imaging findings, new assumptions need to be made about how functional aspects of the model map onto aspects of brain functioning. Thus, models like WEAVER++ may be used to formalize hypotheses about brain function, but assumptions about neural correlates are not a necessary part of the model (see Roelofs (2005) for an extensive discussion).

To test between the conflict-detection and regulative hypotheses about ACC function, Roelofs, Van Turennout, and Coles (2006) conducted an fMRI experiment. A critical prediction made by the conflict-detection hypothesis is that ACC activity should be increased only when conflicting response alternatives are present (e.g., the word RED in blue ink). ACC activity should not differ between congruent trials (e.g., the word BLUE in blue) and neutral trials (e.g., XXX in blue), because competing response alternatives are absent on both trial types. In contrast, the regulative hypothesis predicts not only more ACC activity on incongruent than on neutral trials, but also less ACC activity on congruent than on neutral trials. More ACC activity is predicted for incongruent than for neutral trials, because more top-down regulation is required for incongruent than for congruent stimuli. Less ACC activity is predicted for congruent than for neutral trials, because the correct response is already activated by the distractor on congruent trials and therefore less regulation is required.

Participants were scanned while performing a manual arrow-word version of the Stroop task (e.g., Baldo, Shimamura, & Prinzmetal, 1998), in which they were presented with arrow-word combinations. The arrows were pointing to the left or right, and the words were LEFT or RIGHT. The participants indicated by a left or right button press the direction denoted by the word (word task) or arrow (arrow task). Trials were blocked by task. On incongruent trials, the word and the arrow designated opposite responses. On congruent trials, the word and arrow designated the same response. On neutral trials in the word task, a word was presented in combination with a straight line, so only one response was designated by the stimulus. On neutral trials in the arrow task, an arrow was presented in combination with a row of Xs;

therefore, on these trials also only one response was designated by the stimulus. Congruent, incongruent, and neutral trials were presented rapidly, in a randomly intermixed order to prevent participants from anticipating and changing strategies for the different event types.

Reaction-time data showed that, consistent with earlier findings, responses to words were much slower on incongruent than on neutral trials, and fastest on congruent trials. Responses to arrows were only slightly slower on incongruent than on neutral and congruent trials, while no difference between neutral and congruent trials was obtained. FMRI data demonstrated that activity in the ACC was larger on incongruent than on congruent trials when participants responded to the words. Importantly, ACC responses were larger for neutral than for congruent stimuli, in the absence of response conflict. This result demonstrates that the ACC plays a role in regulation itself. WEAVER++ simulations, instantiating a version of the regulative hypothesis, showed that the model accounted for the empirical findings concerning response latencies and ACC activity.

Summary and conclusions

We discussed the issue of how visual orienting, selective stimulus processing, and vocal response planning are related in Stroop-like tasks. The evidence suggests that visual orienting is dependent on both visual processing and verbal response planning. We also discussed the issue of selective perceptual processing in Stroop-like tasks. The evidence suggests that space-based and object-based attention lead to a Trojan horse effect in the classic Stroop task, which can be moderated by increasing the spatial distance between colour and word and by making colour and word part of different objects. Reducing the presentation duration of the colour-word stimulus or the duration of either the colour or word dimension reduces Stroop interference. This paradoxical finding was correctly simulated by the WEAVER++ model. Finally, we discussed evidence on the neural correlates of executive attention, particularly the ACC. The evidence suggests that the ACC plays a role in regulation itself rather than only signalling the need for regulation.

Acknowledgements

We thank Glyn Humphreys and Kay Bock for helpful comments. The preparation of the article was supported by a VICI grant from the Netherlands Organization for Scientific Research (NWO) to Ardi Roelofs.

References

Ach, N. K. (1905). *Über die Willenstätigkeit und das Denken* [On the activity of the will and on thinking]. Göttingen: Vandenhoeck & Ruprecht.

Baldo, J. V., Shimamura, A. P., & Prinzmetal, W. (1998). Mapping symbols to response modalities: Interference effects on Stroop-like tasks. *Perception and Psychophysics, 60,* 427–437.

Barch, D. M., Braver, T. S., Akbudak, E., Conturo, T., Ollinger, J., & Snyder, A. (2001). Anterior cingulate cortex and response conflict: Effects of response modality and processing domain. *Cerebral Cortex, 11,* 837–848.

Botvinick, M. M., Braver, T. S., Barch, D. M., Carter, C. S., & Cohen, J. D. (2001). Conflict monitoring and cognitive control. *Psychological Review, 108,* 624–652.

Brown, T. L., Gore, C. L., & Carr, T. H. (2002). Visual attention and word recognition in Stroop color naming: Is word recognition "automatic"? *Journal of Experimental Psychology: General, 131,* 220–240.

Deacon, T. W. (1997). *The symbolic species: The co-evolution of language and the brain.* New York: Norton.

Gatti, S. V., & Egeth, H. E. (1978). Failure of spatial selectivity in vision. *Bulletin of the Psychonomic Society, 11,* 181–184.

Glaser, W. R., & Düngelhoff, F.-J. (1984). The time course of picture-word interference. *Journal of Experimental Psychology: Human Perception and Performance, 10,* 640–654.

Glaser, W. R., & Glaser, M. O. (1989). Context effects in Stroop-like word and picture processing. *Journal of Experimental Psychology: General, 118,* 13–42.

Griffin, Z. M. (2001). Gaze durations during speech reflect word selection and phonological encoding. *Cognition, 82,* B1–B14.

Hillyard, S. A., Mangun, G. R., Woldorff, M. G., & Luck, S. J. (1995). Neural systems mediating selective attention. In M. S. Gazzaniga (Ed.), *The cognitive neurosciences* (pp. 665–681). Cambridge, MA: MIT Press.

Holroyd, C. B., & Coles, M. G. H. (2002). The neural basis of human error processing: Reinforcement learning, dopamine, and the error-related negativity. *Psychological Review, 109,* 679–709.

Humphrey, G. (1951). *Thinking: An introduction to its experimental psychology.* London: Methuen.

Kahneman, D., & Henik, A. (1981). Perceptual organization and attention. In M. Kubovy & J. R. Pomerantz (Eds.), *Perceptual organization* (pp. 181–211). Hillsdale, NJ: Lawrence Erlbaum Associates, Inc.

Kanwisher, N., & Wojciulik, E. (2000). Visual attention: Insights from brain imaging. *Nature Neuroscience Reviews, 1,* 91–100.

Kustov, A. A., & Robinson, D. L. (1996). Shared neural control of attentional shifts and eye movements. *Nature, 384,* 74–77.

La Heij, W., Van der Heijden, A. H. C., & Plooij, P. (2001). A paradoxical exposure-duration effect in the Stroop task: Temporal segregation between stimulus attributes facilitates selection. *Journal of Experimental Psychology: Human Perception and Performance, 27,* 622–632.

Levelt, W. J. M., Roelofs, A., & Meyer, A. S. (1999). A theory of lexical access in speech production. *Behavioral and Brain Sciences, 22,* 1–38.

Logan, G. D. (1995). Linguistic and conceptual control of visual spatial attention. *Cognitive Psychology, 28,* 103–174.

Lupker, S. J. (1979). The semantic nature of response competition in the picture-word interference task. *Memory and Cognition, 7,* 485–495.

MacLeod, C. M. (1991). Half a century of research on the Stroop effect: An integrative review. *Psychological Bulletin, 109,* 163–203.

Mandler, J. M., & Mandler, G. (Eds.) (1964). *Thinking: From association to Gestalt.* New York: Wiley.

Merikle, P. M., & Gorewich, N. J. (1979). Spatial selectivity in vision: Field size depends upon noise size. *Bulletin of the Psychonomic Society, 14,* 343–346.

Meyer, A. S., Roelofs, A., & Levelt, W. J. M. (2003). Word length effects in object naming: The role of a response criterion. *Journal of Memory and Language, 48,* 131–147.

Meyer, A. S., Sleiderink, A. M., & Levelt, W. J. M. (1998). Viewing and naming objects. *Cognition, 66,* B25–B33.

Meyer, D. E., & Kieras, D. E. (1997). A computational theory of executive cognitive processes and multiple-task performance. I. Basic mechanisms. *Psychological Review, 104,* 3–65.

Miller, E. K. (2000). The prefrontal cortex and cognitive control. *Nature Reviews Neuroscience, 1,* 59–65.

Müller, G. E. (1913). Zur Analyse der Gedächtnistätigkeit und des Vorstellungsverlaufs [On the analysis of memory and the flow of images]. *Zeitschrift für Psychologie, 8,* 475–489.

Neumann, O. (1986). *How automatic is Stroop interference?* (Rep. No. 109/1986). Bielefeld, Germany: University of Bielefeld.

Norman, D. A., & Shallice, T. (1986). Attention to action: Willed and automatic control of behavior. In R. J. Davidson, G. E. Schwarts, & D. Shapiro (Eds.), *Consciousness and self-regulation. Advances in research and theory,* Vol. 4 (pp. 1–18). New York: Plenum Press.

Paus, T. (2001). Primate anterior cingulate cortex: Where motor control, drive and cognition interface. *Nature Reviews Neuroscience, 2,* 417–424.

Posner, M. I. (1980). Orienting of attention. *Quarterly Journal of Experimental Psychology, 32,* 3–25.

Posner, M. I. (1994). Attention: The mechanisms of consciousness. *PNAS, 91,* 7398–7403.

Posner, M. I., & DiGirolama, G. J. (1998). Executive attention: Conflict, target detection, and cognitive control. In R. Parasuraman (Ed.), *The attentive brain* (pp. 401–423). Cambridge, MA: MIT Press.

Posner, M. I., & DiGirolama, G. J. (2000). Attention in cognitive neuroscience: An overview. In M. Gazzaniga (Ed.), *The new cognitive neurosciences* (2nd ed., pp. 623–631). Cambridge, MA: MIT Press.

Posner, M. I., & Peterson, S. E. (1990). The attentional system of the human brain. *Annual Review of Neuroscience, 13,* 25–42.

Posner, M. I., & Raichle, M. E. (1994). *Images of mind.* New York: W. H. Freeman.

Rayner, K. (1998). Eye movements in reading and information processing: 20 years of research. *Psychological Bulletin, 124,* 372–422.

Roelofs, A. (1992). A spreading-activation theory of lemma retrieval in speaking. *Cognition, 42,* 107–142.

Roelofs, A. (1997). The WEAVER model of word-form encoding in speech production. *Cognition, 64,* 249–284.

Roelofs, A. (2003). Goal-referenced selection of verbal action: Modeling attentional control in the Stroop task. *Psychological Review, 110,* 88–125.

Roelofs, A. (2005). From Popper to Lakatos: A case for cumulative computational modeling. In A. Cutler (Ed.), *Twenty-first century psycholinguistics: Four cornerstones* (pp. 313–330). Hillsdale, NJ: Lawrence Erlbaum Associates, Inc.

Roelofs, A. (submitted). *Saccadic eye movements and the attentional control of spoken word production.*

Roelofs, A., & Hagoort, P. (2002). Control of language use: Cognitive modeling of the hemodynamics of Stroop task performance. *Cognitive Brain Research, 15,* 85–97.

Roelofs, A., Van Turennout, M., & Coles, M. G. H. (2006). Anterior cingulate cortex activity can be independent of response conflict in Stroop-like tasks. *PNAS, 103,* 13884–13889.

Sanders, A. F. (1998). *Elements of human performance: Reaction processes and attention in human skill.* Hove, UK: Lawrence Erlbaum Associates Ltd.

Selz, O. (1913). *Über die Gesetze des geordneten Denkverlaufs* [On the laws of directed thinking]. Stuttgart: Spemann.

Smith, M. C., & Magee, L. E. (1980). Tracing the time course of picture-word processing. *Journal of Experimental Psychology: General, 109,* 373–392.

Stroop, J. R. (1935). Studies of interference in serial verbal reactions. *Journal of Experimental Psychology, 18,* 643–662.

Van der Heijden, A. H., Hagenaar, R., & Bloem, W. (1984). Two stages in postcategorical filtering and selection. *Memory and Cognition, 12,* 458–469.

Van Opstal, A. J. (2002). The gaze control system. In L. J. Van Hemmen, J. D. Cowan, & E. Domany (Eds.), *Models of neural networks, Vol. IV: Early vision and attention* (pp. 47–95). Heidelberg: Springer Verlag.

Watt, H. J. (1905). Experimental contribution to a theory of thinking. *Journal of Anatomy and Physiology, 40,* 257–266.

Wühr, P., & Waszak, F. (2003). Object-based attentional selection can modulate the Stroop effect. *Memory and Cognition, 31,* 983–994.

7 Executive functions in name retrieval: Evidence from neuropsychology

Glyn W. Humphreys, Emer M. E. Forde,
Eleanor Steer, Dana Samson, and
Catherine Connelly
University of Birmingham, UK

Since the pioneering work of Paul Broca (1861), it has been known that damage to the left frontal lobe can have serious consequences for language function. Most typically, patients with damage to this brain region develop a form of nonfluent aphasia characterized by halting speech and poor name retrieval, often affecting most the retrieval of grammatical articles and verbs (e.g., Kertesz, 1979). There are also problems in language processing associated with damage to the right frontal lobe (e.g., Code, 1987). For example, patients with right frontal lesions have been reported to have difficulties in both expressing and comprehending prosody (e.g., Ross, 1981), but, as we shall report here, more subtle deficits in aspects of word selection can also be observed. Damage to the frontal lobes is also known to generate problems in the "executive functions", which operate to control other aspects of information processing. Patients can exhibit poor generation and maintenance of goal-driven behaviour, impulsive responding to stimuli, and abnormal responses to affective stimuli associated with prior rewards or punishments (Humphreys & Samson, 2004; Stuss & Knight, 2002). These deficits may co-occur with intact performance on "basic" tasks requiring (for example) object recognition, spatial coding, and motor programming. Rather than holding that the frontal lobes perform basic cognitive functions, such as object recognition or access to semantic knowledge, many current theories suppose that the frontal lobes play a role in controlling low-level modules—setting the goals and contexts that constrain activation during stimulus and response selection (e.g., Braver & Cohen, 2000; Cooper, 2002; Cooper & Shallice, 2000; Miller, 2000), or, in language tasks, modulating the response set of words and the response criteria set for output (Roelofs, 2003). Alternatively, the frontal lobes may serve as a "global workspace" (cf. Dehaene, Sergent, & Changeux, 2003), supporting the basic operations when tasks become more difficult (e.g., when working-memory requirements are increased) (Duncan & Owen, 2000).

The executive deficits that characterize patients with frontal lobe lesions have often been thought of as distinct from the language impairments that such patients may also suffer. Thus, the language impairments are frequently attributed to the lesions affecting specific parts of a language-processing system, such as lexical retrieval, the representation of abstract words and concepts, or a grammatical parser (Miceli, 1999). Furthermore, this language system itself is frequently described in a way that is quite isolated from generic cognitive processes that serve functions outside language—such as selective attention to a task goal and working memory (though see Daneman & Merikle, 1996). Latterly, however, this view has begun to shift, and a number of authors specifically posit a role for executive processes in language tasks (e.g., Roelofs, 2003). This is supported by emerging neuropsychological and imaging data, where neural regions linked with executive processes appear to be recruited under particular circumstances. For example, Thompson-Schill, D'Esposito, Aguirre, and Farah (1997), and Thompson-Schill, D'Esposito, and Kan (1999) argue that increased activity in the left prefrontal cortex occurs when a selection must be made between competing semantic representations (e.g., when participants have to change their response in a semantic association task, when a generator word is presented for a second time; see also Noppeney, Phillips, & Price, 2004). Converging with this, patients with lesions to the left inferior frontal cortex can have problems that emerge only when selection demands between semantic competitors are high (Thompson-Schill, Swick, Farah, D'Esposito, Kan, & Knight, 1998). Other authors, though, interpret similar data not in terms of selecting between competing representations but rather in terms of the role of the left prefrontal cortex in retrieving semantic knowledge (Demb, Desmond, Wagner, Vaidya, Glover, & Gabrieli, 1995; Gabrieli, Poldrack, & Desmond, 1998; Wagner, Koustaal, Maril, Schacter, & Buckner, 2000; Wagner, Pare-Blagoev, Clark, & Poldrack, 2001), or of the left prefrontal cortex being recruited when deeper semantic analysis takes place (Roskies, Fiez, Balota, Raichle, & Peterson, 2001; Wagner et al., 2001). Note that, on these last interpretations, the left prefrontal cortex is viewed as integral to the language system, but it is not necessarily involved in executive aspects of language (e.g., in controlling selection in language-based tasks). In this chapter, we will reconsider the links between executive function and the particular language functions involved in categorization and name retrieval, and we will argue that, specifically, impaired executive processes (in patients with frontal lobe lesions) can have a significant impact on language performance. Furthermore, and in contradiction to current accounts of executive processes in language, we provide evidence for a role of the right frontal cortex in semantic selection. We suggest that models of language need to specify how executive and language functions interact, to give a complete account of normal language operations.

Patient FK: Executive control, categorization, and naming

Patient FK has been reported in a number of papers, where we have examined different aspects of his cognitive deficits (Forde & Humphreys, 2002, 2005; Humphreys & Forde, 1998, 2005). FK was 30 years old at the time of testing here. He had suffered carbon monoxide poisoning when he was at university studying for an engineering degree (in 1989). An MRI scan revealed bilateral damage to the superior and middle frontal gyri, superior and middle temporal gyri (extending extensively through the temporal lobe, including anterior temporal cortex), and lateral occipital gyri (see Humphreys & Forde, 1998). Following his lesion, FK presented with a number of impairments, including poor object recognition, poor spelling, and aspects of "dysexecutive syndrome", including poor performance on sequential, everyday tasks. His low-level visual processing was preserved, including the ability to match objects presented in different views (e.g., the foreshortened object test from BORB (Riddoch & Humphreys, 1993), in which he scored at a normal level). However, there was clear evidence of a semantic deficit. He performed relatively poorly at the associative matching test from BORB (20/30; more than 2 s.d. below controls), he made errors by pointing to semantically related distractors of target words in the picture-word match task from PALPA (29/40; Kay, Lesser, & Coltheart, 1992), and he fell outside the control range on the Pyramids and Palm Trees test of semantic knowledge (36/52) (Howard & Patterson, 1992). In addition, FK was impaired at naming objects presented in different input modalities (e.g., from vision, touch, and sound) and when different response modalities were used (e.g., speaking and writing). There was also considerable consistency between the items he could and the items he could not identify across the different input modalities and across the different output modalities. This item-specific consistency was not due simply to FK naming only the high-familiarity stimuli or those items with very frequent names—reliable consistency effects were found even when the effects of familiarity and name frequency were factored out (Humphreys & Forde, 2005). This stability of FK's naming deficit, across items and across contrasting input and output modalities, would be expected if it had a locus within a semantic system that is involved in name retrieval irrespective of the input and output modality (cf. Riddoch, Humphreys, Coltheart, & Funnell, 1988). As well as having a semantic impairment, FK typically fared badly on standardized tests of executive function such as the Stroop task and the Wisconsin Card Sort Task (e.g., sorting only into one category in the latter; for data see Humphreys & Forde, 1998). Thus, his case showed evidence of both poor name retrieval and a deficit in the executive control of behaviour. Was there any relationship between these two impairments?

One particularly interesting aspect of FK's case is that, unlike many patients who have a semantic impairment, FK was poor at making a superordinate response to objects that he was unable to identify. Very typically, patients with semantic deficits will provide a superordinate rather than a specific name for an object, and in disorders such as semantic dementia, there is a switch from object-specific to superordinate names over time (e.g., Hodges, Graham, & Patterson, 1995). This tendency to produce superordinate rather than specific names can be attributed to patients losing the distinctive semantic features that separate one object from others within a common category (e.g., Rogers et al., 2004). FK performed in the opposite manner. For example, we (Humphreys & Forde, 2005) gave FK sets of six words or six pictures of objects drawn from two different superordinate categories. He was told the category label for each trial, and he was asked to sort the words into two piles according to the category appropriate to each word. The categories were either relatively distant from one another (e.g., animals vs. clothes), or they were relatively close (clothes vs. body parts). FK was able to perform this task when the categories were distant from one another, demonstrating that he understood the basic concept of the task. His performance with close semantic categories, however, was poor. He was quite likely to classify an item of clothing, such as a glove, as a body part; he also made errors by categorizing a body part, such as a foot, as clothing. His scores were separated according to whether the exemplars were stimuli that FK could consistently name correctly when presented as pictures ("known" stimuli), or whether they were stimuli that he consistently failed to name ("unknown" stimuli). We might expect that FK's semantic representation of known stimuli would be better than that of unknown items, given the evidence for a semantic locus to his deficit (see above; see also Warrington, 1975). However, summing across trials with words and pictures, FK scored 16/30 with known stimuli and 21/30 with unknown stimuli on the superordinate classification task. Overall, FK's performance did not differ from chance ($\chi^2(10) = 1.66$, $p > .05$), and it was not better for known than for unknown items. Similar deficits were found again in other tasks requiring access to superordinate knowledge. For example, he was given trials in which a picture of an object was presented along with either a basic-level name ("dog") or superordinate name ("animal") (half the names matched and half mismatched). His performance at basic-level name–picture matching (115/150 (75%) was better than his performance at superordinate word–picture matching (86/150 (57%)), when he was presented with stimuli that he could consistently name as pictures. With items that he consistently failed to name, there was no difference between basic-level name–picture matching (131/198 (66%)) and superordinate name–picture matching (121/198 (61%)). In both of these examples, FK was impaired at accessing knowledge about the superordinate category that objects belonged to, and for objects he could name, he was worse at accessing superordinate category information than he was at accessing the more specific (base-level) name.

These results have a number of interesting implications. One is that they are hard to reconcile with models that assume a strict hierarchy of recognition processes, in which superordinate information must be accessed prior to information at more specific levels (Collins & Quillian, 1969; Warrington,

1975). If semantic access operated automatically, initially from superordinate knowledge before going to finer-grained knowledge, then superordinate information should be easier to retrieve than item-specific information, as access to semantic knowledge becomes more difficult. This is the typical picture presented in disorders such as semantic dementia (e.g., Hodges et al., 1995; Rogers et al., 2004), but it did not hold for FK. Moreover, it cannot be the case that access to semantic knowledge proceeds from superordinate to other types of knowledge, but that access even to superordinate information is problematic, since access to item-specific semantic knowledge should be at least as poor.

A second implication is that the factors that determine whether FK could access a superordinate name seemed to be divorced from the semantic impairment that limits his ability to generate the correct specific name for an object, since he was no better at superordinate classification for objects he could name than for objects he could not name. That is, access to the specific name did not guarantee access to superordinate information.

One way of thinking about this last problem is that FK has a postsemantic deficit on name retrieval that affects access to superordinate names more than access to basic-level names, perhaps because superordinate names are less familiar, lower-frequency terms. However, this argument is the opposite to that made elsewhere in the literature, where it has been proposed that patients may show better production of superordinate than specific names because superordinate terms are more familiar and frequent (Funnell, 1995). The argument also seems unlikely to hold for FK's particular case, since the objects he could name were quite often low in familiarity and name frequency (indeed, he very often produced these names in response to other, more familiar and frequent, items from the same category; e.g., an individual arthropod, such as an ant or a spider, was typically named as "mosquito").

Alternative accounts seem to be required. One view is that objects are recognized, and associated names made available, by matching stimuli to stored representations of individual exemplars in long-term memory (see Lamberts & Shapiro, 2002). If the number of category-related exemplars has been reduced by FK's lesion, he may be poor at retrieving superordinate names because there remain too few exemplars in regions of his "semantic space" to make similarity comparisons. He then retrieves just the exemplar name. Though this view may account for FK's performance, it is more problematic to explain the opposite pattern, where patients are better at retrieving superordinate than base-level semantic knowledge (Hodges et al., 1995). It is possible that representations of individual exemplars are difficult to raise above threshold, while above-threshold activation may be found by summing across many subthreshold representations to allow superordinate categorization to occur. However, we know of no independent evidence for this "subthreshold" view of such patients.

Another possibility is that this poor naming at a superordinate level reflects two factors: (1) FK's semantic impairment, which disrupts his performance on semantic matching tasks not requiring name retrieval, along with name retrieval itself, and (2) FK's executive deficit, which makes it very difficult for him to select the correct semantic and name information when there is competition at a semantic and name level. Here we assume that FK's semantic impairment can lead to several competing name representations being activated. For example, FK would quite frequently make "associative" errors in naming, in which he produced the name of an object that was associated with the target that he was trying to name but actually belonged to a different category—for example, naming a dog as a "kennel" or a bowl as "soup". This suggests that there was a spread of activation, at either a semantic or a name level, from one representation (e.g., for dog) to other representations of related items (e.g., kennel, bone), and that FK then had difficulty in selecting between the different representations that were activated. The differentiation between the correct semantic representation for the target object, and other representations excited by spreading activation, may be small in FK because there is a loss of semantic features that specify the object, but it may also be due to a lack of executive (top-down) constraint in naming. Normally, we suggest that executive processes, located within the frontal lobes, may help to constrain selection between competing semantic and name representations for objects. For example, there may normally be relatively rapid activation of superordinate information at a semantic level, partly because there can be a correlation between the basic features of a stimulus and its superordinate category (e.g., animals tend to have a head, body, and four legs; see Riddoch & Humphreys, 1987), and partly because the semantic features specifying the superordinate category of an object (e.g., whether an object is animate or inanimate) may be strongly weighted in the object's representation (Rogers et al., 2004). This early-activated semantic information may in turn excite executive control structures in the frontal lobes that constrain the spread of activation within the semantic system, so that there is activation only of semantic representations (and ultimately names) consistent with the superordinate category of the stimulus. For normal participants, the "true" competitors for object naming are items within the same category as the target, not other associates—indeed, to the best of our knowledge there are few instances of associative naming errors in participants without frontal lobe lesions, even when errors are induced by requiring naming to a deadline (e.g., Vitkovitch & Humphreys, 1991). This idea of feedback processes constraining naming is consistent with accounts such as the HIT (hierarchical interactive theory) model, which assume that the role-down re-entrant feedback is important for name selection (Humphreys & Forde, 2001). On this view, FK's frontal lobe damage (and his loss of executive control processes) leads to a relatively unconstrained spread of activation at the semantic level, and poor selection of names, over and above the problems due to damage to the semantic system alone.

Now consider the case of retrieving a superordinate name. If there was unconstrained spreading of activation between items, often going across categories (as with the dog → kennel example), FK may well have had problems in selecting which superordinate name was appropriate for the stimulus. This contrasts with cases of patients with damage that is confined to the semantic system (e.g., as in cases of semantic dementia; Hodges et al., 1995), where executive control processes may still constrain activation to be within the appropriate superordinate domain—indeed, due to the correlations between features linked to superordinate labels, and due to their strong weighting within semantic representations, patients with "pure" semantic deficits are typically better at naming objects at a superordinate level than at generating the specific name for the object. On this view, FK's particular (and unusual) pattern of disturbance is a consequence of a joint deficit in semantic knowledge in the first place, coupled with an impairment in executive selection processes that normally constrain name selection.

DS: Left hemisphere processes in inhibitory control of name selection through semantics

From FK's case, we have argued that executive control processes, localized within the frontal lobes, can play a part in normal name retrieval—in constraining activation to be consistent with the superordinate properties of objects and in helping to select between competing semantic and name representations. FK, however, suffered bilateral lesions to both his temporal and frontal lobes, and it is not clear whether the processes that normally constrain selection processes in language retrieval are confined to the left hemisphere, consistent with left hemisphere language dominance. In functional imaging studies with normal participants, there are grounds for arguing that structures in the left frontal lobe play a particularly important part in name retrieval from semantic knowledge. In a now classic study, Petersen, Fox, Posner, Mintun, and Raichle (1988) had participants either read a word silently (hammer → hammer) or think of a verb associated with the object denoted by the word (hammer → pound). In both cases, participants had to process the word given to them, and in both cases they had to retrieve a name. The conditions differed, however, in whether the name-retrieval process could be by association with the spelling of the word (for word naming) or whether it needed to take place via semantics (when the verb associated with the object had to be retrieved). Petersen et al. (1988) found that there was selective activation of the left inferior frontal lobe when semantically based verb retrieval took place (see also Bookheimer, 2002). These results suggest that the left frontal lobe may play a functional role in a semantically based name-retrieval process; however, it may also be the case that any involvement is found particularly when verb retrieval takes place, either because left frontal structures represent grammatical aspects of language (Miceli, 1999) or because they are involved in the representation of action knowledge (e.g., Grabowski, Damasio, & Damasio, 1998; Grafton, Fadiga, Arbib, & Rizzolatti, 1997). Neuropsychological data can be useful here because patients may be impaired at isolated name-retrieval tasks, where names must be retrieved through semantic knowledge, even when names for verbs or actions are not involved. As we will argue below, the involvement of left frontal lobe structures may be specifically required when semantic representations trigger a number of alternative competing responses, when there is strong competition for name selection.

Our argument for the necessary involvement of frontal lobe control processes in semantically based name retrieval comes from another single case, patient DS. DS suffered a stroke when aged 60 that produced a unilateral lesion of his left dorsolateral prefrontal cortex, including the inferior and middle frontal gyri. DS subsequently had some problems in object naming (e.g., naming 48/76 of the pictures from the object-naming task from the BORB battery; Riddoch & Humphreys, 1993). There were some coordinate semantic errors in object naming (e.g., donkey → horse, cigar → cigarette), but, unlike FK, DS's error did not cross category borders. His reading was also impaired, but particularly when sublexical spelling–sound translation was involved. For example, he read 26 and 25/30 frequency-matched regular and irregular words (PALPA test 35; Kay et al., 1992), but only 4/24 nonwords (PALPA test 36). This suggests that his reading tended to be based either on direct spelling–sound associations at the word level, or on semantics activated from the word, with his nonlexical processing abilities being very deficient. DS was also impaired at some tests of executive function, including the Stroop task and the Wisconsin Card Sorting Task (see Humphreys & Forde, 1998).

We had DS carry out a series of simple arithmetic addition tasks, in conjunction with a working memory task in which he had to remember a series of words (see Figure 7.1). On one trial, DS received an arithmetic problem and a word, both written on the same page. The arithmetic problem could be correct or incorrect (when incorrect, it was always out by a single item; e.g., 4 + 5 = 8). DS was required to read aloud the numbers and then to state whether the depicted answer to the arithmetic problem was correct or wrong. He also had to remember the name on the page. This continued for a series of trials, after which DS was required to remember the words (tested using a recognition memory procedure; see Figure 7.1). Thus, DS had to name numbers under conditions in which his (already impaired) executive control processes were "loaded" by carrying a working memory load. An interesting pattern of performance emerged. Very often (on 67/100 trials where the depicted answer was incorrect), DS produced the correct name for the addition problem (e.g., 4 + 5 = 8 → "four plus five equals nine"), even though he was repeatedly told just to say the numbers that were written (even if the depicted answer was wrong). We term these *"inappropriate completion"* errors. Always on such occasions, we asked DS whether he had named the numerals on the page and he replied that he had. He was also nearly always correct at stating whether the addition sum presented to him was correct or wrong (4 + 5 = 8 → "four plus five equals nine; wrong") (he made only five

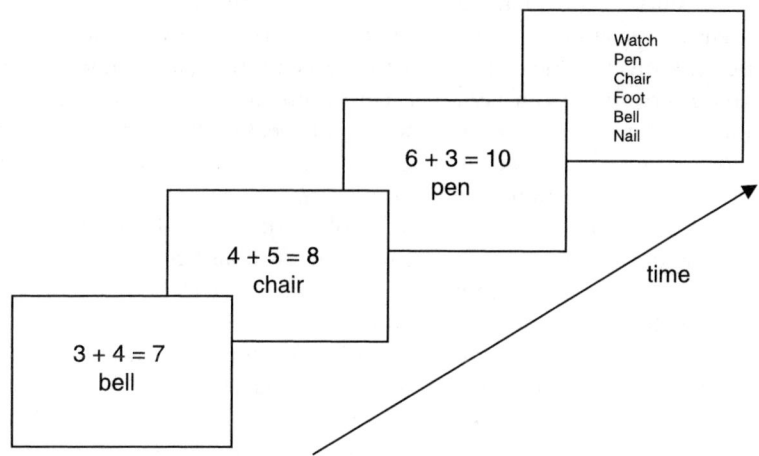

Figure 7.1 Stimuli used with patient DS. DS had to remember each word while also reading out the numbers and judging whether the addition, as expressed, was correct. After a series of these trials, he was presented with multiple words and asked to make a recognition memory judgement on which words were presented.

errors in judging the addition problem, on the 67 trials where he generated the wrong name). In other conditions, though, DS did not generate these naming errors. For example, we presented DS simply with the same stimuli as before, but now he did not have to remember the words on each page, and was required just to read out the numbers and to judge whether the addition were correct or incorrect. Without the working-memory load of the words, DS made 0 errors (now $4 + 5 = 8 \rightarrow$ "four plus five equals eight; wrong"). Hence, it was not the case that DS failed to understand the task, and it was not the case that he was unable to name the numbers involved from their Arabic depiction. We also presented DS with alphabetic versions of the same tasks, where he had to read aloud and judge whether an addition sum was correct (four plus five = eight) while also remembering a simultaneously presented word. We again failed to find any inappropriate completions under this circumstance (e.g., four plus five = eight $\rightarrow$ "four plus five equals eight; wrong"; 100/100 correct). Furthermore, the errors were particular to when the final item was depicted as an Arabic numeral. For example, in another version of the study, we presented the first two numbers in the sum as Arabic digits and the final number in an alphabetic form ($4 + 5 = $ eight); the task was again to read out the numbers and to judge whether the sum was correct, while concurrently remembering a separate word that was present. Here DS made 0/50 inappropriate completions. In contrast, when the first numbers were written alphabetically and the last as an Arabic numeral (four + five = 8), 31/50 inappropriate completions occurred (i.e., to a level comparable to that found when all the numbers were Arabic).

These results suggest that the inappropriate completions arose in a very particular circumstance—namely, when DS was naming an Arabic digit under conditions in which a memory load was imposed, and when there was also strong activation from a competing response (the correct solution to the addition problem). Note that errors did not occur when DS read out the initial Arabic numbers that had to be added together, so there was not a general problem in naming Arabic numbers. The fact, however, that this result did not occur when DS named alphabetic numerals completing the additions, and when a memory load was imposed, also constrains accounts of his performance. For example, let us assume that DS's problems arose because the phonological representations of numerals ("number names") are highly connected together by verbal learning of simple sums ("four plus five equals nine"). Given activation of the phonological forms "four", "plus", and "five", there may be associated activation of the phonological form "nine", even when the stimulus given was "4 + 5 = 8". This activation of the inappropriate (but verbally associated) phonological form "nine" may be difficult to overcome when a memory load is imposed to limit executive control over processing. However, if this was the reason why DS produced the wrong name ("nine"), we would also expect a similar pattern of performance when the phonological forms are activated from alphabetic forms. This was not the case. On this line of reasoning, the competition that DS suffers from the inappropriate completion to the sum does not originate from verbal associations at the level of phonological forms.

An alternative is that the competition originates at a semantic level, and, when this is transmitted to a phonological level, DS has difficulties in selection. For instance, the conceptual magnitude "9" may be activated when DS reads the Arabic numbers for 4 + 5 = 8, in addition to the magnitude for "8" being activated. Note, though, that DS was typically correct in judging that the written magnitude was wrong for such stimuli, so it appears that he could resolve competition at a semantic level. The problems could nevertheless arise because the semantic magnitudes, once activated, also activated their associated phonological forms, and DS had difficulty in resolving competition between the phonological forms. That is, DS had difficulty in resolving semantically driven competition at the level of phonological forms. This is similar to arguments made concerning semantic interference from contextual stimuli on picture naming (e.g., Roelofs, 1992; Starreveld & La Heij, 1996; see Bloem & La Heij, 2003). With alphabetic stimuli, this form of phonological competition would not necessarily arise if there was a contrast in the procedures DS used to read alphabetic and Arabic forms. In particular, semantically driven competition would not occur if DS read the alphabetic forms through a direct (nonsemantic) route, that remained relatively preserved (cf. Coltheart, 2004). With the stimuli "four + five = eight", then, we suggest that the phonological form for "nine" does not get activated from semantics, because the phonological forms for each stimulus are accessed nonsemantically.

A further alternative is that DS reads Arabic numerals nonsemantically and alphabetic numerals semantically. There are arguments that normal participants read Arabic numbers nonsemantically. For example, Ratinckx, Brysbaert, and Fias (2005) have recently reported masked priming from Arabic numerals in a naming task, but not in a number decision task (are these two forms both numbers?: 18 and 1M). Furthermore, priming in naming Arabic numbers behaved in a similar way to masked priming between unrelated letters. Ratinckx et al. (2005) suggest that priming was based on the activation of verbal responses to numbers that were accessed nonsemantically (and so similarly to unrelated letter pairs). However, this account runs into the problem of where competition may arise in naming Arabic numbers. For example, the direct (nonsemantic) reading of Arabic numerals could generate competition at a phonological level if there were verbal associations between the names (as we elaborated above), but then it is difficult to understand why similar phonological competition does not arise from alphanumeric forms, even if they are read semantically (since the phonological forms would need to be contacted for output).

We conclude that executive processes in the left frontal lobe are required to constrain activation between competing names for name retrieval. Such selection processes may be required particularly for semantically based name retrieval, because spreading activation at a semantic level may lead to competitor representations being activated (Bloem & La Heij, 2003). In contrast, a direct route between alphabetic forms and phonology may be based on a one-to-one mapping in which few competitor names are activated—hence, any tendency to generate an inappropriate completion was reduced. It should be noted that we are not arguing against there being a direct (nonsemantic) route for naming Arabic forms in normal participants (Ratinckx et al., 2005), but only that DS does not appear to use this. We should also be cautious in restricting our arguments to the domain of numbers in this case, since there is evidence that conceptual knowledge for numbers may be distinct from conceptual knowledge for other aspects of stimuli (see Cappelletti, Kopelman, Morton, & Butterworth, 2005, for recent evidence). It may be that DS suffers from unresolved competition at a conceptual rather than a name level in object naming, say, leading to the production of semantic errors. Detailed assessment of competition at conceptual and name levels is required here. Nevertheless, within the number domain, DS has a particular problem in resolving competition at the name level.

PW: The role of right hemisphere inhibitory processes

Recently, we (Samson, Connelly, & Humphreys, in press) have studied a patient, who, like FK, had an abnormal problem in selecting the appropriate semantic and name information in language-based tasks. An interesting aspect of this case is that damage was confined to the right hemisphere (affecting the right temporal and dorsolateral frontal cortex). This raises the issue of how any control processes in the right hemisphere may relate to those in the left (as in a patient such as DS, with a unilateral left hemisphere lesion). PW, a 73-year-old former shopkeeper, made striking name-selection errors in both speech production and language comprehension. During a conversation, he would, for instance, say that "flu jabs have been recommended for people *under* the age of 65". He also reported difficulties in card games due to his confusion in saying the words *"higher/lower"*. During a general neuropsychological assessment, PW made similar errors in language comprehension. For example, when asked to *add* two numbers, he would *subtract* one from the other and when asked which day comes *after* a particular day of the week (e.g., what comes after Monday?) he would give the day that comes *before* (despite being able to give the days of the week in the correct forward sequence, when asked to name them all).

On formal testing, it appeared that such errors in meaning/lexical node selection were particularly frequent when the target word was highly associated with another, inappropriate, word. PW was presented with a semantic matching task in which he was shown a target word (e.g., *happy*) and three choice words: a synonym (e.g., *cheerful*), an antonym (e.g., *sad*), and an unrelated word (e.g., *conscious*). PW was asked to choose the word that was closest in meaning to the target. For half of the trials, the antonym was highly associated with the target whereas the synonym was weakly associated with the target (e.g., target = *happy*; correct synonym = *cheerful*; highly associated antonym distractor = *sad*). For the other half of the trials, the antonym was weakly associated with the target, but the synonym was highly associated with the target (e.g., target = *occupied*; correct synonym = *busy*; weakly associated antonym distractor = *vacant*). The strength of association was taken from the Edinburgh Associative Thesaurus (Kiss, Armstrong, Milroy, & Piper, 1973) with strongly associated antonyms or synonyms being those that first came to mind when the subjects heard the target item. PW correctly chose the synonym on 78% of occasions when the antonym distractor was weakly associated with the target, but his score dropped to 57% correct when the antonym distractor was highly associated with the target. In that latter case, PW would choose the antonym rather than the synonym as being the closest in meaning to the target. PW's errors were not limited to opposite meaning distractors, as similar results were obtained in a similar task where the distractor was a nonantonym semantic associate. PW was more likely to choose correctly the synonym when the semantic associate distractor was weakly associated with the target (e.g., target = *garbage*; correct synonym = *rubbish*; weakly associated semantic associate distractor = *bin*), scoring 76% correct, than when the semantic associate distractor was highly associated with the target (e.g., target = *piece*; correct synonym = *slice*; highly associated semantic associate distractor = *cake*), scoring 55% correct in the latter case. PW's responses seemed thus to be strongly driven by word association, even when such an association led to the incorrect/inappropriate response. Note that these errors occurred in a task requiring semantic rather than name production, suggesting a problem in selection at a semantic rather than a name level.

One possible interpretation of these results is that PW lacked the selection abilities that would have allowed him to inhibit the irrelevant meaning, especially when the semantic representation associated with an irrelevant word was strongly activated, as in the case of highly associated pairs of words (e.g., as was evident with the antonym pairs that PW was highly likely to confuse in spontaneous speech production and comprehension, e.g., *high/low, before/after, above/after*). Such impaired selection abilities could be purely linguistic in nature or, alternatively, could be more generally executive in nature. PW's pattern of performance in other tasks favours the latter possibility. Firstly, PW did not make any other type of semantic error in spontaneous conversation, and his performance was perfectly within normal range on tasks that challenge name retrieval (e.g., such as the Category-Specific Names Test; McKenna, 1997). This is not what would have been expected in impairment of purely lexicosemantic selection mechanisms. Moreover, in several tasks measuring executive function, PW showed difficulties in response selection. PW had an impaired score on the Hayling Sentence Completion Test (Burgess & Shallice, 1997), a task in which he was asked to complete a sentence by inhibiting the expected word in order (instead) to produce an unconnected word. Similarly, the production of an incongruent response to a stimulus (saying *two* on seeing one finger raised and saying *one* on seeing two fingers raised), as compared to the production of a congruent response (saying *one* on seeing one finger raised and saying *two* on seeing two fingers raised), yielded high costs to performance (the "cost" of producing an incongruent relative to a congruent response for PW was more than six standard deviations greater that for age-matched controls). PW's general response-inhibition impairment was consistent with the recent finding of the necessary role of the right inferior frontal gyrus for response inhibition (Aron, Fletcher, Bullmore, Sahakian, & Robbins, 2003), but our data go beyond this in suggesting that there is an impact of right frontotemporal damage on selection in the first place. Many current accounts of lexicosemantic selection propose that this process is primarily a function of the left inferior frontal regions (Noppeney et al., 2004; Thompson-Schill et al., 1997, 1998, 1999). However, if selection was completed in such regions, without any necessary contribution from the right hemisphere, then any problem in response inhibition should not arise, because there should not be a competing response to the target to inhibit in the first place. Our results instead suggest that right frontotemporal regions do contribute to selection in linguistic tasks, and particularly under conditions of high competition. Furthermore, the data indicate a problem in resolving competition at a conceptual level in PW, given that his problem was found in matching as well as production tasks.

Conclusions

When semantic information is accessed and name retrieval takes place, we suggest that there is often competition for the appropriate representations to be selected. This competition is normally constrained by several factors—the pragmatics of the situation, the goal of the speaker, and, at a single item level, the information that may be accessed early during online processing (e.g., superordinate information about an object being named). We suggest that these constraints are modulated by executive control structures in the frontal lobes. After frontal lobe damage, patients may present with a variety of problems in name retrieval, due to difficulties in resolving the competition for name selection. This can lead to relatively poor selection of superordinate information about objects (e.g., in patient FK; Humphreys & Forde, 2005), and to problems in overriding strongly activated, competing responses, at both a name level (patient DS, for numbers) and a semantic level (patient PW). Interestingly, our data further suggest that left frontal lobe damage can selectively impair processes that deal with competition during name selection (as in patient DS, who had no problems with semantic judgements about numbers that he nevertheless misnamed), while right frontal and temporal lobe damage (in patient PW) affects the ability to select between highly related, competing representations at a conceptual level.

In all of the individuals reported here, there were deficits affecting executive processes dealing apparently with nonlinguistic functions (e.g., in the Wisconsin Card Sort test), so it is a moot point whether it is these *general* executive functions (of selectively inhibiting competing representations) that critically affect naming, or whether there are also language-specific executive processes that are impaired in the patients. Neuropsychological studies provide one way to address this issue. For instance, if it could be demonstrated that patients with general executive deficits do not have problems in naming when there is competition for name selection, and if patients without problems in nonlinguistic executive processes present with executive deficits in naming, then a strong argument can be mounted for language-specific control processes. At present, the empirical evidence on this is missing. Nevertheless, the present results show that impairments in executive processes can contribute to problems in naming after brain lesion, and these need to be taken into account over and above specific deficits in the representation of linguistic knowledge.

Acknowledgements

This work was supported by grants from the MRC and the Stroke Association (UK).

References

Aron, A. R., Fletcher, P. C., Bullmore, E. T., Sahakian, B. J., & Robbins, T. W. (2003). Stop-signal inhibition disrupted by damage to right inferior frontal gyrus in humans. *Nature Neuroscience, 6*, 115.

Bloem, I., & La Heij, W. (2003). Semantic facilitation and semantic interference in word translation: Implications for models of lexical access in language production. *Journal of Memory and Language, 48*, 468–488.

Bookheimer, S. (2002). Functional MRI of language: New approaches to understanding the cortical organization of semantic processing. *Annual Review of Neuroscience, 25*, 151–188.

Braver, T. S., & Cohen, J. D. (2000). On the control of control: The role of dopamine in regulating prefrontal function and working memory. In S. Monsell & J. Driver (Eds.), *Control of cognitive processes: Attention and performance XVIII* (pp. 713–738). Cambridge, MA: MIT Press.

Broca, P. (1865). Remarques sur le siege de la faculté du langage articulé suivies d'une observation d'aphemie (perte de la parole) [On the locus of articulated language faculty followed by an observation of aphemia (loss of speech)]. *Paris Bulletin de la Société d'Anatomie, 36*, 330–357.

Burgess, P. W., & Shallice, T. (1997). *The Hayling and Brixton Tests.* Bury St Edmunds, UK: Thames Valley Test Company.

Cappelletti, M., Kopelman, M. D., Morton, J., & Butterworth, B. (2005). Dissociations in numerical abilities revealed by progressive cognitive decline in a patient with semantic dementia. *Cognitive Neuropsychology, 22*, 771–793.

Code, C. (1987). *Language, aphasia, and the right hemisphere.* New York: Wiley.

Collins, A. M., & Quillian, M. R. (1969). Retrieval time from semantic memory. *Journal of Verbal Learning and Verbal Behavior, 8*, 240–247.

Coltheart, M. (2004). Are there lexicons? *Quarterly Journal of Experimental Psychology, 57*, 1153–1171.

Cooper, R. (2002). Order and disorder in everyday action: The roles of contention scheduling and supervisory attention. *Neurocase, 8*, 61–79.

Cooper, R., & Shallice, T. (2000). Contention scheduling and the control of routine activities. *Cognitive Neuropsychology, 17*, 297–338.

Daneman, M., & Merikle, P. M. (1996). Working memory and language comprehension: A meta-analysis. *Psychonomic Bulletin and Review, 3*, 422–433.

Dehaene, S., Sergent, C., & Changeux, J. P. (2003). A neuronal network model linking subjective reports and objective physiological data during conscious perception. *PNAS, 100*, 8520–8525.

Demb, J. B., Desmond, J. E., Wagner, A. D., Vaidya, C. J., Glover, G. H., & Gabrieli, J. D. (1995). Semantic encoding and retrieval in the left inferior prefrontal cortex: A function MRI study of task difficulty and process specificity. *Journal of Neuroscience, 15*, 5870–5878.

Duncan, J., & Owen, A. M. (2000). Consistent response of the human frontal lobe to diverse cognitive demands. *Trends in Neurosciences, 23*, 475–483.

Forde, E. M. E., & Humphreys, G. W. (2002). The role of semantic knowledge in short term memory. *Neurocase, 8*, 13–27.

Forde, E. M. E., & Humphreys, G. W. (2005). Is oral spelling recognition dependent on reading or spelling systems? Dissociative evidence from two single case studies. *Cognitive Neuropsychology, 22*, 169–181.

Funnell, E. (1995). Objects and properties: A study of the breakdown of semantic memory. *Memory*, 3, 497–518.

Gabrieli, J., Poldrack, R. A., & Desmond, J. E. (1998). The role of left prefrontal cortex in language and memory. *PNAS*, 95, 906–913.

Grabowski, T. J., Damasio, H., & Damasio, A. R. (1998). Premotor and prefrontal correlates of category-specific lexical retrieval. *Neuroimage*, 7, 232–243.

Grafton, S. T., Fadiga, L., Arbib, M. A., & Rizzolatti, G. (1997). Premotor cortex activation during observation and naming of familiar tools. *Neuroimage*, 6, 231–236.

Hodges, J. R., Graham, N., & Patterson, K. E. (1995). Charting the progression in semantic dementia: Implications for the organisation of semantic memory. *Memory*, 3, 463–496.

Howard, D., & Patterson, K. E. (1992). *The Pyramids and Palm Trees Test*. Bury St Edmonds, UK: Thames Valley Test Company.

Humphreys, G. W., & Forde, E. M. E. (1998). Disordered action schema and action disorganisation syndrome. *Cognitive Neuropsychology*, 15, 771–812.

Humphreys, G. W., & Forde, E. M. E. (2001). Hierarchies, similarity and interactivity in object recognition: On the multiplicity of "category specific" deficits in neuropsychological populations. *Behavioral and Brain Sciences*, 24, 453–509.

Humphreys, G. W., & Forde, E. M. E. (2005). Naming a giraffe but not an animal: Base-level but not super-ordinate naming in a patient with impaired semantics. *Cognitive Neuropsychology*, 22, 539–558.

Humphreys, G. W., & Samson, D. (2004). Attention and the frontal lobes. In M. Gazzaniga (Ed.), *The cognitive neurosciences*. VC3 (pp. 607–619). Cambridge, MA: MIT Press.

Kay, J., Lesser, R., & Coltheart, M. (1992). *PALPA: Psycholinguistic assessments of language processing in aphasia*. Hove, UK: Lawrence Erlbaum Associates Ltd.

Kertesz, A. (1979). *Aphasia and associated disorders*. New York: Grune and Stratton.

Kiss, G. R., Armstrong, C., Milroy, R., & Piper, J. (1973). An associative thesaurus of English and its computer analysis. In A. J. Aitken, R. W. Bailey, & N. Hamilton-Smith (Eds.), *The computer and literary studies*. Edinburgh: Edinburgh University Press.

Lamberts, K., & Shapiro, L. (2002). Exemplar models and category-specific deficits. In E. M. E. Forde & G. W. Humphreys (Eds.), *Category specificity in brain and mind* (pp. 291–314). London: Psychology Press.

McKenna, P. (1997). *Category-specific names test*. Hove, UK: Psychology Press.

Miceli, G. (1999). Grammatical deficits in aphasia. In G. Denes & L. Pizzamiglio (Eds.), *Handbook of clinical and experimental neuropsychology*. London: Psychology Press.

Miller, E. K. (2000). The neural basis of top-down control of visual attention in prefrontal cortex. In S. Monsell & J. Driver (Eds.), *Control of cognitive processes: Attention and performance XVIII* (pp. 511–534). Cambridge, MA: MIT Press.

Noppeney, U., Phillips, J., & Price, C. J. (2004). The neural areas that control the retrieval and selection of semantics. *Neuropsychologia*, 42, 1269–1280.

Petersen, S. E., Fox, P. T., Posner, M. I., Mintun, M., & Raichle, M. (1988). Positron emission tomographic studies of the cortical anatomy of single-word processing. *Nature*, 331, 585–589.

Ratinckx, E., Brysbaert, M., & Fias, W. (2005). Naming two-digit Arabic numerals, evidence from masked priming studies. *Journal of Experimental Psychology: Human Perception and Performance*, 31, 1150–1163.

Riddoch, M. J., & Humphreys, G. W. (1987). Picture naming. In G. W. Humphreys & M. J. Riddoch (Eds.), *Visual object processing: A cognitive neuropsychological approach* (pp. 107–144). Hove, UK: Lawrence Erlbaum Associates Ltd.

Riddoch, M. J., & Humphreys, G. W. (1993). *The Birmingham Object Recognition Battery (BORB)*. Hove, UK: Lawrence Erlbaum Associates Ltd.

Riddoch, M. J., Humphreys, G. W., Coltheart, M., & Funnell, E. (1988). Semantic system or systems? Neurological evidence re-examined. *Cognitive Neuropsychology, 5*, 3–25.

Roelofs, A. (1992). A spreading activation theory of lemma retrieval in speaking. *Cognition, 42*, 107–142.

Roelofs, A. (2003). Goal-referenced selection of verbal action: Modeling attentional control in the Stroop task. *Psychological Review, 110*, 88–125.

Rogers, T. T., Lambon-Ralph, M. A. L., Garrard, P., Bozeat, S., McClelland, J. L., Hodges, J. R., & Patterson, K. E. (2004). Structure and deterioration of semantic memory: A neuropsychological and computational investigation. *Psychological Review, 111*, 205–235.

Roskies, A. L., Fiez, J. A., Balota, D. A., Raichle, M. E., & Petersen, S. E. (2001). Task-dependent modulation of regions in the left inferior frontal cortex during semantic processing. *Journal of Cognitive Neuroscience, 13*, 829–843.

Ross, E. D. (1981). The aprosodias. Functional-anatomic organization of the effective components of language in the right hemisphere. *Archives of Neurology, 38*, 561–569.

Samson, D., Connelly, C., & Humphreys, G. W. (in press). When "happy" means "sad": Neuropsychological evidence for the right prefrontal contribution to executive semantic processing. *Neuropsychologia*.

Starreveld, P. A., & La Heij, W. (1996). Time course analysis of semantic and orthographic context effects in picture naming. *Journal of Experimental Psychology: Learning, Memory and Cognition, 22*, 896–918.

Stuss, D. T., & Knight, R. T. (Eds.) (2002). *Principles of frontal lobe function*. Oxford: Oxford University Press.

Thompson-Schill, S. L., D'Esposito, M., Aguirre, G. K., & Farah, M. J. (1997). Role of left inferior prefrontal cortex in retrieval of semantic knowledge: A reevaluation. *PNAS, 94*, 14792–14797.

Thompson-Schill, S. L., D'Esposito, M., & Kan, I. P. (1999). Effects of repetition and competition on activity in left prefrontal cortex during word generation. *Neuron, 23*, 513–522.

Thompson-Schill, S. L., Swick, D., Farah, M. J., D'Esposito, M., Kan, I. P., & Knight, R. T. (1998). Verb generation in patients with focal frontal lesions: A neuropsychological test of neuroimaging findings. *PNAS, 95*, 15855–15860.

Vitkovitch, M., & Humphreys, G. W. (1991). Perseverative responding in speeded naming to pictures: It's in the links. *Journal of Experimental Psychology: Learning, Memory and Cognition, 17*, 664–680.

Wagner, A. D., Koustaal, W., Maril, A., Schacter, D. L., & Buckner, R. L. (2000). Task-specific repetition priming in left inferior prefrontal cortex. *Cerebral Cortex, 10*, 1176–1184.

Wagner, A. D., Pare-Blagoev, E. J., Clark, J., & Poldrack, R. A. (2001). Recovering meaning: Left prefrontal cortex guides controlled semantic retrieval. *Neuron, 31*, 329–338.

Warrington, E. K. (1975). The selective impairment of semantic memory. *Quarterly Journal of Experimental Psychology, 27*, 635–657.

8   Semantic short-term memory, language processing, and inhibition

Randi C. Martin
Rice University, USA

Introduction

Over the last 10 years, we have been developing a theory of short-term memory (STM) that includes separable semantic and phonological retention capacities (Martin & He, 2004; Martin, Lesch, & Bartha, 1999; Martin & Romani, 1994; Martin, Shelton, & Yaffee, 1994). This claim has been based primarily on different patterns of STM deficits demonstrated by aphasic patients, suggesting that some have a deficit primarily in retaining phonological information and others a deficit primarily in maintaining semantic information. In the past, we have assumed that these deficits derive from overly rapid decay of information in buffers dedicated to the storage of phonological or semantic codes (Martin et al., 1999). Recently, we have obtained evidence that the pattern associated with a semantic STM deficit may result from a deficit in one aspect of executive function—specifically, a deficit in the inhibition of irrelevant information (Hamilton & Martin, 2005). This deficit appears to be specific to the inhibition of irrelevant verbal information, suggesting that inhibition processes are not global, but may be specific to particular domains.

Our past research has demonstrated that phonological and semantic STM deficits are associated with different patterns of impairment in language comprehension and production (Hanten & Martin, 2000; Martin & Freedman, 2001; Martin & He, 2004; Martin & Romani, 1994). The findings on the nature of the STM deficits and their connection to language processing will be reviewed below, with an emphasis on data from language production. The final section will present the findings on inhibition and consider how a deficit in inhibition might be related to the sentence comprehension and production patterns shown by the patients with a semantic STM deficit.

Phonological vs. semantic deficits in STM

A large body of literature has demonstrated that phonological codes are important for retaining verbal information in STM. For instance, memory span is smaller for phonologically similar than dissimilar word lists and smaller for longer than shorter words (Baddeley, Thomson, & Buchanan, 1975; Schweickert, Guentert, & Hersberger, 1990). These are termed the phonological similarity and word-length effects, respectively. These effects are obtained when items are presented auditorily or visually, indicating that written words are translated into a phonological form during STM retention. Patients have been reported who show very reduced STM span and whose pattern of performance implicates a deficit in holding onto phonological information (Vallar & Papagno, 1995). A patient that we have studied for many years, patient EA, shows this pattern (Martin, 1993; Martin et al., 1994). (Table 8.1 provides background information on patient EA and other patients from our laboratory reported here.) Using a criterion of 50% lists correct for determining span length, her span is about 1.5 words or less (see Table 8.2 for a transcription of her repetition of several two-word lists). With visual presentation, her span is somewhat larger—about two words. She fails to show a word-length effect with either auditory or visual presentation. Although she shows a phonological similarity effect with auditory presentation, she fails to show this effect with visual presentation. She is poor at repeating single nonwords if they have more than three phonemes—e.g., she can repeat "lem" but not "danta".

All of these findings are consistent with a deficit in phonological storage,

Table 8.1 Patient background information

	Age	Education	Auditory span	Visual span	PNT[a]	Lesion site[b] (Left hemisphere)
Phonological STM deficit						
EA	64	College	1.5	2.5	94	Temporal/parietal
SJD	59	Master's degree	2.4	3.4	83[c]	Frontal/parietal
Semantic STM deficit						
AB	74	Law school	2.3	1.5	89	Frontal/parietal
ML	60	2 years of college	2.5	1.5	97	Frontal/parietal
GR	54	College	3.3	2.2	84	Frontal/temporal/parietal
Anomic						
MS	29	2 years of college	4.5	—[d]	44	Temporal, diffuse

[a] Philadelphia Naming Test (control mean = 96, S.D. 7).
[b] All but MS sustained a left hemisphere cerebrovascular accident. MS had herpes encephalitis.
[c] SJD's score is from the Boston Naming Test, and was within normal range.
[d] MS was surface dyslexic, and thus was not tested with visually presented words.

Table 8.2 Patient EA list recall

Experimenter: hardship discipline	
EA:	hardship . . . I didn't get the other one
Experimenter: nursery hammer	
EA:	. . . I didn't get either one
Experimenter: cigarette elbow	
EA:	cigarette elbow
Experimenter: railroad valley	
EA:	railroad . . . I didn't get the other one
Experimenter: onslaught virtue	
EA:	onslaught . . . I didn't get the other one

and similar findings have been reported in the literature for several other patients claimed to have a phonological STM deficit. The span advantage shown by these patients for visual over auditory presentation (the reverse of the normal pattern) suggests that they can rely on a visual or orthographic code when presentation is visual. The presence of a phonological similarity effect with auditory presentation might seem inconsistent with a phonological store deficit. However, although phonological storage capacity is severely reduced, the capacity for most patients is not zero. The standard assumption is that with auditory presentation, information is encoded automatically into a phonological form, and recoding into another format is not typically involved (but see Butterworth, Campbell, & Howard, 1986). Thus, patients rely on their impaired phonological storage capacity for auditory presentation, resulting in the phonological similarity effect. With visual presentation, it is assumed that translation to a phonological form is not automatic. Patients do not opt to carry out such recoding because there is no advantage in doing so (Vallar & Baddeley, 1984). They can better rely on visual or orthographic coding.

In our laboratory, we have observed other patients with STM deficits who show a pattern different from that shown by the phonological STM-deficit patients and one that suggests a deficit in retaining semantic information (Freedman & Martin, 2001; Martin et al., 1994; Martin & He, 2004; Martin & Lesch, 1996). These patients do better with auditory than visual presentation and show the standard phonological similarity and word-length effects. However, these patients do not show the advantage for words over nonwords that is shown by normal subjects and patients with a phonological STM deficit. For example, patient AB (see background information in Table 8.1), who showed evidence of a semantic STM deficit, scored 50% items correct for words and 45% items correct for nonwords averaging across two- and three-word lists, a difference which was nonsignificant. Thus, he seemed not to benefit from the lexical and semantic information in the words. In contrast, on the same lists, patient EA (with a phonological STM deficit) scored significantly better on the words (42% items correct) than on the nonwords (18% items correct). A distinction between the phonological and semantic STM deficit patients is also seen in their performance on category vs. rhyme probe tasks. On the category probe task, subjects judge whether a probe word is in the same semantic category as any of the preceding list items. On the rhyme probe task, they judge whether the probe word rhymes with any of the preceding list items. The phonological patients do better on the category than the rhyme probe task, whereas the semantic patients show the reverse. It should be noted, however, that while the phonological retention of the semantic STM-deficit patients is better than that for the patients with a phonological STM deficit, it could not be said to be normal. For instance, nonword span is below normal for patients with a semantic STM deficit.

N. Martin and Saffran (1997) have also reported several aphasic patients showing a dissociation between semantic and phonological STM deficits. They have related their patients' STM deficits to semantic or phonological processing deficits and have examined the relation between these deficits and serial position effects in list recall. Our emphasis has been on patients who show normal performance or only minimal deficits on single word processing tasks (e.g., see Martin & Breedin, 1992; Martin & He, 2004; Martin & Lesch, 1996), and who, despite their good single-word comprehension and production abilities, show dramatically impaired performance on a variety of STM tasks.

Input vs. output phonology

In the earliest papers postulating a separation between phonological and semantic STM capacities, we assumed a single phonological storage capacity (e.g., Martin et al., 1994). More recently, we have argued that the phonological component needs to be divided into two components: one supporting the retention of input phonology and the other supporting the retention of output phonology (Martin et al., 1999). Input phonology refers to phonological codes derived from perception, whereas output phonology refers to phonological codes involved in generating speech output. Some of the earliest studies on patients with STM deficits suggested that the patients' deficit was on the input side. Shallice and Butterworth (1977) reported that a patient, JB, with what they termed an "auditory verbal" STM deficit was normal on various measures of narrative speech production. Although the patient was not tested on the phonological similarity and word-length effects, the patient did show very reduced span and better recall with visual than auditory presentation, suggesting a phonological STM deficit. She also failed to show a recency effect (Warrington, Logue, & Pratt, 1971). In contrast to her very reduced span, JB's speech rate, words per minute, pausing, and hesitations were all within normal range when she was asked to describe her job and two holiday trips. She also produced a large proportion of sentences with

subordinate clauses, well within the range of such sentences for normal subjects. The pattern of errors that she made in production was similar to that
of controls on all measures except that she made a larger number of function
word errors, though the rate of such errors was still quite low. Similar findings on narrative production were obtained in our laboratory for patient EA,
whose STM performance was described earlier (Martin et al., 1994). In telling
the Cinderella story after viewing a picture book with the words covered up,
EA had a normal speech rate and was normal on all measures of structural
and morphological complexity, according to the indices in the Quantitative
Analysis of Production developed by Saffran, Berndt, and Schwartz (1989).
In line with the conclusions of Shallice and Butterworth, we argued that
these findings imply that a different buffer is involved in producing speech
than in perceiving speech. That is, if the planning of speech production
depends on having a buffer for holding several words simultaneously in a
phonological form, one would have expected patients with a phonological
STM deficit to be impaired in production. Their normal performance on
production suggests that a different capacity is involved on the output side. It
should be acknowledged, however, that some current models of production
assume that planning does not proceed very far at the phonological level,
spanning only one or two words (e.g., Meyer, 1996). If so, then EA's normal
production could be attributed to the minimal demands on phonological
storage involved in production.

Another way in which we have provided evidence for separate input and
output phonological stores was by examining the STM performance of a
patient, MS, who was severely anomic (Martin et al., 1999; see Table 8.1). MS
showed preserved comprehension of words but was impaired in producing
names for objects, whether in spontaneous speech, naming to definition, or
picture naming. He showed a strong effect of frequency on picture naming,
as he was 77% correct in naming objects with high-frequency names and
only 27% correct for objects with low-frequency names. (All objects were
easily nameable by control subjects.) When unable to name an object, MS
almost always produced a circumlocution—that is, on 95% of the error
trials, he described the object and its function, but did not produce the name.
For example, for *cane*, he said, "This is something you use to walk with if
you have trouble walking, if you have, you broke your leg or something, and
you need something to help you walk." MS showed excellent performance
on all STM tasks when he was not required to reproduce the list. For instance,
on recognition probe or order probe tasks, he performed at or above the
mean for control subjects. In contrast, his performance when he was asked to
recall word lists aloud was below the range of controls. The errors that MS
made in word list recall mirrored his word-production problems. That is, he
showed a much greater than normal effect of word frequency on his list
recall, with the recall of high-frequency words sometimes within normal
range but the recall of low-frequency words far below normal range. In addition, he was much better able to recall word lists composed of words that he

could produce in picture naming than lists composed of words that he could not produce. Moreover, he sometimes produced circumlocutions in list recall like those he produced in picture naming. For example, for the list "lobster, castle, bagpipe", he said "losser . . . the thing you eat", "the place where kings go in", and "it comes from the place where men dress like women".

MS's normal performance when the tasks did not require output indicates that the input buffer was preserved. His poor performance on tasks requiring output of the lists suggests that either his output buffer was damaged or the representations that would be held in the output buffer were inaccessible. Arguing against an output buffer deficit per se were findings showing that MS's span for nonwords was normal. His excellent list recall with nonwords indicates that he could translate between input and output forms and hold these forms in an output buffer. Consequently, it appears that his deficit for word lists derives from weak output phonological representations, rather than to a buffer disruption. That is, the contents of the buffer were degraded because of his weak access to output phonological representations. (See further discussion in the next section.)

A model of word processing and STM

We have interpreted the findings from MS and other patients in terms of the model shown in Figure 8.1. On the left-hand side is the long-term knowledge representation for words and on the right are STM buffers. The lexical processing network shown on the left-hand side is equivalent to that used by N. Martin and Saffran (1997) in providing an account of the effects of lexical factors such as word frequency and concreteness on STM performance. Their model is closely related to the interactive activation model of word production initially presented by Dell and O'Seaghdha (1992) and used by Dell, Schwartz, Martin, Saffran, and Gagnon (1997) to account for accuracy and error patterns in normal participants' and aphasic patients' picture naming. Their model includes phonological, lexical, and semantic nodes and bidirectional connections between them; however, unlike the lexical network on the left-hand side of Figure 8.1, there is no distinction between input and output phonology.[1] Their model has been applied to data from picture-naming (Dell et al., 1997) and STM deficits (N. Martin et al., 1996; Saffran & Martin, 1997).

The major difference between our approach and theirs is that we have emphasized the role of buffers on the right-hand side of the model that are used to maintain several representations simultaneously (Martin et al., 1999). We have claimed that there are separate buffers for maintaining input phonological representations, output phonological representations, and lexical-semantic representations, and that brain damage can selectively affect these buffers, leaving lexical processing intact. In earlier instantiations of the model, we assumed that representations were copied from the long-term knowledge structures into the buffers; however, in more recent formulations, we have argued that the buffers have nodes that serve as placeholders and these nodes are linked to the appropriate representations in the knowledge structure (Martin et al., 1999). Bidirectional activation between the knowledge structure and the buffers is assumed, such that the attachment of a representation to a placeholder node results in activation of the node, and activation of the placeholder node feeds back activation to the representations in the knowledge structure.

Patients like JB (Shallice & Butterworth, 1977) or EA (Martin et al., 1994) are assumed to have a disruption of the input phonological buffer, whereas patients like AB have a disruption of the lexical-semantic buffer (Martin et al., 1994; Martin & He, 2004). Some patients have been reported who appear to have damage to the output buffer (Romani, 1992; Shallice, Rumiati, & Zadini, 2000). The anomic patient MS does not have damage to the output buffer, given his normal nonword span (Martin et al., 1999). His picture-naming deficits paired with his excellent word comprehension imply that his deficit is in the connection between the lexical nodes and the output phonological nodes in the knowledge structure. That is, due to brain damage, these connections have been weakened, with the consequence that retrieval of low-frequency words is most affected. Since STM depends on the linkage between the output phonological representations and slots in the output buffer, if the output representations themselves are weak or inaccessible, impaired list recall results.

Thus, in this model, impairments in the knowledge structure will result in impairments in recall based on that aspect of the knowledge structure. However, in this model, it is also possible to have damage to the buffers themselves even though the knowledge representations are intact. For instance, patient ML, with a span of about two items and a pattern consistent with a semantic STM deficit, scored above the mean for control subjects on standardized picture-naming and word-comprehension tests (Martin & He, 2004) (see Table 8.1), indicating an intact knowledge structure together with a damaged lexical-semantic buffer. Some patients with phonological STM deficits do show subtle deficits in speech perception. For example, patient EA scored at 90% correct on the discrimination of minimal pairs, which was slightly below the range of controls (94–100%). However, a study by Martin and Breedin (1992) showed that several patients with mild impairments similar to EA's, on minimal pairs and on auditory lexical decision, showed much better STM performance than she did, with one subject scoring within the normal range on STM tasks. Thus, even though EA had some slight impairment related to extracting phonological information from acoustic input, this could not be the source of her severe STM deficit, as the other patients did not show the same STM deficit.

Evidence from patients with damage to the knowledge structures themselves is also consistent with this model. Jefferies, Jones, Bateman, and Lambon Ralph (2005) tested the serial recall of words and nonwords for semantic dementia cases—that is, patients who show a loss of knowledge of semantic representations that is evident in both single-word production and comprehension. They found that several of these patients showed nonword list recall that was within normal range, but showed lexicality effects (i.e., the advantage for words over nonwords) that were nonsignificant or substantially smaller than those of control subjects. Thus, in the model, feedforward and feedback from semantic representations to the placeholders in the semantic buffer would be decreased, due to the lack of integrity of the semantic representations. In a later section, we will provide some consideration of how STM patterns might differ for patients with semantic STM deficits from those with a disruption of semantic knowledge representations.

Relationship of STM deficits to language comprehension

Our research on the nature of STM deficits was initially motivated by suggestions that the sentence-comprehension deficits of aphasic patients might be attributable to their STM deficits (Caramazza, Basili, Koller, & Berndt, 1981; Saffran & Marin, 1975). The first study from my laboratory that looked at this question found that some patients who had very reduced spans nonetheless did well on sentence comprehension, even for sentences with complex centre-embedded relative clause structures (e.g., "The boy that carried the girl had red hair", and "The boy that the girl carried had red hair") (Martin, 1987). In that initial study, aphasic patients were grouped into those who had phonological store deficits and those who had rehearsal deficits but a preserved phonological store. (See also Vallar, Di Betta, and Silveri (1997) for a similar differentiation between store and rehearsal deficits.)

The results of this study showed that patients who were classified as having a rehearsal deficit, but who were not agrammatic speakers, showed good comprehension of complex syntactic structures (Martin, 1987). The one patient who showed evidence of a phonological storage deficit (EA) performed well on simple active and passive sentences and on three of five embedded-clause structures. The sentences on which she performed poorly were those in which the centre-embedded clause had a complex structure— that is, either a passive form ("The boy that was carried by the girl had red hair") or an object relative form ("The boy that the girl carried had red hair"). One hypothesis about the source of this comprehension deficit was that upon encountering the difficult structure in the embedded clause, the patient had either to finish processing the embedded clause while the remainder of the main clause was presented and stored in her defective phonological buffer or else abandon processing of the difficult embedded structure in order to attend to the main clause. In either case, the patient should have difficulty with comprehending the sentence. However, later studies from our laboratory and others showed that some patients with phonological storage deficits did well on processing equally complex structures (Butterworth, Campbell, & Howard, 1986; Caplan & Waters, 1999; Hanten & Martin, 2001). Consequently, it may be the case that EA had some difficulty with the syntax of these complex forms and consequently was more dependent than might otherwise be the case on retaining information downstream in a phonological form because of the greater time needed to process the difficult, embedded-clause structure (see Romani (1992) for relevant discussion).

Martin (1993) examined whether EA's phonological storage deficit would result in sentence comprehension difficulty when words had to be integrated over several intervening words. For example, the distance between a noun and a reflexive pronoun was manipulated in a sentence-acceptability task using sentences such as, "The girl hurt himself" or "The girl fell down the stairs almost once a week and hurt himself." EA performed at the level of controls on this task and scored slightly above the mean for controls for the longer distances. Similarly, she performed within the range of controls when the subjects and objects of verbs were reversed, even when several words intervened between them (e.g., "The world, as everyone knows, divides the equator into two halves"). Thus, EA's phonological retention deficit did not appear to affect her comprehension of sentences that required maintaining word meanings for integration later in a sentence, providing further support for a separation between phonological and semantic STM capacities.

Several other comprehension studies have examined the consequences of phonological vs. semantic STM deficits. Martin et al. (1994) and Martin and He (2004) showed that patients with a semantic STM deficit, but not those with a phonological STM deficit, had difficulty with comprehending attribute questions of the form, "Which is loud, a concert or a library?" Patient EA (with a phonological STM deficit) performed at 100% correct on this task, whereas AB and ML (with semantic STM deficits) performed at or close to chance (AB 50% correct; ML 65% correct). AB and ML showed that they knew the meaning of the nouns and attributes as they performed at 100% correct with the same sentences presented visually, where they were free to look back and forth between different parts of the sentence. They also performed much better (88% correct for ML; 83% correct for AB) with spoken presentation of shortened versions of these sentences (e.g., "Is a library loud?", "Is sandpaper soft?"). These results suggest that maintaining two content words was within the capacity of the semantic STM-deficit patients, but retaining three content words was not. With visual presentation, patients needed to keep only one adjective in mind while comparing it with a noun. If that comparison indicated a mismatch, the patient could make a decision at that point, or proceed to check whether the other adjective matched the noun, again retaining only one adjective and one noun in mind.

Martin and Romani (1994) and Martin and He (2004) assessed comprehension in a sentence-acceptability test, which manipulated the amount of semantic information that had to be held prior to integration of the words into larger units of meaning. Two types of sentence constructions were used: (1) a list of nouns appeared before or after a verb (e.g., "Rocks, trees, and shrubs grew in the yard" vs. "The gardener grew shrubs, trees, and rocks in the yard"); and (2) a list of adjectives appeared before or after a noun (e.g., "The rusty, old, red swimsuit was . . ." vs. "The swimsuit that was old, red, and rusty"). The number of nouns or adjectives varied from one to three items. As discussed in Martin and Romani (1994), in the "before" conditions, integration of word meanings into propositions is delayed if there is more than one noun preceding the verb or more than one adjective preceding the noun. In contrast, in the "after" conditions, integration of the nouns with the verb or adjectives with the noun can be carried out immediately as each is perceived. Consequently, the sentences in the "before" condition placed a greater demand on the retention of individual word meanings prior to integration. Martin and Romani (1994) and Martin and He (2004) showed that patients with semantic STM deficits had difficulty comprehending sentences in which two or three adjectives preceded a noun or two or three nouns preceded a verb. (They did well when only one adjective preceded a noun or one noun preceded a verb.) These patients performed much better in the "after" conditions, in which immediate integration of the adjectives with the noun or the nouns with respect to their role relation to the verb and showed no effect of the number of nouns or adjectives. The patient with a phonological STM deficit (EA) was impaired overall relative to controls, but showed an effect within normal range for the "before" vs. "after" manipulation. Because of the better performance of the patients with a semantic STM deficit in the "after" condition, the results indicate that their deficit was not in maintaining complex conceptual information, but in retaining lexical-semantic information prior to its integration. Consequently, the results indicated that their retention deficit was specifically at a lexical-semantic level rather than at a more general conceptual level. (See Hanten and Martin (2000) for similar findings for children with STM deficits resulting from closed head injury.)

Retention of syntactic information

We have shown that the comprehension deficits of patients with semantic STM deficits are specific to certain sentence types that require the retention of several unintegrated word *meanings*. We have further assessed these patients' ability to retain *syntactic* information across several intervening words in a variety of syntactic constructions (Martin & He, 2004; Martin & Romani, 1994). For instance, the patients were asked to detect the grammatical error in a sentence like "The damaged but valuable jewel will all be sold at the auction tomorrow" vs. a sentence like "The kitten that you brought home from the carnival should all be given milk." In the first sentence, the words signalling the error (i.e., "jewel" and "all") are separated by only one word, whereas in the second, the two words (i.e., "kitten" and "all") are separated by several intervening words. Patients with semantic STM deficits performed at a high level on these grammaticality judgements (89% correct for AB; 85% correct for ML) and showed no significant difference in detecting the errors across short or long distances. The contrast between these findings for maintaining syntactic information vs. retaining unintegrated word meanings supports a separation between the capacities involved in the retention of syntactic and semantic information.

Sentence repetition

The comprehension results indicate that patients with a phonological STM deficit show good sentence comprehension, whereas patients with semantic STM deficits are impaired in the comprehension of certain sentence types. A contrasting pattern of performance is seen with repetition. Here the patients with a phonological STM deficit have considerable difficulty—substituting semantically related words, paraphrasing phrases or clauses, or rearranging the order of clauses (Martin et al., 1994; Saffran & Marin, 1975). Patients with a semantic STM deficit actually perform better in terms of verbatim repetition than the patients with a phonological STM deficit because of their greater ability to maintain phonological information. However, their repetition is marked by the deletion of content information (Martin et al., 1994; see also Hanten & Martin, 2000).

Implications from sentence comprehension and repetition

The findings from patient EA and other patients with a phonological STM deficit showing well-preserved comprehension but poor repetition are consistent with findings from neurally intact individuals supporting *immediacy of processing* (e.g., Marslen-Wilson & Tyler, 1980). That is, listeners do not wait until the end of a clause or even a phrase before attempting syntactic integration or semantic interpretation. Numerous experimental studies have shown that listeners extract semantic and syntactic information on a word-by-word basis and attempt to integrate each word into the developing syntactic structure and into the developing meaning interpretation to the extent possible (e.g., Boland, 1997; Trueswell, Tanenhaus, & Garnsey, 1994). Patients with phonological STM deficits can construct the syntactic structure and integrate word meanings based on this structure and the discourse context (Hanten & Martin, 2001; Martin, 1993). There is apparently no need to maintain the words in terms of their phonological representations in order to integrate later words with earlier words. Instead, what needs to be maintained are the semantic and syntactic representations for each word. Patients with a semantic STM deficit cannot maintain the semantic representations for individual words and thus have difficulty whenever integration is delayed. In sentence repetition, however, retaining the meaning is not enough for accurate performance. Rather, retention of phonological information is critical for verbatim repetition. Thus, the patients with semantic STM deficits, because they have better phonological retention, do better than the patients with phonological STM deficits on repetition.

Recently, Baddeley (2000) has proposed the addition of an episodic buffer to his model of working memory, which previously consisted of a phonological loop, visual-spatial sketchpad, and central executive. This episodic buffer is assumed to be a limited capacity system that maintains a binding of multiple types of codes, including those from the phonological loop and visual-spatial sketchpad and those from long-term memory—including semantic codes. Thus, one might question whether the patients with a semantic STM deficit have, in fact, a deficit to the hypothesized episodic buffer. However, several lines of evidence argue against such a proposal. As discussed above, the patients with semantic STM deficits have deficits specifically to the maintenance of lexical-semantic representations rather than conceptual representations or syntactic representations. Moreover, Romani and Martin (1999) reported that one patient with a semantic STM deficit (AB) performed normally on story memory—and prose comprehension is supposed to be one function supported by the episodic buffer. These findings argue against a generalized deficit in maintaining nonphonological or nonvisual spatial information for the semantic STM-deficit patients.[2]

STM and language production

The model in Figure 8.1 shows a single lexical-semantic buffer but separate buffers for input and output phonology. To the extent that the semantic buffer is involved in both language comprehension and production, one would predict that patients with a semantic STM deficit should have difficulty with language production as well. As discussed earlier, the separation between input and output phonology implies that patients with an input phonological STM deficit could potentially show normal language production. As discussed earlier, in a narrative production task that involves telling the Cinderella story, patient EA, with a phonological STM deficit, scored at a normal level on all indices. In contrast, patients AB and ML, with semantic STM deficits, performed within normal range on the morphological indices, but were impaired on the structural indices (Martin et al., 1994; Martin & He, 2004). Specifically, their speech rate was very slow, their sentence length was reduced, and they showed reduced noun-phrase and verb-phrase complexity. These noun-phrase and verb-phrase complexity measures reflect the number of content words in the phrase.

The reduced noun-phrase and verb-phrase complexity for the two patients with semantic STM deficits might be attributed to difficulty in maintaining the lexical-semantic representation of several content words simultaneously during the planning of a phrase. In order to examine this possibility in a more controlled fashion, we assessed their ability to produce adjective–noun phrases and conjoined noun phrases. These constructions were of particular

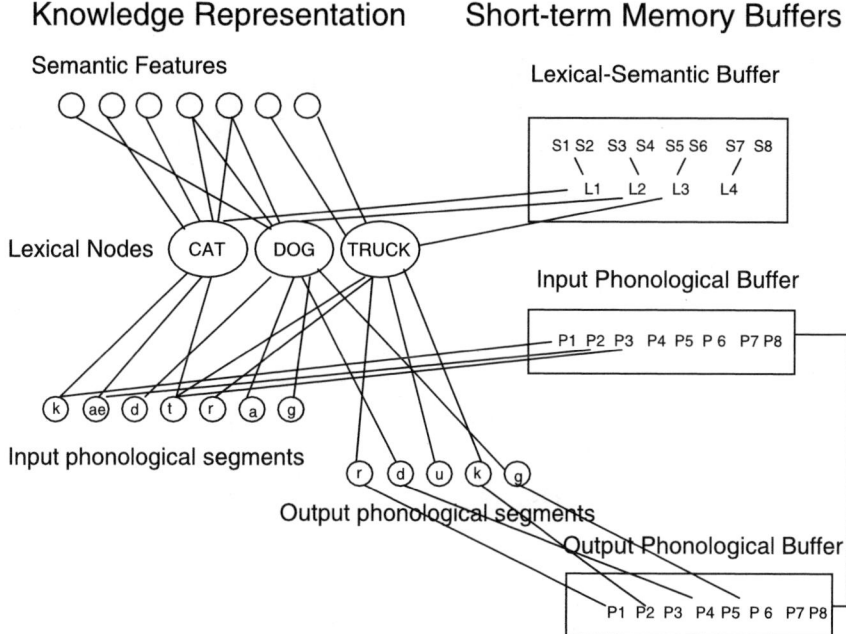

Figure 8.1 Model of short-term memory with separate knowledge representations and short-term memory buffers, reprinted from Martin, Lesch, and Bartha (1999), with permission from Elsevier.

interest, as they have been shown to cause difficulty in comprehension for patients with semantic STM deficits (Martin & He, 2004; Martin & Romani, 1994).

Adjective–noun phrase production

Martin and Freedman (2001) tested production of adjective–noun phrases by using stimuli like those shown in Figure 8.2. Individual pictured objects were used to elicit nouns (Figure 8.2A). To elicit adjectives, a pair of pictured objects was presented with one of the pair highlighted (Figure 8.2B). Subjects were asked to produce an adjective to describe the highlighted object that would differentiate it from the other. These paired objects were also used to elicit adjective–noun phrases. Sets of three pictured objects were used to elicit adjective–adjective–noun phrases (Figure 8.2C). Again, subjects were asked to describe the highlighted picture by adjective–adjective–noun phrases that differentiated the highlighted picture from the other two. The results are shown in Table 8.3. Patient EA, who has a phonological STM deficit, performed at a normal level on all single words and phrases. The two patients with semantic STM deficits (ML and AB) were able to produce all of the individual nouns and adjectives but were very impaired in their ability to

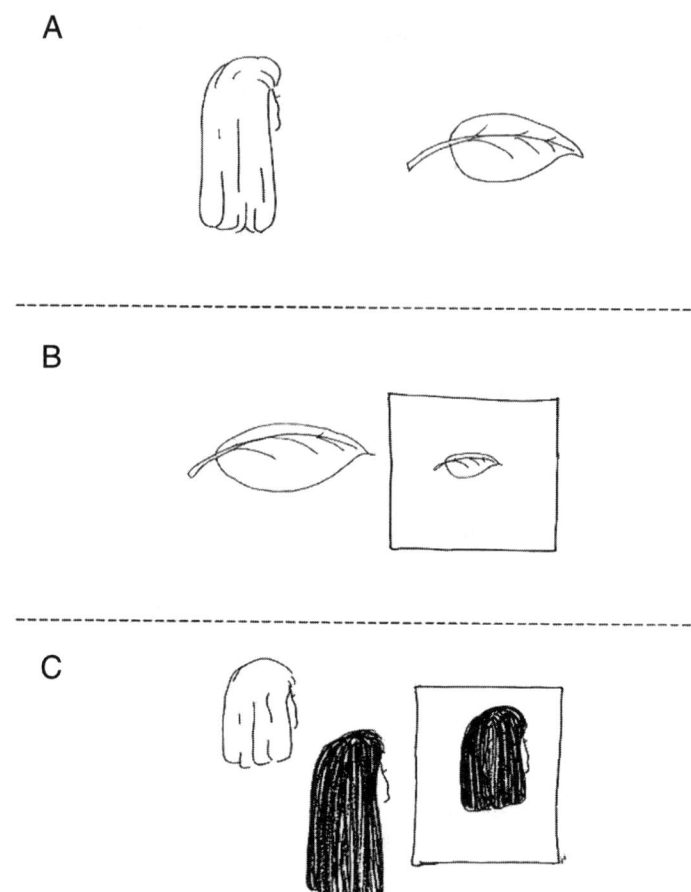

Figure 8.2 Pictures used to elicit (A) single nouns, (B) single adjectives and adjective–
noun phrases, (C) adjective–adjective–noun phrases.

produce the adjective–noun and adjective–adjective–noun phrases. They
would often produce the individual elements of the phrase separately but
struggled to put them together in a phrase. For instance, for the target "short
hair", patient AB said, "Well . . . that's hair. It's short. That's short. . . . I
can't get it."

In order to account for these findings, we hypothesized that individuals
activated and maintained all of the lexical-semantic representations for a
phrase in a lexical-semantic buffer prior to the initiation of articulation.
Such a proposal is consistent with a phrasal scope of planning at a lexical-
semantic level (Smith & Wheeldon, 1999). Patients with a semantic STM
deficit were unable to maintain these representations simultaneously and,
hence, attempted to produce the utterance in a piecemeal fashion, putting the

Table 8.3 Percentage correct on noun phrase production task

	Adjective	Noun	AN	AAN
Controls	100	88	92	77
(n=6)		(93)[a]	(97)	(82)
Phonological STM				
EA	100	90	90	70
		(90)	(100)	(80)
Semantic STM				
AB	100	100	30	0
			(30)	(0)
ML	100	100	20	10
			(80)	(40)

[a] Numbers in parentheses are percentage correct after self-correction.
AN: adjective–noun; AAN: adjective–adjective–noun.

content words in separate phrases. Consequently, we predicted that the semantic STM-deficit patients would do better if the target construction was a sentence such as "The hair is blonde" or "The hair is short and blonde", in which the noun and adjectives were in different phrases. As shown in Figures 8.3A and 8.3B, these predictions were confirmed in terms of accuracy for patient GR (who showed a semantic STM deficit; see Table 8.1) and in terms of onset latencies for patient ML. Patient EA (with a phonological STM deficit) showed a normal pattern of performance for both reaction times and errors. Although ML and GR performed better on the sentence than the phrase conditions, it should be noted that they produced more pauses and longer duration pauses for the sentence than phrase conditions, whereas EA made fewer pauses than they did and showed no significant difference for number or duration of pauses across the phrase and sentence conditions. The pause data suggest that ML and GR were producing the phrases within the sentence in a piecemeal fashion.

It might be argued that the worse performance with the single-phrase versions is due to the greater syntactic complexity of adjective–noun phrases than the corresponding copula constructions. However, Martin and Freedman (2001) showed that patients ML and GR were better able to produce syntactically complex sentences like "It was the frog that bumped the alligator" and "It was the frog that was bumped by the alligator" than adjective–noun phrases. Hence, it seems unlikely that a syntactic deficit is at the root of their difficulty with adjective–noun phrase production. However, as with the copula sentences, they produced more pauses of longer duration for these complex sentences than did EA, again suggesting that they planned and produced one phase (containing one content word) before moving on to the next.

More recently, we have examined the production of conjoined noun phrases, either alone or within a sentence context. Freedman, Martin, and Biegler (2004) manipulated the semantic relatedness of the two nouns within

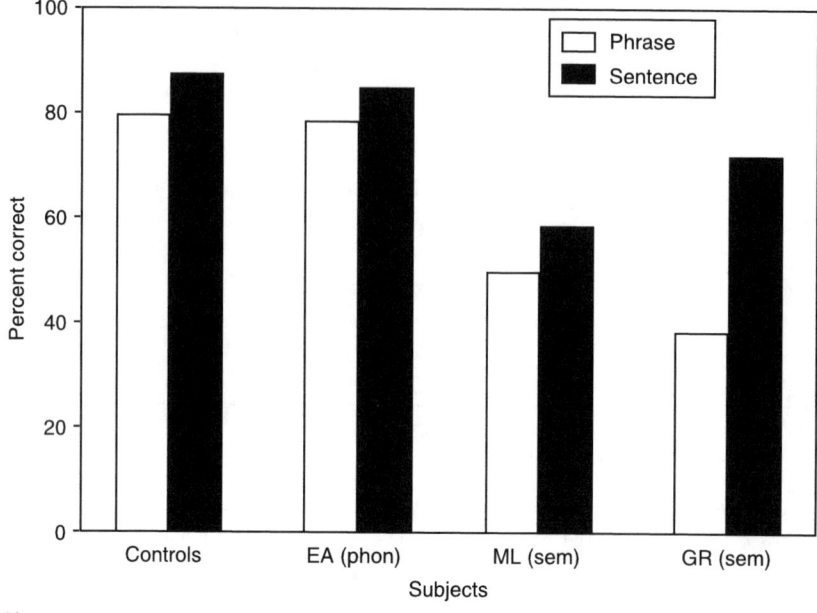

(A)

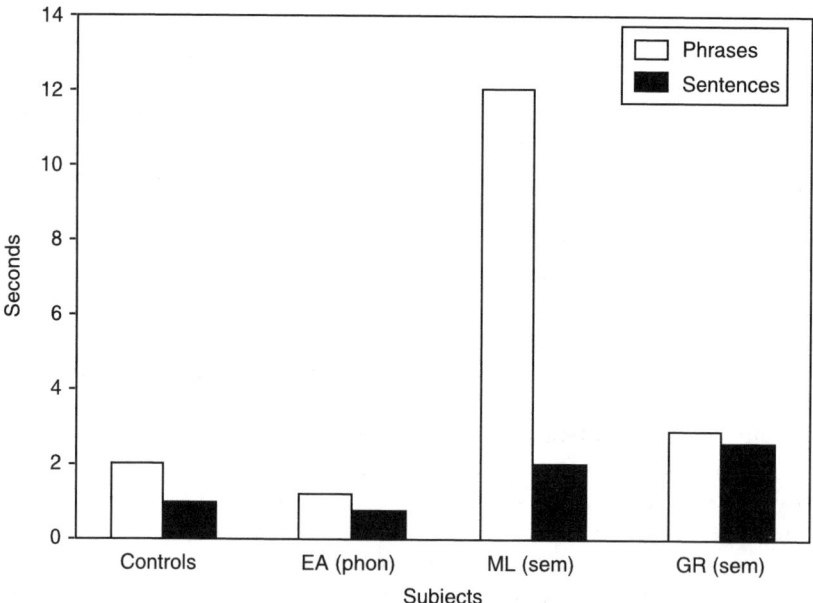

(B)

Figure 8.3 Production of adjective–noun phrases vs. copular sentences for patients with phonological or semantic STM deficits and controls: (A) percent correct; (B) onset latencies. Phon: phonological; Sem: semantic.

the phrase, reasoning that if both nouns were being planned simultaneously, some effect of semantic relatedness should be observed. Patients and controls were asked to name individual pictures or to produce a conjoined noun phrase to describe two pictures (e.g., tree and car). Mean onset latencies are shown in Table 8.4. The results showed that control subjects had longer onset latencies (41 ms longer) for producing conjoined noun phrases describing two related pictures (e.g., dress and shirt) relative to two unrelated pictures (e.g., car and tree) (see Smith and Wheeldon (2004) for related results). Two patients with semantic STM deficits (ML and GR) had greatly exaggerated interference effects, whereas two patients with phonological STM deficits (EA and SJD) had interference effects within normal range. (Onset latencies for the single pictures were similar for the two types of patients.) This exaggerated effect for the semantic STM-deficit patients was attributed to the difficulty in selecting between two semantically related representations at the point of producing the first in the phrase when the representations for each were degraded due to rapid decay in the semantic STM buffer. When words rather than pictures were presented to elicit the phrases, the interference effect for semantic relatedness disappeared for control subjects, and all of the patients showed only small, nonsignificant differences in onset latencies for the related vs. unrelated pairs. The difference between the findings for pictures and words was attributed to the necessity of accessing (and maintaining) semantic information when producing the names for pictures, whereas access to semantics was not required in word reading.

Martin, Miller, and Vu (2004) examined the production of sentences to describe moving objects with constructions such as those below in which the subject noun phrase contained one noun and the predicate noun phrase contained two nouns or the reverse:

(1) simple-complex: The ball moves above the faucet and the tree.
(2) complex-simple: The ball and the faucet move above the tree.

Smith and Wheeldon (1999) had used a similar paradigm with normal subjects to examine the scope of planning in sentence production. Some have

Table 8.4 Onset latencies for naming single pictures and semantically unrelated and related picture pairs

| | Semantic STM deficit | | Phonological STM deficit | | |
	ML	GR	EA	SJD	Controls
Single	1370	1073	1347	1384	758
Unrelated	1788	1363	1588	1222	868
Related	2371	1670	1595	1198	909
Difference	583	307	13	−24	41

argued that planning proceeds at the level of the clause (Garrett, 1975, 1982), but others have argued that planning proceeds on a word-by-word basis (Griffin, 2001; Griffin & Bock, 2000; Meyer, Sleiderink, & Levelt, 1998). If either of these positions were correct, one would expect no differences in onset latencies of the two sentence types shown above. That is, since the sentences are similar in syntactic structure and are matched in the number and identity of content words, onset latencies should be the same if planning is at the clausal level. Since sentences were matched in initial nouns, there should also be no difference if planning is at the word level. However, Smith and Wheeldon found across several experiments that onset latencies were about 70–100 ms longer for the complex-simple sentences, implying that planning was at a phrasal level, rather than at clausal or word levels. Martin et al. (2004) showed that a patient with a semantic STM deficit, ML, showed a greatly exaggerated effect of initial noun phrase complexity, with an onset latency difference of 1027 ms. In contrast, patient EA, who had a phonological STM deficit, showed a difference of only 58 ms, which was close to the mean for controls (66 ms). Although both ML and EA had longer onset latencies than controls, the greatly exaggerated effect for ML could not be attributed to greater slowing for him than EA, as his onset latency for the simple-complex condition (1918 ms) was actually shorter than that for EA (2015 ms).

The results for the patients on the production of conjoined noun phrases provide further evidence that the lexical-semantic buffer that is impaired in comprehension is also involved in production, as the patients with semantic STM deficits showed difficulty in planning two nouns in a single phrase. The results also provide evidence for a phrasal scope of planning at the lexical-semantic level. The normal pattern of results for the phonological STM-deficit patients provides further evidence that the buffer involved in maintaining phonological information on the input side is different from that involved on the production side.

Semantic STM deficits and inhibition

Theorizing about the nature of STM deficits, whether phonological or semantic, has often included the assumption that the source of the deficit is overly rapid decay of representations (Martin & Lesch, 1996; N. Martin & Saffran, 1997). Some findings from the patients with semantic STM deficits, however, challenge that notion. Martin and Lesch noted that both patients AB and ML, with semantic STM deficits, produced a large proportion of intrusions from previous lists during serial recall. In contrast, patient EA, with a phonological STM deficit, showed only one such intrusion in recalling the same lists. The intrusions shown by the patients with semantic STM deficits seem inconsistent with a rapid loss of information, instead suggesting abnormal persistence of previous list information and difficulty inhibiting that information.[3] The findings from Freedman et al. (2004) showing exaggerated interference for semantic STM-deficit patients when producing semantically related words could also be interpreted in terms of a deficit in inhibition rather than from overly rapid decay. That is, when the two lexical-semantic representations being held in STM are related, each would serve to activate the other due to spreading activation. However, when having to produce the two words in order, it would be necessary to select one and, presumably, to inhibit the other. Difficulty with such inhibition for semantically related items that are highly activated could also be the basis of the very long onset latencies shown by patients with semantic STM deficits in producing semantically related picture names.

Recently, Hamilton and Martin (2005) investigated the possibility of an inhibition deficit for patient ML, one of the patients with a semantic STM deficit. ML's performance was examined on two verbal tests and two non-verbal tests thought to require inhibition. One of the verbal tasks was the "recent negatives" short-term recognition task (Monsell, 1978). In this task, subjects receive a short list of letters or unrelated words and judge whether a probe item matches an item in the current list. On some trials, termed "recent negatives", the probe does not match a current list item but does match an item from the immediately previous list. Times to reject these probes are longer than times to reject probes that match items presented four lists back (nonrecent negatives). This longer time for recent negatives has been attributed to difficulty in overcoming the proactive interference from the previous list. On a version of this task that used word lists sampled from a set of 16 words, control participants showed a 91-ms interference effect for recent vs. nonrecent negatives for reaction times and a 4.2% effect for accuracy. In contrast, ML's interference effects were 731 ms for reaction times and 25% for error rates. He was only 63% correct on the recent negatives compared to 88% correct on the nonrecent negatives.

The results for ML suggest that he had difficulty inhibiting previous list items when presented with subsequent lists. To determine whether his difficulties with inhibition were limited to inhibiting information in STM, we examined his performance on the standard Stroop task involving the naming of the ink colours of printed words, in which there is no STM requirement (Stroop, 1935). ML showed a 969-ms interference effect for incongruent trials (e.g., the word "red" printed in blue ink) vs. neutral trials (i.e., naming the colour of a row of Xs). This effect was 12.4 standard deviations above the mean interference effect for controls (197 ms) and well outside their range (101–279 ms).

Thus, both the recent negatives and the Stroop tasks showed that ML had difficulty inhibiting irrelevant information, at least within the verbal domain. To determine whether this difficulty would extend to nonverbal tasks, ML was tested on a visual-spatial analogue of the Stroop task, which involved pressing a button to indicate whether an arrow was pointing to the left or right. Conflict or congruence was created by positioning the arrow on the left or right of a rectangle that spanned the computer screen. On neutral trials, the arrow was presented in the centre of the rectangle. (For a similar task, see Clark and Brownell (1975) and experiment 3 of Lu and Proctor (1994).) On this task, ML showed an interference effect of 106 ms, which was slightly greater than the mean for controls (75 ms), but well within their range (27–129 ms). Both ML and the controls were highly accurate on this task, scoring at or close to 100% correct.

The high accuracy of the controls might be taken to indicate that this nonverbal Stroop analogue was simply an easier task and that perhaps the contrast between ML's verbal and nonverbal Stroop derives from differences in task difficulty. Arguing against this conclusion are the findings from a second nonverbal task requiring inhibition—the antisaccade task (Roberts, Hager, & Heron, 1994). In this task, a cue appears on one side of a display, and the target appears briefly on the opposite side of the display, followed by a mask. In order to detect the target, subjects have to inhibit a reflexive eye movement toward the cue. In the prosaccade version of this task, the cue and the target appear in the same location. The antisaccade task is quite difficult. Control subjects in our study scored at only 72% correct on the antisaccade task compared to 97% correct on the prosaccade task (where 33% would be chance for each). ML performed both of these tasks at a normal level and was actually faster and more accurate than the mean for controls on the antisaccade task.

Thus, the results of this study indicate that ML has difficulty with inhibition in the verbal domain, but not in the nonverbal domain. These findings suggest that executive functions may not be global functions, but may be specific to particular processing domains (see Hamilton & Martin (2005) for discussion). ML's difficulty with inhibition in the verbal domain leads to the notion that this difficulty could be the source of his STM deficit. That is, proactive interference from previous lists as well as from items in the current list might be the source of his poor list recall (see May, Hasher, and Kane (1999) for similar claims with regard to the effects of ageing on list recall). Exactly why this verbal inhibition deficit should manifest itself as more difficulty with semantic than phonological retention is not obvious. One possibility is that there are two mechanisms affecting the retention of phonological information. One is a phonological buffer, which is subject to decay, and which plays the role of the phonological store component of the phonological loop of Baddeley's (1986) model. Operation of this loop would not be dependent on an inhibition mechanism. Neuropsychological data suggest that this phonological store is localized in the left temporal-parietal area, with the region of greatest lesion overlap being the left supramarginal gyrus (Vallar & Papagno, 1995). In addition to the phonological store, there are components of verbal STM that depend on the operation of control functions such as inhibition and selection, which are tied to left frontal regions (Jonides, Smith, Marshuetz, Koeppe, & Reuter-Lorenz, 1998; Thompson-Schill, D'Esposito, Aguirre, & Farah, 1997). These mechanisms may operate on semantic representations as well as on the phonological representations maintained in the phonological store.[4] In fact, the patients we have reported as having semantic STM deficits do not show normal phonological retention. Their nonword span is below the normal range, despite the fact that they may show both phonological similarity and word-length effects on span (Martin et al., 1994). Thus, damage to the phonological store results in a severe deficit in maintaining phonological information because the phonological store is damaged and because the frontal mechanisms have nothing on which to operate in the phonological domain. Patients with damage to the frontal mechanisms may show impairments in both phonological and semantic retention. However, because they have preservation of the phonological store component, they show better retention of phonological information than do patients who have damage to the phonological store.

The hypothesis that the semantic STM deficits that we have identified derive from a disruption of frontal control mechanisms that operate on verbal representations leads to a means of distinguishing these deficits from those of patients with semantic disruptions per se (as in semantic dementia). As has already been established, phonological retention may be at a normal or near normal level in the semantic dementia cases, whereas it would be expected to be reduced in patients with a verbal inhibition deficit (e.g., Jefferies et al., 2005; Martin et al., 1994). Furthermore, one would not expect to see the inhibitory deficits shown for ML in verbal Stroop tasks or tasks tapping proactive interference (like the recent negatives task) in patients with a disruption of semantic knowledge representations.

Relation of inhibition deficits to language-processing deficits

Reinterpreting the source of semantic STM deficits as deficits in inhibition implies that the corresponding language comprehension and production deficits should also derive from deficits in inhibition. Some proposals along these lines are considered in the next sections.

Language production and inhibition

In language production, one means of providing an inhibitory deficit account is to assume that the difficulty in production is specifically related to impairments in producing words in the proper order. Several models of serial behaviour have implicated inhibitory functions. For instance, Estes' (1972) hierarchical model of serial recall assumes that elements to be recalled are connected to control elements and that serial output depends on inhibitory connections between successive elements (and between successive control elements). As shown in Figure 8.4A, element 1 under one control element inhibits all of the following elements under the same control element. Once this control element has been recalled, its activation is set to zero (indicated as self-inhibition in the figure). At this point, the second element would have

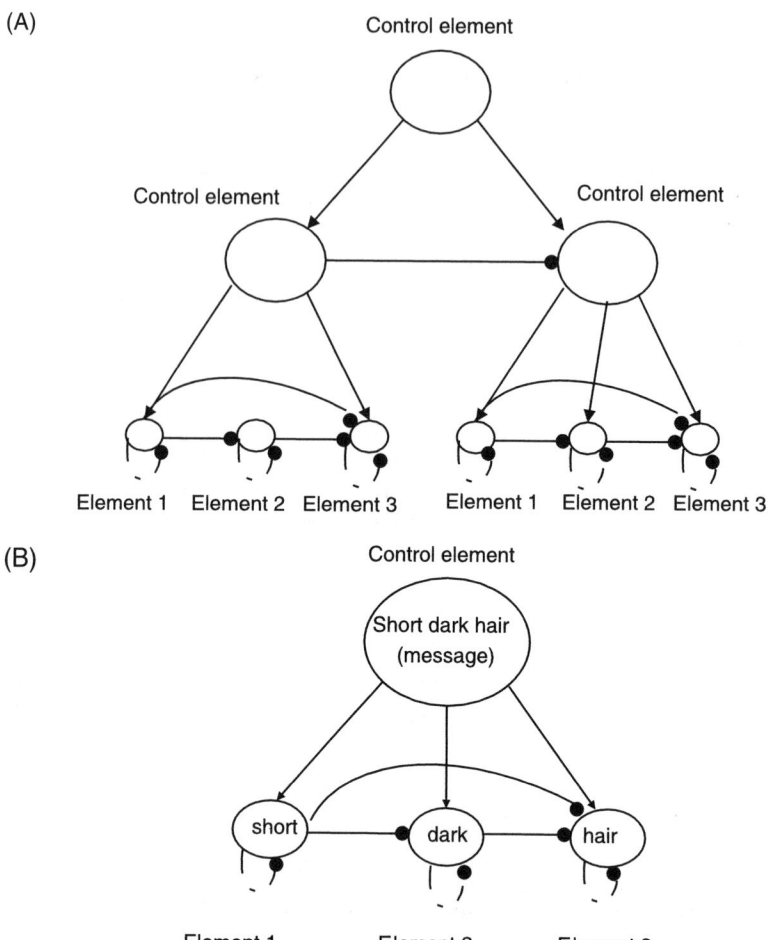

(A)

(B)

Figure 8.4 Estes' (1972) hierarchical model of serial behaviour: (A) general model; (B) applied to noun phrase production.

the highest activation, as it is no longer inhibited by element 1 and it is inhibiting elements 3 and 4. Although this model was created to account for patterns in serial recall of verbal materials, Estes indicates that it could be applied to other domains, such as language production. Figure 8.4B presents an application to the production of an adjective–noun phrase. Models with somewhat similar structure have been presented by MacKay (1982, 1987) and Eikmeyer and Schade (1991) specifically to model language production. In these models, there is a separation between the nodes that represent the sequencing of word classes and the specific lexical elements that are attached to these sequencing elements. In the MacKay (1987) model, lateral inhibition

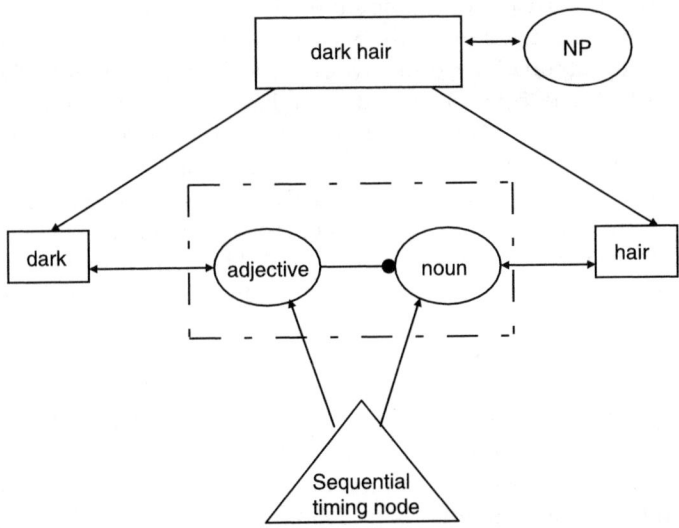

Figure 8.5 MacKay's (1987) model of language production. Rectangles are content nodes and circles are sequencing nodes. All nodes self-inhibit after selection.

is assumed to occur between the sequential structural elements, such as adjective and noun, rather than between specific lexical representations (Figure 8.5). Dell, Burger, and Svec (1997) proposed a general model, similar to the MacKay model in several respects. On one side, content elements are connected to a plan based on long-term weights and, on the other side, are connected to a structural frame. While there are no inhibitory links between content elements, Dell et al. state that one possible mechanism for ordering the activation of the elements in the structural frame would be forward lateral inhibition, as in the Estes and MacKay approaches. Furthermore, in the Dell et al. model, activation to the past from the frame is set at zero, which is equivalent to self-inhibition.

In order to apply models like those of MacKay (1987) or Dell et al. (1997) to the performance of ML (with a semantic STM deficit and verbal inhibition deficit), one would have to assume some difficulty in the inhibitory connections and self-inhibition within elements in the frame. As these frames are used to ensure proper sequencing of word classes, they are related to syntactic processing rather than to maintaining semantic representations per se. It seems unlikely, however, that ML's deficits in production are specifically related to syntactic processes involved in the ordering of words. As discussed earlier, the findings of Martin and Freedman (2001) indicated that ML did well in producing cleft sentences like "It was the frog that was pushed by the elephant", which certainly require at least as much in the way of ordering words as does the production of adjective–noun phrases such as "short blond hair". However, most of the words in the cleft sentences are function words. Perhaps some account could be given that would allow for correct ordering of function words, but not content words. For instance, one might assume that function words have direct connections to syntactic frames (Garrett, 1975) and consequently do not have to compete for selection. Alternatively, one might argue that function words readily assume their correct position within a frame because they typically have very high frequency and consequently high levels of resting activation, which allow them to win out over competitors even when the competitors are not strongly inhibited. In this view, then, increased competition (and thus more need for inhibition and selection) would exist among those semantic representations that fill content word slots rather than between function words and content words. Consequently, a patient with an inhibition deficit would show a selective difficulty for producing sequences of content words. While such an account of ML's production deficit seems intriguing, it should be acknowledged that ML's performance on the recent negatives task and on the Stroop task indicates that his difficulty with inhibition is evident even on tasks that make no demands on the retention or production of serial order. However, one might claim that he simply has difficulty with all types of inhibition in the verbal domain—whether related to serial order or not.

Another type of inhibitory explanation for a production impairment was offered by Robinson, Blair, and Cipolotti (1998). They reported a patient ANG with a left inferior frontal lesion who showed what they termed "dynamic aphasia". The patient's verbal output was severely reduced, but was grammatically well formed. They found that the patient was impaired in generating sentences using provided words or word pairs. When asked to complete a sentence with a word, she was much more impaired when there were many response options than when there were few. They attributed her production impairment to a difficulty in selecting among response options, which would seem to be the flip side of a deficit in inhibiting alternatives.

Several other patients with left frontal lesions have been reported who have been argued to have deficits in control processes involved in language processing. These patients have difficulty with speech-production tasks, though their performance on standardized picture-naming tasks may be at least relatively well preserved. For example, McCarthy and Kartsounis (2000) and Wilshire and McCarthy (2002) reported patients that performed poorly during repeated naming of a small set of items, particularly when the set of items were semantically related and when the presentation rate was fast. This problem was attributed to difficulty in selecting among competing lemma representations (i.e., lexical representations that contain syntactic, but not phonological information). Similarly, Schwartz and Hodgson (2002) reported a patient (MP) who was much more impaired in producing the names of pictured objects when describing several presented in a scene than when naming the same pictures presented singly. They hypothesized a deficit in syntactic control processes that serve to boost the activation of an appropriate lemma representation when it is to be selected for production.

It is tempting to attribute all of these cases to difficulty with inhibition of competing lexical representations. This competition may stem from selecting among several semantically related items. Similarly, in phrase or sentence production, a single item appropriate for a syntactically specified serial position might need to be selected from a set of activated items. However, in other experiments with ML using materials from the studies cited above, ML did not show many of the features demonstrated by these other cases (see Crowther et al., 2005). Thus, it seems likely that there are a variety of control mechanisms involved in language processing that are localized in left frontal regions, with different mechanisms affected in different patients.

Language comprehension and inhibition

An even greater challenge in linking language-processing impairments to inhibition is in providing an account of the sentence-comprehension patterns of patients with semantic STM deficits (Hanten & Martin, 2000; Martin & He, 2004; Martin et al., 1994). As discussed earlier, such patients had difficulty with attribute judgement questions (e.g., "Which is quiet, a concert or a library?") and with the sentence anomaly judgements that manipulate the number of nouns coming before or after a verb or the number of adjectives coming before or after a noun. For the attribute judgements, one might argue that after finding a mismatch between the attribute and the first noun, that noun would have to be suppressed and the second noun's match to the attribute would then be evaluated and the second noun produced. The difficulty might come with suppressing the first noun's representation after having activated it sufficiently to address its fit to the attribute. If suppression of the first noun were the source of the difficulty, one might have expected performance to be better for the trials in which the first noun was the correct one, since a match would indicate that the first noun could be produced without evaluating the second. However, both patients showed a similar level of performance whether the first or second noun was the correct choice. It is possible that the patients treated these questions as comparatives (e.g., "Which is quieter?" rather than "Which is quiet?"), in which case both nouns would have to have been evaluated for all sentences—making it necessary to suppress the incorrect choice after deep semantic processing of both nouns on every trial.

For the sentence anomaly judgements with the before/after manipulation, the decay interpretation seems intuitively plausible. That is, if the nouns come before the verb or the adjectives before the noun, it is difficult for patients to maintain their semantic representations long enough (particularly for the earlier ones in the sequence) to process the associated verb or noun and determine the degree of fit. In the after condition, each noun or adjective can be evaluated for semantic fit as it is perceived. If the list of nouns or adjectives stayed abnormally active, it seems that this should help rather than hurt comprehension. However, the exact sequence of processes that is carried out to determine a mismatch in the "before" condition is unclear. In the "after" condition, serial processing of each word in the list of nouns or adjectives can be carried out as each is perceived. In the before condition, with two or three words in the noun or adjective lists, the fit of each of the list words to the target verb or noun needs to be evaluated after the target word is processed. If this evaluation is done in parallel, it may be difficult to suppress a judgement that the sentence is plausible when one out of two or two out of three list items do fit with the target word (as was the case in our materials). If this evaluation is done serially, it may be difficult to select one word (and suppress the other activated words) in order to evaluate each word's fit with the target word. In either case, a deficit in inhibition cannot be ruled out as a source of poor performance in the "before" condition.

While these possible explanations involving inhibition may have at least some plausibility, the challenge for the future will be to design experiments that can decide between the decay and inhibition accounts.

Summary and conclusions

Work in our laboratory over the last 10 years or so has indicated a differentiation between memory-span deficits that involve a disruption of the retention of semantic vs. phonological information. A phonological STM deficit has remarkably few consequences for language comprehension, but has a dramatic negative effect on sentence repetition. The good comprehension of patients with phonological STM deficits is consistent with immediacy of processing findings in neurally intact individuals (Marslen-Wilson & Tyler, 1980). That is, these patients are able to access semantic and syntactic representations immediately, as each word is processed, and are able to maintain these representations despite the loss of phonological representations. A semantic STM deficit is associated with deficits in comprehension for certain sentence types that require maintaining several individual word meanings prior to their integration into larger units of meaning. It is also associated with deficits in the production of phrases that contain several content words—specifically, adjective–noun phrases and conjoined noun phrases. In speech production, patients with an input phonological store deficit may show normal speech production—and this is one source of evidence for a separation between input and output buffers.

Recently, we have been investigating the extent to which the semantic STM-deficit pattern might be associated with a deficit in inhibiting irrelevant semantic representations. A case report of patient ML revealed that he showed greatly exaggerated interference effects on verbal tasks (i.e., the standard Stroop effect and the recent negatives task) but performed normally on two nonverbal inhibition tasks (i.e., spatial Stroop test and antisaccade task) (Hamilton & Martin, 2005). Although it is fairly easy to provide an explanation of how this inhibition deficit might underlie ML's STM deficit, it is more of a challenge to relate this inhibition deficit to his deficits in language production and comprehension. On the production side, an inhibition deficit could plausibly be related to difficulty in selecting words in a phrase to appear in their proper order (MacKay, 1987). On the comprehension side, decay of semantic representations seems to provide a more plausible account of the findings, although it is possible to hypothesize a role for inhibition. Clearly, additional patients need to be tested to determine whether a semantic STM-deficit pattern is necessarily associated with an inhibition deficit or whether the two just happened to coexist in the one patient that has been tested extensively so far. Specific tests will also need to be carried out to determine whether decay or inhibition provides a better account of the production and comprehension patterns.

With regard to anatomical specifications, there is fairly good evidence that the left supramarginal gyrus plays an important role in maintaining phonological information (Vallar & Papagno, 1995). It seems likely that left prefrontal regions play an important role in acting on semantic representations—either in maintaining these representations, or in selecting or inhibiting them (Fiez, 1997; Thompson-Schill et al., 1997). Currently, functional neuroimaging studies are being carried out in our laboratory to determine whether converging evidence for these anatomical claims can be obtained from studying language comprehension and production in neurally intact individuals for phrases and sentences that make different demands on STM.

Acknowledgements

This research was supported in part by US National Institutes of Health grant DC-00218 to Rice University. The author would like to thank Cris Hamilton and Rachel Hull for their comments on an earlier version of this chapter.

References

Baddeley, A. (2000). The episodic buffer: A new component of working memory? *Trends in Cognitive Sciences, 4,* 417–423.

Baddeley, A. D. (1986). *Working memory.* New York: Oxford.

Baddeley, A. D., Thomson, N., & Buchanan, M. (1975). Word length and the structure of short-term memory. *Journal of Verbal Learning and Verbal Behavior, 14,* 575–589.

Boland, J. (1997). The relationship between syntactic and semantic processes in sentence comprehension. *Language and Cognitive Processes, 12,* 423–484.

Butterworth, B., Campbell, R., & Howard, D. (1986). The uses of short-term memory: A case study. *Quarterly Journal of Experimental Psychology, 38A,* 705–737.

Caplan, D., & Waters, G. (1999). Verbal working memory and sentence comprehension. *Behavioral and Brain Sciences, 22,* 77–126.

Caramazza, A., Basili, A. G., Koller, J., & Berndt, R. S. (1981). An investigation of repetition and language processing in a case of conduction aphasia. *Brain and Language, 14,* 235–271.

Clark, H. H., & Brownell, H. H. (1975). Judging up and down. *Journal of Experimental Psychology: Human Perception and Performance, 1,* 339–352.

Crowther, J., Biegler, K., & Martin, R. C. (2005). Deficits in naming in context: The role of semantic STM vs. control of word retrieval. *Brain and Language, 95,* 48–49.

Dell, G. S., Burger, L. K., & Svec, W. R. (1997). Language production and serial order: A functional analysis and a model. *Psychological Review, 104,* 123–147.

Dell, G. S., & O'Seaghdha, P. G. (1992). Stages of lexical access in language production. *Cognition, 42,* 287–314.

Dell, G. S., Schwartz, M. F., Martin, N., Saffran, E. M., & Gagnon, D. A. (1997). Lexical access in aphasic and nonaphasic speakers. *Psychological Review, 104,* 801–838.

Devlin, J. T., Matthews, P. M., & Rushworth, M. F. S. (2003). Semantic processing in the left inferior prefrontal cortex: A combined functional magnetic resonance imaging and transcranial magnetic stimulation study. *Journal of Cognitive Neuroscience, 15,* 71–84.

Eikmeyer, H.-J., & Schade, U. (1991). Sequentialization in connectionist language production models. *Cognitive Systems, 3,* 128–138.

Estes, W. K. (1972). An associative basis for coding and organization in memory. In A. W. Melton & E. Martin (Eds.), *Coding processes in human memory* (pp. 161–190). Washington, DC: Winston.

Fiez, J. (1997). Phonology, semantics, and the role of the left inferior prefrontal cortex. *Human Brain Mapping, 5,* 79–83.

Freedman, M. L., & Martin, R. C. (2001). Dissociable components of short-term memory and their relation to long-term learning. *Cognitive Neuropsychology, 18,* 193–226.

Freedman, M., Martin, R. C., & Biegler, K. (2004). Semantic relatedness effects in conjoined noun phrase production: Implications for the role of short-term memory. *Cognitive Neuropsychology, 21,* 245–265.

Garrett, M. F. (1975). The analysis of sentence production. In G. H. Bower (Ed.), *The psychology of learning and motivation* (pp. 133–177). New York: Academic Press.

Garrett, M. F. (1982). Production of speech: Observations from normal and pathological language use. In A. W. Ellis (Ed.), *Normality and pathology in cognitive functions* (pp. 19–76). London: Academic Press.

Griffin, Z. M. (2001). Gaze durations during speech reflect word selection and phonological encoding. *Cognition, 82,* B1–B14.

Griffin, Z. M., & Bock, K. (2000). What the eyes say about speaking. *Psychological Science, 11,* 274–279.

Hamilton, A. C., & Martin, R. C. (2005). Dissociations among tasks involving inhibition: A single case study. *Cognitive, Affective, and Behavioral Neuroscience, 5,* 10–13.

Hanten, G., & Martin, R. (2000). Contributions of phonological and semantic short-term memory to sentence processing: Evidence from two cases of closed head injury in children. *Journal of Memory and Language, 43,* 335–361.

Hanten, G., & Martin, R. (2001). A developmental short-term memory deficit: A case study. *Brain and Cognition, 45,* 164–188.

Jefferies, E., Jones, R. W., Bateman, D., & Lambon Ralph, M. A. (2005). A semantic contribution to nonword recall? Evidence for intact phonological processes in semantic dementia. *Cognitive Neuropsychology, 22,* 183–212.

Jonides, J., Smith, E. E., Marshuetz, C., Koeppe, R. A., & Reuter-Lorenz, P. A. (1998).

Inhibition in verbal working memory revealed by brain activation. *PNAS, 95,* 8410–8413.

Lu, C.-H., & Proctor, R. W. (1994). Processing of an irrelevant location dimension as a function of the relevant stimulus dimension. *Journal of Experimental Psychology: Human Perception and Performance, 20,* 286–298.

MacKay, D. G. (1982). The problems of flexibility, fluency and speed-accuracy trade-off in skilled behaviors. *Psychological Review, 89,* 483–506.

MacKay, D. G. (1987). *The organization of perception and action: A theory for language and other cognitive skills.* New York: Sprague.

Marslen-Wilson, W., & Tyler, L. (1980). The temporal structure of spoken language understanding. *Cognition, 8,* 1–71.

Martin, N., & Saffran, E. (1997). Language and auditory-verbal short-term memory impairments: Evidence for common underlying processes. *Cognitive Neuropsychology, 14,* 641–682.

Martin, N., Saffran, E. M., & Dell, G. S. (1996). Recovery in deep dysphasia: Evidence for a relation between auditory-verbal STM capacity and lexical errors in repetition. *Brain and Language, 52,* 83–113.

Martin, R. C. (1987). Articulatory and phonological deficits in short-term memory and their relation to syntactic processing. *Brain and Language, 32,* 137–158.

Martin, R. C. (1990). Neuropsychological evidence on the role of short-term memory in sentence processing. In G. Vallar & T. Shallice (Eds.), *Neuropsychological impairments of short-term memory* (pp. 390–427). Cambridge: Cambridge University Press.

Martin, R. C. (1993). Short-term memory and sentence processing: Evidence from neuropsychology. *Memory and Cognition, 21,* 176–183.

Martin, R. C., & Breedin, S. (1992). Dissociations between speech perception and phonological short-term memory. *Cognitive Neuropsychology, 9,* 509–534.

Martin, R. C., & Freedman, M. L. (2001). Short-term retention of lexical-semantic representations: Implications for speech production. *Memory, 9,* 261–280.

Martin, R. C., & He, T. (2004). Semantic short-term memory deficit and language processing: A replication. *Brain and Language, 89,* 76–82.

Martin, R. C., & Lesch, M. (1996). Associations and dissociations between language processing and list recall: Implications for models of short-term memory. In S. Gathercole (Ed.), *Models of short-term memory* (pp. 149–178). Hove, UK: Lawrence Erlbaum Associates Ltd.

Martin, R. C., Lesch, M. F., & Bartha, M. C. (1999). Independence of input and output phonology in word processing and short-term memory. *Journal of Memory and Language, 41,* 1–27.

Martin, R. C., Miller, M., & Vu, H. (2004). Lexical-semantic retention and speech production: Further evidence from normal and brain-damaged participants for a phrasal scope of planning. *Cognitive Neuropsychology, 21,* 625–644.

Martin, R. C., & Romani, C. (1994). Verbal working memory and sentence comprehension: A multiple-components view. *Neuropsychology, 8,* 506–523.

Martin, R. C., Shelton, J., & Yaffee, L. S. (1994). Language processing and working memory: Neuropsychological evidence for separate phonological and semantic capacities. *Journal of Memory and Language, 33,* 83–111.

May, C. P., Hasher, L., & Kane, M. J. (1999). The role of interference in memory span. *Memory and Cognition, 27,* 759–767.

McCarthy, R. A., & Kartsounis, L. D. (2000). Wobbly words: Refractory anomia with preserved semantics. *Neurocase, 6,* 487–497.

Meyer, A. (1996). Lexical access in phrase and sentence production: Results from picture-word interference experiments. *Journal of Memory and Language, 33,* 83–111.

Meyer, A., Sleiderink, A., Levelt, W. (1998). Viewing and naming objects: Eye movements during noun phrase production. *Cognition, 66,* B25–B33.

Monsell, S. (1978). Recency, immediate recognition memory, and reaction time. *Cognitive Psychology, 10,* 465–501.

Neath, I., & Suprenant, A. (2003). *Human memory: An introduction to research, data, and theory* (2nd ed.). Belmont, CA: Wadsworth.

Poldrack, R. A., Wagner, A. D., Prull, M. W., Desmond, J. D., Glover, G. H., & Gabrieli, J. D. (1999). Functional specialization for semantic and phonological processing in the left inferior prefrontal cortex. *Neuroimage, 10,* 15–35.

Roberts, R. J., Hager, L. D., & Heron, C. (1994). Prefrontal cognitive processes: Working memory and inhibition in the antisaccade task. *Journal of Experimental Psychology: General, 123,* 374–393.

Robinson, G., Blair, J., & Cipolotti, L. (1998). An inability to select between competing verbal responses. *Brain, 121,* 77–89.

Romani, C. (1992). Are there distinct input and output buffers? Evidence from an aphasic patient with an impaired output buffer. *Language and Cognitive Processes, 7,* 131–162.

Romani, C., & Martin, R. (1999). A deficit in the short-term retention of lexical-semantic information: Forgetting words but remembering a story. *Journal of Experimental Psychology: General, 128,* 56–77.

Saffran, E. M., Berndt, R. S., & Schwartz, M. F. (1989). The quantitative analysis of agrammatic production: Procedure and data. *Brain and Language, 37,* 440–479.

Saffran, E. M., & Marin, O. S. M. (1975). Immediate memory for word lists and sentences in a patient with deficient auditory short-term memory. *Brain and Language, 2,* 420–433.

Schwartz, M. F., & Hodgson, C. (2002). A new multiword naming deficit: Evidence and interpretation. *Cognitive Neuropsychology, 19,* 263–288.

Schweickert, R., Guentert, L., & Hersberger, L. (1990). Phonological similarity, pronunciation rate, and memory span. *Psychological Science, 1,* 74–77.

Shallice, T., & Butterworth, B. (1977). Short-term memory impairment and spontaneous speech. *Neuropsychologia, 15,* 729–735.

Shallice, T., Rumiati, R. I., & Zadini, A. (2000). The selective impairment of the phonological output buffer. *Cognitive Neuropsychology, 17,* 517–546.

Smith, M., & Wheeldon, L. R. (1999). High level processing scope in spoken sentence production. *Cognition, 73,* 205–246.

Smith, M., & Wheeldon, L. R. (2004). Horizontal information flow in spoken sentence production. *Journal of Experimental Psychology: Learning, Memory and Cognition, 30,* 675–686.

Stroop, J. R. (1935). Studies of interference in serial verbal reactions. *Journal of Experimental Psychology, 18,* 643–662.

Thompson-Schill, S. L., D'Esposito, M., Aguirre, G. K., & Farah, M. J. (1997). Role of left inferior prefrontal cortex in retrieval of semantic knowledge: A re-evaluation. *PNAS, 94,* 14792–14797.

Trueswell, J., Tanenhaus, M., & Garnsey, S. (1994). Semantic influences on parsing: Use of thematic role information in syntactic ambiguity resolution. *Journal of Memory and Language, 33,* 285–318.

Vallar, G., & Baddeley, A. D. (1984). Fractionation of working memory: Neuropsychological evidence for a phonological short-term store. *Journal of Verbal Learning and Verbal Behavior, 23,* 151–162.

Vallar, G., Di Betta, A. M., & Silveri, M. C. (1997). The phonological short-term store-rehearsal system: Patterns of impairment and neural correlates. *Neuropsychologia, 35,* 795–812.

Vallar, G., & Papagno, C. (1995). Neuropsychological impairments of short-term memory. In A. D. Baddeley, B. Wilson, & F. Watts (Eds.), *Handbook of memory disorders* (pp. 135–165). Chichester, UK: Wiley.

Warrington, E. K., Logue, V., & Pratt, R. T. C. (1971). The anatomical localisation of selective impairment of auditory-verbal short-term memory. *Neuropsychologia, 9,* 377–387.

Wilshire, C. E., & McCarthy, R. A. (2002). Evidence for a context-sensitive word retrieval disorder in a case of nonfluent aphasia. *Cognitive Neuropsychology, 19,* 165–186.

Notes

1   Although the model used by Dell et al. (1997) did not include a separation between input and output phonology, they found that in order to model repetition in addition to naming they had to assume separate links between phonological and lexical nodes on the input and output sides. That is, repetition was better than would have been predicted from the naming results and the implied damage in the lexical to phonological links required to model the naming results. To model repetition, they assumed perfect perception even for patients who showed poor access to phonology on the output side.

2   In fact, these findings call into question the value of hypothesizing something like the episodic buffer (see also Neath and Suprenant (2003) for a general critique of the approach).

3   These intrusions in list recall seem related to perseverative errors that are observed in some aphasic patients. Neither AB nor ML demonstrated perseverative errors in other tasks, such as picture naming, as both were highly accurate. However, recent evidence from patient ML suggests that he may have difficulty in inhibiting previous responses in picture naming, though the effect shows up in latencies rather than errors. Specifically, he shows a great exaggeration of the normal effect of longer picture-naming latencies when pictures are drawn repeatedly from the same semantic category (Crowther, Biegler, & Martin, 2005). This effect could be attributed to the strong persistence of the lexical-semantic representations of previously produced names, resulting in very long times when trying to select the appropriate name from a set of highly activated semantically related competitors.

4   Some neuroimaging evidence is consistent with the notion that operations on both semantic and phonological representations involve the left inferior frontal gyrus—with the more anterior portion being involved in semantic processing and the more posterior portion being involved in phonological processing (Devlin, Matthews, & Rushworth, 2003; Poldrack, Wagner, Prull, Desmond, Glover, & Gabrieli, 1999).

9 The importance of memory and executive function in aphasia: Evidence from the treatment of anomia using errorless and errorful learning

Matthew A. Lambon Ralph and
Joanne K. Fillingham
University of Manchester, UK

Introduction

Neural plasticity, that is, the ability of the brain to change its function, is a current and fundamental issue in neuroscience (e.g., Buonomano & Merzenich, 1998; Tallal, Merzenich, Miller, & Jenkins, 1998). Work at this level of basic science has shown that the mature brain is, in principle, capable of "rewiring" itself so that new functions can be learnt by brain areas that previously performed other processes (Buonomano & Merzenich, 1998). This basic science has been extended to the applied level (e.g., Tallal et al., 1998; Wilson & Evans, 1996). This applied research suggests that a particular form of therapy/remediation programme, known as errorless learning, might have advantages over more traditional trial-and-error methods. The basic premise behind errorless learning is that learning/recovery may be limited by patients' errors in that, not only may they correctly reinforce the link between stimulus and correct responses but they might also reinforce the association with erroneous responses. By adjusting the intervention such that the patients are much less likely to make errors, better learning arises because the patients reinforce only the correct response. In turn, computational neuroscience is beginning to provide a link between clinical application of errorless learning and basic neuroscience. This work has shown that the functioning of neuron-like processing units does not alter if the system reinforces its own errors, but change can follow in circumstances like errorless learning (McClelland, Thomas, McCandliss, & Fiez, 1999).

Errorless learning has a long history. It was first studied and proved effective in the area of animal learning. Under standard procedures, pigeons demonstrate very poor learning of red–green visual discrimination even after repeated exposures. Terrace (1963) found that if an errorless learning method was adopted, pigeons' learning of the same discrimination was very much better. Since then, it has been used as a rehabilitation method in a variety of areas. It has been used as a behaviour-modification technique with children and adults (Brownjohn, 1988; Cipani & Spooner, 1997; Ducharme, 1996; Ducharme, Atkinson, & Poulton, 2000). These methods have been used to teach auditory discrimination skills to children with language-based learning impairments and to children and adults with Down's syndrome (Brownjohn, 1988; Duffy & Wishart, 1987, 1994; McCandliss, Fiez, Protopapas, Conway, & McClelland, 2002; Merzenich, Jenkins, Johnston, Schreiner, Miller, & Tallal, 1996; Tallal et al., 1998). It has been used with people with psychiatric illnesses to teach a variety of tasks, including naming (Kern, 1996; O'Carroll, Russell, Lawrie, & Johnstone, 1999; Wykes, Reeder, Corner, Williams, & Everitt, 1999). The occupational therapy literature reports it as a technique for dyspraxia intervention (Jackson, 1999). More recently, studies have found that errorless training methods are more successful when teaching golf putting to normal adults (Maxwell, Masters, Kerr, & Weedon, 2001).

Baddeley (1992) suggested that errorless learning was a possible principle for the practice of memory rehabilitation, and it is in the domain of amnesia that much of the recent literature has been focused. Wilson and colleagues have studied the use of errorless learning extensively and compared this with errorful methods. With this technique they have taught people with amnesia and memory impairment to do a variety of tasks, including learning names of objects and people, programming an electronic aid, remembering orientation items, and learning items of general knowledge (Baddeley & Wilson, 1994; Clare, Wilson, Breen, & Hodges, 1999; Clare, Wilson, Carter, Breen, Gosses, & Hodges, 2000; Evans et al., 2000; Wilson & Evans, 1996; Wilson, Baddeley, Evans, & Shiel, 1994). Squires, Hunkin, Parkin, and colleagues have also examined errorless and errorful learning. They taught people with amnesia word associations, names of objects and people, and basic commands and procedures associated with use of a word-processing package (Hunkin, Squires, Aldrich, & Parkin, 1998; Hunkin, Squires, Parkin, & Tidy, 1998; Parkin, Hunkin, & Squires, 1998; Squires, Hunkin, & Parkin, 1997).

Wilson and colleagues pioneered the use of errorless learning for the treatment of memory impairment across a range of people (Clare et al., 1999; Wilson et al., 1994). The existing literature provides many demonstrations that amnesic subjects are better able to learn new and relearn old information by errorless techniques. The errorless method has been successfully applied to a variety of learning situations, including relearning proper nouns and object names. These studies can be split into two types: experimental and therapeutic. In the experimental studies, Wilson and colleagues have directly compared errorless and errorful learning. They have asked people with amnesia to learn arbitrary associations (paired associate learning and stem completion) and have found that patients consistently do better if the learning paradigm prevents patients from making errorful responses. For example, Wilson et al. (1994) taught PS, a patient with dense amnesia following a thalamic stroke, the names of fictitious people by errorful and errorless techniques. Ten first names and 10 surnames were trained with each technique. Three successive learning trials were given for each technique followed by nine test trials, spread over a 30-minute period. In the errorful condition, PS was given the first letter of the name and was asked to guess. If, after three guesses, he was still incorrect, the correct name was given, and he was asked to write it down. In the errorless condition, PS was told the first letter, and then the name and was asked to write it down. Wilson et al. (1994) found that in eight of the nine test trials, errorless learning resulted in superior learning. In the therapeutic studies, Wilson and colleagues have extended these experimental findings and have shown that people with amnesia can learn to use memory aids, learn new tasks, or relearn the names of objects or people by the use of errorless learning. For example, Clare et al. (1999) retaught VJ, a man in the early stages of Alzheimer's disease, the names of 11 members of his social club by an errorless technique. The therapy comprised the following elements: learning a mnemonic for each person; completing the name with a step-by-step reduction of the letters provided (vanishing cues); writing the name by filling in the gaps; recalling the mnemonic used; repeating the name; and, finally, recall at short but gradually increasing intervals. The therapy consisted of 21 sessions twice weekly. VJ also practised the same procedure with family members at home three times a day, and he was encouraged to name the members while he was at his social club. VJ was tested on the 11 names after each therapy session. These continual assessments showed that the proportion of faces correctly named increased from 22% at baseline to 98% after training. Additional testing found that this benefit was maintained after 9 months.

If we consider results from beyond the amnesia literature, however, it is clear that errorless learning is advantageous for people other than just those with impaired memory. For a complete account, other aspects of the processes that underpin learning (and relearning) need to be considered. For example, it can be very difficult for adults to learn to perceive certain speech contrasts that their native language does not use. Native Japanese people have persistent difficulty in distinguishing the English liquids [r] and [l]. Even after years of exposure to English, Japanese adults are still markedly poorer at discriminating between these sounds than native English speakers. Recent studies (see below) have been able to remediate these persistent perceptual difficulties by errorless learning. Such demonstrations are important because these participants are entirely neurologically normal, and yet errorless learning can induce plasticity in their mature language system.

McClelland et al. (1999) used a computational model to test the hypothesis that the Japanese adults' poor learning was due to a general learning mechanism that reinforces perceptual categories learnt early in life but prevents new learning. More specifically, Hebbian learning might maintain pre-established perceptual representations even in the face of new experience. McClelland et al. (1999) trained computational, Kohonen networks in English-like and Japanese-like environments. In the English version, the model was trained to discriminate between six different abstract "phonological" representations, including /l/ and /r/. Tokens of these two phonemes were sampled from two similar but somewhat different distributions. The Japanese version was identical except that the distributions of /l/ and /r/ were identical to mirror the fact that there is no distinction between these two phonemes in the real Japanese language. After training, the representational layer of the English model had been structured to reflect six different phonemes, including separate spaces for /l/ and /r/. Unsurprisingly, the representational space in the Japanese model contained only five distinctions with /l/ and /r/ occupying the same part. In the next, critical step, McClelland et al. (1999) switched the Japanese model to the English-like environment in which tokens of /l/ and /r/ were drawn from overlapping but nonidentical distributions. Despite this switch, the model, like Japanese people, failed to learn the /l/–/r/ discrimination. This followed because both /l/ and /r/ inputs were captured by the same, single phonological representation, and this incorrect association was continually reinforced by the Hebbian learning used in this model. Although the model, like Japanese people, appeared to be perpetually stuck, McClelland et al. (1999) were able to demonstrate that plasticity and effective learning were possible, given the right circumstances. Instead of presenting the model with the standard English-like environment, McClelland et al. (1999) included exaggerated tokens of /l/ and /r/, thus increasing the separation of their distributions. In these circumstances, the model no longer collapsed /l/ and /r/ into the same single representation but altered the representational layer to include six separate phonemes. Most importantly, when the model was returned to the English-like environment with overlapping /l/ and /r/ distributions, it was able to accurately discriminate between the two phonemes.

These simulations provide the obvious prediction that the use of exaggerated contrasts might prove effective for human subjects. Previous work suggests that this type of training regime can be useful for children with language-learning impairments (Merzenich et al., 1996; Tallal et al., 1998). McCandliss et al. (2002) conducted an empirical study with Japanese adults in order to test the prediction of the simulations more directly. This study contrasted two important factors: errorless vs. errorful and with feedback vs. without feedback. The errorless condition used an adaptive training method. Japanese subjects began with exaggerated tokens of /l/ and /r/ embedded within a simple word frame (*lock* and *rock*). A staircase method was used to move the tokens gradually toward those found in normal English. Closer tokens of /l/ and /r/ were used once the subject had made eight successive correct discriminations, while more disparate examples were used if the subject made only one error. This asymmetric staircase method provided an "error-reduction" intervention in which errors were deliberately controlled and minimized. In contrast, in the errorful condition, the Japanese subjects were presented with standard tokens of /l/ and /r/ throughout the training sessions. These two training regimes were crossed with the feedback factor. Half the subjects were told whether their discrimination choice was correct while the remainder received no feedback. In the no-feedback condition, the prediction of the computational model was upheld. The adaptive, error-reduction method produced significant improvement in /l/–/r/ discrimination, while the errorful method produced no benefit relative to control. McCandliss et al. (2002) also found that feedback was a critical factor: subjects in the errorful condition who received feedback about their discriminations learned as well as those people in the adaptive, error-reducing condition.

When this study is taken together with those described above, it is clear that there is a wide range of learning situations and of participants/patients for which errorless learning is beneficial. In addition, the McCandliss et al. (2002) study demonstrates that some subjects are able to use feedback to control for the inherent problems associated with learning in an errorful situation. While amnesia may be an important factor when choosing between an errorful or errorless intervention (Baddeley & Wilson, 1994), memory impairments do not provide a complete explanation for the whole literature: there are a range of situations in which neurologically intact subjects benefit from an errorless technique (Maxwell et al., 2001; McCandliss et al., 2002). In addition, there are certain circumstances in which even normal subjects with feedback available still perform better with an errorless method (e.g., when learning a complex motor skill; Maxwell et al., 2001).

Review of previous therapy studies for treating aphasic word-finding difficulties

The amnesia studies raise the possibility that errorless learning might be a technique that could be used to treat aphasic word-finding difficulties (anomia) and, perhaps, a wide variety of acquired language deficits. Studies of children with developmental disorders and normal Japanese adults (McCandliss et al., 2002; Tallal et al., 1998) also indicate that errorless learning methods can be successfully extended from the memory to the language domain. As far as we are aware, the aphasia treatment literature contains no studies that have directly investigated the use of errorless learning. A closer look at the literature, however, highlights a number of studies that are comparable to the errorless method. For example, Morris, Franklin, Ellis, Turner, & Bailey (1996) conducted a study designed to treat word deafness that is analogous to other reports in the errorless learning literature (McCandliss et al., 2002; Tallal et al., 1998). Morris et al.'s (1996) investigation highlights the fact that although the aphasic therapy literature contains no studies that have set out to examine errorless learning specifically, it does include interventions that either reduce or eliminate errors. Given that the amnesia literature contains many examples of therapies aimed at treating word-finding problems, an obvious question is whether errorless techniques might also prove effective for treating anomia in people with aphasia. This would be especially interesting given that word-finding difficulties are perhaps one of the most common and disabling aphasic symptoms (Lambon Ralph, Moriarty, & Sage, 2002).

We undertook, therefore, a review of the anomia treatment literature, starting from the seminal paper by Howard, Patterson, Franklin, Orchard Lisle, and Morton (1985). Studies were categorized into one of three classifications: *error elimination* (patient errors are completely eliminated from the therapy), *error reduction* (the therapy is designed to reduce or minimize patient errors), and *errorful learning* (no control is exerted over patient errors). The relative merits of each approach were considered in terms of three efficacy measures—improvement immediately after therapy, residual benefit after a period of no therapy (follow-up testing), and generalization to untreated items. Studies were then split by aphasia type (fluent vs. nonfluent aphasia), principal impairment (expressive vs. both receptive and expressive aphasia), and therapy method (receptive or expressive therapy) to test for variation in outcome for these important factors.

It is becoming increasingly recognized that cognition is an important factor in determining recovery outcome (Helm-Estabrooks, 2002). Robertson and Murre (1999) argued that not only are age and education determinants of recovery, but there is now evidence that attentional control and level of awareness are also predictors. These cognitive factors may, in turn, reflect the integrity of frontal lobe function. The aphasia and amnesia literatures are such that it is difficult to make comparisons and theoretical predictions about the role of cognitive processes in language recovery/rehabilitation. This is because aphasia studies rarely assess cognition, while language testing is generally very limited, or nonexistent, in investigations of people with amnesia (Hinckley, 2002). As noted above, previous studies of errorless learning suggest that memory and feedback can be important determinants of therapy outcome. It is important, therefore, to assess the more general cognitive abilities of people with aphasia and to relate these to therapy outcomes. It would have been interesting, therefore, to investigate the possibility that concurrent cognitive impairment, e.g. amnesia or executive-attentional deficits, influences the efficacy of errorful and errorless interventions. Unfortunately, too few studies reported sufficient background neuropsychology to be certain about the status of these cognitive systems in people with aphasia.

The review of the anomia treatment literature highlighted a reasonable number of studies that can be classified as error reducing. Although the number of therapies utilizing errorful techniques outweighed those with some form of errorless learning, the rate of success was equivalent for both types of therapy. Although the number of studies prevented formal statistical analysis, the review found evidence to suggest that errorless approaches are just as likely to achieve a positive outcome (in terms of immediate effect, follow-up testing, and generalization). This did not seem to vary if the studies were split by therapy type, principal impairment, or patient type. There were, however, a number of areas where there was very little information. For example, there were very few examples of errorless learning for treating anomia with a receptive technique. Likewise, there was only one study that used an error-reducing approach with a nonfluent patient. It is also notable that many errorless learning studies did not report long-term effects and generalization.

It is not surprising to find that only two therapies used the potentially optimal, error-eliminating approach. This may be because articles did not report error rate, or it may be that, in practice, it is extremely difficult to prevent people from making mistakes. The review showed that error-reducing techniques do have positive effects for people with word-finding difficulties. However, there is limited information on which to judge whether this technique is significantly advantageous over errorful approaches for treating word-finding difficulties—though the review did show that error-reducing techniques are at least as good as the more traditional trial-and-error interventions. In addition, there was very little information about the effects of error-reducing methods on untreated items and whether there was a lasting effect of training because very few studies included the necessary measures (Fillingham, Hodgson, Sage, & Lambon Ralph, 2003).

Novel therapy studies designed to compare errorless and errorful learning directly

Word-finding difficulties are a key and frustrating symptom of Alzheimer's disease that typically follow the initial period of amnesia (Lambon Ralph, Patterson, Graham, Dawson, & Hodges, 2003). Word-finding difficulties are also commonly found in people with aphasia after stroke (Lambon Ralph et al., 2002). A key aim of therapy/intervention is to tackle these word-finding difficulties that otherwise cause frustration, embarrassment, and disability. We wanted to test the efficacy of errorless learning for aphasic word-finding difficulties and to begin to address some of the issues associated with the application and theory of errorless learning in this domain. Knowing which techniques are advantageous for which people would be extremely valuable knowledge for speech and language therapists (Nickels, 2002). We investigated the efficacy of errorless learning for the amelioration of anomia and directly contrasted this technique with errorful learning (trial and error), which is more traditionally used as a rehabilitation technique with people with aphasia. The specific research questions were as follows:

(1) Is errorless learning an effective therapy for anomia in people with aphasia? (Is it better than an equivalent intervention using traditional trial-and-error techniques?)
(2) Does the advantage of errorless learning depend on aphasia severity?

(3) Does the effectiveness of errorless learning depend on neuro-psychological severity?
(4) Does therapy generalize to untreated items?
(5) Does the advantage for errorless learning depend on the ability to use feedback?
(6) Is the positive effect of errorless learning dependent on the number of items in the training set?

To answer these questions, a sequence of three targeted therapy studies was carried out. The three therapy studies were designed to be linked to enable comparisons to be made across them. All participants were asked to complete the same battery of tests so that direct comparisons between participants could be made, and the severity of different underlying impairments could be related to therapy outcome. In order to maintain this link, the same participants were kept, and the core methodology was repeated, with some manipulation to enable specific research questions to be addressed. A case series design was used to facilitate this methodology (Lambon Ralph et al., 2002).

Basic methodology

A case series of people with aphasia with varying anomia severity, underlying cause of word-finding difficulty, and neuropsychological skill was used for each of the three studies. Not all of the participants from study 1 were able to complete studies 2 and 3. Each participant was selected by criteria (see Fillingham, Sage, & Lambon Ralph, 2005a) that allowed a wide variety of aphasia severity to be investigated. The participants' age ranged from 40 to 80 (mean 68), and the year of their cerebral vascular accident ranged from 1987 to 2001 (mean 1997). Each participant undertook a comprehensive battery of neuropsychological and aphasiological assessment. These revealed a phonological impairment in all cases except for SC. Formal assessment with semantic tasks revealed at least some comprehension/semantic problems in many of the cases too (with the exception of ME, HA, and GP). Some patients also had impaired comprehension. Interestingly, all patients were impaired on simple tests of divided attention and varied in their ability on classical tests of executive function (which turned out to be important—see below). The methods used in the previous amnesia and anomia studies informed the nature of the therapies adopted such that they were representative of previous errorless learning techniques and were akin to clinical practice. An unelaborated method was used so that errorless and errorful techniques were directly comparable and efficacy could be judged against the language and neuropsychological measures for the case series of participants. Phonemic and orthographic cues were combined together with the picture so that all modalities were being used. The therapy tasks included sets of pictures that were matched for phoneme length, number of syllables, and frequency, within studies and across studies. In each of the studies, the two forms of intervention were run in a standard therapy procedure. The core methodology remained the same over the course of the three studies; how-ever, there were small changes made. Table 9.1 shows the similarities and differences between the three studies.

Table 9.1 Summary of methodology for the three studies

Study no.	1 (Fillingham et al., 2005a)	2 (Fillingham, Sage, & Lambon Ralph, 2006)	3 (Fillingham, Sage, & Lambon Ralph, 2005b)
Participants	HF, FO, RD, EW, RR, JS, RH, ME, HA, GP, SC	HF, RD, RR, JS, ME, HA, SC	HF, RR, JS, RH, ME, HA, SC
No. items per condition	30	20	20
No. sessions	10	10	10
Method	Consecutively	Concurrently	Concurrently
No. items per session	30	40	40
*Therapy**	EL—read and/or repeat EF—progressive phonological and orthographic cueing	EL—read and/or repeat EF—first phoneme and grapheme cue	EL—read and/or repeat EF—first phoneme and grapheme cue
No. attempts at each item during therapy	90—errorless 120 (potentially)—errorful	30	90
Feedback	Yes	No	No

* EL: errorless learning; EF: errorful learning.

Study 1

In study 1 (Fillingham et al., 2005a), errorless therapy consisted of providing the patient with the picture along with its spoken and written name to ensure the correct response was made. The patient was told, "I am going to ask you to name the picture. First, I will tell you the name. Then I will show you the picture. The name will be written underneath the picture. We will do this three times." In errorful therapy, subjects were asked to name the picture, and if the response was incorrect, they were provided with progressive phonemic and orthographic cueing (Herbert, Best, Hickin, Howard, & Osborne, 2001; Lambon Ralph et al., 2002; Lambon Ralph, Sage, & Roberts, 2000). If the word was monosyllabic, the first phoneme and letter were given initially. If they were still unable to name the item, the first two phonemes and letters were given. If they were still incorrect, the whole word was given to repeat and/or read. If the word was multisyllabic, the first phoneme and letter were given, then the first syllable (spoken and written), and finally the whole word spoken and written (repeat/read). The 30 items were cycled through three times in each therapy session, which lasted 25–40 minutes. In study 1, errorless learning proved to be as effective as the more traditional errorful learning (the raw scores were extremely similar for both methods across all patients: see Figure 9.1). The most striking finding was that language skill did not predict therapy outcome. Nor did any specific aspect of the patients' language profile (e.g., degree of phonological or semantic impairment). Instead, the participants that responded better overall had better recognition memory, executive/problem-solving skills, and monitoring ability. It was concluded that these factors are essential cognitive components for providing effective monitoring and feedback systems to a more general learning mechanism. However, there were two main issues, one methodological and the other theoretical, which could have affected the results. First, the order of therapies was not counterbalanced across the participants. We chose to order the therapies so that the participants were given an initial period of therapy in which no errors occurred (errorless learning therapy was carried out first), to accustom them to this different form of therapy. This means, of course, that there might have been effects of this specific order on the results. Secondly, it was thought that feedback was available to the participants implicitly during errorful therapy (they knew when they had produced the correct answer because they moved onto the next item no matter what stage of the cueing process they were at). In other studies, the feedback reduced the underlying difference between the two, such that errorful learning produced equivalent results to errorless learning (McCandliss et al., 2002).

The aphasia literature contains very little information about the role of feedback. There appears to be no studies that have manipulated the use of feedback, or, if they have, it has not been the focus of such studies (Fink, Brecher, Schwartz, & Robey, 2002). Even discussion of therapy practice gives contradictory advice about the utility of feedback. For example, Schuell's stimulation approach suggests that "Feedback about response accuracy should be provided when such feedback appears beneficial. The necessity for feedback may vary from patient to patient, but it generally is advisable" (Duffy, 1986, p. 150). However, it also argues: "It seems that confirmation of adequate performance may be helpful and encouraging and generally represents good clinical practice. Explanation and correction, on the other hand, should be carefully controlled and concise, bearing in mind that such feedback may be of little value, may waste time, and may be counterproductive" (Duffy, 1986, p. 165). Empirical studies for the role of feedback are clearly required.

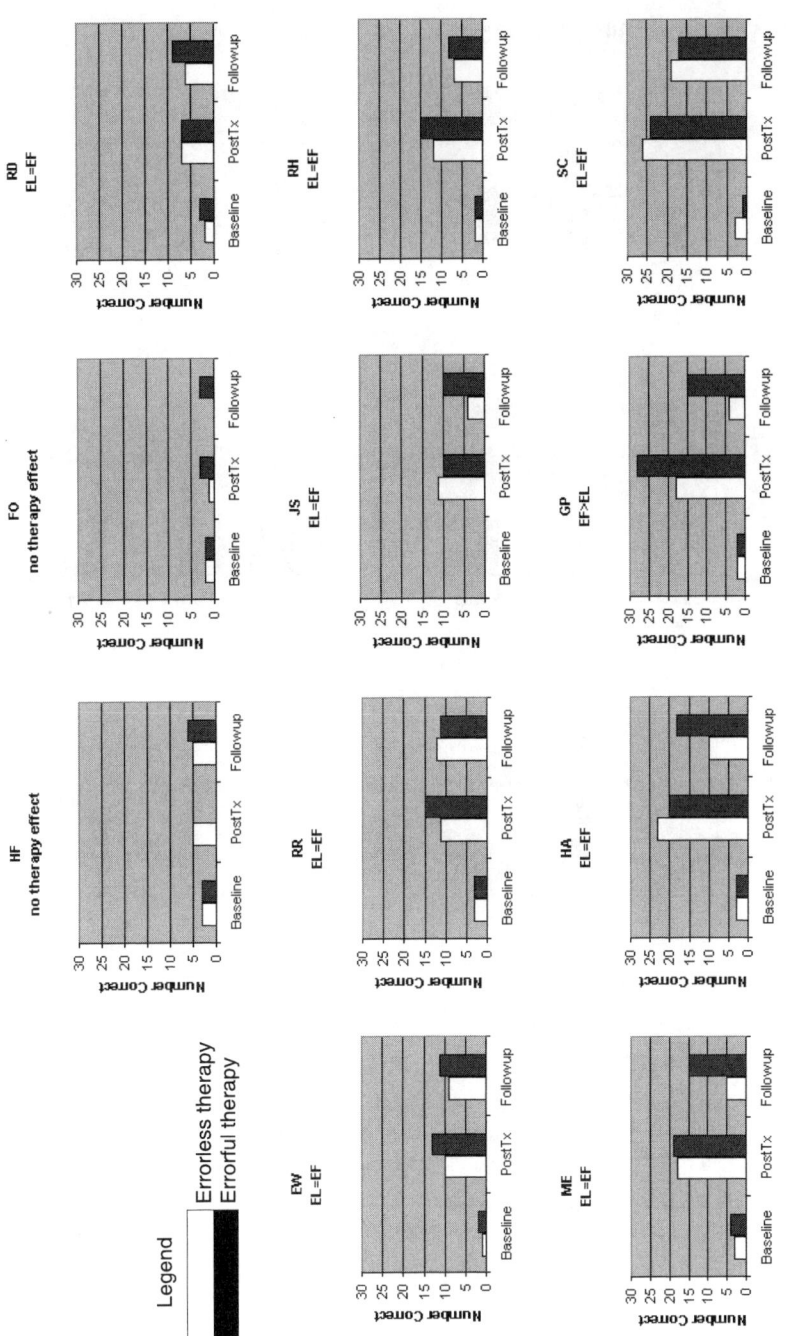

Figure 9.1 Individual patient results from study 1, EL: errorless; EF: errorful.

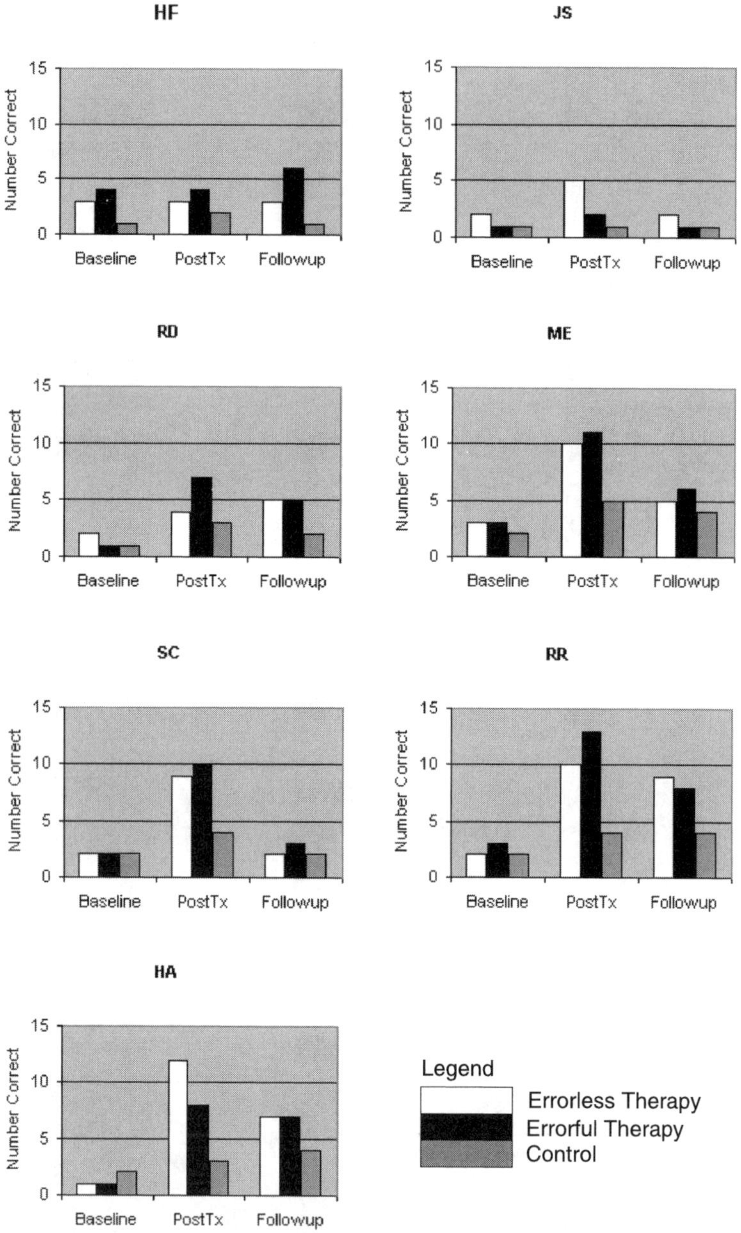

Figure 9.2 Individual patient results from study 2.

Study 2

These potential confounds were addressed in study 2 (Fillingham, Sage, & Lambon Ralph, 2005b). In this investigation, errorless and errorful learning therapies were given simultaneously and feedback was eliminated. Errorless therapy consisted of providing the participant with the picture along with its spoken and written name to ensure the correct response was made. The participant repeated and/or read the name once. In errorful therapy, the participant was given the picture along with the first phoneme and grapheme and asked to name the picture. For both therapies, whether the response was correct or not, no feedback was given, and the next item was attempted. The 20 items were cycled through three times in each therapy session, which lasted 25–40 minutes.

The pattern of results was unchanged; both therapies were equally effective after therapy and at follow-up (Figure 9.2). Therefore, there was no indication that the order adopted in the original study had any particular effect on the results. Again, executive/problem-solving skills and monitoring ability predicted immediate naming improvements, not language skill or specific aspects of the patients' language profile. Surprisingly, there was no effect of omitting feedback on the equivalence of each technique. It is thought that feedback is used to aid learning (Duffy, 1986); however, there are no empirical data for this patient group to support this view. However, in comparing the overall results immediately after treatment against the original study, it was clear that there was a reduction in the overall amount of learning in study 2. There were three methodological changes that could have contributed to this reduction in therapy effectiveness; feedback was omitted, the number of naming attempts per session for each item was reduced, and there was an increase in the number of items for learning in each therapy session.

Study 3

Study 3 (Fillingham, Sage, & Lambon Ralph, 2006) (Figure 9.3) was carried out to replicate the previous findings, that errorless and errorful learning produce equivalent results and executive/problem-solving skills and monitoring ability predict therapy outcome, and to find out what contributed to the reduction in therapy from study 1 to study 2. The methodology from study 2 was replicated with the exception that the number of naming attempts per session was increased to match the number of naming attempts in study 1. Errorless therapy consisted of providing the participant with the picture along with its spoken and written name to ensure the correct response was made. The participant repeated and/or read the name three times. In errorful therapy, the participant was given the picture along with the first phoneme and grapheme and asked to name the picture. This was done three times. For both therapies, whether the response was correct or not,

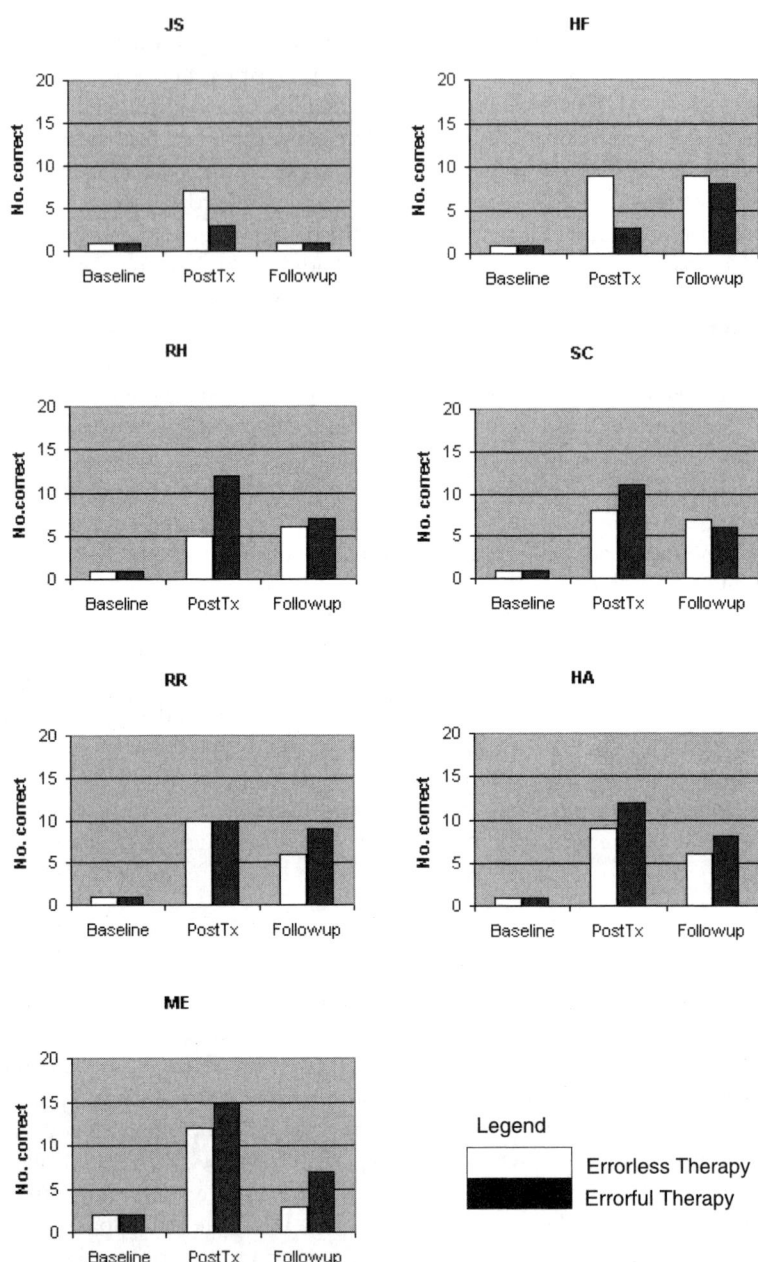

Figure 9.3 Individual patient results from study 3.

no feedback was given and the next item was attempted. The 20 items were cycled through three times in each therapy session, which lasted 30–45 minutes. The results replicated the previous findings that errorless and errorful learning produce equivalent results immediately after treatment and at follow-up. Moreover, executive/problem-solving skills, monitoring ability, and recall memory predict immediate naming improvement, whereas the status of the participants' language skills do not.

When overall learning was compared over the three studies, two important findings emerged: (1) The greater the number of naming attempts at an item during therapy, the greater the success at learning the item; (2) giving or withdrawing feedback made no difference to therapy outcome. Figure 9.4 illustrates overall learning for all participants in each study.

General discussion

These findings pose a puzzle. Why are the two types of therapy equivalent for people with anomic aphasia, yet errorless learning appears to be better for people with memory impairment? The current literature does not contain a direct answer to this question. There are a number of variations between the amnesia studies and the anomia studies. The obvious differences between the two literatures are the diagnosis (aphasia/amnesia) and type of neurological disease (stroke/Alzheimer's disease). Another difference is the type of task. Wilson and colleagues have only ever directly compared the two types of learning in experimental tasks (e.g., stem completion); for therapeutic interventions, they have always used errorless learning alone. There are clear and potentially important differences between these tasks. During experimental studies involving stem completion, the participants are

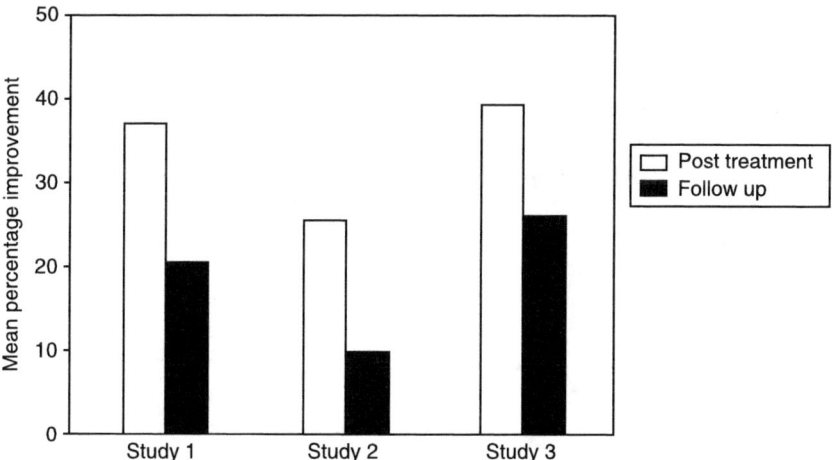

Figure 9.4 The mean percentage improvement for all participants, for each study, immediately after treatment and at follow-up.

required to learn novel associations between fully formed, normal representations—that is, between the stem and a word in the person's existing vocabulary. During therapeutic intervention, the emphasis is on restoring damaged representations. One possibility, therefore, is that errorless learning is beneficial for some types of learning (e.g., novel associations) and not others (e.g., relearning representations). There is need for future research to address these issues by crossing the factors: people with aphasic anomia and people with Alzheimer's disease vs. experimental tasks and therapeutic intervention. Because there are no empirical data to answer such questions, it will be assumed, for now, that experimental tasks and therapeutic tasks are tapping into the same learning/relearning system.

If this is the case, then the overall findings from the amnesia literature indicate that errorless learning produces superior performance to errorful learning. Currently, there are two explanations arising from the literature as to why this may be. The first, proposed initially by Wilson and colleagues, is one of a memory deficit (Baddeley & Wilson, 1994). They proposed that errorless learning was effective as it capitalized on the intact implicit memory skills of people with amnesia. This has been debated by Squires et al. (1997), who argue that errorless learning profits from the residual explicit memory of people with amnesia. The second explanation is one of a source-monitoring difficulty—the patients are unable to determine whether the correct answer was their own self-generated incorrect guess or the experimenter's correction (O'Carroll et al., 1999).

However, errorless learning is advantageous for people other than those with memory impairment. As noted above, a recent study of learning in a normal adult system found that Japanese adults, who find it difficult to learn the distinction between the phonemes /l/ and /r/ even after years of exposure to the English language, could learn the distinction if they were taught by an errorless technique. They also found that if feedback was introduced into the errorful paradigm, the adults would learn the distinction equally well in both errorless and errorful learning. McCandliss et al. (2002) concluded, therefore, that a model based solely on Hebbian learning (like McClelland et al., 1999) required an additional mechanism to capture the positive effects found in the feedback condition. Two possible mechanisms were proposed: Hebbian learning combined with error-correcting learning methods or Hebbian learning modulated by outcome information, as in reinforcement learning. This evidence indicates that memory impairments do not provide a complete explanation for the whole literature, as there are situations in which neurologically intact subjects benefit from an errorless learning technique.

The results from the three case-series studies presented here produced consistent findings. Although the participants varied greatly in the degree and type of aphasia, the two therapies produced equivalent results immediately after treatment, at follow-up, and for generalization. However, if a clinical judgement had to be made about which technique to use, then it was important to take into account the fact that *all* participants reported errorless learning as the preferable technique. Fillingham et al. (2003) noted that errorless learning is inherently monotonous and might suffer from being a passive treatment. Our experience suggests that participants were as likely to engage in the errorless learning therapy as any other. Indeed, the participants strongly preferred errorless treatment, as they found it less frustrating and more rewarding. This is probably because the errorless learning technique removes the need for people with aphasia, with some-times severe expressive difficulties, to provide a spoken name repeatedly through each therapy trial. In this study, the participants were not bored by errorless therapy. There is, however, a danger that it may be inherently tedious for the therapist. If the positive results of errorless learning found here are replicated in future studies, alternative methods such as computer-assisted therapy may prove to be the most effective way to deliver this type of intervention (see Fink et al. (2002) for an example). Another finding was that the outcome of immediate naming improvement can be predicted by the status of the participants' cognitive skills (executive/problem solving, monitoring ability, and memory), not language skills per se. Perhaps the most striking example of the lack of a relationship between language skills and therapy outcome was found in the results of participant JS. He was the most severe aphasic in our series (a global aphasic), yet he was in the middle of the range with respect to the size of his therapy effect. This interim position aligns closely with his performance on the Wisconsin Card Sorting Test (Grant & Berg, 1993)—an assessment that almost per-fectly ranks the participants for therapy outcome (see Fillingham et al., 2005a). This result replicates a finding that has been shown previously for rehabilitation in other neurologically damaged patients, namely, that frontal executive systems are crucial for rehabilitation (Robertson & Murre, 1999). Over the course of the three studies, we also found that a greater number of naming attempts at an item during therapy influenced learning success, while giving or withdrawing feedback makes no difference to therapy outcome.

Toward a complete account and theoretical framework

To devise a complete account, the following findings need to be taken into consideration:

(1) People with amnesia learn better with an errorless technique.
(2) Japanese adults, who are neurologically intact, also learn better with an errorless technique, but they can learn equally well when feedback is given in an errorful situation.
(3) People with aphasia, who have varying degrees of attentional-executive skills, either fail to learn with either technique or, for those that do learn, show an outcome that is equivalent for both techniques.
(4) The outcome of immediate naming improvement, for people with

aphasia, can be predicted by the status of attentional-executive skills and, to a lesser extent, memory.

(5) The number of naming attempts per session influences the outcome of therapy in people with aphasia.

(6) Feedback during an errorless and errorful technique, for people with aphasia, makes no difference to therapy outcome.

In an attempt to unify these various findings, we offer the following simple generic framework (Figure 9.5). The framework represents a single learning system made up of two component elements. The left-hand side (shown in boxes with roman font) represents a simplified information-processing framework in which input is transferred to output according to a series of internal representations. For example, during picture naming, there may be a series of representations involved, including visual, semantics, and phonology, all of which are required to drive speech production from a picture input.

The right-hand side of the model (depicted by lines and circles with italic

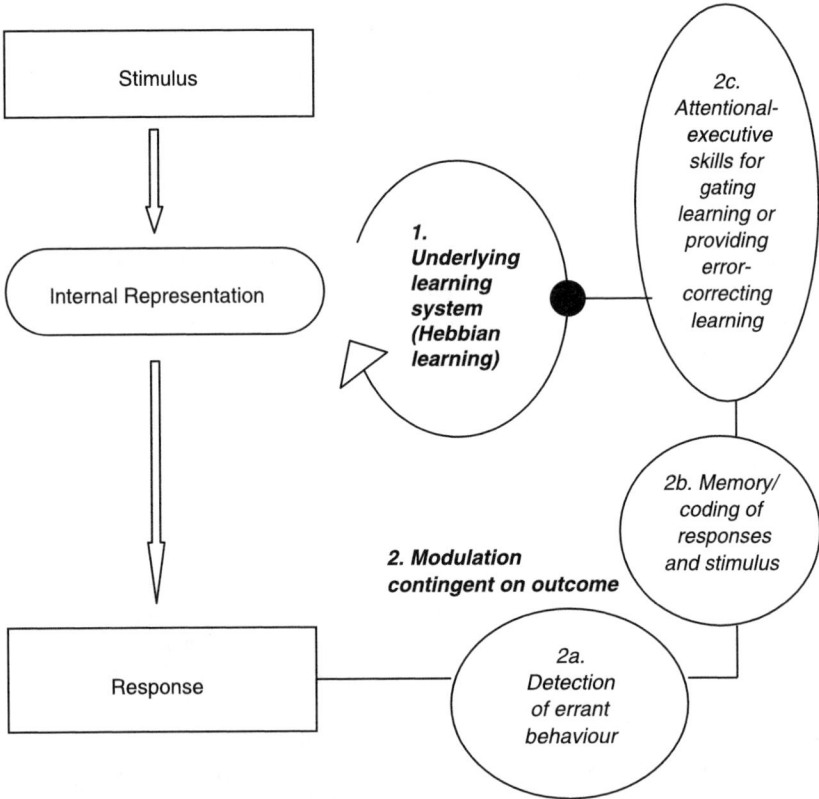

Figure 9.5 A framework for learning in errorless and errorful situations.

font) involves components that adjust these internal representations. The adjustment of representations might be based on a Hebbian learning process (depicted as item 1 on Figure 9.5) that operates at the neural level in much the same way as the computational model of McClelland et al. (1999). This learning system is modulated by outcome (depicted as item 2 on Figure 9.5) through a series of linked components (shown as items 2a, 2b, and 2c on Figure 9.5). If this modulatory process is intact, learning should proceed and be equivalent for errorless and errorful learning. If any one of these components is compromised, then, unless learning stops altogether, errorless learning would be expected to be the superior method because it can rely solely upon Hebbian learning.

Modulation of learning probably requires the following elements. The initial stage is one of detection—that is, is the response correct or incorrect? The first part of this stage may simply be the detection of a difference between intended and observed outcome. If patients are unable to detect that, for example, their erroneous speech is not leading to the desired outcome, there may be no internal impetus for learning. This would seem to explain why patients with very poor attentional-executive skills show the poorest recovery (Robertson & Murre, 1999), and why some of the people with aphasia that we studied did not improve with therapy. If patients can detect that something has gone awry with their response, learning is turned on in an attempt to adjust the internal representations.

For good learning in an errorful situation, the underlying Hebbian process needs to be gated appropriately. For this to happen, the response must be coded and distinguished from any alternatives, and the system must be able to distinguish correct responses from errors so that only the correct form is reinforced. These elements will be reliant on the status of internal representations (to distinguish correct from incorrect responses), memory, and attentional-executive mechanisms. Memory may be a key element in that, for learning to occur, patients may need to encode the stimulus, their response, and any therapist feedback. There are at least two ways that a gating process could operate (see McClelland et al., 1999). The first, much simpler version proposes that when a response is detected as correct, Hebbian learning continues to reinforce this correct stimulus–response pairing. If the response is detected as incorrect, learning is switched off. In this way, the system will gradually move toward an internal representation that is more likely to make a correct response and less likely to make an error. The second possible explanation involves an error-correcting learning mechanism that switches on when a trial leads to an erroneous response but continues with Hebbian learning to reinforce correct responses. These accounts need more investigation. Specifically, there is a need for a detailed computational model of learning to distinguish whether a simple gating system is enough for learning or whether the gating needs a mechanism for correcting errors.

How might this generic framework account for the six key findings listed above?

(1) The findings from the amnesia literature fit with this account in the following way. Unlike some of the participants in this study, the people with amnesia at some level know that they need to learn and/or that they are in a learning situation, so their learning system is switched on. However, their poor memory affects their ability to code and maintain representations for the stimulus and their response (see item 2b on Figure 9.5). In this way, their poor memory skills disable the gating process, so that it is either functioning poorly or is dysfunctional. Consequently, the system is reliant on the basic Hebbian learning system—that is, learning will be better in an errorless situation.

(2) This account also explains why Japanese adults are poor at the auditory discrimination of /l/ and /r/ even after years of exposure to English. Clearly, the Japanese adults know that they are failing, so their learning system is switched on. Their underlying representations for the receptive task cannot distinguish correct and incorrect responses (see item 2b on Figure 9.5); therefore, the system has no basis for detecting errors. So even though they are not amnesic (they may have some memory for the auditory form and their response), they have no basis on which to gate learning. This means that they can use Hebbian learning, but they cannot engage effective modulation, as they do not know when to gate the system—much like the source-monitoring difficulty described by O'Carroll et al. (1999). Therefore, they—like the people with amnesia—benefit from errorless learning, but for a slightly different reason. Their difficulty can be overcome by replacing the gating with external feedback, such that they are able to learn in an errorful situation when they are told whether their response is correct or not.

(3) and (4) The people with aphasia we studied have a damaged internal representation. On the whole, they have intact memory skills but vary in attentional-executive ability. The participants with the poorest attentional-executive skills do not detect that anything is wrong (see item 2a on Figure 9.5) and therefore have no need to switch on their learning system. Consequently, they do not benefit from therapy by either errorless or errorful learning. The more attentional-executive skills people with aphasia have, the more likely they are to be able to realize that something is wrong. They are able to and do switch on their learning system. Given that these people with aphasia have at least a degree of attentional-executive abilities and, on the whole, good memory (see items 2b and 2c on Figure 9.5), they can engage all elements of the gating system, and thus they are able to learn in an errorful situation. This enables learning to occur equivalently in both an errorless and errorful situation.

(5) The account for the influence of the number of naming attempts and

learning is relatively straightforward. Much like frequency effects in normal subjects, the more attempts at an item during learning, the more opportunity there is for the correct stimulus-response to be reinforced.

(6) The influence of experimenter/therapist feedback can be considered within this framework. For the Japanese adults, feedback effectively replaces the internal system(s) that would normally detect and distinguish errors from correct responses. In the people with aphasia, it seems possible that, apart from those participants who do not learn at all, the gating system is relatively intact and the therapist feedback is superfluous.

In conclusion, we believe that the combination of experimental neuropsychology with speech and language therapy provides a very productive partnership. In doing so, we have been able to bring insights from the neuropsychology of amnesia and contemporary findings from neuroscience to bear upon the treatment of a disabling and frustrating symptom of aphasia. In turn, the therapy studies have brought new information and insights not only specifically about the nature of relearning in the language domain but also more generally, about the plasticity of the human brain.

Acknowledgement

This work was supported by the Health Foundation (Award ref. no. 1727/1000).

References

Baddeley, A., & Wilson, B. A. (1994). When implicit learning fails: Amnesia and the problem of error elimination. *Neuropsychologia, 32,* 53–68.

Baddeley, A. D. (1992). Implicit memory and errorless learning: A link between cognitive theory and neuropsychological rehabilitation? In L. R. Squire, & N. Butters (Eds.), *Neuropsychology of memory* (2nd ed.) (pp. 309–314). New York: Guilford Press.

Brown, P., Lupker, S. J., & Colombo, L. (1994). Interacting sources of information in word naming: A study of individual differences. *Journal of Experimental Psychology: Human Perception and Performance, 20,* 537–554.

Brownjohn, M. D. (1988). Acquisition of Makaton symbols by a young man with severe learning difficulties. *Behavioural Psychotherapy, 16,* 85–94.

Buonomano, D. V., & Merzenich, M. M. (1998). Cortical plasticity: From synapses to maps. *Annual Review of Neuroscience, 21,* 149–186.

Cipani, E., & Spooner, F. (1997). Treating problem behaviors maintained by negative reinforcement. *Research in Developmental Disabilities, 18,* 329–342.

Clare, L., Wilson, B. A., Breen, K., & Hodges, J. R. (1999). Errorless learning of face-name associations in early Alzheimer's disease. *Neurocase, 5,* 37–46.

Clare, L., Wilson, B. A., Carter, G., Breen, K., Gosses, A., & Hodges, J. R. (2000). Intervening with everyday memory problems in dementia of Alzheimer type: An errorless learning approach. *Journal of Clinical and Experimental Neuropsychology,* 22, 132–146.

Ducharme, J. M. (1996). Errorless compliance training: Optimizing clinical efficacy. *Behavior Modification, 20,* 259–280.

Ducharme, J. M., Atkinson, L., & Poulton, L. (2000). Success-based, noncoercive treatment of oppositional behavior in children from violent homes. *Journal of the American Academy of Child and Adolescent Psychiatry, 39,* 995–1004.

Duffy, J. R. (1986). Schuell's stimulation approach to rehabilitation. In E. D. Chapey (Ed.), *Language intervention strategies in adult aphasia* (pp. 146–174). Baltimore, MD: Williams and Wilkins.

Duffy, L., & Wishart, J. G. (1987). A comparison of two procedures for teaching discrimination skills to Down's syndrome and non-handicapped children. *British Journal of Educational Psychology, 57,* 265–278.

Duffy, L. A., & Wishart, J. G. (1994). The stability and transferability of errorless learning in children with Down's syndrome. *Down Syndrome: Research and Practice, 2,* 51–58.

Evans, J. J., Wilson, B. A., Schuri, U., Andrade, J., Baddeley, A., Bruna, O., Canavan, T., Della Sala, S., Green, R., Laaksonen, R., Lorenzi, L., & Taussik, I. (2000). A comparison of "errorless" and "trial-and-error" learning methods for teaching individuals with acquired memory deficits. *Neuropsychological Rehabilitation, 10,* 67–101.

Fillingham, J. K., Hodgson, C., Sage, K., & Lambon Ralph, M. A. (2003). The application of errorless learning to aphasic disorders: A review of theory and practice. *Neuropsychological Rehabilitation, 13,* 337–363.

Fillingham, J. K., Sage, K., & Lambon Ralph, M. A. (2005a). Further explorations and an overview of errorless and errorful therapy for anomia: The number of naming attempts during therapy affects outcome. *Aphasiology, 19,* 597–614.

Fillingham, J. K., Sage, K., & Lambon Ralph, M. A. (2005b). The treatment of anomia using errorless learning vs. errorful learning: Are frontal executive skills and feedback important? *International Journal of Language and Communication Disorders, 40,* 505–524.

Fillingham, J. K., Sage, K., & Lambon Ralph, M. A. (2006). The treatment of anomia using errorless learning. *Neuropsychological Rehabilitation, 16,* 129–154.

Fink, R. B., Brecher, A., Schwartz, M. F., & Robey, R. R. (2002). A computer-implemented protocol for treatment of naming disorders: Evaluation of clinician-guided and partially self-guided instruction. *Aphasiology, 16,* 1061–1086.

Grant, D. A., & Berg, E. A. (1993). *Wisconsin Card Sorting Test.* Odessa, FL: Psychological Assessment Resources, Inc.

Helm-Estabrooks, N. (2002). Cognition and aphasia: A discussion and a study. *Journal of Communication Disorders, 35,* 171–186.

Herbert, R., Best, W., Hickin, J., Howard, D., & Osborne, F. (2001). Phonological and orthographic approaches to the treatment of word retrieval in aphasia. *International Journal of Language and Communication Disorders, 36,* 7–12.

Hinckley, J. (2002). Models of language rehabilitation. In P. Eslinger (Ed.), *Neuropsychological interventions: Clinical research and practice* (pp. 182–221). New York: Guilford Press.

Howard, D., Patterson, K., Franklin, S., Orchard Lisle, V., & Morton, J. (1985). Treatment of word retrieval deficits in aphasia—a comparison of 2 therapy methods. *Brain, 108,* 817–829.

Hunkin, N., Squires, E., Parkin, A., & Tidy, J. (1998). Are the benefits of errorless learning dependent on implicit memory? *Neuropsychologia, 36,* 25–36.

Hunkin, N. M., Squires, E. J., Aldrich, F. K., & Parkin, A. J. (1998). Errorless learning and the acquisition of word processing skills. *Neuropsychological Rehabilitation, 8,* 433–449.

Jackson, T. (1999). Dyspraxia: Guidelines for intervention. *British Journal of Occupational Therapy, 62,* 321–326.

Kern, R. (1996). Cognitive rehabilitation of people with mental illness. *Psychiatric Rehabilitation Skills, 1,* 65–73.

Lambon Ralph, M. A., Moriarty, L., & Sage, K. (2002). Anomia is simply a reflection of semantic and phonological impairments: Evidence from a case-series study. *Aphasiology, 16,* 56–82.

Lambon Ralph, M. A., Patterson, K., Graham, N., Dawson, K., & Hodges, J. R. (2003). Homogeneity and heterogeneity in mild cognitive impairment and Alzheimer's disease: A cross-sectional and longitudinal study of 55 cases. *Brain, 126,* 2350–2362.

Lambon Ralph, M. A., Sage, K., & Roberts, J. (2000). Classical anomia: A neuropsychological perspective on speech production. *Neuropsychologia, 38,* 186–202.

Maxwell, J. P., Masters, R. S. W., Kerr, E., & Weedon, E. (2001). The implicit benefit of learning without errors. *Quarterly Journal of Experimental Psychology, 54,* 1049–1068.

McCandliss, B., Fiez, J., Protopapas, A., Conway, M., & McClelland, J. (2002). Success and failure in teaching the /r/–/l/ contrast to Japanese adults: Tests of a Hebbian model of plasticity and stabilization in spoken language perception. *Cognitive, Affective, and Behavioural Neuroscience, 2,* 89–108.

McClelland, J., Thomas, A. G., McCandliss, B., & Fiez, J. (1999). Understanding failures of learning: Hebbian learning, competition for representational space, and some preliminary data. *Progress in Brain Research, 121,* 75–80.

Merzenich, M., Jenkins, W., Johnston, P., Schreiner, C., Miller, S., & Tallal, P. (1996). Temporal processing deficits of language-learning impaired children ameliorated by training. *Science, 271,* 77–84.

Morris, J., Franklin, S., Ellis, A. W., Turner, J. E., & Bailey, P. J. (1996). Remediating a speech perception deficit in an aphasic patient. *Aphasiology, 10,* 137–158.

Nickels, L. (2002). Therapy for naming disorders: Revisiting, revising, and reviewing. *Aphasiology, 16,* 935–979.

O'Carroll, R. E., Russell, H. H., Lawrie, S. M., & Johnstone, E. C. (1999). Errorless learning and the cognitive rehabilitation of memory-impaired schizophrenic patients. *Psychological Medicine, 29,* 105–112.

Parkin, A. J., Hunkin, N. M., & Squires, E. J. (1998). Unlearning John Major: The use of errorless learning in the reacquisition of proper names following herpes simplex encephalitis. *Cognitive Neuropsychology, 15,* 361–375.

Robertson, I. H., & Murre, J. M. J. (1999). Rehabilitation of brain damage: Brain plasticity and principles of guided recovery. *Psychological Bulletin, 125,* 544–575.

Squires, E. J., Hunkin, N. M., & Parkin, A. J. (1997). Errorless learning of novel associations in amnesia. *Neuropsychologia, 35,* 1103–1111.

Tallal, P., Merzenich, M., Miller, S., & Jenkins, W. (1998). Language learning impairments: Integrating basic science, technology, and remediation. *Experimental Brain Research, 123,* 210–219.

Terrace, H. S. (1963). Discrimination learning with and without "errors". *Journal of the Experimental Analysis of Behavior, 6,* 1–27.

Wilson, B., & Evans, J. (1996). Error-free learning in the rehabilitation of people with memory impairments. *Journal of Head Trauma Rehabilitation*, *11*, 54–64.

Wilson, B. A., Baddeley, A., Evans, J., & Shiel, A. (1994). Errorless learning in the rehabilitation of memory impaired people. *Neuropsychological Rehabilitation*, *4*, 307–326.

Wykes, T., Reeder, C., Corner, J., Williams, C., & Everitt, B. (1999). The effects of neurocognitive remediation on executive processing in patients with schizophrenia. *Schizophrenia Bulletin*, *25*, 291–307.

10 The mismatch negativity as an objective tool for studying higher language functions

Friedemann Pulvermüller and
Yury Shtyrov
Medical Research Council, Cognition and Brain Sciences Unit, UK

Introduction

The mismatch negativity (MMN), a well-known index of automatic acoustic change detection, is also a sensitive indicator of long-term memory traces for native language sounds. This may suggest that it is a more general index of the existence of memory traces or neuronal assemblies for learned engrams that play a role in cognitive processing. Here, we review recent work done to test this idea. When comparing MMNs to words and meaningless pseudo-words, we found larger MMN amplitudes for words than for meaningless items, thus indicating the presence of long-term memory networks for the former, a finding now replicated by different groups using different languages. The MMN also shows differences in the brain response to individual words that even reflect aspects of the referential semantics of these words. This suggests that cortical memory networks of individual lexical items can be investigated using the MMN. In other studies, we found evidence that the MMN reflects automatic syntactic processing commencing as early as ~100 ms after relevant information becomes available in the acoustic input. In summary, neurophysiological imaging of the MMN response provides a unique opportunity to see subtle spatiotemporal dynamics of language processing in the human cortex in lexical, semantic, and syntactic domains. The chapter briefly reviews the current state of the art in the neurophysiology of language, provides motivations for studying language function with the MMN, and offers a detailed review of findings which are discussed in the framework of distributed action-perception networks underlying language and other cognitive processes.

The MMN: Change detection and memory trace indicator

Neurophysiological recordings of neuronal mass activity by electroencephalogram (EEG) and magnetoencephalogram (MEG) offer a unique opportunity to monitor the exact spatiotemporal characteristics of cognitive brain processes. In cognitive neuroscience, one of the most revealing neuronal mass responses is the MMN, which is elicited by an infrequent acoustic event, the so-called deviant stimulus, occasionally occurring among frequently repeated sounds, the standard stimuli. When the MMN was discovered (Näätänen, Gaillard, & Mäntysalo, 1978), elementary acoustic events (brief tone pips) were the stimuli, and the rare deviant stimuli differed from the repetitive standard stimuli in pitch or length. In these experiments, the MMN was considered an indicator of acoustic change detection, which, surprisingly, was present regardless of whether subjects focused their attention on the stimuli or not, and it can therefore be considered to be an automatic brain response (Näätänen, Tervaniemi, Sussman, Paavilainen, & Winkler, 2001; Näätänen & Winkler, 1999). More recently, linguistically interesting stimuli were probed, and it emerged that sounds representing typical examples of a phoneme category of a given language elicit an enhanced MMN in speakers of that language. Interestingly, the MMNs to these same sounds were reduced in speakers of languages lacking a phoneme category matching the stimuli (Dehaene-Lambertz, 1997; Näätänen et al., 1997; Winkler et al., 1999b), and it therefore appeared that the phonological MMN adds to the change detection MMN elicited by the sounds per se. These results indicate that, on top of its known role as an automatic index of acoustic change detection, the MMN may reflect the existence of learned neuronal representations or memory traces, conceptualized as large, connected neuron ensembles, for the phonemes of languages one is familiar with (Winkler et al., 1999a). The strong internal connections within the neuron ensemble may provide the basis for corticocortical bottom-up and top-down activation following the presentation of learned acoustic elements, and this provides a tentative explanation for the enhancement of the MMN (Pulvermüller, 2001).

Subsequent research showed that the MMN can indicate processes at other, "higher" levels of language processing as well. Here, we highlight MMN changes with the lexical status of a stimulus, with the grammaticality of a word string, and with the meaning of words used as deviant stimuli. We propose that the MMN is a tool for investigating these higher language processes as they are elicited by spoken language stimuli, regardless of whether subjects attend to them or not. We use the results to draw careful conclusions on the time course of the cortical activation processes that manifest lexical access and selection, syntactic analysis, and semantic access. We also consider the brain loci of these processes as suggested by neurophysiological source localization.

Motivations for investigating brain processes of language with the MMN

Why should we investigate the MMN elicited by speech to study the brain basis of language? Are there not numerous dependent measures for doing this already? Here are our three main answers to this question.

First, the MMN is automatic. This means, once again, that, for eliciting the MMN, it is not necessary that subjects perform an overt task or focus their attention on the stimuli, or on a specific processing aspect of these stimuli. Subjects can even be distracted—for example, they can read a book or watch a silent movie—while the acoustic stimuli are played. In spite of this distraction, the MMN is being elicited. Even heavy distraction is possible, as by having subjects engage in a demanding video game or by streaming their attention away from the stimuli, and still there is an MMN, and sometimes even an unattenuated one (Surakka, Tenhunen-Eskelinen, Hietanen, & Sams, 1998; Woods, Alho, & Algazi, 1992). This makes the MMN a measure that can monitor processes not influenced by the attentional biases and strategies so characteristic of cognitive tasks. For example, in a language task where subjects have to indicate the meaningfulness of phoneme sequences or the grammaticality or intelligibility of word strings, it is likely that different stimulus types put different attentional demands on the cognitive system. Identifying a lexical representation or a syntactic structure for a well-formed stimulus may require less processing resources than searching the lexicon or syntactic rule space to find finally a lexical or syntactic mismatch. Even if no task is used and subjects are allowed to "just listen" to speech stimuli under investigation, it appears natural that different stimuli are approached with different strategies. For example, subjects may spend more effort on finding a match for an unknown pseudo-word than on listening to a familiar word, or they may contemplate grammatical errors in an ungrammatical string and how best to fix them, but prepare for the next trial immediately after a well-formed sentence. This also implies differences in the amount of attention directed to different stimulus types. These differences in task and attentional strategies between stimulus types can have a manifestation in behavioural responses, such as response times or error rates, and can clearly also have a neurophysiological reflection picked up in the brain response—although they are of little relevance to those interested in the language processes necessary for achieving word or sentence comprehension. Here, an automatic brain response such as the MMN can help: It can be recorded while subjects are discouraged from processing stimuli actively; therefore, the danger that different strategies are used to process stimuli of different kinds is minimized. This probability is not zero, but, as we would like to argue, the MMN paradigm with its characteristic distraction from the stimuli is the best possible approach to avoid attentional, task, or strategic biases toward one stimulus type. The first reason for choosing the MMN when studying speech processing is therefore that it can be elicited in the absence of attention directed to the stimuli.

If we say that the MMN response is automatic, we mean that it is present even in the absence of focused attention, in the extreme even in coma (Fischer, Morlet, & Giard, 2000). Some groups have still reported that it can be modulated by attention (e.g. Szymanski, Yund, & Woods, 1999), and some results on the enhancement of the MMN could therefore also relate to modulation of attention. However, as we see MMN enhancement to phonemes and lexical items (see the first and third sections of this chapter) compared with pseudo-phonemes and pseudo-words occurring in the same contexts, it would be a necessary condition for this attentional modulation that a cortical representation of a phoneme or words be accessed in the first place. We suggest that the access to cortical memory networks or cell assemblies implies activation enhancement, which becomes visible at the behavioural and cognitive level, as stimulus-induced attention. This issue is discussed further in the conclusions section of this chapter.

The second reason for using the MMN in the investigation of language processes is its earliness. We know from psycholinguistic behavioural studies that crucial information about incoming words and their context is processed within the first ~200 ms after a critical word can be recognized (Marslen-Wilson, 1973, 1987; Mohr & Pulvermüller, 2002; Rastle, Davis, Marslen-Wilson, & Tyler, 2000). The neurophysiological mass responses most frequently studied in current brain-imaging research on language, however, have peak latencies of 400–600 ms, which raises doubt of whether they are appropriate for exploring the early brain processes crucial for language comprehension. In view of the early effects of spoken words, as documented, for example, in cross-modal priming (Moss, McCormick, & Tyler, 1997; Tyler, Moss, Galpin, & Voice, 2002), where semantic knowledge could be demonstrated to be present well before the end of a spoken word and within 200 ms after the acoustic signal allows for unique word identification, it appears more likely that this information uptake is revealed by a brain response with a short latency of ~200 ms or even less. Therefore, the short latency of the MMN, which peaks at 100–250 ms after the deviant stimulus differs from the standard stimulus (physical divergence point), makes it a potential tool for studying the physiological basis of the early speech-comprehension processes demonstrated by behavioural studies.

The third reason for using the MMN in language research is that it can reveal the brain basis of the processing of individual language stimuli. Why should this be an advantage? In most brain-imaging studies of language, large groups of stimuli are investigated and compared with each other, and the average curves are used to draw generalized conclusions on all language materials falling into a certain category. However, this inference scheme is flawed, because, if averages over large stimulus groups yield a result, as in most neurophysiological and neuroimaging studies, this does not demonstrate that all members of the group contribute equally. Rather, it could be that effects are due to a fraction of the group members, to a few outliers in the extreme. Even more devastating problems are entailed by the fact that words differ in their physical features. For example, the earliest brain responses to long written words may be almost twice as large as those to short ones (see, e.g., Assadollahi & Pulvermüller, 2001), and the vast variability of physical features of spoken words probably leads to even more substantial variation. Controlling for such variation is utterly impossible if large stimulus groups of 50 or more words are under study. The problem that arises is that the variation in physical stimulus features unavoidably leads to variability in the early brain responses, and if these are to reflect the neural basis of the early cognitive processes of language comprehension, this variability acts as noise masking the cognitive potentials and fields. We call this the physical variance problem (for discussion, see Pulvermüller, 1999). An additional specific problem of stimulus group studies of spoken language is that speech unfolds in time, and the psycholinguistic processes of interest follow word onset at variable latencies. However, the neurophysiological brain responses are usually calculated from the onset of the critical word or phrase. This raises problems, since, if lexical, syntactic, or semantic processes are under investigation, the relevant point in time is not the onset of a critical word, but rather the point in time when the word becomes distinct from its lexical competitor environment and can therefore be recognized with certainty, the word-recognition point (Marslen-Wilson, 1987). Now one may argue that, to reveal physiological-linguistic correspondence, one can always relate the average word-recognition point for a stimulus group to the peak latency of the averaged physiological response, as we and others have done in the past (e.g., Pulvermüller, Mohr, & Schleichert, 1999). However, this strategy is still flawed for the following reason: If word recognition points differ between stimuli, word comprehension and the other "higher" syntactic and semantic processes will occur at different points in time for different stimuli. If the brain responses reflecting the higher processes are early and therefore short-lived, this temporal variance reduces or even removes any effect in the average. We call this the psycholinguistic variance problem, and it is clear that, apart from word-recognition latencies, the variability of numerous other psycholinguistic variables could play a role in reducing early brain responses (cf. Pulvermüller, 1999). Considering the physical and psycholinguistic variance problems, it is not surprising that many studies following the "mix and average" strategy could reveal late, long-lasting, and widespread language-related responses, such as the N400 or the P600, but not early, brief, and focal lexical, syntactic, and semantic effects. The only way out is to reduce stimulus variance, and it has therefore been proposed to keep factors known to influence early brain response, such as word length, lexical frequency, and recognition latency, to a minimum in word group studies that aim at documenting early linguistic brain activity (Pulvermüller, 1999). The maximal reduction of such variance can be achieved in studies of single items where all relevant physical and psychophysiological factors have been carefully controlled. This means adopting a strategy with a long tradition in psychoacoustics (Micheyl, Carlyon, Shtyrov, Hauk, Dodson, & Pulvermüller, 2003) when investigating the neurophysiological basis of psycholinguistic processes (Pulvermüller et al., 2001c; Shtyrov, Pulvermüller, Näätänen, & Ilmoniemi, 2003). Demonstrating the physiological basis of a psycholinguistic process for an individual speech stimulus provides an existence proof for such a correspondence. It does not in itself allow for generalized conclusions for all stimuli of the same kind, but replicating results for different individual stimuli can provide a basis for generalized conclusions. The single-item approach to the neurophysiology of spoken language would, as we would like to suggest, avoid some of the shortcomings of the conventional stimulus group approach, especially the physical and psycholinguistic variance problems. We therefore believe that stronger conclusions on early cognitive brain responses can be based on single-item studies than on the stimulus-group approach. At the very least, single-item studies are necessary to complement neurophysiological studies of speech stimulus groups. On the other hand, because, naturally, also the single-item strategy has its limitations—for example, those grounded in the fact that stimuli must be repeated within the experiment—it would be ideal to confirm results from single-item studies by investigations of low-variance stimulus groups.

In a design applying the single-item approach, a single standard item will be presented repeatedly (similar to conventional MMN paradigm) and occasionally replaced by another item. A potential concern inherent to this approach is the known reduction of responses to repetitive stimulus presentation. However, this caveat exists for repetitive standard stimuli and, to a lesser degree, also for the language-specific effects in MMN studies, which are mostly found for rare unexpected deviants. These deviant stimuli are presented much more infrequently than the standard stimuli, but can still be repeated over 100 times within one experiment and will fall outside the scope of short-term memory. The ERP attenuation due to repetition should be compensated for by increasing the number of events over which averages are calculated, to increase signal-to-noise-ratios. And it is equally important to balance critical conditions with regard to the number of repetitions of critical items, so that the repetition factor does not become a confound of between-stimulus differences. In carefully planned experimental designs, repetition effects would therefore be equal for different conditions/test stimuli, and should thus not bias the final results. Still, if repetition effects differ between stimulus groups, this could have an influence on their MMN.

In sum, we propose to use the MMN in neuropsycholinguistic studies of spoken language, because it does not require focused attention (automaticity), has short latency (earliness), and can be used to study individual speech stimuli exactly matched for physical and psycholinguistic features. There are other early neurophysiological brain responses that share these advantages, but are primarily driven by physical stimulus features. In contrast, the MMN's unique role as an index of early cognitive processes ("primitive intelligence"; Näätänen et al., 1978, 2001) suggests exploring its usefulness in the study of "higher" aspects of human language.

Theoretical issues: Functional seriality or parallelism in spoken language processing?

If we conceptualize the speech-perception system in a traditional way, as suggested by many serial and parallel cognitive models, we may envisage the level of phonological analysis to follow the level of acoustic information extraction. "Above" these "basement" and "ground-floor" systems, "higher" levels can be envisaged, one for word, or lexical, processing, which some like to conceptualize as the "look-up" of a lexical item in a "mental lexicon" comprising only word forms, but not their meaning or other word-related information. A second level may exist for semantic information defining the meaning of words and longer utterances by listing their essential semantic features, but not arbitrary memories attached to language elements. Finally, a third level can be envisaged for syntax and the grammatical information linked to words. This "town-house model" of language comprehension is an echo of early psycholinguistic models (Dell, 1986; Fromkin, 1973; Garrett, 1980; MacKay, 1987; Morton, 1969) also resonating in current approaches to speech comprehension and production (Levelt, Roelofs, & Meyer, 1999; Norris, McQueen, & Cutler, 2000). There is some discussion on whether the individual components should be added, omitted, or merged with others (e.g., Caramazza & Miozzo, 1998), or arranged differently (Gaskell & Marslen-Wilson, 2002), but it is clear that these types of information are being processed when words and sentences are to be comprehended. The general question of where in the brain these different information types are processed is still under discussion, in spite of much imaging work done in recent years. For example, the cortical locus of semantics has been discussed controversially, and, although several researchers now attribute semantic information processing to areas in the inferior temporal lobe (Price, 2000; Rogers et al., 2004), there is evidence for a contribution of frontal lobes to semantics as well (Bak, O'Donovan, Xuereb, Boniface, & Hodges, 2001; Hauk, Johnsrude, & Pulvermüller, 2004). The other linguistic processes are probably all localized in the perisylvian cortex and lateralized to the dominant hemisphere.

Psycholinguistic models allow for predictions on the time course of information processing, and for testing these, the slow-imaging methods are not appropriate, but fast, neurophysiological imaging studies, for example, those using EEG and MEG, are necessary. A great debate in psycholinguistics, between models according to which processing of these information types is stepwise, that is, serial or cascaded, so that their access onsets differ substantially in time, and models implying that these processes take place near-simultaneously, can potentially be decided on the basis of neurophysiological data. Physical (20–200-ms latencies; Krumbholz, Patterson, Seither-Preisler, Lammertmann, & Lutkenhoner, 2003; Lutkenhoner, Krumbholz, Lammertmann, Seither-Preisler, Steinstrater, & Patterson, 2003) and phonological (100–200-ms latencies; Obleser, Lahiri, & Eulitz, 2004; Poeppel et al., 1996; van den Brink, Brown, & Hagoort, 2001) processes are reflected in the brain response already before 200 ms after the relevant stimulus information is available. According to the step models, the "higher" processes follow later. The N400 component, which peaks around 400 ms after the onset of a critical visual word (Kutas & Hillyard, 1980), is traditionally considered the main index of semantic processes. This component, or perhaps a slightly earlier peaking subcomponent of it called N350, is also considered to be an index of lexical processing (Holcomb & Neville, 1990; Pylkkanen & Marantz, 2003; Stockall, Stringfellow, & Marantz, 2004). For syntax, an even later component, the P600, has been reported that differentiates between well-formed and grammatically incorrect word strings (Hagoort, Brown, & Groothusen, 1993; Osterhout & Holcomb, 1992), but an early component, the early left anterior negativity (ELAN), peaking at 100–250 ms, has also been found to be associated with grammaticality (Friederici, Pfeifer, & Hahne, 1993; Neville, Nicol, Barss, Forster, & Garrett, 1991). Therefore, the classical neurophysiological studies allow us to label tentatively the different linguistic information types with the putative times (in milliseconds after the respective information is present in the input) of the neurophysiological processes that manifest their access in the brain (Table 10.1). These data appear to support stepwise, serial, or cascaded access to linguistic information types. Phonological and, for written language, orthographic processing seems to precede lexical and semantic access, with a potential serial alignment of the latter two processes as well (Bentin, Mouchetant-Rostaing, Giard, Echallier, & Pernier, 1999). The N350 index of lexical processes seems to peak slightly earlier than the semantic N400. Syntactic processing has at least two temporal loci within this sequence, probably reflecting initial access to syntactic information and grammatical reanalysis, respectively (Friederici, 2002).

Table 10.1 summarizes what is still sometimes declared the mainstream view on the neurophysiology of information access in language recognition. A different picture of the linguistic information-processing sequence arises from neurophysiological studies looking in detail at the early brain responses peaking at 50–250 ms after the critical information is available in the

Table 10.1 Classical ERP components and language processes. Time course of the processing of different linguistic information types according to classical studies of event-related potentials (ERPs). The scalp topographies, typical latencies, and labels are indicated for a selection of components that reflect processing of acoustic, phonological, lexical, semantic, and syntactic information. Latencies are relative to onset of the critical stimuli. The letters N and P in component labels, respectively, indicate negative- or positive-going ERP components

Information type	Topography	Delay (ms)	Component
Syntactic	Left anterior/ Centroparietal	100–250/500–700	ELAN/LAN/P600
Semantic	Centroparietal	300–500	N400
Lexical	Centroparietal	250–500	N350
Phonological	Frontocentral/ Central/ Centroparietal	100–400	N100, N200
Acoustic	Variable	20–200	P20–N100

input. In these studies, lexicality and word frequency effects were seen at 100–250 ms after visual word onset (Assadollahi & Pulvermüller, 2003; Hauk & Pulvermüller, 2004a; Sereno & Rayner, 2003; Sereno, Rayner, & Posner, 1998), shortly after the effect of physical stimulus features. Neurophysiological differences between lexicosyntactic categories, such as content and function words or nouns and verbs, were also seen early (150–250 ms; Preissl, Pulvermüller, Lutzenberger, & Birbaumer, 1995; Pulvermüller, Lutzenberger, & Birbaumer, 1995), as were brain reflections of semantic properties of single words (80–250 ms; Pulvermüller, Assadollahi, & Elbert, 2001a; Pulvermüller, Hummel, & Härle, 2001b; Pulvermüller et al., 1999; Skrandies, 1998; Skrandies & Chiu, 2003). A brain response peaking around 250 ms, called the recognition potential (Rudell, 1992), could also be shown to be sensitive to lexical status (Martin-Loeches, Hinojosa, Gomez-Jarabo, & Rubia, 1999), word frequency (Rudell, 1999), lexical category (Hinojosa et al., 2001), and word semantics (Martin-Loeches, Hinojosa, Fernandez-Frias, & Rubia, 2001). As mentioned in the last paragraph, there is also evidence for early syntactic processing (100–250 ms; Friederici et al., 1993; Neville et al., 1991). These results speak in favour of parallel models postulating near synchronous access to all types of linguistic information in word and sentence comprehension (Marslen-Wilson & Tyler, 1980; Pulvermüller, 2001). Near simultaneous information access would, accordingly, occur at 100–250 ms, the exact point in time probably depending on stimulus and task properties. However, most of these results are based on studies of written language. The lion's share of neurophysiological studies of spoken language is still consistent with stepwise information access. For the reasons mentioned earlier, we consider it necessary to use the MMN to explore properly the neurophysiological side of the time course of linguistic information types in spoken language comprehension.

MMN evidence

Here, we will focus on the time course of higher language processes, that is, on lexical, semantic, and syntactic processing, as they are revealed by the MMN brain response. Separate sections will be devoted to words as units stored in memory or in a "mental" lexicon (lexical processing), to word meaning (semantic processing), and to sentence structure (syntactic processing). A final section will focus on the possible role of attention in the neurophysiological study of language.

Lexical access and selection

When does a spoken word presented in the input activate its lexical entry? The "lexical entry" can be conceptualized as a network of neurons that has formed during learning, which is probably housed in the perisylvian (especially inferior frontal plus superior temporal) cortex and lateralized to the language-dominant hemisphere. For convenience, we can call the connected neuronal network of the lexical entry a word-related cell assembly (Hebb, 1949) or word web (Pulvermüller, 2003). The activation of a strongly connected neuronal set leads to spreading of activity within the feedforward and feedback connections within this set. Due to this feedback and feedforward activation, the amount of overall neuronal activity should therefore be larger when a cell assembly is being activated than in a condition where no such network becomes active.

To investigate properly the distinction between activation of a lexical representation and the failure of such activation, it is necessary to compare physically identical stimuli that nevertheless differ in their lexical status (in being either a word or not). Otherwise, the physical stimulus differences, which are, as we argued above, near impossible to control, will confound what may appear to be a lexicality difference.

We solved this problem by placing the same syllables in contexts where they either completed words or failed to do so and thus terminated meaningless pseudo-words in the testing language. A fully crossed design was applied to control for the influence of context and critical syllables. We used Finnish as the testing language, since this language is one of the few in which long pauses within words can have the linguistic status of a phonological distinctive feature. Geminate stop consonants of Finnish include a pause of 200–250 ms followed by the chirp of the stop sound. In neurophysiological studies, this pause makes it possible to record a prestimulus baseline before the first acoustic signal of the critical syllable is presented. All words under study had their recognition points at 30–40 ms after onset of the critical acoustic signal, that is, after the pause of the geminate stop consonant.

When comparing the neurophysiological responses elicited by the syllable [ka] completing the Finnish word *pakko* ("compulsion") with that elicited by the identical syllable stimulus completing the pseudo-word *takko*, we found a larger MMN in the word context than in the pseudo-word context. A larger MMN in word context than in pseudo-word context was also seen for the syllable [ku], which, in sharp contrast to [ko], forms a word with the syllable [ta] (*takku*: "tangle"), but not [pa]. Note that this design controls not only for physical differences between the critical syllables eliciting the MMN and their preceding context syllables, but also for possible effects of the sequential probabilities with which phonemes follow each other. The results rule out an explanation in terms of bi- or trigram frequencies of the critical phonemes.

The lexical enhancement of the MMN was confirmed by a series of studies performed by our group (Pulvermüller et al., 2001c; Pulvermüller, Shtyrov, Kujala, & Näätänen, 2004; Shtyrov, Pihko, & Pulvermüller, 2005; Shtyrov & Pulvermüller, 2002) and by other colleagues (Endrass, Mohr, & Pulvermüller, 2004; Korpilahti, Krause, Holopainen, & Lang, 2001; Kujala et al., 2002; Pettigrew et al., 2004a, 2004b; Sittiprapaporn, Chindaduangratn, Tervaniemi, & Khotchabhakdi, 2003). Wunderlich and Cone-Wesson did not find larger MMNs to CVC words (e.g., [bæd]) than to CV pseudo-words ([bæ]), but physical stimulus properties were obviously not matched here; the study focused on psychoacoustic issues (Wunderlich & Cone-Wesson, 2001). Jacobsen and colleagues did not replicate the lexical MMN enhancement, although they claim to have matched all relevant factors (Jacobsen, Horvath, Schröger, Lattner, Widmann, & Winkler, 2004). On closer examination, however, it turns out that what they used as their German pseudo-word was, in fact, a word with low lexical frequency ([ʃaːp], an imperative form of the verb *schaben*: "scrape"). Our own studies indicated that the lexical status of the deviant stimulus was relevant for eliciting the MMN, but the lexical status of the standard stimulus did not significantly affect MMN amplitude (Shtyrov & Pulvermüller, 2002). However, others have reported that the event-related brain response evoked by the speech standard stimulus is also affected by its lexical status (Diesch, Biermann, & Luce, 1998; Jacobsen et al., 2004), but it is difficult to decide to what degree physical acoustic differences between standard stimuli contributed to the observed differences between meaningful words and meaningless pseudo-words.

In most studies, we found the lexical enhancement of the MMN around 130–150 ms after stimulus information allowed unique word identification. There was some variation between studies, and, in some cases, a longer-lasting effect persisted up to 250 ms. Later wordness effects were inconsistent between stimuli (Pulvermüller et al., 2004). The main cortical sources of the word-evoked MMN revealed by equivalent current dipole analysis were in the superior temporal cortex, anterior to Heschl's gyrus. Distributed source analysis indicated a spread-out superior temporal source and an additional inferior frontal one peaking shortly after the former ($\Delta t \sim 20$ ms) (see Figure 10.1 [in colour plate section] and Figure 10.2) (Pulvermüller, Shtyrov, & Ilmoniemi, 2003).

There may be a seeming controversy between the conventional MMN as an increased response to unexpected acoustic stimulus, on the one hand, and its enhancement in response to known words, on the other hand. This is resolved by the interpretation of this enhancement as stemming from the activation of long-term memory traces for these words. This activation takes place in addition to any acoustic change-detection MMN, which must be present in any acoustic oddball task, language included. This once again stresses the importance of balancing the experimental design such that the acoustic contrasts do not confound the language-related activity, and this, in our view, is best done by incorporating identical physical contrasts into different linguistic contexts.

On the basis of the above data, we hypothesized that the MMN might include information about the point in time when cortical memory networks for lexical items become active. This leads to the prediction that the point of word recognition in the acoustic signal has a correlate in the MMN. This issue could be approached by using physically different word stimuli with different word-recognition latencies. However, in such a design, physical differences between stimuli would be an unavoidable confound. We therefore

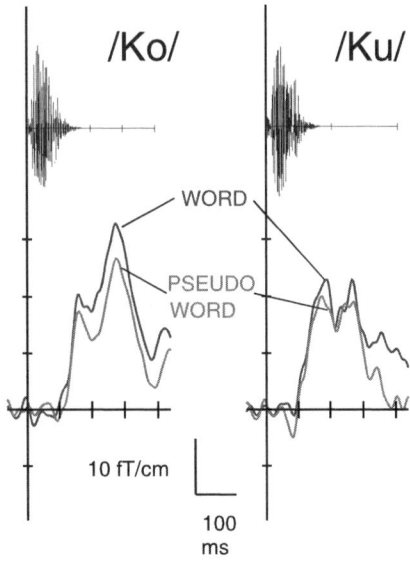

Figure 10.2 The magnetic MMN elicited by a syllable is enhanced in word context relative to pseudo-word context. The syllable (Kim et al., 2002) forms a word together with the preceding syllable [pa], but not with [ta]. Context effects are reversed for [ku], where only preceding [ta] yields a word (Pulvermüller et al., 2001c).

chose to look at stimuli for which speakers showed massive differences in the use of subphonemic coarticulatory cues, so that different subjects identified the same words at different latencies. With this design, it was possible to compare the different time courses of psycholinguistic processes in different speakers while keeping physical stimulus properties constant. In a gating task, word-recognition points were determined for each stimulus word and subject separately, and an acoustic discrimination task was used to examine psychoacoustic processes elicited by the stimuli. In addition, MMNs were recorded to the same stimuli in each subject. The correlation between word-recognition points and peak latencies of the MMN sources in the left superior temporal lobe was significant, therefore suggesting that MMN latency indexes word-recognition processes (Pulvermüller, Shtyrov, Ilmoniemi, & Marslen-Wilson, 2006).

We therefore conclude that MMN amplitude and latency can reveal information about cortical processes of lexical access and selection. The latency at which the lexical selection process becomes manifest neurophysiologically varies slightly between studies but was, in most cases, present around 130–150 ms after the acoustic input allowed identification of the critical word. External validation for early brain indicators of lexical access and selection comes from conventional EEG studies of written word processing (Assadollahi & Pulvermüller, 2001, 2003; Compton, Grossenbacher, Posner,

& Tucker, 1991; Hauk & Pulvermüller, 2004a; Sereno & Rayner, 2003; Sereno et al., 1998) and from studies of intracortical recordings (Halgren, Baudena, Heit, Clarke, Marinkovic, & Clarke, 1994).

Semantic processes

When in the course of spoken language understanding is the specific semantic information tied to a lexical item accessed in the brain, and could the MMN help to reveal this process? Some brain models of language postulate that semantic concepts linked to words are housed in different brain regions (Martin & Chao, 2001; Pulvermüller & Preissl, 1991; Warrington & Shallice, 1984). If correct, this provides a basis for neurophysiological experiments of meaning access, because one could then make specific predictions from aspects of a word's meaning about the brain areas it activates and investigate the time course of this excitation (Pulvermüller, 1996).

We tried this strategy with a pair of words clearly differing in meaning, a concrete, visually well-imageable word (the Finnish word *lakki*: "cap") and a more abstract and less imageable word (*lakko*: "strike, walkout"), hypothesizing that only the concrete imageable word would elicit strong, right-hemispheric brain activity (Pulvermüller, 1996). We controlled for the physical differences between the stimuli by comparing the MMN to the word final syllable to that elicited by a pseudo-word ending in the same syllable. Again, physically identical control stimuli were used and the preceding context syllables were also identical between the two pseudo-words. The words *lakki* and *lakko* were compared with the pseudo-words *vakki* and *vakko*. All stimuli included a pause of 250 ms as part of the "double k".

Source estimates of the lexical MMN enhancement elicited by the two words showed primarily left-lateralized sources for the abstract word and a bilateral, slightly right-lateralized source constellation for the concrete, imageable word, thus supporting the prediction. It is not clear, however, whether word meaning was indeed reflected by the brain response, because the word pair was not matched for standardized lexical frequency. However, assuming that a word-frequency difference cannot explain a rightward shift of word-evoked sources (cf. Assadollahi & Pulvermüller, 2003; Hauk & Pulvermüller, 2004a), the semantic explanation of the observed difference in cortical generators appears plausible. The between-word differences were present already at 100–150 ms, suggesting surprisingly early access to aspects of word semantics. This study also makes it clear that the previous findings of predominantly left-hemispheric (Pulvermüller et al., 2001c) vs. right-hemispheric sources (Kujala et al., 2002) of the lexical MMN are compatible with each other and may be grounded in word-specific differences, possibly in their semantics.

In further studies, we used action words referring to different body parts, such as "pick" and "kick". Referential meaning is an integral part of a word's semantics (Frege, 1980), and these words' regular usage for referring to arm/hand actions or leg/foot actions, respectively, is therefore an essential characteristic of their meaning, although their semantics can certainly not be exhaustively described by these features. If lexical representations become manifest cortically as perisylvian cell assemblies, and the motor actions referred to by these words are laid down in motor areas of the brain, in particular, the premotor and primary motor areas, the semantic links between neuronal sets in these cortical regions should realize the semantic relationship between the word forms and their actions (somatotopy of action word model; Pulvermüller, 2001). Crucially, this leads to the specific prediction that action words with different reference domains in the body also activate the corresponding areas of motor cortex, a claim which receives strong support from conventional neuroimaging studies (Hauk et al., 2004; Hauk & Pulvermüller, 2004b). We used the MMN to determine whether meaning access in word recognition requires focused attention and, if so, when semantic access in spoken action word recognition takes place (Shtyrov, Hauk, & Pulvermüller, 2004).

Two MMN experiments were performed, one using 64-channel EEG and English stimuli ("pick" and "kick") and one using 306-channel MEG and the Finnish words (*hotki* and *potki*: "eat" and "kick"). In both experiments, the classical superior temporal MMN sources were seen at the usual time, at 130–150 ms. Activation elicited by the words referring to face and/or arm movements activated inferior frontocentral areas in the vicinity of the cortical representation of the upper body. Critically, the leg words elicited a stronger superior central source—compatible with leg area activation (Figure 10.3, see colour plate section). This leg-word-specific superior frontocentral activation was seen later than the inferior frontocentral activation predominating for face- and arm-related words. In one of the studies, inferior frontocentral activation was seen 140–150 ms after the word-recognition point, whereas the superior activation focus evoked by leg words was maximal at 170–180 ms ($\Delta t = 30$ ms). These spatiotemporal characteristics suggest that MMN sources in perisylvian areas, along with near simultaneous activation distant from the sylvian fissure, can reflect access to word meaning in the cortex. The minimal delays between area activations may be mediated by cortical conduction delays caused by the travelling of action potentials. The fast, myelinated axons of 0.5–1 mm diameter, which are known to be the most frequent corticocortical axon type and therefore to carry the main burden of long-range communication within the cortex, would cause a delay of ~20 ms for a travelling distance of ~10 cm and can therefore explain the delays measured (see also Figure 10.1, colour plate section).

From these data, we suggest that the processing of semantic features of action words is reflected in the MMN as early as 140–180 ms after acoustic signals allow unique word recognition. Like lexical access and selection, meaning access may therefore be an early brain process occurring within the first 200 ms. The two processes can be conceptualized as near simultaneous. Slightly increased delays seen for the presumably semantically related activations (relative to lexical ones) can, in part, be explained by the larger cortical distances that need to be bridged when the distributed neuronal networks binding word form and meaning are being accessed. External validation for early semantic access in word recognition comes from EEG and MEG studies converging on the result that semantic features of a word are reflected within 200 ms after written word onset (Hauk & Pulvermüller, 2004b; Pulvermüller et al., 1999, 2001a, 2001b; Skrandies, 1998; Skrandies & Chiu, 2003). Our finding of early semantic processes reflecting aspects of word meaning does not devaluate earlier findings about the N400 response as an index of semantics. However, it may be that the early responses reflect initial access to word-specific semantic information, whereas the later responses could index other semantic processes, such as the effort spent in integrating a word's meaning into a meaningful context or the secondary thought processes arising from confrontation with unlikely cognitive links.

Syntactic processes

A conventional way of studying syntactic processing in the brain is to compare the responses with well-formed grammatical sentences to those of ungrammatical strings. We used this strategy in MMN experiments to look at syntactic processing under conditions where subjects were discouraged from attending to language stimuli and directed to focus their attention on other tasks. Would the syntax indicators, such as the early left-anterior negativity and the late positivity at 600 ms, persist under such attentional withdrawal?

We looked at neurophysiological indicators of syntactic agreement, because this grammatical phenomenon has earlier been reported to elicit both early and late neurophysiological grammar indicators (e.g., Deutsch & Bentin, 2001; Gunter, Friederici, & Schriefers, 2000; Hagoort et al., 1993; Münte, Matzke, & Johannes, 1997; Osterhout, McKinnon, Bersick, & Corey, 1996). To control exactly for physical stimulus properties, we once again presented identical, naturally spoken linguistic stimuli in different contexts. In these experiments, the critical word occurred after a context word with which it matched in syntactic features or mismatched syntactically. The context word was a pronoun and the critical word a noun so that subject–noun agreement was the syntactic feature of interest, or agreement between determiner and noun was chosen. To be able to draw generalized conclusions, we again used different methods (EEG and MEG) and languages (Finnish, German, and English). One experiment looked at the neurophysiological difference between the Finnish translation of "I bring" ending in a verb suffix, which agreed with the pronoun in person and number. This grammatical string was compared with the same critical word "bring" plus first person singular suffix placed after the Finnish "you" representing the ungrammatical string. The same contexts were also used for the verb terminating in its second person singular suffix, thus yielding a crossed design orthogonally varying physical and grammatical string properties.

The results showed an increase of the magnetic MMN to words in ungrammatical context compared with the MMNs to the same words in grammatical context. Similar results were also seen for English and German stimuli. The latencies where grammaticality effects were found varied somewhat between studies but generally were present within 200 ms after the word-recognition point, sometimes starting as early as 100 ms (Pulvermüller & Shtyrov, 2003; Shtyrov et al., 2003). The cortical locus where the main sources of the syntactic MMN were localized varied. MEG studies indicated a distributed superior temporal main source and some weak effects in inferior frontal cortex, whereas EEG studies suggested the opposite, a most pronounced grammaticality effect in the inferior frontal cortex. This slight divergence matches well the neuroimaging literature on the cortical basis of syntax, where this module is sometimes localized in frontal areas (e.g., Musso et al., 2003) and sometimes in temporal lobes (e.g., Meyer, Friederici, & von Cramon, 2000). The best way to make sense of this state of affairs seems to us to assume that different areas in the perisylvian cortex contribute to grammatical and syntactic processing.[1]

The early syntactic MMN resembles the ELAN component (Friederici et al., 1993; Neville et al., 1991), which has been interpreted as an index of syntactic structure building (Friederici, 2002). Our results converge on this interpretation and further show that the early syntactic brain response does not require that attention be directed to language stimuli. In this sense, early syntactic processing seems to be automatic. Because the MMN paradigm failed to reveal late grammatically related differences resembling the late positivity characteristic of syntactic violations in experiments where subjects are encouraged to attend to speech stimuli, these results confirm that the late positivity is under strong influence of attention (Hahne & Friederici, 1999). Therefore, the late positivity may reflect second, controlled attempts at parsing a string after initial analysis has failed (Friederici, 2002; Osterhout & Holcomb, 1992).

Varying attentional withdrawal in the study of language

One may argue that demonstrating language-related effects in a paradigm where subjects are instructed to attend to a video film or book while language stimuli are presented does not control strictly for attentional withdrawal. To draw conclusions on the automaticity of the processes investigated from such studies, subjects must strictly follow the instruction to try to ignore the speech stimuli. It would be desirable to control for the attentional withdrawal in each subject throughout the experiment. Therefore, we performed an experiment to investigate further the role of attention in language processing by comparing the classic MMN paradigm with its moderate attentional withdrawal by a silent video film with a distraction task where subjects had to perform continuously an acoustic detection task. Language stimuli were played only through the right ear while acoustic stimuli were delivered to the left ear. In a streaming condition, subjects had to press a button to a "deviant" acoustic stimulus in the left ear while, at the same time, the language stimuli were played to the right ear. The probability of deviants in both streams was equal; more importantly, the target acoustic event in the attended stream was positioned at the point in the same time (end of stimulus) as the contrast of interest in the nonattended linguistic input to maximize the distraction. In the other condition, subjects were allowed to watch a video as usual, without further distraction, while the same stimuli, sounds, and language stimuli were played. Results showed a replication of the grammaticality effect; that is, stronger MMNs to ungrammatical word strings than to ungrammatical ones up to a latency of ~150 ms. There was no difference between task conditions varying attentional withdrawal. Only later, we found significant interactions of the task and attention factors, indicating that at these later stages the grammar processes revealed by the MMN were influenced by attention and task demand. We interpret this as strong evidence for the attention independence of the early part of the MMN and for the automaticity of early syntactic analysis.

Conclusions

The time course of information access in spoken language comprehension

MMN studies on language processes suggest that all types of linguistic information are processed near-simultaneously shortly after incoming acoustic stimuli allow for identification of a critical word. The lexical MMN with its superior temporal and inferior frontal sources was generated in the superior temporal and possibly inferior frontal cortex at 130–150 ms. Correlates of semantic meaning access in action word recognition were seen at 140–180 ms in cortical areas further away from the sylvian fissure. The syntactic MMN was seen in several time windows, starting as early as 100 ms and extending up to above 200 ms. Phonological MMN indicators of vowel processing were also seen in a wider time interval at 150–200 ms (Näätänen et al., 1997), but also at 120–150 ms (Obleser et al., 2004), after stimulus onset. These latencies were extracted from studies with methodological differences, such as different stimulus intensities and using artificially generated or naturally spoken speech. These and other methodological features can influence the latency of the MMN (see, e.g., Tiitinen, May, Reinikainen, & Näätänen, 1994), and it is therefore not feasible to make comparisons in the millisecond range between studies. However, it clearly emerges from MMN research on language that specific neural processes reflecting lexical, syntactic, and semantic processing can be documented within the first 200 ms after auditory information allows recognition of critical lexical items, and that the early processing indicators of different kinds of linguistic information occur near-simultaneously. Potential latency differences documented within studies can be explained on the basis of conduction delays related to corticocortical information transmission. Latencies are even comparable between basic acoustic MMN and the processing of "higher" linguistic information (Shtyrov et al., 2005).

There is an obvious incompatibility between the serial interpretation of linguistic information processing, as put forward on the basis of classical, mainly N400- and P600-based evidence (Table 10.1), and the parallel processing perspective opened by recent MMN studies (Table 10.2). As discussed above, the MMN studies are complemented by work in the visual modality that further establishes early neurophysiological indicators of lexical, semantic, and syntactic processes within 200 ms after stimulus information allows word identification. It may therefore be that these early neurophysiological indicators of lexical, semantic, and syntactic information processing reflect the early access to stored linguistic representations. An MMN would thus indicate the match or mismatch between a stimulus and its corresponding brain circuit or cell assembly. Speech-elicited activity patterns coming in through sensory modalities may activate their matching neuronal circuits even if subjects try to ignore these speech stimuli and focus their attention elsewhere. The early information access and selection reflected by early neurophysiological components, especially the MMN, may be followed by later secondary thought processes that can be triggered by the access to memory representations, but depend on attention and task-related strategies. The late optional processes (latencies >250 ms) may be related to the classical language potentials N400 and P600.

Table 10.2 Time course of language processing according to MMN studies. Latencies and main cortical sources of neurophysiological indicators of acoustic, phonological, lexical, semantic, and syntactic information processing as revealed by the MMN. Latencies are given relative to critical stimulus onset; for "higher" linguistic processes, numbers marked by asterisks indicate latencies relative to the point in time when stimulus information allows unique identification of the critical words

Information type	Cortical sources	Latency (ms)	Example reference
Syntactic	Left inferior frontal and superior temporal	*100–250 130–280	(Pulvermüller & Shtyrov, 2003)
Semantic	Left inferior to superior frontocentral	*140–180 170–210	(Shtyrov et al., 2004)
Lexical	Left inferior frontal and superior temporal	*130–150 160–190	(Pulvermüller et al., 2001c)
Phonological	Left superior temporal	150–200	(Näätänen et al., 1997)
Acoustic	Superior temporal and right frontal	90–170	(Opitz et al., 2002)

The contribution of the frontocentral cortex to language comprehension

What is the specific role of frontal circuits in the early automatic access to linguistic information? What do the frontal activity "blobs" actually tell the cognitive scientist?

One possibility is that they reflect attention; that is, not selective attention as it emerges when subjects prepare for processing a stimulus or making a response, but rather automatic reorientation of attention triggered by a stimulus (Näätänen, 1990). It could therefore be that the occurrence of a meaningful word in the input leads to activation of a cortical cell assembly and therefore to stronger activity than the presentation of a pseudo-word, which, in turn, triggers frontal attention networks more strongly. However, this view would predict similar frontal activation patterns for different types of linguistic information, possibly engaging the same frontal attention system (Posner & Raichle, 1995) to different degrees for different linguistic information types. The topographically distinct patterns of frontal activation seen for different types of linguistic information access remain unexplained by this approach.

An alternative interpretation is offered by brain theories inspired by recent findings about the cortical processing of actions and their corresponding perceptual patterns. Mirror neurons in the inferior frontal lobe (Gallese, Fadiga, Fogassi, & Rizzolatti, 1996; Rizzolatti, Fadiga, Gallese, & Fogassi, 1996), but possibly more widely scattered throughout different parts of the premotor and other areas (Buccino et al., 2001), appear to be a cortical basis of knowledge about actions. These mirror neurons may bind perceptual and action-related information, thus playing a role in both perception and action. This is reminiscent of language theories in the tradition of the motor theory of speech perception claiming that action-related mechanisms play a crucial role in phoneme perception (Liberman & Whalen, 2000). Likewise, a strong linkage within the phonological loop, between articulatory and acoustic phonological components, probably housed in the perisylvian cortex, was postulated to be the basis of short-term verbal memory (Baddeley, 2003). Neurophysiological evidence obtained from monkeys provided direct support for frontotemporal perisylvian neuronal assemblies that bind action-related and perceptual information and form the biological basis of memories kept active in the short term (Fuster, 2003). Distributed perisylvian neuronal assemblies for words binding perceptual information in the superior temporal cortex and articulatory action information in the inferior frontal cortex were first postulated to account for double dissociations and symptom co-occurrence in aphasic syndromes (Pulvermüller & Preissl, 1991). Since these circuits predicted the near simultaneous activation of distant cortical areas in language comprehension (Figure 10.1, colour plate section), and, especially, the different patterns of frontocentral activation elicited by different types of linguistic information (Pulvermüller, 2001), we propose the following interpretation.

Word-related inferior frontal activation, which follows superior temporal activation elicited by spoken words, may index the activation of stored action programs related to word articulation within distributed lexical circuits. Differential activation along the motor and premotor cortex in the fronto-central cortex elicited by action words related to different parts of the body may reflect the specific semantic coupling of word forms and the representations of nonlinguistic actions critical for action words. Inferior frontal activation related to syntactic anomaly may reflect the motor component of circuits for serial alignment and hierarchical or heterarchical structuring of words and morphemes in sentences. In this view, the different frontal fields activated when specific linguistic information types are being processed are related to different types of action programs intimately linked to and therefore contributing to language comprehension.

Summary

We reviewed MMN studies of lexical, semantic, and syntactic processing. These studies suggest that the different "higher" linguistic information types are accessed and processed near simultaneously within 200 ms after stimulus information allows unique identification of the critical meaningful language unit. This time range overlaps with and may be identical to that of the MMN, reflecting phonological and acoustic stimulus features. This evidence, together with other neurophysiological studies of early language-related brain responses, calls into question serial models of language comprehension and weighs in favour of parallel models.

The MMN indicated early linguistic information access that does not require that subjects focus their attention on language or intentionally perform lexical, semantic, or grammar tasks. In this sense, the MMN reflects early automatic processes of lexical access and selection, semantic information processing, and syntactic analysis. The frontal sources of the MMN, whose locus varied with linguistic information type under processing, may indicate the automatic access to action-related information relevant in the language comprehension process at different levels of processing.

Acknowledgements

This research was supported by the MRC and the EU.

References

Assadollahi, R., & Pulvermüller, F. (2001). Neuromagnetic evidence for early access to cognitive representations. *Neuroreport, 12*, 207–213.

Assadollahi, R., & Pulvermüller, F. (2003). Early influences of word length and frequency: A group study using MEG. *Neuroreport, 14*, 1183–1187.

Baddeley, A. (2003). Working memory: Looking back and looking forward. *Nature Reviews Neuroscience, 4*, 829–839.

Bak, T. H., O'Donovan, D. G., Xuereb, J. H., Boniface, S., & Hodges, J. R. (2001). Selective impairment of verb processing associated with pathological changes in Brodmann areas 44 and 45 in the motor neurone disease–dementia–aphasia syndrome. *Brain, 124*, 103–120.

Bentin, S., Mouchetant-Rostaing, Y., Giard, M. H., Echallier, J. F., & Pernier, J. (1999). ERP manifestations of processing printed words at different psycholinguistic levels: Time course and scalp distribution. *Journal of Cognitive Neuroscience, 11*, 235–260.

Buccino, G., Binkofski, F., Fink, G. R., Fadiga, L., Fogassi, L., Gallese, V., Seitz, R. J., Zilles, K., Rizzolatti, G., & Freund, H. J. (2001). Action observation activates premotor and parietal areas in a somatotopic manner: An fMRI study. *European Journal of Neuroscience, 13*, 400–404.

Caramazza, A., & Miozzo, M. (1998). More is not always better: A response to Roelofs, Meyer, & Levelt. *Cognition, 69*, 231–241.

Compton, P. E., Grossenbacher, P., Posner, M. I., & Tucker, D. M. (1991). A cognitive-anatomical approach to attention in lexical access. *Journal of Cognitive Neuroscience, 3*, 304–312.

Dehaene-Lambertz, G. (1997). Electrophysiological correlates of categorical phoneme perception in adults. *Neuroreport, 8*, 919–924.

Dell, G. S. (1986). A spreading-activation theory of retrieval in sentence production. *Psychological Review, 93*, 283–321.

Deutsch, A., & Bentin, S. (2001). Syntactic and semantic factors in processing gender agreement in Hebrew: Evidence from ERPs and eye movements. *Journal of Memory and Language, 45*, 200–224.

Diesch, E., Biermann, S., & Luce, T. (1998). The magnetic mismatch field elicited by words and phonological non-words. *Neuroreport, 9*, 455–460.

Endrass, T., Mohr, B., & Pulvermüller, F. (2004). Enhanced mismatch negativity brain response after binaural word presentation. *European Journal of Neuroscience, 19*, 1653–1660.

Fischer, C., Morlet, D., & Giard, M. (2000). Mismatch negativity and N100 in comatose patients. *Audiology & neuro-otology, 5*, 192–197.

Frege, G. (1980). Über Sinn und Bedeutung (first published in 1892). In G. Patzig (Ed.), *Funktion, Begriff, Bedeutung* (pp. 25–50). Göttingen: Huber.

Friederici, A., Pfeifer, E., & Hahne, A. (1993). Event-related brain potentials during natural speech processing: Effects of semantic, morphological and syntactic violations. *Cognitive Brain Research, 1*, 183–192.

Friederici, A. D. (2002). Towards a neural basis of auditory sentence processing. *Trends in Cognitive Sciences, 6*, 78–84.

Fromkin, V. A. (1973). The non-anomalous nature of anomalous utterances. In V. A. Fromkin (Ed.), *Speech errors as linguistic evidence* (pp. 215–242). The Hague: Mouton.

Fuster, J. M. (2003). *Cortex and mind: Unifying cognition.* Oxford: Oxford University Press.

Gallese, V., Fadiga, L., Fogassi, L., & Rizzolatti, G. (1996). Action recognition in the premotor cortex. *Brain, 119*, 593–609.

Garrett, M. (1980). Levels of processing in sentence production. In Butterworth, B. (Ed.), *Language production I* (pp. 177–220). London: Academic Press.

Gaskell, M. G., & Marslen-Wilson, W. D. (2002). Representation and competition in the perception of spoken words. *Cognitive Psychology, 45*, 220–266.

Gunter, T. C., Friederici, A. D., & Schriefers, H. (2000). Syntactic gender and semantic expectancy: ERPs reveal early autonomy and late interaction. *Journal of Cognitive Neuroscience, 12,* 556–568.

Hagoort, P., Brown, C., & Groothusen, J. (1993). The syntactic positive shift (SPS) as an ERP-measure of syntactic processing. *Language and Cognitive Processes, 8,* 439–483.

Hahne, A., & Friederici, A. D. (1999). Electrophysiological evidence for two steps in syntactic analysis. Early automatic and late controlled processes. *Journal of Cognitive Neuroscience, 11,* 194–205.

Halgren, E., Baudena, P., Heit, G., Clarke, J. M., Marinkovic, K., & Clarke, M. (1994). Spatio-temporal stages in face and word processing. I. Depth-recorded potentials in the human occipital, temporal and parietal lobes [corrected]. *Journal of Physiological Paris, 88,* 1–50.

Hauk, O., Johnsrude, I., & Pulvermüller, F. (2004). Somatotopic representation of action words in the motor and premotor cortex. *Neuron, 41,* 301–307.

Hauk, O., & Pulvermüller, F. (2004a). Effects of word length and frequency on the human event-related potential. *Clinical Neurophysiology, 115,* 1090–1103.

Hauk, O., & Pulvermüller, F. (2004b). Neurophysiological distinction of action words in the fronto-central cortex. *Human Brain Mapping, 21,* 191–201.

Hebb, D. O. (1949). *The organization of behavior. A neuropsychological theory.* New York: Wiley.

Hinojosa, J. A., Martin-Loeches, M., Casado, P., Munoz, F., Carretie, L., Fernandez-Frias, C., & Pozo, M. A. (2001). Semantic processing of open- and closed-class words: an event-related potentials study. *Brain Research: Cognitive Brain Research, 11,* 397–407.

Holcomb, P. J., & Neville, H. J. (1990). Auditory and visual semantic priming in lexical decision: A comparison using event-related brain potentials. *Language and Cognitive Processes, 5,* 281–312.

Jacobsen, T., Horvath, J., Schröger, E., Lattner, S., Widmann, A., & Winkler, I. (2004). Pre-attentive auditory processing of lexicality. *Brain and Language, 88,* 54–67.

Kim, Y. H., Ko, M. H., Parrish, T. B., & Kim, H. G. (2002). Reorganization of cortical language areas in patients with aphasia: A functional MRI study. *Yonsei Medical Journal, 43,* 441–445.

Korpilahti, P., Krause, C. M., Holopainen, I., & Lang, A. H. (2001). Early and late mismatch negativity elicited by words and speech-like stimuli in children. *Brain and Language, 76,* 332–339.

Krumbholz, K., Patterson, R. D., Seither-Preisler, A., Lammertmann, C., & Lutkenhoner, B. (2003). Neuromagnetic evidence for a pitch processing center in Heschl's gyrus. *Cerebral Cortex, 13,* 765–772.

Kujala, A., Alho, K., Valle, S., Sivonen, P., Ilmoniemi, R. J., Alku, P., & Näätänen, R. (2002). Context modulates processing of speech sounds in the right auditory cortex of human subjects. *Neuroscience Letters, 331,* 91–94.

Kutas, M., & Hillyard, S. A. (1980). Reading senseless sentences: Brain potentials reflect semantic incongruity. *Science, 207,* 203–205.

Levelt, W. J. M., Roelofs, A., & Meyer, A. S. (1999). A theory of lexical access in speech production. *Behavioral and Brain Sciences, 22,* 1–75.

Liberman, A. M., & Whalen, D. H. (2000). On the relation of speech to language. *Trends in Cognitive Science, 4,* 187–196.

Lutkenhoner, B., Krumbholz, K., Lammertmann, C., Seither-Preisler, A., Steinstrater, O., & Patterson, R. D. (2003). Localization of primary auditory cortex in humans by magnetoencephalography. *Neuroimage, 18,* 58–66.

MacKay, D. G. (1987). *The organization of perception and action. A theory of language and other cognitive skills.* New York: Springer-Verlag.

Marslen-Wilson, W. (1973). Linguistic structure and speech shadowing at very short latencies. *Nature, 244,* 522–523.

Marslen-Wilson, W. D. (1987). Functional parallelism in spoken word-recognition. *Cognition, 25,* 71–102.

Marslen-Wilson, W. D., & Tyler, L. K. (1980). The temporal structure of spoken language understanding. *Cognition, 8,* 1–71.

Martin, A., & Chao, L. L. (2001). Semantic memory and the brain: Structure and processes. *Current Opinion in Neurobiology, 11,* 194–201.

Martin-Loeches, M., Hinojosa, J. A., Fernandez-Frias, C., & Rubia, F. J. (2001). Functional differences in the semantic processing of concrete and abstract words. *Neuropsychologia, 39,* 1086–1096.

Martin-Loeches, M., Hinojosa, J. A., Gomez-Jarabo, G., & Rubia, F. J. (1999). The recognition potential: An ERP index of lexical access. *Brain and Language, 70,* 364–384.

Meyer, M., Friederici, A. D., & von Cramon, D. Y. (2000). Neurocognition of auditory sentence comprehension: event related fMRI reveals sensitivity to syntactic violations and task demands. *Cognitive Brain Research, 9,* 19–33.

Micheyl, C., Carlyon, R. P., Shtyrov, Y., Hauk, O., Dodson, T., & Pulvermüller, F. (2003). The neurophysiological basis of the auditory continuity illusion: A mismatch negativity study. *Journal of Cognitive Neuroscience, 15,* 747–758.

Mohr, B., & Pulvermüller, F. (2002). Redundancy gains and costs in cognitive processing: Effects of short stimulus onset asynchronies. *Journal of Experimental Psychology: Learning, Memory, and Cognition, 28,* 1200–1223.

Morton, J. (1969). The interaction of information in word recognition. *Psychological Review, 76,* 165–178.

Moss, H. E., McCormick, S. F., & Tyler, L. K. (1997). The time course of activation of semantic information during spoken word recognition. *Language and Cognitive Processes, 12,* 695–731.

Münte, T., Matzke, M., & Johannes, S. (1997). Brain activity associated with syntactic incongruencies in words and pseudo words. *Journal of Cognitive Neuroscience, 9,* 318–329.

Musso, M., Moro, A., Glauche, V., Rijntjes, M., Reichenbach, J., Buchel, C., & Weiller, C. (2003). Broca's area and the language instinct. *Nature Neuroscience, 6,* 774–781.

Näätänen, R. (1990). The role of attention in auditory information processing as revealed by event-related potentials and other brain measures of cognitive function. *Behavioral and Brain Sciences, 13,* 201–288.

Näätänen, R., Gaillard, A. W., & Mäntysalo, S. (1978). Early selective-attention effect on evoked potential reinterpreted. *Acta Psychologica, 42,* 313–329.

Näätänen, R., Lehtokoski, A., Lennes, M., Cheour, M., Huotilainen, M., Iivonen, A., Valnio, A., Alku, P., Ilmoniemi, R. J., Luuk, A., Allik, J., Sinkkonen, J., & Alho, K. (1997). Language-specific phoneme representations revealed by electric and magnetic brain responses. *Nature, 385,* 432–434.

Näätänen, R., Tervaniemi, M., Sussman, E., Paavilainen, P., & Winkler, I. (2001). "Primitive intelligence" in the auditory cortex. *Trends in Neurosciences, 24,* 283–288.

Näätänen, R., & Winkler, I. (1999). The concept of auditory stimulus representation in cognitive neuroscience. *Psychological Bulletin, 12,* 826–859.

Neville, H., Nicol, J. L., Barss, A., Forster, K. I., & Garrett, M. F. (1991). Syntactically based sentence processing classes: Evidence from event-related brain potentials. *Journal of Cognitive Neuroscience, 3*, 151–165.

Norris, D., McQueen, J. M., & Cutler, A. (2000). Merging information in speech recognition: Feedback is never necessary. *Behavioral and Brain Sciences, 23*, 299–370.

Obleser, J., Lahiri, A., & Eulitz, C. (2004). Magnetic brain response mirrors extraction of phonological features from spoken vowels. *Journal of Cognitive Neuroscience, 16*, 31–39.

Opitz, B., Rinne, T., Mecklinger, A., von Cramon, D. Y., & Schroger, E. (2002). Differential contribution of frontal and temporal cortices to auditory change detection: fMRI and ERP results. *Neuroimage, 15*, 167–174.

Osterhout, L., & Holcomb, P. J. (1992). Event-related brain potentials elicited by syntactic anomaly. *Journal of Memory and Language, 31*, 785–806.

Osterhout, L., McKinnon, R., Bersick, M., & Corey, V. (1996). On the language specificity of the brain response to syntactic anomalies: Is the syntactic positive shift a member of the P300 family? *Journal of Cognitive Neuroscience, 8*, 507–526.

Pettigrew, C. M., Murdoch, B. E., Ponton, C. W., Finnigan, S., Alku, P., Kei, J., Sockalingam, R., & Chenery, H. J. (2004a). Automatic auditory processing of English words as indexed by the mismatch negativity, using a multiple deviant paradigm. *Ear and Hearing, 25*, 284–301.

Pettigrew, C. M., Murdoch, B. M., Kei, J., Chenery, H. J., Sockalingam, R., Ponton, C. W., Finnigan, S., & Alku, P. (2004b). Processing of English words with fine acoustic contrasts and simple tones: A mismatch negativity study. *Journal of the American Academy for Audiology, 15*, 47–66.

Poeppel, D., Yellin, E., Phillips, C., Roberts, T. P., Rowley, H. A., Wexler, K., & Marantz, A. (1996). Task-induced asymmetry of the auditory evoked M100 neuromagnetic field elicited by speech sounds. *Brain Research: Cognitive Brain Research, 4*, 231–242.

Posner, M. I., & Raichle, M. E. (1995). Precis of "images of mind". *Behavioral and Brain Sciences, 18*, 327–383.

Preissl, H., Pulvermüller, F., Lutzenberger, W., & Birbaumer, N. (1995). Evoked potentials distinguish nouns from verbs. *Neuroscience Letters, 197*, 81–83.

Price, C. J. (2000). The anatomy of language: Contributions from functional neuroimaging. *Journal of Anatomy, 197* (Pt 3), 335–359.

Pulvermüller, F. (1996). Hebb's concept of cell assemblies and the psychophysiology of word processing. *Psychophysiology, 33*, 317–333.

Pulvermüller, F. (1999). Words in the brain's language. *Behavioral and Brain Sciences, 22*, 253–336.

Pulvermüller, F. (2001). Brain reflections of words and their meaning. *Trends in Cognitive Sciences, 5*, 517–524.

Pulvermüller, F. (2003). *The neuroscience of language*. Cambridge: Cambridge University Press.

Pulvermüller, F., Assadollahi, R., & Elbert, T. (2001a). Neuromagnetic evidence for early semantic access in word recognition. *European Journal of Neuroscience, 13*, 201–205.

Pulvermüller, F., Hummel, F., & Härle, M. (2001b). Walking or talking?: Behavioural and neurophysiological correlates of action verb processing. *Brain and Language, 78*, 143–168.

Pulvermüller, F., Kujala, T., Shtyrov, Y., Simola, J., Tiitinen, H., Alku, P., Alho, K., Martinkauppi, S., Ilmoniemi, R. J., & Näätänen, R. (2001c). Memory traces for words as revealed by the mismatch negativity. *Neuroimage, 14*, 607–616.

Pulvermüller, F., Lutzenberger, W., & Birbaumer, N. (1995). Electrocortical distinction of vocabulary types. *Electroencephalography and Clinical Neurophysiology, 94*, 357–370.

Pulvermüller, F., Mohr, B., & Schleichert, H. (1999). Semantic or lexico-syntactic factors: What determines word-class specific activity in the human brain? *Neuroscience Letters, 275*, 81–84.

Pulvermüller, F., & Preissl, H. (1991). A cell assembly model of language. *Network: Computation in Neural Systems, 2*, 455–468.

Pulvermüller, F., & Shtyrov, Y. (2003). Automatic processing of grammar in the human brain as revealed by the mismatch negativity. *Neuroimage, 20*, 159–172.

Pulvermüller, F., Shtyrov, Y., & Ilmoniemi, R. J. (2003). Spatio-temporal patterns of neural language processing: An MEG study using minimum-norm current estimates. *Neuroimage, 20*, 1020–1025.

Pulvermüller, F., Shtyrov, Y., Ilmoniemi, R. J., & Marslen-Wilson, W. (2006). Tracking speech comprehension in space and time. *Neuroimage, 31*, 1297–1305.

Pulvermüller, F., Shtyrov, Y., Kujala, T., & Näätänen, R. (2004). Word-specific cortical activity as revealed by the mismatch negativity. *Psychophysiology, 41*, 106–112.

Pylkkanen, L., & Marantz, A. (2003). Tracking the time course of word recognition with MEG. *Trends in Cognitive Science, 7*, 187–189.

Rastle, K., Davis, M. H., Marslen-Wilson, W. D., & Tyler, L. K. (2000). Morphological and semantic effects in visual word recognition: A time-course study. *Language and Cognitive Processes, 15*, 507–537.

Rizzolatti, G., Fadiga, L., Gallese, V., & Fogassi, L. (1996). Premotor cortex and the recognition of motor actions. *Cognitive Brain Research, 3*, 131–141.

Rogers, T. T., Lambon Ralph, M. A., Garrard, P., Bozeat, S., McClelland, J. L., Hodges, J. R., & Patterson, K. (2004). Structure and deterioration of semantic memory: a neuropsychological and computational investigation. *Psychological Review, 111*, 205–235.

Rudell, A. P. (1992). Rapid stream stimulation and the recognition potential. *Electroencephalography and Clinical Neurophysiology, 83*, 77–82.

Rudell, A. P. (1999). The recognition potential and the word frequency effect at a high rate of word presentation. *Brain Research: Cognitive Brain Research, 8*, 173–175.

Sereno, S. C., & Rayner, K. (2003). Measuring word recognition in reading: Eye movements and event-related potentials. *Trends in Cognitive Sciences, 7*, 489–493.

Sereno, S. C., Rayner, K., & Posner, M. I. (1998). Establishing a time line for word recognition: Evidence from eye movements and event-related potentials. *NeuroReport, 13*, 2195–2200.

Shtyrov, Y., Hauk, O., & Pulvermüller, F. (2004). Distributed neuronal networks for encoding category-specific semantic information: The mismatch negativity to action words. *European Journal of Neuroscience, 19*, 1083–1092.

Shtyrov, Y., Pihko, E., & Pulvermüller, F. (2005). Determinants of dominance: Is language laterality explained by physical or linguistic features of speech? *Neuroimage, 27*, 37–47.

Shtyrov, Y., & Pulvermüller, F. (2002). Neurophysiological evidence of memory traces for words in the human brain. *Neuroreport, 13*, 521–525.

Shtyrov, Y., Pulvermüller, F., Näätänen, R., & Ilmoniemi, R. J. (2003). Grammar processing outside the focus of attention: An MEG study. *Journal of Cognitive Neuroscience, 15*, 1195–1206.

Sittiprapaporn, W., Chindaduangratn, C., Tervaniemi, M., & Khotchabhakdi, N. (2003). Preattentive processing of lexical tone perception by the human brain as indexed by the mismatch negativity paradigm. *Annals of the New York Academy of Sciences, 999*, 199–203.

Skrandies, W. (1998). Evoked potential correlates of semantic meaning—a brain mapping study. *Cognitive Brain Research, 6*, 173–183.

Skrandies, W., & Chiu, M. J. (2003). Dimensions of affective semantic meaning— behavioural and evoked potential correlates in Chinese subjects. *Neuroscience Letters, 341*, 45–48.

Stockall, L., Stringfellow, A., & Marantz, A. (2004). The precise time course of lexical activation: MEG measurements of the effects of frequency, probability, and density in lexical decision. *Brain and Language, 90*, 88–94.

Surakka, V., Tenhunen-Eskelinen, M., Hietanen, J. K., & Sams, M. (1998). Modulation of human auditory information processing by emotional visual stimuli. *Brain Research: Cognitive Brain Research, 7*, 159–163.

Szymanski, M. D., Yund, E. W., & Woods, D. L. (1999). Phonemes, intensity and attention: differential effects on the mismatch negativity (MMN). *The Journal of the Acoustical Society of America, 106*, 3492–3505.

Tiitinen, H., May, P., Reinikainen, K., & Näätänen, R. (1994). Attentive novelty detection in humans governed by pre-attentive sensory memory. *Nature, 372*, 90–92.

Tyler, L. K., Moss, H., Galpin, A., & Voice, J. K. (2002). Activating meaning in time: The role of imageability and form-class. *Language and Cognitive Processes, 17*, 471–502.

van den Brink, D., Brown, C. M., & Hagoort, P. (2001). Electrophysiological evidence for early contextual influences during spoken-word recognition: N200 versus N400 effects. *Journal of Cognitive Neuroscience, 13*, 967–985.

Warrington, E. K., & Shallice, T. (1984), Category specific semantic impairments. *Brain, 107*, 829–854.

Winkler, I., Kujala, T., Tiitinen, H., Sivonen, P., Alku, P., Lehtokoski, A., Czigler, I., Csepe, V., Ilmoniemi, R. J., & Näätänen, R. (1999a). Brain responses reveal the learning of foreign language phonemes. *Psychophysiology, 36*, 638–642.

Winkler, I., Lehtokoski, A., Alku, P., Vainio, M., Czigler, I., Csepe, V., Aaltonen, O., Raimo, I., Alho, K., Lang, H., Iivonen, A., & Näätänen, R. (1999b). Pre-attentive detection of vowel contrasts utilizes both phonetic and auditory memory representations. *Cognitive Brain Research, 7*, 357–369.

Woods, D. L., Alho, K., & Algazi, A. (1992). Intermodal selective attention. I. Effects on event-related potentials to lateralized auditory and visual stimuli. *Electroencephalography and Clinical Neurophysiology, 82*, 341–355.

Wunderlich, J. L., & Cone-Wesson, B. K. (2001). Effects of stimulus frequency and complexity on the mismatch negativity and other components of the cortical auditory-evoked potential. *Journal of the Acoustic Society of America, 109*, 1526–1537.

Note

1   MEG and EEG are differentially sensitive to different spatial aspects of dipolar electric activity in the cortex (tangentially vs. radially oriented sources), thus providing mutually complementary information. In the most extreme cases such as here, some sources may be visible only with one of the two methods, possibly implying differential geometrical configuration of the sources involved.

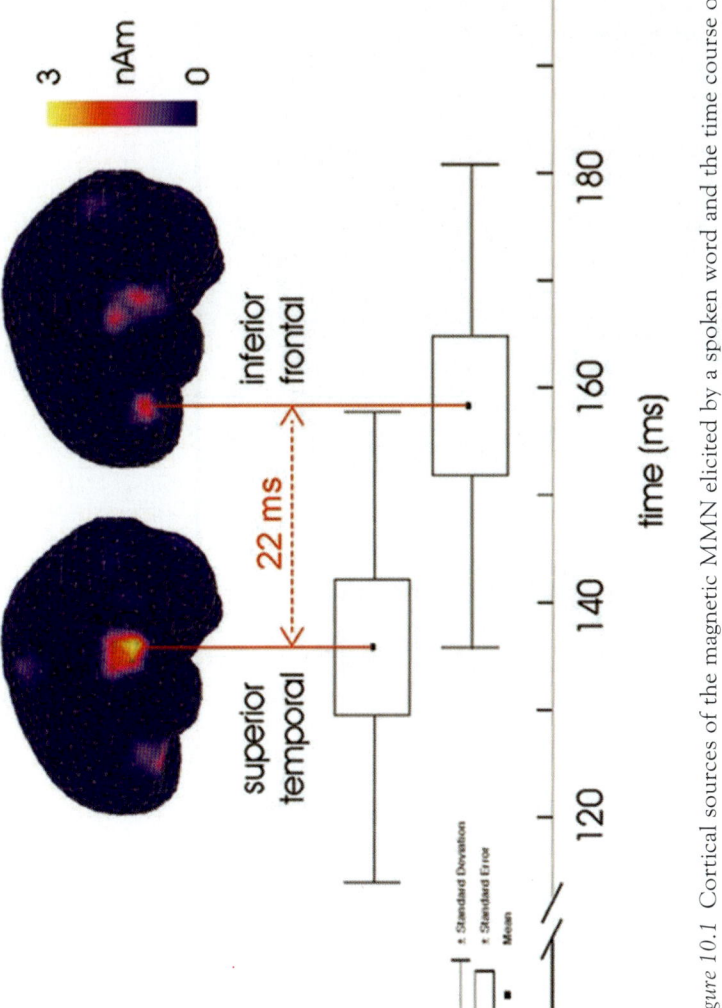

Figure 10.1 Cortical sources of the magnetic MMN elicited by a spoken word and the time course of maximal activation of these sources. Time is given relative to the recognition point of the word presented as the deviant stimulus in a passive oddball paradigm. Note that a superior temporal source peaked at 130–140 ms, closely followed by an inferior frontal source at 150–160 ms. This spatiotemporal pattern of cortical activation may be related to the activation of a word-related neuronal assembly (Pulvermüller et al., 2003).

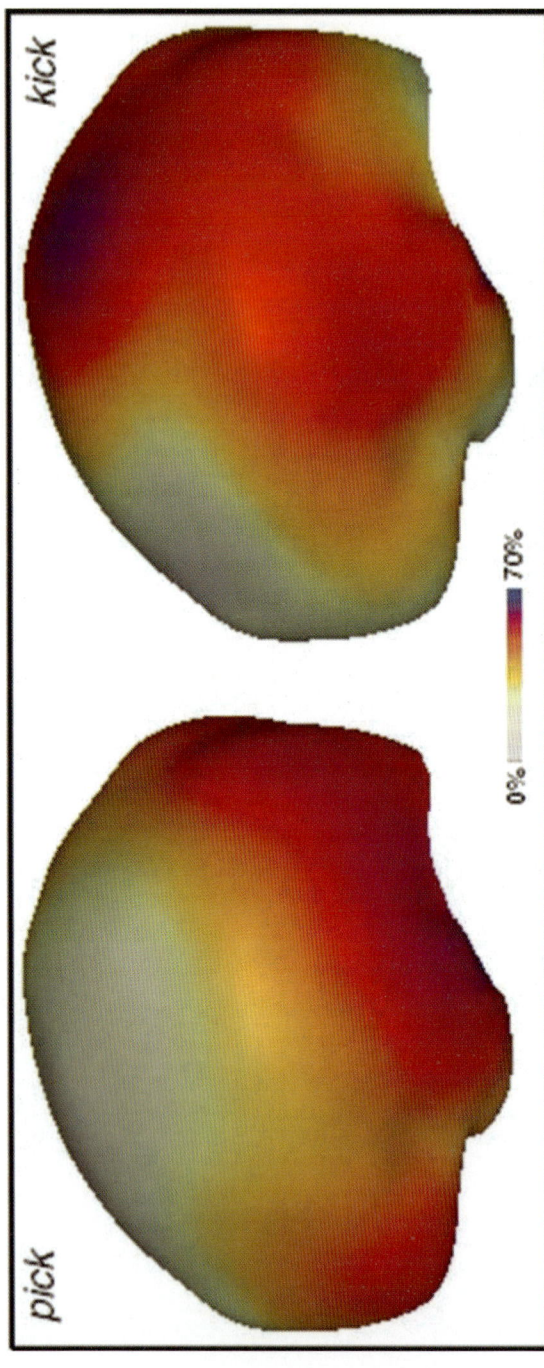

Figure 10.3 Cortical source constellations activated by the action words "pick" and "kick" presented as deviant stimuli in an MMN experiment. Note the difference in the topographies of cortical sources, especially the superior frontocentral activation elicited by the leg word (Shtyrov et al., 2004).

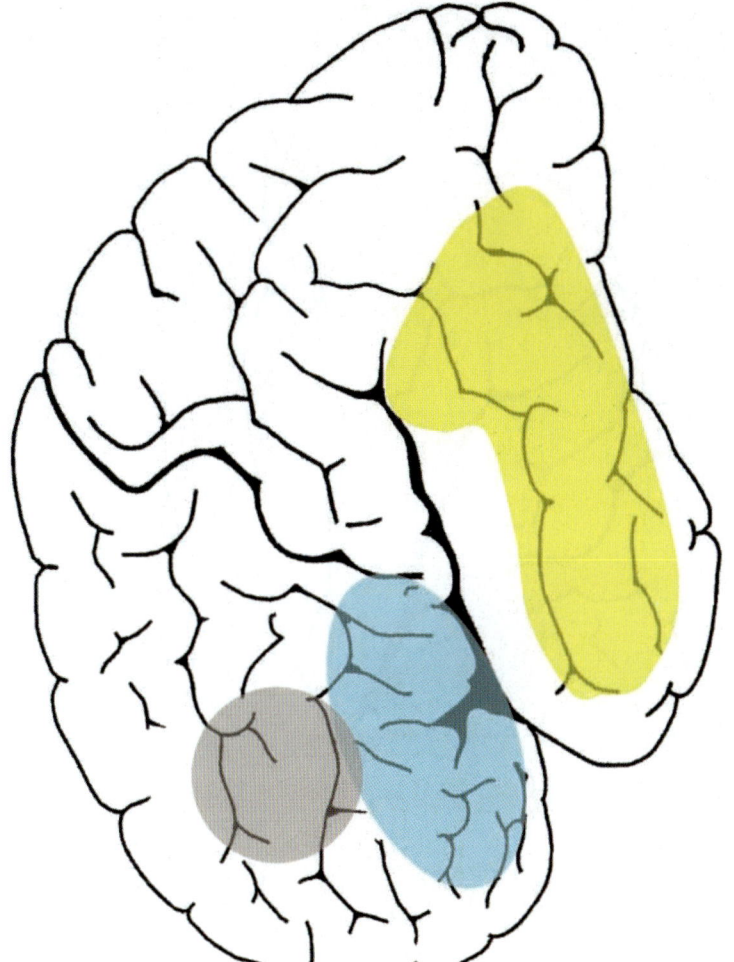

Figure 11.1 The three components of the MUC model projected onto a lateral surface of the left hemisphere: memory (yellow) in the left temporal cortex, unification (blue) in Broca's complex, and control (grey) in the dorsolateral prefrontal cortex. The ACC (part of the control component) is not shown.

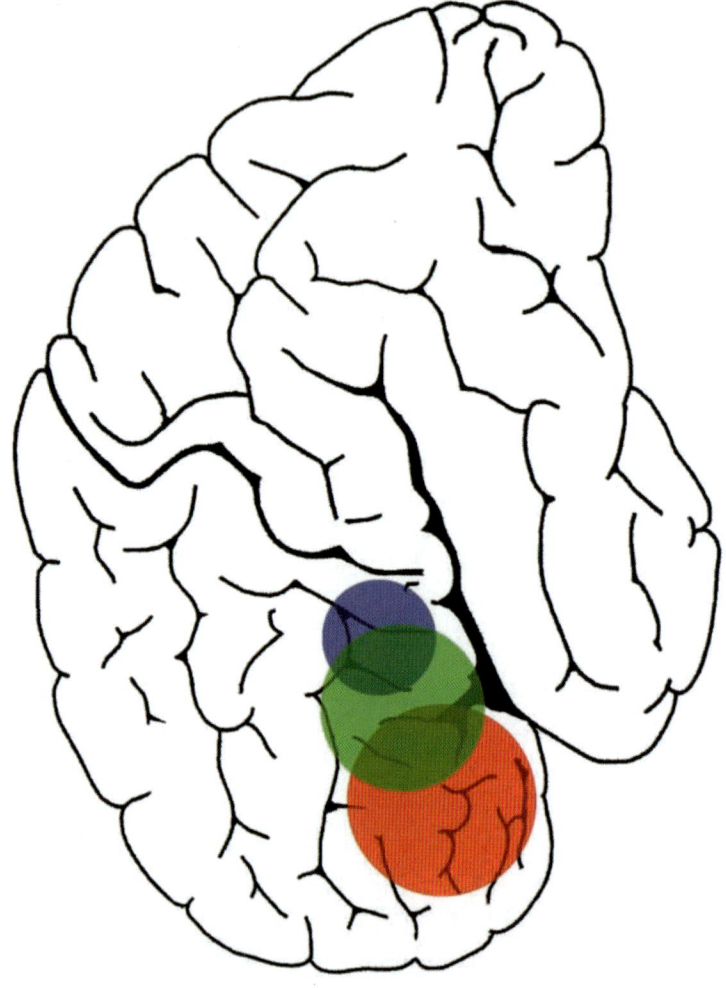

Figure 11.10 The unification gradient in the left inferior frontal cortex. Activations and their distribution are shown, related to semantic (red), syntactic (green), and phonological (blue) processing. Areas are based on the meta-analysis in Bookheimer (2002).

11 The memory, unification, and control (MUC) model of language

Peter Hagoort
Radboud University Nijmegen,
The Netherlands

Models of language processing distinguish between retrieval of information from long-term memory (the mental lexicon) and operations that combine lexical information into larger structures. Memory retrieval and combinatorial operations occur at the levels of meaning, syntax, and phonology. These combinatorial operations result in the unification of the conceptual, syntactic, and phonological building blocks that are retrieved from memory. While the left temporal cortex plays an important role in lexical retrieval, Broca's area and the adjacent cortex seem to be relevant to unification.

The MUC (memory, unification, and control) model provides a framework for a neurobiologically plausible account of language processing. It connects psycholinguistically motivated processing components to their neuronal substrate, guided by knowledge about brain function across domains of cognition. The model distinguishes three functional components of language processing. The memory component comprises a specification of the different types of language information stored in long-term memory, and of their retrieval operations. The unification component refers to the integration of lexically retrieved information into a representation of multiword utterances. The control component relates language to action.

According to the MUC model, the left temporal cortex plays a critical role in storage and retrieval of linguistic information that language acquisition has laid down in memory. This refers to the phonological/phonetic properties of words; their syntactic features such as grammatical gender and word class (verb, noun, etc.), including the syntactic frames; and finally the conceptual specifications of the 60,000 or so words that a native speaker of a language such as English has stored in memory. Activations related to phonological/phonetic properties are reported for the central to posterior superior temporal gyrus (STG) extending into the superior temporal sulcus (STS) (Aleman, Formisano, Koppenhagen, Hagoort, De Haan, & Kahn, 2005; Indefrey & Cutler, 2004; Scott & Johnsrude, 2003).

Semantic information is presumably distributed over a number of brain areas, but most likely different parts of the left middle and inferior temporal gyri may be crucially involved in lexical-semantic processing (Damasio,

Grabowski, Tranel, Hichwa, & Damasio, 1996; Indefrey & Cutler, 2004; Indefrey & Levelt, 2000; Saffran & Sholl, 1999).

Hardly anything is known about the brain areas involved in the lexical retrieval of a word's syntactic specifications. On the basis of the meta-analysis of a large series of imaging studies on syntactic processing (Indefrey, 2004), the hypothesis is that the left posterior superior temporal cortex (Wernicke's area) is involved in the retrieval of lexical-syntactic information.

The memory component thus seems to be distributed mainly over the left temporal cortex. The control component of the model accounts for the fact that the language system operates in the context of communicative goals and actions. For example, attentional control allows individuals to speak while seeing irrelevant objects or hearing interlocutors; to take turns in conversational settings; or, in case of bilingualism, to select the correct language in a particular communicative setting. The issue of verbal control has so far mostly been studied in the context of a Stroop task (Botvinick, Cohen, & Carter, 2004; Bush, Luu, & Posner, 2000; MacLeod & MacDonald, 2000; Roelofs & Hagoort, 2002). These studies suggest that a network of areas consisting of the anterior cingulate cortex (ACC) and the dorsolateral prefrontal cortex (DLPC, BA 46/9) is involved in verbal action planning and attentional control.

Figure 11.1 (see colour plate section) summarizes the network of areas subserving the three central components (memory, unification, and control) of human language in action. The precise effective connectivity between these areas is a topic for further research.

Hereafter I will mainly focus on the processing principles behind unification. First, I will discuss syntactic unification and then semantic unification. In addition, the neural architecture of unification will be discussed.

Syntactic unification

Recent accounts of the human language system (Jackendoff, 1999, 2002; Levelt, 1999) assume a cognitive architecture, which consists of separate processing levels for conceptual/semantic information, orthographic/phonological information, and syntactic information. Based on this architecture, most current models of language processing agree that, in online sentence processing, different types of constraints are very quickly taken into consideration during speaking and listening/reading. Constraints on how words can be structurally combined operate alongside qualitatively distinct constraints on the combination of word meanings, on the grouping of words into phonological phrases, and on their referential binding into a discourse model.

Moreover, in recent linguistic theories, the distinction between lexical items and traditional rules of grammar is vanishing. For instance, Jackendoff (2002) proposes that the only remaining rule of grammar is *unify pieces*, "and all the pieces are stored in a common format that permits unification" (p. 180).

The unification operation clips together lexicalized patterns with one or more variables in it. The operation MERGE in Chomsky's minimalist program (Chomsky, 1995) has a similar flavour. Thus, phonological, syntactic, and semantic/pragmatic constraints determine how lexically available structures are glued together.

In models of language processing, there exists a fairly wide agreement on the types of constraints that are effective during the formulation and the interpretation of sentences and beyond. However, disagreement prevails with respect to exactly how these are implemented in the overall sentence-processing architecture. One of the key issues is when and how the assignment of a syntactic structure to an incoming string of words and the semantic integration of single-word meanings interact during listening/reading. The by now classical view is that, in sentence comprehension, the syntactic analysis is autonomous and initially not influenced by semantic variables (Frazier, 1987). Semantic integration can be influenced by syntactic analysis, but it does not contribute to the initial computation of syntactic structure. An alternative view maintains that lexical-semantic and discourse information can guide or contribute to the syntactic analysis of the utterance. This view is mainly supported by studies showing that the reading of syntactically ambiguous sentences is immediately influenced by lexical or more global semantic information (e.g., Altmann & Steedman, 1988; Trueswell, Tanenhaus, & Garnsey, 1994; Trueswell, Tanenhaus, & Kello, 1993; Tyler & Marslen-Wilson, 1977).

Some of the discrepancies between the different views on this topic are due to the fact that no clear distinction is made between cases where the syntactic constraints are, at least temporarily, indeterminate with respect to the structural assignment (syntactic ambiguity), and cases where these constraints are sufficient to determine the syntactic analysis. In the former case, there is a substantial body of evidence for an immediate influence of non-syntactic context information on the structure that is assigned (Tanenhaus & Trueswell, 1995; Van Berkum, Brown, & Hagoort, 1999a). However, for the latter case, although it has not been studied as intensely, the available evidence seems to provide some support for a certain level of syntactic autonomy (Hagoort, 2003; O'Seaghdha, 1997; but see Ferreira, 2003).

A more recent version of the autonomous syntax view is proposed by Friederici (2002). Based on the time course of different language-relevant event-related brain potentials (ERP) effects, she proposes a three-phase model of sentence comprehension. The first phase is purely syntactic in nature. An initial syntactic structure is formed on the basis of information about the word category (noun, verb, etc.). During phase two, lexical-semantic and morphosyntactic processes take place, which result in thematic role assignments. In the third phase, integration of the different types of information takes place, and the final interpretation results. This proposal is mainly based on findings in ERP studies on language processing. The last decade has seen an increasing number of ERP studies on syntactic processing, triggered by the discovery some 10 years ago of an ERP effect on syntactic violations that was clearly different from the well-known N400 effect on semantic violations (Hagoort, Brown, & Groothusen, 1993; Osterhout & Holcomb, 1992).

These studies have been followed up by a large number of ERP studies on syntactic processing that have provided a wealth of data. Here I will connect the known syntax-related ERP effects to a computational model of parsing (Vosse & Kempen, 2000). This model was developed to account for a large portion of behavioural findings in the parsing literature and for deficit patterns in aphasic patients. In the context of considerations based on brain organization, it makes the right distinction between lexicalized patterns and a unification component. However, before discussing the model, I will first discuss the relevant ERP results, and then present some data that are more compatible with an immediacy model than a syntax-first model. Later in this chapter, I will indicate how the model connects to relevant brain areas for syntactic processing, and to data from lesion studies.

Language-relevant ERP effects

The electrophysiology of language as a domain of study started with the discovery by Kutas and Hillyard (1980) of an ERP component that seemed especially sensitive to semantic manipulations. Kutas and Hillyard observed a negative-going potential with an onset at about 250 ms and a peak around 400 ms (hence the N400), whose amplitude was increased when the semantics of the eliciting word (i.e., *socks*) mismatched with the semantics of the sentence context, as in *He spread his warm bread with socks*. Since 1980, much has been learned about the processing nature of the N400 (for extensive overviews, see Kutas & Van Petten, 1994; Osterhout & Holcomb, 1995). As Hagoort and Brown (1994) and many others have observed, the N400 effect does not depend on a semantic violation. Subtle differences in semantic expectancy, as between *mouth* and *pocket* in the sentence context, "Jenny put the sweet in her *mouth/pocket* after the lesson", can modulate the N400 amplitude (Figure 11.2) (Hagoort & Brown, 1994).

The amplitude of the N400 is most sensitive to the semantic relations between individual words, or between words and their sentence and discourse context. The better the semantic fit between a word and its context, the more reduced the amplitude of the N400. Modulations of the N400 amplitude are generally viewed as directly or indirectly related to the processing costs of integrating the meaning of a word into the overall meaning representation that is built up on the basis of the preceding language input (Brown & Hagoort, 1993; Osterhout & Holcomb, 1992). This holds equally when the preceding language input consists of a single word, a sentence, or a discourse, indicating that semantic unification operations might be similar in word, sentence, and discourse contexts (Van Berkum, Brown, & Hagoort, 1999b). In addition, recent evidence indicates that sentence verification against world

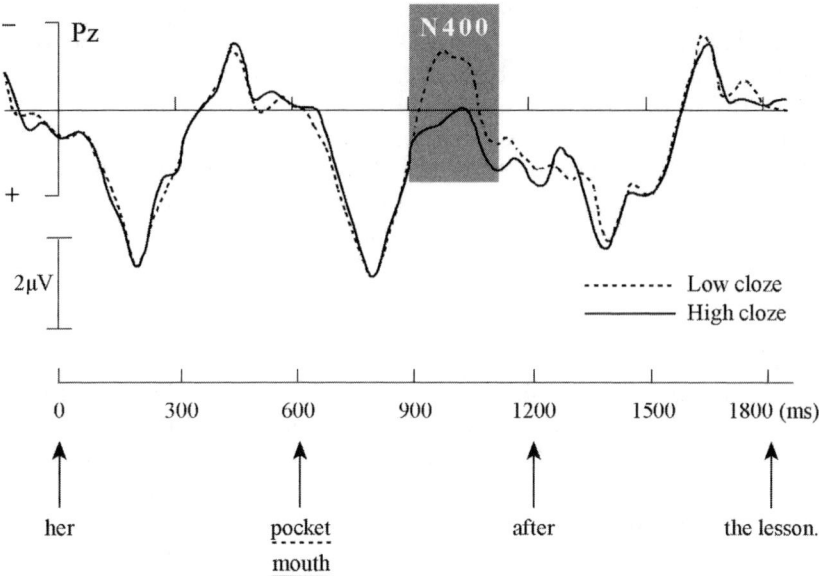

Figure 11.2 Modulation of the N400 amplitude as a result of a manipulation of the semantic fit between a lexical item and its sentence context. The grand-average waveform is shown for electrode site Pz (parietal midline), for the best-fitting word (high cloze; solid line), and for a word that is less expected in the given sentence context (low cloze; dashed line). The sentences were visually presented word by word, every 600 ms. In the figure, the critical words are preceded and followed by one word. The critical word is presented at 600 ms on the time axis. Negativity is up. (Adapted from Hagoort and Brown (1994). Copyright © 1994 Erlbaum, reprinted by permission).

knowledge in long-term memory modulates the N400 in the same way (Hagoort, Hald, Bastiaansen, & Petersson, 2004).

In recent years, a number of ERP studies have been devoted to establishing ERP effects that can be related to the processing of syntactic information. These studies have found ERP effects to syntactic processing that are qualitatively different from the N400. Even though the generators of these effects are not yet well determined and not necessarily language-specific (Osterhout & Hagoort, 1999), the existence of qualitatively distinct ERP effects to semantic and syntactic processing indicates that the brain honours the distinction between semantic and syntactic unification operations. Thus, the finding of qualitatively distinct ERP effects for semantic and syntactic processing operations supports the claim that these two levels of language processing are domain specific. However, domain specificity should not be confused with modularity (Fodor, 1983). The modularity thesis makes the much stronger claim that domain-specific levels of processing operate autonomously without interaction (informational encapsulation). Although domain specificity is widely assumed in models of language processing, there is much less agreement about the organization of the cross-talk between different levels of sentence processing (cf. Boland & Cutler, 1996).

ERP studies on syntactic processing have reported a number of ERP effects related to syntax (for an overview, see Hagoort, Brown, & Osterhout, 1999). The two most salient syntax-related effects are an anterior negativity, also referred to as LAN, and a more posterior positivity, here referred to as P600/SPS.

LAN

A number of studies have reported negativities that are different from the N400, in that they usually show a more frontal maximum (but see Münte, Matzke, & Johannes, 1997), and are sometimes larger over the left than the right hemisphere, although in many cases the distribution is bilateral (Hagoort, Wassenaar, & Brown, 2003). Moreover, the conditions that elicit these frontal negative shifts seem to be more strongly related to syntactic processing than to semantic integration. Usually, LAN effects occur within the same latency range as the N400, that is, at 300–500 ms after a stimulus (Friederici, Hahne, & Mecklinger, 1996; Kluender & Kutas, 1993; Münte, Heinze, & Mangun, 1993; Osterhout & Holcomb, 1992; Rösler, Friederici, Pütz, & Hahne, 1993). But in some cases the latency of a left-frontal negative effect is reported to be much earlier, approximately 100–300 ms (Friederici, 2002; Friederici, Pfeifer, & Hahne, 1993; Neville, Nicol, Barss, Forster, & Garrett, 1991).

In some studies, LAN effects have been reported to violations of word-category constraints (Friederici et al., 1996; Hagoort et al., 2003; Münte et al., 1993). That is, if the syntactic context requires a word of a certain syntactic class (e.g., a noun in the context of a preceding article and adjective), but, in fact, a word of a different syntactic class is presented (e.g., a verb), early negativities are observed. Friederici and colleagues (e.g., Friederici, 1995; Friederici et al., 1996) have tied the early negativities specifically to the processing of word-category information. However, in other studies, similar early negativities are observed with number, case, gender, and tense mismatches (Münte & Heinze, 1994; Münte et al., 1993). In these violations, the word category is correct but the morphosyntactic features are wrong. Friederici (2002) has recently attributed the very early negativities that occur approximately between 100 and 300 ms (ELAN) to violations of word category, and the negativities at 300–500 ms to morphosyntactic processing.

LAN effects have also been related to verbal working memory in connection to filler-gap assignment (Kluender & Kutas, 1993). This working memory account of the LAN is compatible with the finding that lexical, syntactic, and referential ambiguities seem to elicit very similar frontal negativities (Hagoort & Brown, 1994; Van Berkum et al., 1999a; Kaan & Swaab, 2003b; King & Kutas, 1995). Lexical and referential ambiguities are clearly not syntactic in nature, but can be argued to tax verbal working memory more heavily than sentences in which lexical and referential ambiguities are absent. Syntactic ambiguities might also tax working memory stronger than their unambiguous counterparts. Future research should indicate whether or not these two functionally distinct classes of LAN effects can be dissociated at a more fine-grained level of electrophysiological analysis.

P600/SPS

A second ERP effect that has been related to syntactic processing is a later positivity, nowadays referred to as P600/SPS (Coulson, King, & Kutas, 1998; Hagoort et al., 1999; Osterhout, Bersick, & McKinnon, 1997). One of the antecedent conditions of P600/SPS effects is a violation of a syntactic constraint. If, for instance, the syntactic requirement of number agreement between the grammatical subject of a sentence and its finite verb is violated (see item (1) below, with the critical verb form in italics; the asterisk indicates the ungrammaticality of the sentence), a positive-going shift is elicited by the word that renders the sentence ungrammatical (Hagoort et al., 1993). This positive shift starts at about 500 ms after the onset of the violation and usually lasts for at least 500 ms. Given the polarity and the latency of its maximal amplitude, this effect was originally referred to as the P600 (Osterhout & Holcomb, 1993) or, on the basis of its functional characteristics, as the syntactic positive shift (SPS) (Hagoort et al., 1993).

(1) *The spoilt child *throw* the toy on the ground.

An argument for the independence of this effect from possibly confounding semantic factors is that it also occurs in sentences where the usual semantic/ pragmatic constraints have been removed (Hagoort & Brown, 1994). This results in sentences like (2a) and (2b) in which one is semantically odd but grammatically correct, whereas the other contains the same agreement violation as in (1):

(2) a. The boiled watering can *smokes* the telephone in the cat.
     b. *The boiled watering can *smoke* the telephone in the cat.

If one compares the ERPs to the italicized verbs in (2a) and (2b), a P600/SPS effect is visible with the ungrammatical verb form (Figure 11.3). Despite the fact that these sentences do not convey any conventional meaning, the ERP effect of the violation demonstrates that the language system is nevertheless able to parse the sentence into its constituent parts.

Similar P600/SPS effects have been reported for a broad range of syntactic

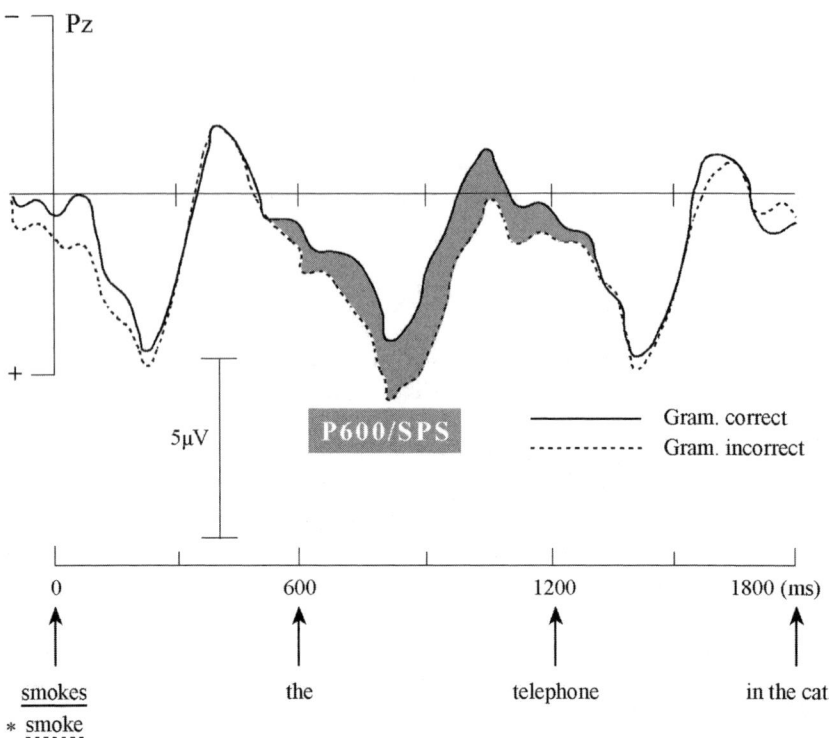

Figure 11.3 ERPs to visually presented syntactic prose sentences. These are sentences without a coherent semantic interpretation. A P600/SPS is elicited by a violation of the required number agreement between the subject-noun phrase and the finite verb of the sentence. The averaged waveforms for the grammatically correct (solid line) and the grammatically incorrect (dashed line) words are shown for electrode site Pz (parietal midline). The word that renders the sentence ungrammatical is presented at 0 ms on the time axis. The waveforms show the ERPs to this and the following two words. Words were presented word by word, with an interval stimulus onset asynchrony (SOA) of 600 ms. Negativity is plotted upward (adapted from Hagoort & Brown (1994). Copyright © 1994 Erlbaum, reprinted by permission.)

violations in different languages (English, Dutch, and German), including phrase-structure violations (Hagoort et al., 1993; Neville et al., 1991; Osterhout & Holcomb, 1992); subcategorization violations (Ainsworth-Darnell, Shulman, & Boland, 1998; Osterhout, Holcomb, & Swinney, 1994); violations in the agreement of number, gender, and case (Coulson et al., 1998; Hagoort et al., 1993; Münte et al., 1997; Osterhout & Mobley, 1995); and violations of subjacency (McKinnon & Osterhout, 1996; Neville et al., 1991) and of the empty-category principle (McKinnon & Osterhout, 1996).

Recently, a P600/SPS is also reported in relation to thematic role animacy violations (Kuperberg, Sitnikova, Caplan, & Holcomb, 2003). Moreover, a P600/SPS can be found with both written and spoken input (Friederici et al., 1993; Hagoort & Brown, 2000; Osterhout & Holcomb, 1993).

Recently, a P600/SPS is also reported in relation to thematic role assignment (Kim & Osterhout, 2005; Kuperberg et al., 2003; Van Herten, Kolk, & Chwilla, 2005; Wassenaar & Hagoort, accepted). In this case, a P600/SPS is elicited to verbs when constraints for grammatical role assignment conflict with thematic role biases.

In summary, two classes of syntax-related ERP effects have been consistently reported. These two classes differ in their polarity and topographic distribution, and in their latency characteristics. In terms of latency, the first class of effects is an anterior negativity. Apart from LANs related to working memory, anterior negativities are mainly seen with syntactic violations. In a later latency range, positive shifts occur which are elicited not only by syntactic violations, but also in grammatically well-formed sentences that vary in complexity (Kaan, Harris, Gibson, & Holcomb, 2000), as a function of the number of alternative syntactic structures that are compatible with the input at a particular position in the sentence (syntactic ambiguity) (Osterhout et al., 1994; Van Berkum et al., 1999a), or when constraints for grammatical role assignment are overwritten by thematic role biases (Kim & Osterhout, 2005).

Since these two classes of effects are now well established in the context of language processing, and are clearly different from the N400 effect, the need arises to account for these effects in terms of a well-defined model of language processing.

Broadly speaking, models of sentence processing can be divided into two types. One type of model assumes a precedence of syntactic information. That is, an initial syntactic structure is constructed before other information (e.g., lexical-semantic, discourse information) is taken into account (Frazier, 1987). I will refer to this type of model as a *syntax-first model*. The alternative broad set of models claims that the different information types (lexical, syntactic, phonological, and pragmatic) are processed in parallel and influence the interpretation process incrementally, that is, as soon as the relevant pieces of information are available (Jackendoff, 2002; Marslen-Wilson, 1989; Zwitserlood, 1989). I will refer to this type of model as the *immediacy model*. Overall, the behavioural data, although not decisive, are more in favour of the second type of model than the first. I will first present some recent ERP data that support the immediacy model.

Evidence against the syntax-first principle

The strong version of a syntax-first model of sentence processing assumes that the computation of an initial syntactic structure precedes semantic unification operations, because structural information is necessary as input for thematic role assignment. In other words, if no syntactic structure can be built up, semantic unification will be impaired. Recent electrophysiological evidence has been taken as evidence for this syntax-first principle (Friederici, 2002). Alternative models (MacDonald, Pearlmutter, & Seidenberg, 1994; Marslen-Wilson & Tyler, 1980) claim that semantic and syntactic information is immediately used as it becomes available without priority for syntactic information over other information types.

ERP evidence for an autonomous syntax-first model in sentence processing is derived from a series of studies in which Friederici and colleagues found an ELAN to auditorily presented words whose prefix is indicative of a word category violation. For instance, Hahne and Jescheniak (2001) and Friederici et al. (1993) had their subjects listen to sentences such as "Die Birne wurde im *gepflückt*" ("The pear was being in-the *plucked*") or "Die Freund wurde im *besucht*" ("The friend was being in-the *visited*"), where the prefixes "ge-" and "be-", in combination with the preceding auxiliary "wurde", are indicating a past participle where the preposition "im" requires a noun. In this case, a very early (100–300 ms) left anterior negativity is observed that precedes the N400 effect.

Although this evidence is compatible with a syntax-first model, it is not necessarily incompatible with an immediacy model of sentence processing. As long as word-category information can be derived earlier from the acoustic input than semantic information, as was the case in the above-mentioned studies, the immediacy model predicts that it will be used as it comes in. The syntax-first model, however, predicts that even in cases where word-category information comes in later than semantic information, this syntactic information will nevertheless be used earlier than semantic information in sentence processing, or semantic integration will not succeed. In line with their version of this model, Hahne and Friederici (2002) claim that their data "suggest that semantic integration processes are not initiated automatically in the case of a phrase structure violation" (p. 352), and "thus, the comprehension system does not seem to attempt at integrating the element eliciting a phrase structure violation on a semantic level" (p. 353). As they conclude, "the processing of phrase structure information has priority over that of lexical-semantic information", and "the syntactic feature of an incorrect word category may block the semantic integration of that particular word" (p. 353).

Van den Brink and Hagoort (2004) designed a strong test of the syntax-first model, in which semantic information precedes word-category information. In many languages, information about the word category is often encapsulated in the suffix rather than the prefix of a word. In contrast to an immediacy model, a syntax-first model would in such a case predict that semantic processing (particularly semantic unification) is postponed until after the information about the word category has become available, or it will not take place at all.

In their study, Van den Brink and Hagoort (2004) compared correct Dutch sentences (see item 3a below) with their anomalous counterparts (see 3b) in which the critical word (italicized in 3a/b) both was a semantic violation in the context and had the incorrect word category. However, in contrast to the experiments by Friederici and colleagues, word-category information was encoded in the suffix "-de".

(3) a. Het vrouwtje veegde de vloer met een oude *bezem* gemaakt van twijgen.
("The woman wiped the floor with an old *broom* made of twigs.")

b. *Het vrouwtje veegde de vloer met een oude *kliederde* gemaakt van twijgen.
("The woman wiped the floor with an old *messed* made of twigs.")

Figure 11.4 shows the waveform of the spoken verb form "kliederde" (messed). This verb form has a duration of approximately 450 ms. The stem already contains part of the semantic information. However, the onset of the suffix "-de" is at about 300 ms into the word. Only at this point will it be clear that the word category is a verb, and not a noun as required by the context. We define this moment of deviation from the correct word category as the category violation point (CVP), because only at this time is information provided on the basis of which it can be recognized as a verb, which is the incorrect word category in the syntactic context. Although in this case semantic information can be extracted from the spoken signal before word category information, the syntax-first model predicts that this semantic information can not be used for semantic unification until after the assignment of word category.

Figure 11.5 shows the averaged waveforms that are time-locked to the CVP

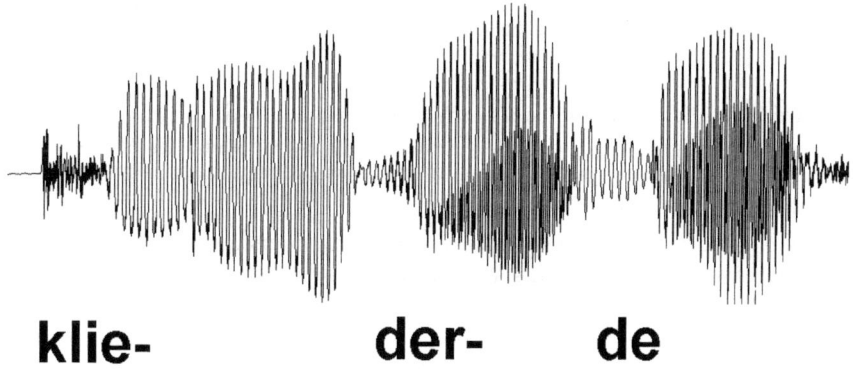

klie-   der-   de

Figure 11.4 A waveform of an acoustic token of the Dutch verb form "kliederde" (messed). The suffix "-de" indicates past tense. The total duration of the acoustic token is approximately 450 ms. The onset of the suffix "-de" is at approximately 300 ms. Only after 300 ms of signal can the acoustic token be classified as a verb. Thus, for a context that does not allow a verb in that position, the category violation point (CVP) is at 300 ms into the verb (see text).

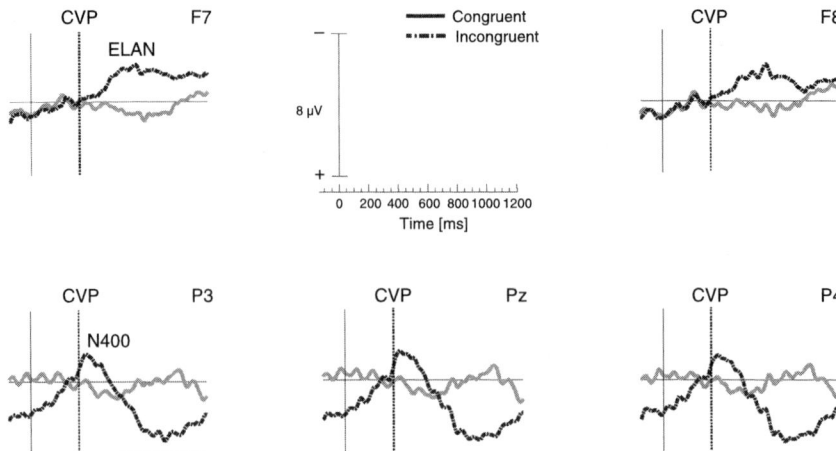

Figure 11.5 Connected speech. Grand-average ERPs from two frontal electrode sites (F7, F8) and three posterior electrode sites (Pz, P3, P4) to critical words that were semantically and syntactically congruent with the sentence context (congruent: solid line), or semantically and syntactically incongruent (incongruent: alternating dashed/dotted line). Grand-average waveforms were computed after time locking on a trial-by-trial basis to the moment of word-category violation (CVP: category violation point). The baseline was determined by averaging in the 180–330-ms interval, corresponding to a 150-ms interval preceding the CVP in the incongruent condition. The time axis is in milliseconds, and negativity is upward. The ELAN is visible over the two frontal sites; the N400 and the P600/SPS over the three posterior sites. The onset of the ELAN is at 100 ms after the CVP; the onset of the N400 effect precedes the CVP by approximately 10 ms (after Van den Brink & Hagoort, 2004).

for two frontal sites where usually the ELAN is observed, and two posterior sites that are representative of N400 effects. As can be seen, the N400 effect clearly precedes the ELAN in time. Whereas the ELAN started at approximately 100 ms after the CVP, the N400 effect was already significant before the CVP. To my knowledge, this is the clearest evidence so far for the claim that semantic unification can start before word-category information is provided. This is strong evidence for the immediacy assumption: information available in the signal is immediately used for further processing. In contrast to what a strong version of the syntax-first model predicts, semantic unification does not need to wait until an initial structure is built on the basis of word-category information. Only when a syntax-first model allows prediction of word category could it be claimed that this prediction was falsified only at the CVP, and thus initially semantic unification could be started up. However, this weaker version of a syntax-first model has given up the characteristic of bottom-up priority and assumes an interaction between syntactic context and lexical processing. One can then ask which feature of the processing architecture guarantees that interaction between context and lexical processing is restricted to syntax.

In summary, the evidence so far indicates that distinct ERP effects are observed for semantic integration (N400) and syntactic analysis ((E)LAN, P600/SPS). The ERP data presented argue against a syntax-first model of sentence processing. Rather, as soon as semantic or syntactic information is available, it is used for the purpose of interpretation. This is in line with the assumptions of the immediacy model. The triggering conditions of the syntax-related ERP effects are becoming more clear. Apart from the LAN effects related to working memory, so far (E)LAN effects have mainly been seen in response to syntactic *violations*. These violations can be word-category violations that are sometimes seen early (ELAN), but they can also be morphosyntactic violations that are usually observed within the same time frame as the N400 effects (300–500 ms). The anterior negativities are normally followed by a P600/SPS. In contrast to the (E)LAN, the P600/SPS is seen not only in syntactic violations but also in syntactically less preferred structures (i.e., in the case of syntactic ambiguity; Van Berkum et al., 1999a; Osterhout et al., 1994), and in syntactically more complex sentences (Kaan et al., 2000). In many cases, the P600/SPS occurs without a concomitant early negativity. For straightforward syntactic violations, the distribution of the P600/SPS seems to be more posterior than the P600/SPS reported in relation to syntactic ambiguity resolution and syntactic complexity (Hagoort et al., 1999; Kaan & Swaab, 2003a, 2003b).

The unification model

The increasing numbers of ERP studies on syntactic processing in the last decade have resulted in a substantial number of data that are in need of a coherent, overall account. I will propose an explicit account of syntax-related ERP effects based on a computational model of parsing developed by Vosse and Kempen (2000), here referred to as the unification model. This proposal is certainly not the end stage, but only a beginning. The model needs to be adapted and the account of the ERP data needs to be refined. Nevertheless, I believe that progress will be made only if we attempt to connect not only the behavioural data but also data from electrophysiology and neuroimaging to explicit computational accounts. I will first describe the general architecture of this model.

According to the unification model, each word form in the lexicon is associated with a structural frame. This structural frame consists of a three-tiered, unordered tree, specifying the possible structural environment of the particular lexical item (Figure 11.6). (For details concerning the computation of word order, see Harbusch & Kempen, 2002.)

This so-called root node is connected to one or more functional nodes (e.g., subject, head, direct object) in the second layer of the frame. The third layer contains again phrasal nodes to which lexical items or other frames can be attached.

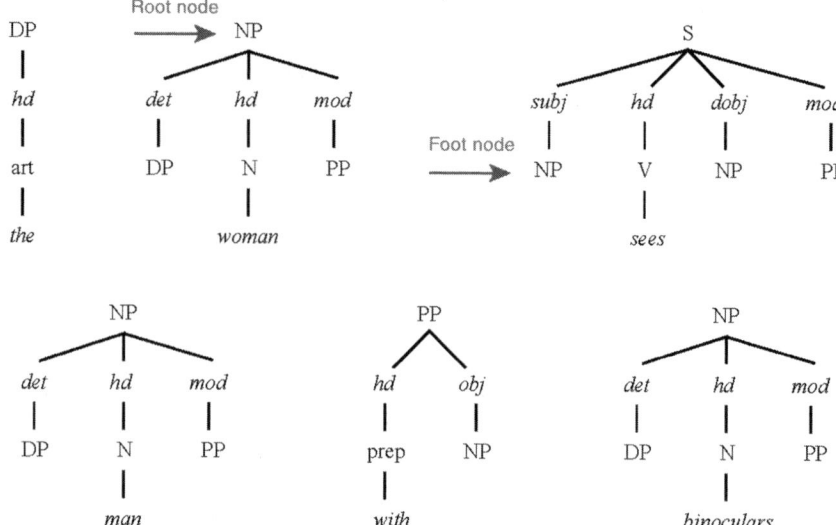

Figure 11.6 Syntactic frames in memory (the mental lexicon). Frames are retrieved on the basis of the word form input for the sentence, *The woman sees the man with the binoculars.* DP: Determiner Phrase; NP: Noun Phrase; S: Sentence; PP: Prepositional Phrase; art: article; hd: head; det: determiner; mod: modifier; subj: subject; dobj: direct object.

This parsing account is 'lexicalist' in the sense that all syntactic nodes (e.g., S, NP, VP, N, V, etc.) are retrieved from the mental lexicon. In other words, chunks of syntactic structure are stored in memory. There are no syntactic rules that introduce additional nodes. In the online comprehension process, structural frames associated with the individual word forms incrementally enter the unification workspace. In this workspace, constituent structures spanning the whole utterance are formed by a unification operation. This operation consists of linking up lexical frames with identical root and foot nodes (Figure 11.7), and checking agreement features (number, gender, person, etc.). It specifies what Jackendoff (2002) refers to as the only remaining "grammatical rule", unify pieces.

The resulting unification links between lexical frames are formed dynamically, implying that the strength of the unification links varies over time until a state of equilibrium is reached. Due to the inherent ambiguity in natural language, alternative unification candidates will usually be available at any point in the parsing process. That is, a particular root node (e.g., PP) often finds more than one matching foot node (i.e., PP) with which it can form a unification link (Figure 11.8).

Ultimately, one phrasal configuration results. This requires that among the alternative unification candidates only one remains active. The required state of equilibrium is reached through a process of lateral inhibition between two or more alternative unification links. In general, due to gradual decay of acti-

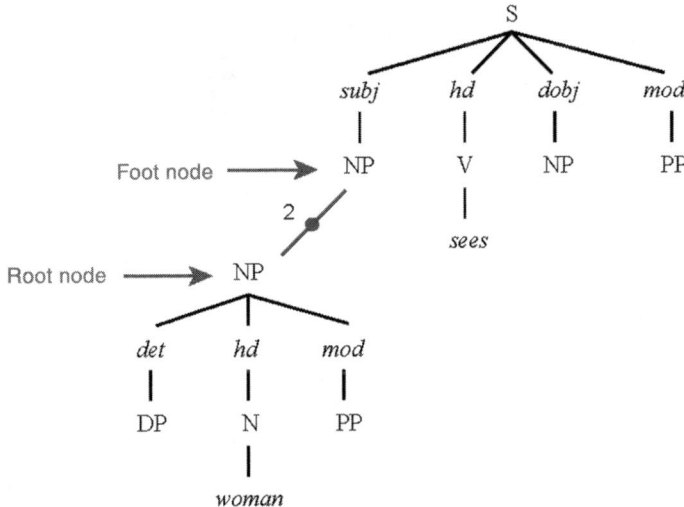

Figure 11.7 The unification operation of two lexically specified syntactic frames. The unification takes place by linking the root node NP to an available foot node of the same category. The number 2 indicates that this is the second link that is formed during online processing of the sentence, *The woman sees the man with the binoculars.*

vation, more recent root nodes will have a higher level of activation than the ones that entered the unification space earlier. This is why the likelihood of an attachment of the PP into the syntactic frame of the verb "sees" is higher than into the syntactic frame for "woman" (see Figure 11.7). In addition, strength levels of the unification links can vary in function of plausibility (semantic) effects. For instance, if instrumental modifiers under S-nodes have a slightly higher default activation than instrumental modifiers under an NP-node, lateral inhibition can override the recency effect. For our example sentence (see Figure 11.8), it means that the outcome of lateral inhibition is that the PP may be linked to the S-frame (unification link 7) rather than to the more recent NP-node of "man" (U-link 8) (for details, see Vosse & Kempen, 2000).

The unification model accounts for sentence complexity effects known from behavioural measures, such as reading times. In general, sentences are harder to analyse syntactically when more potential unification links of similar strength compete with each other. Sentences are easy when the number of U-links is small and of unequal strength.

The advantage of the unification model is that (1) it is computationally explicit, (2) it accounts for a large series of empirical findings in the parsing literature (but presumably not for all the locality phenomena in Gibson, 1998) and in the neuropsychological literature on aphasia, and (3) it belongs to the class of lexicalist parsing models that have found increasing support in recent years (Bresnan, 2001; Jackendoff, 2002; Joshi & Schabes, 1997; MacDonald et al., 1994).

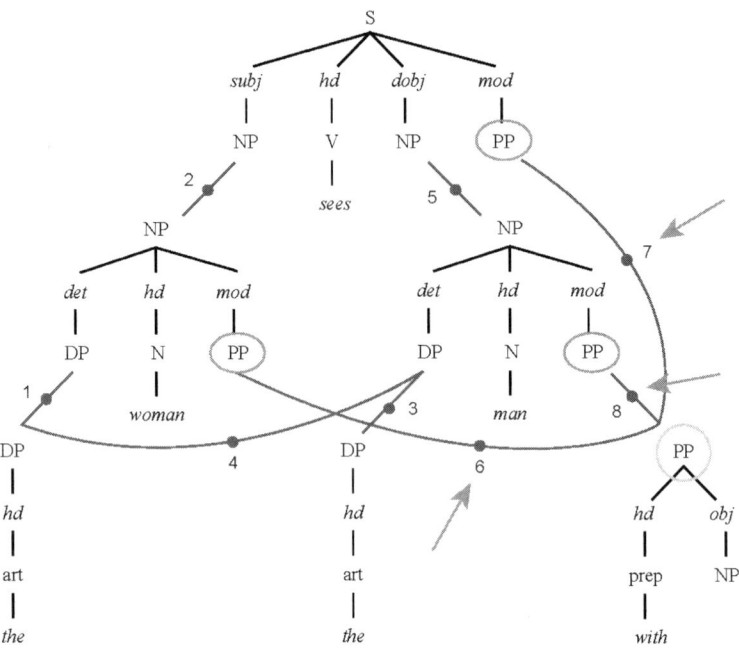

Figure 11.8 Lateral inhibition between three different PP-foot nodes that are candidate unification sites for the PP-root node of the preposition "with". The three possible unification links are indicated by arrows. Lateral inhibition between these three possible unifications (6, 7, and 8) ultimately results in one unification that wins the competition and remains active.

This model also nicely accounts for the two classes of syntax-related ERP effects reported in this and many other studies. In the unification model, binding (unification) is prevented in two cases. One case is when the root node of a syntactic building block (e.g., NP) does not find another syntactic building block with an identical foot node (i.e., NP) to bind to. The other case is when the agreement check finds a serious mismatch in the grammatical feature specifications of the root and foot nodes. The claim is that a (left) anterior negativity (AN) results from a failure to bind, as a result of a negative outcome of the agreement check or a failure to find a matching category node. For instance, the sentence, "The woman sees the man because with the binoculars", does not result in a completed parse, since the syntactic frame associated with "because" does not find unoccupied (embedded) S-root nodes that it can bind. As a result, unification fails.

In the context of the unification model, I propose that the P600/SPS is related to the time it takes to establish unification links of sufficient strength. The time it takes to build up the unification links until the required strength is reached is affected by competition between alternative unification options (syntactic ambiguity), by syntactic complexity, and by semantic influences.

The amplitude of the P600/SPS is modulated by the amount of competition. Competition is reduced when the number of alternative unification options is smaller, or when lexical, semantic, or discourse context biases the strengths of the unification links in a particular direction, thereby shortening the duration of the competition. Violations result in a P600/SPS as long as unification attempts are made. For instance, a mismatch in gender or agreement features might still result in weaker unification in the absence of alternative options. However, in such cases, the strength and build-up of U-links will be affected by the partial mismatch in syntactic feature specification. Compared to less complex or syntactically unambiguous sentences, in more complex and syntactically ambiguous sentences, it takes longer to build up U-links of sufficient strength. The latter sentences, therefore, result in a P600/SPS in comparison to the former ones.

In summary, it seems that the unification model provides an acceptable preliminary account of the collective body of ERP data on syntactic processing. Moreover, it does not assume a syntax-first architecture. It is, therefore, a better account of the empirical data, both behavioural and electrophysiological, than models that assume a syntax-first phase.

Semantic unification

Next to syntactic unification, semantic unification operations have to take place. Neuropsychological patient studies, as well as data from neuroimaging studies, suggest that semantic representations might be distributed with the involvement of areas that support the most salient aspects of a concept (e.g., visual, kinesthetic, linguistic/propositional) (Allport, 1985; Saffran & Sholl, 1999). Context can differentially activate/select the saliency of meaning aspects (as in "The girl gave a wonderful performance on the old *piano*" vs. "Four men were needed to transport the old *piano*"). At the same time, the semantic aspects retrieved on the basis of lexical access have to be integrated into a coherent interpretation of a multiword utterance. This I will refer to as *semantic unification*. It turns out that the left lateral prefrontal cortex is also crucial for semantic unification (see below). Binding-relevant areas within the left prefrontal cortex (LPC) might overlap, at least to some degree, for syntactic and semantic unification. But there is also evidence that semantic unification might involve more ventral areas (especially Brodmann's area 47) than syntactic unification. More research is needed to determine commonalities and differences in the LPC between areas involved in phonological, syntactic, and semantic unification. However, the qualitative differences between ERP effects of semantic (N400) and syntactic (LAN, P600) unification suggest that the brain honours the distinction between these two types of unification operations.

The level of semantic unification: Sentence vs. discourse

A central issue for semantic unification is whether or not a semantic representation at the sentence-level is built up first, before, in a second step, semantic information is integrated into a discourse model. For instance, in their blueprint of the listener, Cutler and Clifton (1999) assume that, based on syntactic analysis and thematic processing, utterance interpretation takes place first, before, in a next processing step, integration into a discourse model follows. Kintsch (Ericsson & Kintsch, 1995; Kintsch, 1998) has made similar claims. To investigate this issue, we conducted an ERP study to investigate how and when the language-comprehension system relates an incoming word to semantic representations of the unfolding local sentence and the wider discourse (Van Berkum et al., 1999b). In the first experiment, subjects were presented with short stories, of which the last sentence sometimes contained a critical word that was semantically anomalous with respect to the wider discourse (e.g., *Jane told the brother that he was exceptionally slow* in a discourse context where he had in fact been very quick). Relative to a discourse-coherent counterpart (e.g., *quick*), these discourse-anomalous words elicited a large N400 effect (i.e., a negative shift in the ERP that began at about 200–250 ms after word onset and peaked around 400 ms).

Next to the discourse-related anomalies, sentence-semantic anomaly effects were elicited under comparable experimental conditions. We found that the ERP effects elicited by both types of anomalies were highly similar. Relative to their coherent counterparts, discourse- and sentence-anomalous critical words elicited an N400 effect with an identical time-course and scalp topography (Figure 11.9). The similarity of these effects, particularly in polarity and scalp distribution, is compatible with the claim that they reflect the activity of a largely overlapping or identical set of underlying neural generators, indicating similar functional processes.

In summary, there is no indication that the language-comprehension system is slower in relating a new word to the semantics of the wider discourse than in relating it to local sentence context. Our data clearly do not support the idea that new words are related to the discourse model *after* they have been evaluated in terms of their contribution to local sentence semantics. The speed with which the discourse context affects processing of the current sentence appears to be at odds with recent estimates of how long it would take to retrieve information about prior discourse from long-term memory. In Van Berkum et al.'s materials, the relative coherence of a critical word usually hinged on rather subtle information that was implicit in the discourse and that required considerable inferencing about the discourse topic and the situation it described. Kintsch (Ericsson & Kintsch, 1995; Kintsch, 1998) has suggested that during online text comprehension, such subtle discourse information is not immediately available and must be retrieved from "long-term working memory" when needed. This is estimated to take some 300–400 ms at least. However, the results of our experiments suggest that the

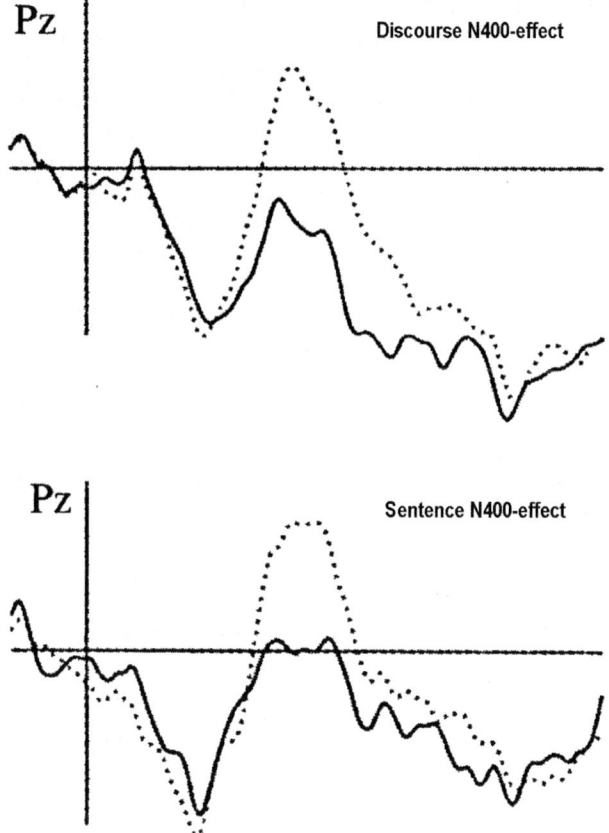

Figure 11.9 N400 effects triggered by discourse-related and sentence-related anomalies. Waveforms are presented for a representative electrode site. The latencies of the N400 effect in discourse and sentence contexts (both onset and peak latencies) are the same (after Van Berkum et al., 1999b).

relevant discourse information can be brought to bear on local processing within at most 200–250 ms.

The observed identity of discourse- and sentence-level N400 effects is most parsimoniously accounted for in terms of a processing model that abandons the distinction between sentence- and discourse-level semantic unification. This is compatible with the notion of *common ground* (Clark, 1996; Stalnaker, 1978). The analysis of Clark clearly demonstrates that the meaning of linguistic utterances cannot be determined without taking into account the knowledge that speaker and listener share and mutually believe they share. This common ground includes a model of the discourse itself, which is continually updated as the discourse unfolds. If listeners and readers always immediately evaluate new words relative to the discourse model and the associated information in common ground (i.e., immediately compute "contextual meaning"), the identity of the ERP effects generated by sentence- and discourse anomalies has a natural explanation. With a single sentence, the relevant common ground includes only whatever discourse and world knowledge has just been activated by the sentence fragment presented so far. With a sentence presented in discourse context, the relevant common ground will be somewhat richer, now also including information elicited by the specific earlier discourse. But the process that maps incoming words onto the relevant common ground can run into trouble either way. The N400 effects observed in the Van Berkum et al. study (1999b) reflect the activity of this unified unification process. Of course, this is not to deny the relevance of sentential structure for semantic interpretation. In particular, how the incoming words are related to the discourse model is co-constrained by sentence-level syntactic devices (such as word order, case marking, local phrase structure, or agreement) and the associated mapping onto thematic roles. However, this is fully compatible with the claim that there is no separate stage during which word meaning is exclusively evaluated with respect to "local sentence meaning", independent of the discourse context in which that sentence occurs.

The neural implementation of unification in language

In the context of the language system, the binding problem refers to the following issue: How is information that is incrementally retrieved from the mental lexicon unified into a coherent overall interpretation of a multiword utterance? Most likely, unification needs to take place at the conceptual, syntactic, and phonological levels, as well as between these levels (Jackendoff, 2002). So far, I have discussed the features of the cognitive architecture for syntactic and semantic unification. In this section, I will argue that the left inferior prefrontal cortex might have the characteristics necessary for performing the unification operations at the different levels of the language system.

One requirement for solving the binding problem for language is the availability of cortical tissue that is particularly suited for maintaining information online while unification operations take place. The prefrontal cortex seems to be especially well suited for doing exactly this. Areas in the prefrontal cortex are able to hold information online (Mesulam, 2002), and to select among competing alternatives (Thompson-Schill, D'Esposito, & Kan, 1999). Electrophysiological recordings in the macaque monkey have shown that this area is important for sustaining information triggered by a transient event for many seconds (Miller, 2000). This allows the prefrontal cortex to establish unifications between pieces of information that are perceived or retrieved from memory at different moments in time.

I will make some tentative suggestions about how the different components of the unification model for syntactic unification that I discussed above could be connected to our knowledge about the neural architecture.

This proposal is not yet explicitly tested, but, as I will argue, it makes good sense in the light of our current knowledge about the contributions of the areas involved. In a recent meta-analysis of 28 neuroimaging studies, Indefrey (2004) found two areas that were critical for syntactic processing, independent of the input modality (visual in reading, auditory in speech). These two supramodal areas for syntactic processing were the left posterior superior temporal gyrus and the left posterior inferior frontal cortex.

As is known from lesion studies in aphasic patients, lesions in different areas of the left perisylvian cortex can result in syntactic processing deficits in sentence comprehension (Caplan, Hildebrandt, & Makris, 1996). The idea that modality-independent grammatical knowledge was mainly represented in Broca's area (Zurif, 1998) has thus been proven to be incorrect. At the same time, the left posterior temporal cortex is known to be involved in lexical processing (Indefrey & Cutler, 2004). In connection to syntactic unification, this part of the brain might be important for the retrieval of the syntactic frames that are stored in the lexicon.

The unification space where individual frames are connected into a phrasal configuration for the whole utterance might be localized in the left frontal part of the syntax-relevant network of brain areas. One of the main specializations of the prefrontal cortex is the holding online and binding of information (Mesulam, 2002). It might be the right area for providing the computational resources for binding together the lexical-syntactic frames through the dynamics of creating unification links between them (cf. Duncan & Miller, 2002). It thus seems that the components of the unification model and the areas known to be crucial for syntactic processing can be connected in a relatively natural way, with the left superior temporal cortex relevant to storage and retrieval of syntactic frames, and the left prefrontal cortex important for binding these frames together.

The need for combining independent bits and pieces into a single coherent percept is not unique for syntax. Models for semantic/conceptual unification and phonological unification could be worked out along similar lines as the unification model for syntax. Recent neuroimaging studies (cf. Bookheimer, 2002) suggest that parts of the prefrontal cortex in and around Broca's area might be involved in conceptual and phonological unification, with Brodmann's areas (BA) 47 and 45 involved in semantic unification, BA 45 and 44 in syntactic unification, and BA 44 and ventral BA 6 in phonological unification (Figure 11.10, see colour plate section).

Neuropsychological studies (Martin & He, 2004; Martin & Romani, 1994) further support the distinction between semantic and syntactic unification. These authors report patients that have difficulty either in integrating semantic information with increasing semantic load, or in maintaining structural information when it must be integrated across several intervening words. However, as often in patients studies, the lesion data lack the required precision to make strong claims about the crucial brain areas for these respective unification operations.

Seven principles of the processing architecture

In analogy to other domains of cognitive neuroscience, for language comprehension, I have made a distinction between memory retrieval and unification or binding. I have discussed features of the processing architecture for syntactic and semantic unification. Evidence from neuroimaging studies seems to support the distinction between brain areas recruited for memory retrieval and brain areas crucial for unification. From the evidence discussed in the preceding sections, I propose the following seven general architectural principles for comprehension beyond the single word level:

(1) The brain honours the distinction between syntactic and semantic unification. However, both involve contributions from the left prefrontal cortex (in and around Broca's area), as the workspace where unification operations take place. It is quite possible that this area is not language specific, but subserves other functions as well (e.g., binding in music; see Patel, 2003). The left prefrontal cortex is suggested to maintain the activation state of representational structures retrieved from memory (the mental lexicon), and to provide the necessary neuroanatomical space for unification operations.

(2) Immediacy is the general processing principle of unification. Semantic unification does not wait until relevant syntactic information (such as word class information) is available, but starts immediately with what it derives on the basis of the bottom-up input and the left context. The corollary of immediacy is incrementality: Output representations are built up from left to right in close temporal contiguity to the input signal.

(3) There does not seem to be a separate stage during which word meaning is exclusively integrated at the sentence level. Incremental interpretation is for the most part done by an immediate mapping onto a discourse model (Clark, 1996).

(4) In parsing, lexically specified structures enter the unification space. Lexical information (e.g., animacy), discourse information, and, according to recent data, other-modality inputs (e.g., visual world, gesture) immediately influence the competition between alternative unification options, and can change the unification links. However, in the absence of competing unification sites, assignment of structure is not influenced by nonsyntactic information types.

(5) There is no evidence for a privileged position of syntax and/or a processing priority for syntax, as assumed in syntax-first models. The different processing levels (phonological, syntactic, and semantic/pragmatic) operate in parallel, and, to some degree, independently. Where necessary, cross-talk takes place, and this is again characterized by the immediacy principle. That is, cross-talk takes place on a more or less moment-to-moment basis.

(6) The comprehension system operates according to the "loser-takes-all" principle. That is, if the syntactic cues are stronger than the semantic cues (e.g., thematic biases), the processing problem will be at the level of semantic unification. If the semantic cues are stronger than the syntactic cues, the processing problem will be shifted to the assignment of syntactic structure.

(7) Within certain limitations, the language-comprehension system can adapt the weight of evidence in the light of system-internal or system-external noise. The degrees of freedom in language comprehension are much greater than in language production.

References

Ainsworth-Darnell, K., Shulman, H., & Boland, J. (1998). Dissociating brain responses to syntactic and semantic anomalies: Evidence from event-related potentials. *Journal of Memory and Language*, 38, 112–130.

Aleman, A., Formisano, E., Koppenhagen, H., Hagoort, P., De Haan, E. H. F., & Kahn, R. S. (2005). The functional neuroanatomy of metrical stress evaluation of perceived and imagined spoken words. *Cerebral Cortex*, 15, 221–228.

Allport, D. A. (1985). Distributed memory, modular subsystems and dysphasia. In S. K. Newman & R. Epstein (Eds.), *Current perspectives in dysphasia* (pp. 32–60). Edinburgh: Churchill Livingstone.

Altmann, G. T. M., & Steedman, M. (1988). Interaction with context during human sentence processing. *Cognition*, 30, 191–238.

Boland, J. E., & Cutler, A. (1996). Interaction with autonomy: Multiple output models and the inadequacy of the great divide. *Cognition*, 58, 309–320.

Bookheimer, S. (2002). Functional MRI of language: New approaches to understanding the cortical organization of semantic processing. *Annual Review of Neuroscience*, 25, 151–188.

Botvinick, M. B., Cohen, J. D., & Carter, C. S. (2004). Conflict monitoring and anterior cingulate cortex: An update. *Trends in Cognitive Sciences*, 8, 539–546.

Bresnan, J. W. (2001). *Lexical-functional syntax*. Oxford: Blackwell.

Brown, C., & Hagoort, P. (1993). The processing nature of the N400: Evidence from masked priming. *Journal of Cognitive Neuroscience*, 5, 34–44.

Bush, G., Luu, P., & Posner, M. I. (2000). Cognitive and emotional influences in anterior cingulate cortex. *Trends in Cognitive Sciences*, 4, 215–222.

Caplan, D., Hildebrandt, N., & Makris, N. (1996). Location of lesions in stroke patients with deficits in syntactic processing in sentence comprehension. *Brain*, 119, 933–949.

Chomsky, N. (1995). *The minimalist program*. Cambridge, MA: MIT Press.

Clark, H. H. (1996). *Using language*. Cambridge: Cambridge University Press.

Coulson, S., King, J. W., & Kutas, M. (1998). Expect the unexpected: Event-related brain response to morphosyntactic violations. *Language and Cognitive Processes*, 13, 21–58.

Cutler, A., & Clifton, C. E. (1999). Comprehending spoken language: A blueprint of the listener. In C. M. Brown & P. Hagoort (Eds.), *The neurocognition of language* (pp. 123–166). Oxford: Oxford University Press.

Damasio, H., Grabowski, T. J., Tranel, D., Hichwa, R. D., & Damasio, A. D. (1996). A neural basis for lexical retrieval. *Nature, 380,* 499–505.

Duncan, J., & Miller, E. K. (2002). Cognitive focus through adaptive neural coding in the primate prefrontal cortex. In D. T. Stuss & R. T. Knight (Eds.), *Principles of frontal lobe function* (pp. 278–292). Oxford: Oxford University Press.

Ericsson, K. A., & Kintsch, W. (1995). Long-term working memory. *Psychological Review, 102,* 211–245.

Ferreira, F. (2003). The misinterpretation of noncanonical sentences. *Cognitive Psychology, 47,* 164–203.

Fodor, J. D. (1983). *The modularity of mind.* Cambridge, MA: MIT Press.

Frazier, L. (1987). Sentence processing: A tutorial review. In M. Coltheart (Ed.), *Attention and performance XII* (pp. 559–585). Hove, UK: Lawrence Erlbaum Associates Ltd.

Friederici, A. D. (1995). The time course of syntactic activation during language processing: A model based on neuropsychological and neurophysiological data. *Brain and Language, 50,* 259–281.

Friederici, A. D. (2002). Towards a neural basis of auditory sentence processing. *Trends in Cognitive Sciences, 6,* 78–84.

Friederici, A. D., Hahne, A., & Mecklinger, A. (1996). Temporal structure of syntactic parsing: Early and late event-related brain potential effects. *Journal of Experimental Psychology: Learning, Memory, and Cognition, 22,* 1219–1248.

Friederici, A. D., Pfeifer, E., & Hahne, A. (1993). Event-related brain potentials during natural speech processing: Effects of semantic, morphological and syntactic violations. *Cognitive Brain Research, 1,* 183–192.

Gibson, E. (1998). Linguistic complexity: Locality of syntactic dependencies. *Cognition, 68,* 1–76.

Hagoort, P. (2003). Interplay between syntax and semantics during sentence comprehension: ERP effects of combining syntactic and semantic violations. *Journal of Cognitive Neuroscience, 15,* 883–899.

Hagoort, P., & Brown, C. M. (1994). Brain responses to lexical ambiguity resolution and parsing. In C. Clifton Jr, L. Frazier, & K. Rayner (Eds.), *Perspectives on sentence processing* (pp. 45–81). Hillsdale, NJ: Lawrence Erlbaum Associates, Inc.

Hagoort, P., & Brown, C. M. (2000). ERP effects of listening to speech compared to reading: The P600/SPS to syntactic violations in spoken sentences and rapid serial visual presentation. *Neuropsychologia, 38,* 1531–1549.

Hagoort, P., Brown, C. M., & Groothusen, J. (1993). The syntactic positive shift (SPS) as an ERP measure of syntactic processing. *Language and Cognitive Processes, 8,* 439–483.

Hagoort, P., Brown, C., & Osterhout, L. (1999). The neurocognition of syntactic processing. In C. M. Brown & P. Hagoort (Eds.), *The neurocognition of language* (pp. 273–317). Oxford: Oxford University Press.

Hagoort, P., Hald, L., Bastiaansen, M., & Petersson, K. M. (2004). Integration of word meaning and world knowledge in language comprehension. *Science, 304,* 438–441.

Hagoort, P., Wassenaar, M., & Brown, C. M. (2003). Syntax-related ERP-effects in Dutch. *Cognitive Brain Research, 16,* 38–50.

Hahne, A., & Friederici, A. D. (2002). Differential task effects on semantic and syntactic processes as revealed by ERPs. *Cognitive Brain Research, 13,* 339–356.

Hahne, A., & Jescheniak, J. D. (2001). What's left if the Jabberwock gets the semantics? An ERP investigation into semantic and syntactic processes during auditory sentence comprehension. *Cognitive Brain Research, 11,* 199–212.

Harbusch, K., & Kempen, G. (2002). *A quantitative model of word order and movement in English, Dutch and German complement constructions.* Paper presented at the 19th international conference on computational linguistics (COLING-2002), San Francisco.

Indefrey, P. (2004). Hirnaktivierungen bei syntaktischer Sprachverarbeitung: Eine Meta-Analyse. In G. Rickheit & H. M. Mueller (Eds.), *Neurokognition in der Sprache* (pp. 31–50). Tübingen: Stauffenburg Verlag.

Indefrey, P., & Cutler, A. (2004). Prelexical and lexical processing in listening. In M. D. Gazzaniga (Ed.), *The cognitive neurosciences* (3rd ed., pp. 759–774). Cambridge, MA: MIT Press.

Indefrey, P., & Levelt, W. J. M. (2000). The neural correlates of language production. In M. S. Gazzaniga (Ed.), *The new cognitive neurosciences* (2nd ed., pp. 845–865). Cambridge, MA: MIT Press.

Jackendoff, R. (1999). The representational structures of the language faculty and their interactions. In C. M. Brown & P. Hagoort (Eds.), *The neurocognition of language* (pp. 37–79). Oxford: Oxford University Press.

Jackendoff, R. (2002). *Foundations of language: Brain, meaning, grammar, evolution.* Oxford: Oxford University Press.

Joshi, A. K., & Schabes, Y. (1997). Treeadjoining grammars. In A. Salomma & G. Rosenberg (Eds.), *Handbook of formal languages and automata* (Vol. 3, pp. 69–124). Heidelberg: Springer-Verlag.

Kaan, E., Harris, A., Gibson, E., & Holcomb, P. (2000). The P600 as an index of syntactic integration difficulty. *Language and Cognitive Processes, 15,* 159–201.

Kaan, E., & Swaab, T. Y. (2003a). Electrophysiological evidence for serial sentence processing: A comparison between non-preferred and ungrammatical continuations. *Cognitive Brain Research, 17,* 621–635.

Kaan, E., & Swaab, T. Y. (2003b). Repair, revision and complexity in syntactic analysis: An electrophysiological differentiation. *Journal of Cognitive Neuroscience, 15,* 98–110.

Kim, A., & Osterhout, L. (2005). The independence of combinatory semantic processing: Evidence from event-related potentials. *Journal of Memory and Language, 52,* 205–225.

King, J. W., & Kutas, M. (1995). Who did what and when? Using word- and clause-level ERPs to monitor working memory usage in reading. *Journal of Cognitive Neuroscience, 7,* 376–395.

Kintsch, W. (1998). *Comprehension: A paradigm for cognition.* Cambridge: Cambridge University Press.

Kluender, R., & Kutas, M. (1993). Subjacency as a processing phenomenon. *Language and Cognitive Processes, 8,* 573–633.

Kuperberg, G. R., Sitnikova, T., Caplan, D., & Holcomb, P. J. (2003). Electrophysiological distinctions in processing conceptual relationships within simple sentences. *Cognitive Brain Research, 17,* 117–129.

Kutas, M., & Hillyard, S. A. (1980). Reading senseless sentences: Brain potentials reflect semantic anomaly. *Science, 207,* 203–205.

Kutas, M., & Van Petten, C. K. (1994). Psycholinguistics electrified: Event-related brain potential investigations. In M. A. Gernsbacher (Ed.), *Handbook of psycholinguistics* (pp. 83–143). San Diego, CA: Academic Press.

Levelt, W. J. M. (1999). Producing spoken language: A blueprint of the speaker. In

C. M. Brown & P. Hagoort (Eds.), *The neurocognition of language* (pp. 83–122). Oxford: Oxford University Press.

MacDonald, M. C., Pearlmutter, N. J., & Seidenberg, M. S. (1994). Lexical nature of syntactic ambiguity resolution. *Psychological Review, 101*, 676–703.

MacLeod, C. M., & MacDonald, P. A. (2000). Interdimensional interference in the Stroop effect: Uncovering the cognitive and neural anatomy of attention. *Trends in Cognitive Sciences, 4*, 383–391.

Marslen-Wilson, W. (1989). Access and integration: Projecting sound onto meaning. In W. Marslen-Wilson (Ed.), *Lexical representation and process* (pp. 3–24). Cambridge, MA: MIT Press.

Marslen-Wilson, W., & Tyler, L. K. (1980). The temporal structure of spoken language understanding. *Cognition, 8*, 1–71.

Martin, R. C., & He, T. (2004). Semantic short-term memory and its role in sentence processing: A replication. *Brain and Language, 89*, 76–82.

Martin, R. C., & Romani, C. (1994). Verbal working memory and sentence comprehension: A multiple-component view. *Neuropsychology, 8*, 506–523.

McKinnon, R., & Osterhout, L. (1996). Constraints on movement phenomena in sentence processing: Evidence from event-related brain potentials. *Language and Cognitive Processes, 11*, 495–523.

Mesulam, M.-M. (2002). The human frontal lobes: Transcending the default mode through contingent encoding. In D. T. Stuss & R. T. Knight (Eds.), *Principles of frontal lobe function* (pp. 8–31). Oxford: Oxford University Press.

Miller, E. K. (2000). The prefrontal cortex and cognitive control. *Nature Review Neuroscience, 1*, 59–65.

Münte, T. F., & Heinze, H. J. (1994). ERP negativities during syntactic processing of written words. In H. J. Heinze, T. F. Münte, & H. R. Mangun (Eds.), *Cognitive electrophysiology* (pp. 211–238). Boston, MA: Birkhauser.

Münte, T. F., Heinze, H. J., & Mangun, G. R. (1993). Dissociation of brain activity related to syntactic and semantic aspects of language. *Journal of Cognitive Neuroscience, 5*, 335–344.

Münte, T. F., Matzke, M., & Johannes, S. (1997). Brain activity associated with syntactic incongruities in words and pseudo-words. *Journal of Cognitive Neuroscience, 9*, 300–311.

Neville, H., Nicol, J. L., Barss, A., Forster, K. I., & Garrett, M. F. (1991). Syntactically based sentence processing classes: Evidence from event-related brain potentials. *Journal of Cognitive Neuroscience, 3*, 151–165.

O'Seaghdha, P. G. O. (1997). Conjoint and dissociable effects of syntactic and semantic context. *Journal of Experimental Psychology, 23*, 807–828.

Osterhout, L., Bersick, M., & McKinnon, R. (1997). Brain potentials elicited by words: Word length and frequency predict the latency of an early negativity. *Biological Psychology, 46*, 143–168.

Osterhout, L., & Hagoort, P. (1999). A superficial resemblance doesn't necessarily mean you're part of the family: Counterarguments to Coulson, King, & Kutas (1998) in the P600/SPS debate. *Language and Cognitive Processes, 14*, 1–14.

Osterhout, L., & Holcomb, P. J. (1992). Event-related brain potentials elicited by syntactic anomaly. *Journal of Memory and Language, 31*, 785–806.

Osterhout, L., & Holcomb, P. J. (1993). Event-related potentials and syntactic anomaly: Evidence of anomaly detection during the perception of continuous speech. *Language and Cognitive Processes, 8*, 413–438.

Osterhout, L., & Holcomb, P. J. (1995). Event-related potentials and language comprehension. In M. D. Rugg & M. G. H. Coles (Eds.), *Electrophysiology of mind* (pp. 171–215). Oxford: Oxford University Press.

Osterhout, L., Holcomb, P. J., & Swinney, D. A. (1994). Brain potentials elicited by garden-path sentences: Evidence of the application of verb information during parsing. *Journal of Experimental Psychology: Learning, Memory, and Cognition, 20,* 786–803.

Osterhout, L., & Mobley, L. A. (1995). Event-related brain potentials elicited by failure to agree. *Journal of Memory and Language, 34,* 739–773.

Patel, A. D. (2003). Language, music, syntax and the brain. *Nature Neuroscience, 6,* 674–681.

Roelofs, A., & Hagoort, P. (2002). Control of language use: Cognitive modeling the hemodynamics of Stroop task performance. *Cognitive Brain Research, 15,* 85–97.

Rösler, F., Friederici, A. D., Pütz, P., & Hahne, A. (1993). Event-related brain potentials while encountering semantic and syntactic constraint violations. *Journal of Cognitive Neuroscience, 5,* 345–362.

Saffran, E., & Sholl, A. (1999). Clues to the functional and neural architecture of word meaning. In C. M. Brown & P. Hagoort (Eds.), *The neurocognition of language* (pp. 241–273). Oxford: Oxford University Press.

Scott, S. K., & Johnsrude, I. S. (2003). The neuroanatomical and functional organization of speech perception. *Trends in Neurosciences, 26,* 100–107.

Stalnaker, R. C. (1978). Assertion. In P. Cole (Ed.), *Syntax and semantics 9: Pragmatics* (pp. 315–332). New York: Academic Press.

Tanenhaus, M. K., & Trueswell, C. (1995). Sentence comprehension. In J. L. Miller & P. D. Eimas (Eds.), *Speech, language, and communication* (pp. 217–262). San Diego, CA: Academic Press.

Thompson-Schill, S. L., D'Esposito, M., & Kan, E. P. (1999). Effects of repetition and competition on activity in left prefrontal cortex during word generation. *Neuron, 23,* 513–522.

Trueswell, J. C., Tanenhaus, M. K., & Garnsey, S. M. (1994). Semantic influences on parsing: Use of thematic role information in syntactic ambiguity resolution. *Journal of Memory and Language, 33,* 285–318.

Trueswell, J. C., Tanenhaus, M. K., & Kello, C. (1993). Verb-specific constraints in sentence processing: Separating effects of lexical preference from garden-paths. *Journal of Experimental Psychology: Learning, Memory, and Cognition, 19,* 528–553.

Tyler, L. K., & Marslen-Wilson, W. D. (1977). The on-line effects of semantic context on syntactic processing. *Journal of Verbal Learning and Verbal Behavior, 16,* 683–692.

Van Berkum, J. J., Brown, C. M., & Hagoort, P. (1999a). Early referential context effects in sentence processing: Evidence from event-related brain potentials. *Journal of Memory and Language, 41,* 147–182.

Van Berkum, J. J., Brown, C. M., & Hagoort, P. (1999b). When does gender constrain parsing? Evidence from ERPs. *Journal of Psycholinguistic Research, 28,* 555–571.

Van den Brink, D., & Hagoort, P. (2004). The influence of semantic and syntactic context constraints on lexical selection and integration in spoken-word comprehension as revealed by ERPs. *Journal of Cognitive Neuroscience, 16,* 1068–1084.

Van Herten, M., Kolk, H. H. J., & Chwilla, D. J. (2005). An ERP study of P600 effects elicited by semantic anomalies. *Cognitive Brain Research, 22,* 241–255.

Vosse, T., & Kempen, G. A. M. (2000). Syntactic structure assembly in human parsing: A computational model based on competitive inhibition and lexicalist grammar. *Cognition, 75,* 105–143.

Wassenaar, M., & Hagoort, P. (2005). Word-category violations in patients with Broca's aphasia: An ERP study. *Brain and Language, 92,* 117–137.

Wassenaar, M., & Hagoort, P. (accepted). Thematic role assignment in patients with Broca's aphasia: sentence-picture matching electrified. *Neuropsychologia.*

Zurif, E. B. (1998). The neurological organization of some aspects of sentence comprehension. *Journal of Psycholinguistic Research, 27,* 181–190.

Zwitserlood, P. (1989). The locus of the effects of sentential-semantic context in spoken-word processing. *Cognition, 32,* 25–64.

Author index

Subject index